The Ohio Frontier

A History of the Trans-Appalachian Frontier

Walter Nugent and Malcolm Rohrbough, general editors

Andrew L. Cayton. *Frontier Indiana*
James Davis. *A History of the Illinois Frontier*
Mark Wyman. *The Wisconsin Frontier*

The Ohio Frontier

Crucible of the
Old Northwest,
1720–1830

R. Douglas Hurt

Indiana University Press   Bloomington & Indianapolis

This book is a publication of

Indiana University Press
601 North Morton Street
Bloomington, IN 47404-3797 USA

http://www.indiana.edu/~iupress

Telephone orders 800-842-6796
Fax orders 812-855-7931
Orders by e-mail iuporder@indiana.edu

First paperback edition 1998
© 1996 by R. Douglas Hurt

The paper used in this publication meets the minimum
requirements of American National Standard for Information
Sciences—Permanence of Paper for Printed Library
Materials, ANSI Z39.48-1984.

Manufactured in the United States of America

Library of Congress Cataloging-in-Publication Data

Hurt, R. Douglas.
    The Ohio Frontier: crucible of the Old Northwest, 1720–1830 / R.
Douglas Hurt.
        p.   cm. — (A history of the Trans-Appalachian frontier)
    Includes bibliographical references and index.
    ISBN 0-253-33210-9 (alk. paper). — 0-253-21212-x (pbk. : alk. paper)
    1. Ohio—History—To 1787. 2. Ohio—History—1787–1865.
3. Frontier and pioneer life—Ohio. I. Series.
F495.H87   1996

997.1—dc20
                                            95-53278

4 5 6 7 8 09 08 07 06 05 04

FOR

Mary Ellen, Adlai, and Austin

OHIOANS

✇ Contents

Foreword

For most Americans, the phrase "the American West"conjures up the western half of the nation. From the Great Plains across the Rockies and the Intermontane Plateaus to the Pacific Ocean came a flood of popular images, from trappers, cowboys, miners, and homesteading families to the "Marlboro Man" and country-western music. This has been "the West" since the California Gold Rush and the migration of '49ers propelled this region into the national consciousness.

But it was not always so. There was an earlier American West, no less vivid and dramatic. Here the fabled figures were not John Charles Fremont but Daniel Boone, not Geronimo but Tecumseh, not Calamity Jane but Rachel Jackson, not "Buffalo Bill" Cody but Davy Crockett. This earlier West ran, geographically, from the crest of the Appalachian Mountains to the Mississippi River, from the border with Canada to the Gulf of Mexico. It was the West of Euro-American expansion from before the American Revolution until the middle of the nineteenth century, when the line of frontier settlement moved through it toward that next, farther West.

In its initial terms, the story of the First American West involved two basic sets of characters: first, the white people of European origin (and south of the Ohio River, many African American slaves), who spread relentlessly westward; second, the original settlers, the Native Americans, who retreated grudgingly before this flood. These first Europeans, French and Spanish, appeared on this landscape in the 1600s and early 1700s, where their interactions with the original native peoples involved both cooperation and conflict. The English arrived a half-century later. In numbers, the Europeans were almost always a minority, and so both sides sought not conquest or annihilation but mutual accommodation, a joint occupation of the land and joint use of its resources, a system of contact allowing both sides to survive and even to benefit from one another's presence. Trade developed and intermarriage followed; so did misunderstandings and violence. But a delicate balance, supported by mutual interests, often characterized relations among Europeans and native peoples.

When Anglo-Americans began moving through the Cumberland Gap from Virginia into what hunters called the Kentucky country in the 1750s, they soon tilted the balance between the two cultures, occupying large portions of Kentucky and pressing against native groups from Ohio south to Georgia. By 1780, the Anglo-Americans had also occupied the former French settlements of Cahokia in Illinois and Vincennes in Indiana. Despite strong resistance by several native groups, the seemingly unending reinforcements of white families made their gradual occupation of the trans-Appalachian frontier inevitable.

In the 1780s the infant American government issued ordinances spelling out how the land between the Great Lakes and the Ohio River was to be acquired, subdivided, and sold to the citizens of the new republic, and how a form of government organization would lead to statehood and equal membership in the Union. A parallel process was soon set up for Kentucky, Tennessee, and the lands south to the Gulf.

In the 1830s and 1840s, the remaining native groups east of the Mississippi were removed to the West. The expansion of settlement into the trans-Appalachian frontier now continued unchecked into Illinois, Wisconsin, Michigan, and the great cotton lands and hill country of Alabama, Mississippi, and Florida. The frontier period had been completed—as early as the 1820s in Kentucky, and within the next twenty years over much of the Old Northwest and in the Old Southwest.

In brief terms, this is the story of the trans-Appalachian frontier. Over scarcely three generations, the trickle of settler families across the mountains had become more than four million, both white and black. Beginning with Kentucky in 1792 and running through Florida in 1845 and Wisconsin in 1848, a dozen new states had entered the American Union. Each territory/state had its own story, and it is appropriate that each should have a separate volume in this series. The variations are large. Florida's first European arrived in 1513, and this future state had both Spanish and American frontier experiences over 350 years. Missouri had a long French and Spanish history before the arrival of American settlers. Kentucky and Ohio did not, and Americans in large numbers came there quickly through the Cumberland Gap.

The opening and closing of the settlement frontier is the subject of each of these volumes. Each begins with the world that existed when Europeans made contact with native peoples. Each describes and analyzes the themes associated with the special circumstances of the individual territories/states. And each concludes with the closing of the frontier.

The editors have selected these authors because of their reputations as scholars and interpreters of their individual territories/states. We believe that you will find this history informative and lively, and we are confident that you will enjoy this and other volumes in the Trans-Appalachian Frontier series.

R. Douglas Hurt's book on the frontier period in Ohio's history begins early in the eighteenth century and continues to about 1830, when Ohio had become a nearly settled state and was starting to ship many of its young people to territories farther west. In truth his story begins in the late 1500s with conflict between the Iroquois Confederation and the Erie Indians. Shawnees, Wyandots, and other Native American groups complicated the picture, and the arrival of the French in the mid-1600s produced an extremely complex mix of accommodation, conflict, warfare, and mutual economic advantage. Still more players—the British by 1750 and the newly independent Americans after 1775—muddied matters even further. Hurt introduces us to the great Indian diplomat Pontiac, who led a nearly successful defense against British aggression in 1764; to the Indian killer Jeffrey Amherst; to Daniel Boone and the American soldiers George Rogers Clark and "Mad" Anthony Wayne; to dozens of speculators and settlers who swooped down upon Ohio from the 1780s on, people such as Ebenezer Zane of Zane's Trace and Zanesville; to Shakers and Quakers; to Tecumseh's resistance of 1811; and finally to fugitive African American slaves and immigrant canal-builders.

R. Douglas Hurt is already the author of several books, including *Indian Agriculture in America* and other works on Ohio history and the history of agriculture. For many years on the staffs of the historical societies of Missouri and then Ohio, and now professor of history at Iowa State University and editor of the journal *Agricultural History*, he is eminently qualified to write an accurate and compelling history of frontier Ohio. This he has done. Let him take you on a tour of the Ohio country from its earliest Indian days to the beginning of the modern state.

WALTER NUGENT
University of Notre Dame

MALCOLM J. ROHRBOUGH
University of Iowa

Preface

This is the story of the Ohio frontier from approximately 1720 to about 1830. In little more than a century, the portion of the frontier that became the Northwest Territory and the state of Ohio changed dramatically from a region inhabited by newly arrived Indian immigrants to a community of farms, towns, and a few cities, settled by white immigrants from New England, Virginia, Pennsylvania, and Kentucky. On the Ohio frontier, the federal government wrought an Indian policy that provoked incredible violence before essentially achieving the complete removal of the Native Americans from the state. Rapid mobility, both economic and geographic, also characterized the frontier in Ohio. Men and women enjoyed an economic democracy based on relatively easy access to land. Relocation often meant that the frontier people were moving to take advantage of new opportunities rather than to escape failure. Speculators helped settle the frontier by making land available at reasonable prices and in tracts small enough to be affordable, yet with enough acreage to support both safety-first agriculture and commercial farming, based on land ownership.

The Ohio frontier also provided men and women with private and group opportunities to seek their own salvation, or to take their chances however they pleased. Politically they fought about the purpose of government and the nature of humankind. Some favored central control by an elite and a strong national government, while others advocated the locus of power in the legislature and expanded democratic action. After statehood, the frontier people in Ohio gave more attention to local elections than to presidential politics until near the end of the frontier period. Always, however, the Ohio frontier was linked to national and international affairs. Although isolated at first, the Ohio River linked the frontier people with the market economy on the eastern seaboard and in Europe as well as with the politics that emanated from Philadelphia, Washington, D.C., Paris, and London.

The frontier in Ohio served as a borderland between the settled East and the relatively uninhabited lands to the west. The men and women who made their way on that frontier lived in a constant state of becoming. By 1840, however, the Ohio frontier as a borderland had essentially passed. Settlers had established farms and towns across Ohio, and newspapers reached every area of the state. Two canals transected the state, and people were beginning to move out of Ohio. The northwest proved to be the only exception to a growing settled community. There, the Black Swamp prevented settlement until new technology enabled it to be drained during the late nineteenth century. Settlement and the development of the state's lands, towns, agriculture, manufacturing, and commerce, together with the further transition of its social and religious institutions, would continue after 1840, but that change would occur within the context of settled communities and a maturing economy.

This study has been written for the general reader who is interested in the history of Ohio and the American frontier. In the preparation of this book, I have accumulated a number of debts for advice and various professional services. At the Ohio Historical Society, Don Hutslar provided several essential documents as well as a wealth of knowledge about Ohio that helped add depth and color to this book. Judy Gallagher went beyond her normal responsibilities to send crucial rolls of microfilm that I could not obtain elsewhere. Gary Arnold shared his extensive expertise about appropriate manuscript collections, and Steve Gutgesell provided crucial information regarding Ohio's frontier newspapers. Stephen C. Gordon sent a copy of his master's thesis on the pork-packing industry, and Jim Richards helped with the sources for Simon Girty. Joan Jones, Glenn Longacre, and Ann Thomas aided with general reference questions. Christopher S. Duckworth granted permission for me to draw upon several articles that I published in *Timeline*, a publication of the Ohio Historical Society. Those works are "Mount Pleasant," 1 (October–November 1984); "Ripley," 1 (December 1984–January 1985); "Hudson," 2 (March 1985); "Plymouth," 2 (August–September 1985); and "'A' is for Apple . . . by the Bushel, by the Barrel," 2 (October–November 1985). Laurel Shannon sent pertinent indexes for that publication, which led me to some of the most current research and writing about the Ohio frontier. David Simmons shared important bibliography about various aspects of military affairs. The Canton Public Library also provided an old but useful master's thesis on Zoar, the original copy of which disappeared from the Ohio State University Library long ago.

Eric Hinderaker at the University of Utah graciously sent me a copy of his manuscript on patriotism and loyalism in the Ohio Valley during the American Revolution. At Iowa State University, Wayne Pederson, Susan Congdon, and Mary Jane Thune provided their usual excellent service in the Interlibrary Loan Department. My research assistants Stephanie Carpenter and Kirk Hutson helped locate essential sources. I am grateful for the expertise, generosity, and good will of everyone who helped with this project.

The Ohio Frontier

I.

THE FIRST SETTLERS

In 1843, the July sun fell heavy on the Wyandots, and the dust rose in a haze from beneath the horses' hooves and wagon wheels as they moved slowly south toward Cincinnati and the waiting steamboats that would take them from Ohio forever. The Wyandots had once been a powerful people, but since the Treaty of Fort Meigs, which they had signed on September 29, 1817, they had been confined to reservation lands in northwestern Ohio. In 1832, political pressure by whites to gain access to those rich lands resulted in a new treaty that extinguished all title to their lands except for a "Grand Reserve" of 146,316 acres near Upper Sandusky to be shared with the Senecas and Shawnees. Still, whites cast a covetous eye on these Indian lands, and they continued to pressure the state and federal governments to reach a new accommodation with the Indians that would further alienate the lands. Congress did not turn a deaf ear, and on April 23, 1836, the federal government struck a new treaty that further reduced the lands to 109,144 acres in a tract twelve by fourteen miles.

The land cession in 1836, however, did not satisfy the insatiable hunger for Indian lands in Ohio, and Native American contact with white civilization often proved intimidating, humiliating, and demoralizing. By 1839, only the Wyandots remained, and they did not have the political power to resist white encroachments much longer. In March 1840, the Wyandots were comforted when the federal government appointed John Johnston to negotiate with them for the cession of their remaining lands. Johnston had considerable experience working as an Indian agent for the federal government in Ohio, and he had gained a reputation for honesty and trustworthiness. With his help, they might make the best of a bad situation. Although delays occurred, Johnston and the Wyandots signed a treaty at Upper Sandusky on March 17, 1842.

In the Wyandot Treaty of 1842, the tribe agreed to terminate all title to their Ohio lands in exchange for 148,000 acres west of the Mississippi River, a perpetual annuity of $17,500 annually, and $10,000 to pay for removal to their new home as well as financial support for a school. The federal government also agreed to pay for the improvements that the Wyandots had made on their lands as well as to assume the tribal debt, which amounted to $23,860. During the course of the next year, the Wyandots made plans for removal and disposal of their property. When they congregated on Sunday, July 9, for their trek south to Cincinnati and the awaiting steamboats that would take them to present-day Kansas, however, Subagent Purdy McElvain told them they still had saved too much. During the next two days they looked on heartbroken as the agent sold many of their personal belongings at public auction. By Wednesday everything was ready, and 674 men, women, and children, 120 wagons, 300 horses, and a contingent of buggies headed south. About 50 Wyandots remained behind because they were too ill to travel, but some of the sick were loaded on the wagons to make do as best they could during the long journey ahead.

The Wyandots moved slowly south toward the river without a fight or any resistance. McElvain said they showed only "perfect resignation." Charles Dickens, traveling though western Ohio on his way from St. Louis to New York, saw the Wyandots on the road and likened them to the "meaner sort of gipsies." Had he seen them in England, Dickens remarked, he would have thought them to be a "wandering and restless people." No matter who saw the Wyandots or how they judged them, all agreed that the sight was a "melancholy one," and a far cry from the days when these Huron people were known as the "Iroquois of the West," and when they controlled the northern half of Ohio with a ferocity that few tribes challenged. Now, in July 1843, their council fires had been cold for a long time.

When the Wyandots passed through Logan on Thursday after a day on the trail, the local editor remarked, "Most of them are noble looking fellows, stout of limb, athletic and agile; devoted in their attachments to their squaws and families and brave and generous to a fault. Among the squaws are some really beautiful women." He did not note, as did another editor from Cincinnati, that many in the entourage were white men with Wyandot wives and white women with Indian husbands as well as a host of mixed-bloods. That observer believed that the Wyandots as a people would have disappeared in the "process of amalgamation" within a decade if they had been allowed to remain in Ohio. Some of the young women wore the fashions of "white belles" and had their forms "shaped into civilized proportions" with tightly cinched corsets. During the two days that it took the Wyandots to pass through Logan, they conducted themselves with "decorum." Only one drunken Indian marred the event for the curious onlookers, who felt "more or less sympathy" for them and who came from the surrounding countryside to see history in the making. Indeed, they realized that the Wyandots no longer belonged to Ohio and that their mutual ties through history were now broken.

When the Wyandots passed through Xenia on Sunday morning, an observer noted that they were all "decently dressed," mostly in the clothes of white civilization. Half of them allegedly practiced Christianity, and on that Sabbath, few could look upon them without praying that the "Great Spirit would guide and protect them on their journey, and carefully preserve them as a people in the far, far west." When they reached Cincinnati on Wednesday the 19th, one hardened newspaperman thought that they looked like "sheep among wolves." By then, several Wyandots were drunk, and as they camped on the landing while waiting to board the steamboats the next day, one drowned. After seven days of the trail, the Wyandots were now a "sorry specimen" of the "Noble Indian." With few exceptions, they were tired and "dirty and greasy"—an observation that reflected a prejudice that would not die. The weariness on their faces now betrayed their inner feelings and revealed the "canker of secret grief." On Thursday, July 20, they all boarded the steamboats with their few possessions, and the paddle wheels of the *Nodaway* and *Republic* churned white wakes down the Ohio River. Soon they were out of sight. The last remnant of Ohio's Indian people were gone.

During the long struggle to control and settle the Ohio country—a conflict fraught with violence, cruelty, and hardship on all sides—the Native Americans became the symbol of that frontier. Although the Ohio frontier had ended at least a decade before the removal of the Wyandots, these Native Americans had remained a visible symbol of a bygone age. But now, in the summer of 1843, Indian Ohio ceased to exist. Thereafter, the Ohio frontier lived only in memory and history.

* * *

The Native Americans who migrated to the Ohio country during the early eighteenth century found a land of rugged hills, dense forest, and open prairies. Above all, however, the forest dominated the landscape, and it spread with both grandeur and foreboding across Ohio like a heavy green blanket. Where the foothills of the Appalachians formed the southeastern third of Ohio, a forest of red and white oak (many six feet or more in diameter and fifty to sixty feet in height), sugar maple, hickory, black walnut, sycamore, hemlock, cedar, beech, and buckeye trees covered the rolling landscape. In this unglaciated region, steep hills, narrow ravines, and sluggish streams provided an unsurpassed area for hunting and fishing to sustain Indian families. Later these lands proved less than desirable, with the exception of the rich soils in the river valleys, for white settlers who wanted to use the land for farming.

The glaciated till plains that spread to the west also had a forest cover consisting primarily of beech, elm, cherry, and ash. Along the river bottoms natural meadows occasionally opened, where deer, elk, and bison grazed on a luxuriant cover of bluegrass, white clover, and wild rye. The soils in the till plains proved the richest and most productive. Not long after the close of the frontier period, when the Indians no longer hunted over this area, it became the eastern edge of the Corn Belt. In the glaciated western and north-central portions of Ohio, the latter area known as the Lake Plains, prairies that extended several miles occasionally provided a welcome relief from the forest's canopy, and sunlight enabled the grass to grow as high as a horse's back. In the northwestern corner, the Great Black Swamp that spread 40 miles wide and 120 miles long loomed as a barrier to settlement either Indian or white. It became inhabitable only after drainage in the late nineteenth century, well after the close of the frontier. Across these Ohio lands approximately thirty-eight inches of precipitation fall annually, and the growing season ranges from 120 to 200 days, climatic features that became more important to the white immigrants who followed the Indians into Ohio.

Retreating glaciers created a visually imperceptible continental divide that runs roughly from east to west approximately thirty to fifty miles south of Lake Erie. The northern-flowing waters, such as the Maumee, Auglaize, St. Joseph, Tiffin, Grand, Portage, Sandusky, Vermillion, Black, and Cuyahoga, run north into Lake Erie and the Great Lakes–St. Lawrence River system, while the southern-flowing rivers, such as the Tuscarawas, Kokosing, Licking, Muskingum, Scioto, Hocking, Olentangy, Great Miami, Killbuck, and Whitewoman's, drain into the Ohio-Mississippi river valleys. Lake Erie and the Ohio River provided transportation for both Indians and whites, and both cultures viewed these waters as their own.

Although the white-tailed deer was the most numerous and important animal to both Indian and white immigrants, black bears, wolves, and pumas also roamed the countryside. Wild turkeys, grouse, quail, Canadian geese, ducks, passenger pigeons, Carolina parakeets, and gray squirrels lived in abundance in the forests and river valleys, while catfish, muskellunge, walleye, perch, sturgeon, and bass thrived in the river and streams. Deer provided the most important food source for the Indians who migrated into Ohio, and skins quickly became a commodity for trade with whites. The Indians also used the black bear for meat and cooking grease and its hide for trade, but white immigrants who came later would consider the black bears and timber wolves to be animals worthy only of extermination, because the former raided pig pens, while the latter played havoc with flocks of sheep.

Similarly, where the Indians would gain limited control of their environment by maintaining natural meadows in the forest, along river valleys, or on the open prairies by using fire to kill woody plants that would choke the grass and prevent cultivation, white settlers would use both fire and ax to remove the trees in great blocks from the landscape in order to use the land for commercial agriculture rather than for hunting and subsistence farming. With the arrival of white settlers, bounties would be paid for wolf and panther scalps, and on some occasions for those of the Native Americans. Many boys, both Indians and white, sharpened their rifle skills on squirrels that scolded from above or too carelessly peeked over a hickory branch. While the Native Americans considered deer, bears, wolves, passenger pigeons, Carolina parakeets, and other animals and birds part of the environment, where nature struck a balance between all living things, white settlers saw them as a menace to agriculture and sought to eliminate many of the native birds and animals as quickly as possible. Although the Native Americans used the environment and changed it (notably with the use of fire to clear land and to drive game), white settlers changed it for all time by essentially destroying the forest, tilling the land, and driving many animals and birds either away or to extinction. The Native Americans and whites who migrated into Ohio, then, used the environment for their own purposes. Neither kept Ohio's environment in an entirely natural state, but after the arrival of white settlers, it would never look as it did when the Native Americans first moved into the Ohio country.

* * *

Nearly two centuries passed between the first European contact with the Ohio country and the close of the frontier soon after the end of the War of 1812. During that time, the Native Americans left an indelible mark on the history of Ohio, which they stamped with both peace and war. Until the mid-seventeenth century, however, the Ohio country remained a vast "no man's land," occasionally marked by mysterious monuments of ancient peoples whose civilizations had disappeared long before. Few Native Americans hunted in Ohio, although the Iroquois considered it their land by right of conquest. The contest for the control of Ohio and the clash of cultures that it wrought did not come until the 1730s, when the Wyandots, Shawnees, and Delawares moved into the region and claimed it as their own, while both France and Great Britain cast their own designs upon it. Until that conflict began, few Europeans ventured into the Ohio country, and their knowledge of the Native American inhabitants depended on reports given to them by other Indians.

Apparently, at the time of French contact and development of the fur trade in present-day Canada and New York, a Native American people lived along the southern shore of Lake Erie, perhaps as far west as the Cuyahoga River and present-day Cleveland. Known as the Erie, they were an Iroquoian-speaking people who lived in forty villages and fortified towns. Most of the population of approximately twelve thousand lived between present-day Erie and Buffalo, but a few settlements extended west into the Ohio country. The French first learned about the Erie, or "Eriehronon" as they were called by the Huron, in 1623. A decade later, the French referred to them as "la Nation du Chat," the Cat Nation, more appropriately translated as the "Raccoon Nation." Indeed, it was from these masked bandits that the Erie secured much of their food and the skins for their robes and blankets, which they fringed with the animals' ringed tails.

About 1575, Hiawatha forged the Iroquois Confederation in central New York. Known as the League of Five Nations, based on the membership of the Mohawks, Onondagas, Cayugas, Oneidas, and Senecas, the Iroquois, who numbered between twenty and thirty thousand, became dependent on trade with the French during the early seventeenth century. As with other Native Americans who would learn the advantages of iron axes and knives, brass cooking pots, wool blankets, guns, black powder, and lead, their wants became insatiable, and the French proved willing traders for a price. At first the French, and later the English and Dutch, wanted so little in return for the goods that made Indian life easier and more secure—beaver skins. The streams and lakes had plentiful beaver populations, and the trapping and hunting of these animals that provided fashionable pelts for hatmakers in Europe proved relatively easy. Quickly, beaver became the first cash crop of North America and beaver skins the monetary medium of exchange. The Iroquois, however, took too many beaver, and their home country became trapped out by the 1640s. Consequently, the Iroquois sought control of the fur trade that originated deep in the interior of Canada and the Ohio country.

Iroquois pressure to gain control of the fur country to the west culminated with the "Beaver Wars" or the "Wars of the Iroquois," which began in 1649. With speed and brutal force, the Iroquois destroyed the Huron, the Tobacco Nation, the Neutral Nation, and the Attiwandaron, who resisted their control along the Niagara River and north of Lakes Erie and Ontario and east of Lake Huron in an area known as the "Ontario Peninsula." By 1654, this area had become the Iroquois preserve for hunting beaver, deer, bear, and elk. Then, with a diplomatic guile that surely impressed the Machiavellian French at Montreal, they established themselves as the power brokers and chief suppliers of the fur trade and welcomed the black-robed Jesuits to their villages. Only the Erie stood in the way of their gaining complete control of the fur trade from the Great Lakes region.

The Five Nations did not take the Erie lightly. The Cat Nation had experienced leaders and a well-organized tribe. Most important, they had defeated the Iroquois in the past. The Dutch considered them to be better fighters than the Iroquois and called them "satanas" or devils. Yet the Erie suffered from a monumental disadvantage that resulted from the fur trade and the long contact of the Iroquois with European civilization. By the mid-seventeenth century, the Erie essentially remained a Stone Age people and isolated from the European technology dispensed at Montreal. They fought primarily with bows and arrows, while the Iroquois had guns, which they acquired from the British and Dutch.

During the spring of 1654, the Iroquois moved to consolidate their control of the fur trade along Lake Erie. In May they informed the French at Montreal that the Erie had recently burned a Seneca village, killed members of an Onondaga war party returning from the west, and captured an Onondaga chief. The Iroquois could not let these challenges pass unanswered, and they told the French that while they would no longer wage war against them, they would fight the Erie. Besides, they noted, their young men were too "warlike to abandon that pursuit," and they planned to wage a war against the Erie that summer. Prophetically, they told the French: "The earth is trembling yonder and here all is quiet." Although the French recognized this ingenious explanation to gain control of the fur trade in the Ohio country, they were delighted that the Iroquois professed peace with them and intended to deliver the goods, that is furs, to Montreal. Although the Erie sent a party of thirty emissaries on a peace mission to the Seneca, their hosts executed all but five in retaliation for a recent killing of a Seneca by an Erie. With encouragement from the French, the Iroquois sent nearly eighteen hundred warriors west in August with their faces painted red and black for war.

Although the Erie villages fell to the Iroquois war parties, the Cat Nation did not crumble easily or immediately. As they fled west, one Jesuit reported that "they fight like Frenchmen, bravely sustaining the first discharge of the Iroquois, who are armed with our muskets, and then falling upon them with a hailstorm of poisoned arrows, which they discharge eight or ten times before a musket can be reloaded." Soon, however, the Iroquois destroyed the major towns, but sporadic fighting continued for the next two years as the Iroquois sought and destroyed the remote villages to the west. By the spring of 1656, the war had ended. Most of the Erie had been killed in battle or tortured to death as captives. The Five Nations absorbed those who remained into their tribes, and the Erie disappeared as a nation during the early 1680s.

Although the Erie had never occupied more than a portion of northeastern Ohio before contact with European civilization, after the Iroquois defeated them, Ohio came under the nominal control of the Five Nations. Yet the Iroquois did not establish villages south of Lake Erie before 1700, in part because the Andaste people who lived south and east of Lake Erie prevented them from doing so. By the 1680s, the territory along the southern shore of Lake Erie served only as a commonly used warpath for the Iroquois going west to strike the Miami, Illinois, and other tribes and for the Illinois and Miami warriors raiding eastward. Although the Iroquois sent hunting parties into the region, one Frenchman wrote that it was "very dangerous to stop there." The war road, then, prevented steady use or settlement of the Ohio country by any Native Americans. Essentially, Ohio remained unoccupied. Still, the Iroquois claimed this ambiguous empire by the right of the conqueror, and they attempted to hold it by military force until the early eighteenth century, when it became a refuge and a homeland for other tribes who fled both the Iroquois and French and British encroachment and domination.

* * *

Between the late 1730s and the early 1750s, the Shawnees, Wyandots, and Delawares moved into the Ohio country and claimed it as their own. Of these three cultural groups, the Shawnees personified the Native Americans on the Ohio frontier and exemplified their aggressiveness and bravery as well as their reserve and reasonableness. They did so primarily because they fought the longest and because the actions and fate of their leaders, such as Cornstalk and Tecumseh, became common knowledge among Ohio's frontier people. The Iroquois called them "Ontouagannaha," a people who spoke an unintelligible language, while the Shawnees referred to themselves as "sa wanna," which meant "person of the South." Linked linguistically to the Algonquian, the Shawnees may have originated in the Ohio country from the Fort Ancient culture. Or they may have migrated into Ohio from the northeastern Great Lakes region, perhaps driven by the Iroquois before European contact. Whatever its origin, Shawnee culture was centered in the Cumberland River valley by the mid-seventeenth century.

By 1692, the Shawnees had established settlements in Pennsylvania along the Delaware and Susquehanna river valleys, where they lived peacefully near the Quakers. When William Penn, who had tried to follow a humanitarian policy by treating the Indians fairly in matters of land acquisition and human relationships, died in 1718, Shawnee relations with the colonial government began to deteriorate. In 1736, Pennsylvania granted the Iroquois hegemony over all other tribes in the colony because of their military power and successful brokerage as middlemen in the fur trade between the western tribes and the English and Dutch. Pennsylvania authorities intended to use the Iroquois to control the other tribes in the colony in order to forge a military force that would deter French expansion in the Ohio country. The Pennsylvanians believed that the nation that achieved the strongest Indian alliance would have the balance of power tipped in its favor. For them, the Iroquois provided more than a counterbalance in the contest for empire. At the same time that the Iroquois prevented French encroachments, the League of Five Nations would also keep the peace and ensure cooperation among the tribes by creating a "Covenant Chain" or "chain of friendship" in which each tribe would provide the essential links.

The Shawnees and later the Delawares, however, thought less about peaceful cooperation with the Iroquois than about their festering grievances against them that demanded resolution, either by fight or by flight. Increased population growth and pressure for Indian lands along the Delaware and Susquehanna rivers gave another push to the Shawnees, while French overtures pulled them west to trade on more favorable terms than with the British. In 1728, the Marquis de Beauharnois, governor of New France, reported: "It would promote in considerable degree the prosperity and security of the Colony, could these Indians settle between Lake Erie and the Ohio River." He did not need to add that in doing so, they would help France secure its claim to the Ohio country.

Pennsylvania's action merely followed the policy of New York, which in 1701 recognized the Iroquois claim to the Ohio country, subject to ultimate British sovereignty, and promised protection of this hunting ground from seizure by the French. The Shawnees, however, had suffered the wrath of Iroquois war parties in Ohio and the Illinois country after the defeat of the Erie. Consequently, when the Iroquois began to consolidate their control over the tribes in Pennsylvania during the 1720s, the Shawnees began to move west, perhaps crossing the Ohio River by 1730. Although the government of Pennsylvania tried to lure the Shawnees back near the settlements where it could more easily regulate the fur trade and keep a watchful eye and shield them from French influence, it failed. When the Iroquois also ordered the Shawnees to return to the colony, they too met rejection.

Although the Iroquois had a long arm that could reach into the Ohio country, it was not well muscled. In fact, the Iroquois, who by now had become known as the Six Nations after the Tuscaroras joined the league during the early eighteenth century, had limited influence in the Ohio country. The "Covenant Chain" among the tribes had become little more than a series of temporary agreements.

Moreover, the Iroquois could not unite on many matters of policy, which further weakened their diplomatic and military effectiveness in the western country. By the early 1730s, the Ohio country was less an Iroquois empire than a refuge from the Six Nations for a host of tribes, none of whom claimed the right to use Ohio exclusively as their own. Tanacharison, a Seneca headman, called it the "country in between."

While the Iroquois theoretically exercised control over the Ohio country, and while some tribes such as the Senecas and Cayugas held specific land claims based on use and occupation in northeastern Ohio, the region had little order except that which the Shawnees and other migrating tribes gave it. In 1732 the Iroquois finally ordered the Shawnees out of Pennsylvania and "back toward Ohio, the place from whence you came," because they would not join an alliance to curb colonial expansion. But the Iroquois had little power to enforce their will in the West, and the Shawnees were leaving anyway. On the Ohio frontier, distance became the great equalizer of military power. Soon the Shawnees developed their own economic network with traders from Pennsylvania and Virginia, some, such as George Croghan, operating from Pennsylvania as far west as the shore of Lake Erie and the Maumee and Miami river valleys.

By 1738, the Shawnees had founded a town at the mouth of the Scioto. This settlement began the regathering of the tribe and the creation of a quasi-Shawnee republic which by late 1747 had kindled its own council fire and, thereby, symbolically and literally cast off all claims of the Six Nations to manage its affairs. When the French party, under Pierre-Joseph de Céloron de Blainville, visited this Lower Shawnee Town in late August 1749, they found it a "pleasant" location of about sixty houses and partially inhabited by Iroquois, Delawares, and Miamis and others from "nearly all the nations of the Upper County," who had been drawn there by the "lavish markets of the English." Although the Shawnees had been pro-French at the time of their settlement in Ohio, they were now "entirely devoted to the English."

Céloron ordered the five English traders at Lower Shawnee Town to leave, and they agreed, but those traders still remained when the French continued down the Ohio River. Céloron wisely recognized that he did not have sufficient power to seize their goods, and, given their protection by the Shawnees, an attack would have "brought discredit on the French." Father Bonnecamps, a priest traveling with Céloron's party, noted that "la belle riviere," or "beautiful river," as the French called the Ohio, was "little known to the French and, unfortunately, too well known to the English," who relied on a "crowd of savages," such as these Shawnees, for protection. By the mid-eighteenth century, then, the Shawnees were well established at the junction of the Ohio and Scioto rivers, where they had become "great Friends to the English."

In the winter of 1752–53, a flood destroyed Lower Shawnee Town, and the residents moved out of the river bottom to higher ground and rebuilt the village on the site of present-day Portsmouth. The Shawnees established other towns along the Ohio and Muskingum rivers, the village of Wakatomica on the site of present-day Dresden being the most important on the latter river. When they abandoned Lower Shawnee Town, they also moved up the Scioto River valley to establish the town of Chillicothe, also known as Upper Shawnee Town, on the plains about fifteen miles south of Circleville. This town became one of five villages so named in Ohio, including one near present-day Chillicothe. Unlike white settlers, the Indians did not give every town a unique name. Rather, they associated their villages with some quality or feature. The Chillicothe towns, for example, simply meant that the Shawnees of the Chillicothe division lived there. By the mid-1760s, the Shawnees had migrated westward and established towns on the Little Miami and Mad rivers. At "Old Chillicothe," located on the Little Miami River near modern-day Xenia, Daniel Boone and Simon Kenton would one day be held prisoner. A dozen miles to the north, the Shawnees also founded another Chillicothe town near Pickawillany, on a site previously occupied by the Miamis. The village was the probable birthplace of Tecumseh in 1768. About 1780, the Shawnees renamed it Piqua. Wherever the Shawnees went, however, the English traders operating out of Pennsylvania quickly followed with the intent of tying them to the British Empire and preventing an alliance with the French.

Other Native Americans settled in northern Ohio about the same time that the Shawnees migrated to the Scioto and Muskingum river valleys. The people whom the British called "Wyandot" and whom the French knew as the Tionontati or Petun (Tobacco) Hurons had been driven west from southern Ontario to the Upper Great Lakes by the Iroquois during the mid-seventeenth century. In 1701, when Antoine Laumet de la Mothe Cadillac built Fort Pontchartrain and established the nucleus of the French outpost at Detroit, he intended to gain the support of the Wyandots and the other tribes who lived in the region to help keep the British out of the Ohio Valley. Not long after the Wyandots settled near Detroit, they began hunting south of Lake Erie in the Sandusky and Maumee river valleys for both food and furs to trade at Detroit. From their winter camps in northwestern Ohio, the Wyandots also ranged southward to the upper branches of the Scioto and the western reaches of the Muskingum rivers. Perhaps as early as 1738, a band of Wyandots under the leadership of Nicholas Orontony settled near present-day Castalia, a few miles below modern Sandusky.

The British did not concede the Ohio country to French territorial claims and control of the fur trade. To lure the Wyandots away from French influence at Detroit, the British sent traders from Pennsylvania, and by 1747 they had built a blockhouse at the Wyandots' settlement at Sandusky to facilitate trade, provide protection, and help ensure their claims to the region. Still, the relationship of the Wyandots to the French and British remained fluid, and they skillfully drifted toward one or the other as their needs or circumstances dictated. In 1747, for example, they moved closer to the British camp when five French traders returning from hunting and trapping along the Cuyahoga River in northeastern Ohio, a region known as the White River country, were killed and their furs stolen along Sandusky Bay. Although the French never learned the identity of the Indians, they assumed the Sandusky Wyandots had made the attack. In late August of that year, Nicholas, probably encouraged by the British, also planned to attack Detroit and, with the help of other tribes in the area, drive the French from the Great Lakes region. But when the French learned of this plot, the conspiracy failed and the Wyandots withdrew.

During the winter of 1747–48, British traders visited the Wyandots twice and perhaps, together with the hostility of the French, persuaded them to move closer to them on the Cuyahoga River. Or perhaps the Wyandots grew weary of the French, because they complained in 1748 to Conrad Weiser, a German-born agent for Pennsylvania, that they were tired of their "hard Usage" by the French, and because the French took their young men to war yet charged them "dear" prices for their trade goods. Indeed, the French officers and traders gained a notorious reputation for speculation and corruption by trying to gain exorbitant profits from the fur trade. Whatever the reason for their removal from Sandusky, Nicholas had burned his village by March 1748 and moved his people, including 119 warriors and more than 300 women, children, and old men, to the mouth of the Cuyahoga.

In November 1750, George Croghan reported to the governor of Pennsylvania that the Wyandots were "Steady and well attached to the English interest." Given the work of the Pennsylvania traders to win their friendship, he believed the French would "make but a poor hand of those Indians." Croghan, who was usually right in his assessment of Indian affairs, missed his mark this time. During the French and Indian War, which began only a few years later, the Wyandots fought with the French against the British, but their loyalty shifted back to the British during the American Revolution. In the War of 1812, the Sandusky Wyandots would side with the Americans, while those near Detroit gave their allegiance to Tecumseh and his Indian confederacy.

By December 1750, the Wyandots under Nicholas had moved south along the Tuscarawas and down the Muskingum rivers, where they established a town, known as "Conchake" to the French or "Muskingum" to the English, near the present site of Coshocton. At that time Christopher Gist, an agent for the Ohio Company of Virginia, who scouted in Ohio to find good lands, reported that the town consisted of a hundred families. He also discovered that George Croghan already had built a trading post for the Wyandots and that he and Nicholas flew "English Colours" above their houses to signify a safe haven for other English traders operating out of Pennsylvania. The Wyandots stayed at Conchake until 1753, when most of them returned to the Sandusky Bay area. The last Wyandots moved back north two years later. In early January 1751, a trader reported that the Wyandots had told him that the French claimed all the rivers that drained into Lake Erie but that the tributaries of the Ohio belonged to them and "their Brothers the English, and that the French had no Business there."

The Delawares became the third major Native American people to migrate to the Ohio country. These Algonquian-speaking Indians called themselves Lenni Lenape, which means "common people." The Dutch, Swedes, and English discovered the Lenape in the Delaware River valley when they began colonization during the mid-seventeenth century. The origin of these people remains a mystery. Perhaps, as tribal tradition contends, they migrated from west of the Mississippi River; or perhaps they descended from the Paleo-Indians who lived along the Atlantic seaboard. In any event, when the English settlers named the Delaware Bay in honor of Thomas West, Lord de la Warr, whom the Crown appointed governor of Virginia in 1610, the river that emptied into it and the Native Americans who lived along it in time also became known as Delaware.

The Delawares were a peaceful people who maintained a loose association and lived in semi-permanent villages in present-day Pennsylvania, southwestern New York, western New Jersey, and northern Delaware. They did not form a "Delaware Nation" or recognize an authoritarian chief or ruler who spoke for them. Instead, they submitted to the domination of the Iroquois, who represented the Delawares on all diplomatic matters with whites and prohibited them from making war or peace with either whites or Indians without their permission. The Iroquois also spoke of them as "women." Although the Delawares greatly resented this humiliation, the Iroquois were too powerful to resist. After Pennsylvania took most of the Delawares' land during the 1740s by purchasing it from the Iroquois, they began to move into western Pennsylvania and the Ohio country. There, the French supplied them with guns and provisions and urged them to attack the white settlers on the Pennsylvania frontier. By the 1750s, the Delawares had allied with the Shawnees, and their war parties asserted tribal independence from the Six Nations. Few frontiersmen considered the Delawares to be effeminate fighters. Indeed, the Delaware war parties operating from the Ohio country became the most feared on the frontier. With great confidence they told the Six Nations: "We are men and are determined not to be ruled any longer by you as Women, and we are determined to cut off all the English, except those that may make their Escape from us in Ships."

Although the Wyandots claimed all land immediately west of the Ohio River and north to Lake Erie as well as the right to light all intertribal council fires, they had granted the Shawnees permission to hunt in that region, and they now came to the aid of the Delawares by permitting them to settle in eastern Ohio. They may have done so based on Native American cultural tradition that allowed the temporary loan of hunting lands during time of need by others. Or the Wyandots may have used the dispossessed Delawares to create a buffer between them and the already relentlessly westering frontiersmen. By 1750, the Delawares had established major villages along the Tuscarawas. There, an abundance of elk browsed in the river valley. In mid-January 1751, Christopher Gist reported several small Delaware towns in south-central Ohio, including Hockhocking or French Margaret's Town at present-day Lancaster, and Maguck, located on the Pickaway Plains near modern Circleville, all of which contained only a few families.

The Delawares established other towns in eastern and southern Ohio. In 1752, Shingas, chief of the Turkey division, whom Pennsylvania frontiersmen called "Shingas the Terrible," established a village known as Shingas Town at the mouth of the Big Sandy Creek on the Tuscarawas near present-day Bolivar. In 1764, after tribal authority had passed to his brother "King Beaver," it became known as Beaver's Town. At that same time, Netawatwees or New Comer, chief of the Turtle division, who founded a town on the Cuyahoga River near present-day Cuyahoga Falls in 1759, established Newcomer's Town east of Coshocton. He called it "Gekelmukpechunk," which means "still water," but it soon became Newcomerstown to the white traders and settlers and the largest Delaware town on the Tuscarawas River. In 1771 it had a hundred dwellings, including the Great Council house; by the American Revolution approximately seven hundred Delawares lived there. At that time, the Delawares also had villages on the Mahoning River near Warren and Youngstown as well as on the Kokosing, Walhonding, and Cuyahoga rivers and their branches. When the Wyandots abandoned Conchake, the Delawares occupied that site, and Coshocton became the tribal center. By 1765, Delaware villages were so common that British

Brigadier General Henry Bouquet referred to the Upper Muskingum region as the "Country of the Delawares," and George Croghan estimated that three thousand Delawares lived between the Ohio and Lake Erie. With an estimated fighting force of five hundred men, and reported to be "firmly attached to the English Interest," they too pledged that they would not "hear the Voice of any other Nation" except their "Brothers the English."

The Christian Delawares were the last major group of Native Americans to settle in Ohio. These Indians were under the influence of the church of the Unity of the Brethren, commonly known as the Moravians. In the summer of 1772, David Zeisberger and John Heckewelder led a group of Delawares from Friedensstadt, Pennsylvania, to the Tuscarawas River, where other Delawares under the leadership of Beaver had settled earlier. Zeisberger selected a site about two miles southeast of present-day New Philadelphia for their settlement, and he called it Schoenbrunn, which means "beautiful spring." The Delawares called it Welhik-Tupeek. The Moravians, whom the Delawares called "Blackcoats," and who, in turn, referred to the Indians as "Brown Brethren," had been invited to Ohio along with the "praying Indians" by Netawatwees, the first among equals of the Delaware chiefs, to strengthen the tribal force at one location, both Christians and nativists (that is, those who observed traditional religious practices) alike. Earlier, in 1761, the Moravians had sent the Reverend Christian Frederick Post to the Muskingum River country to spread the Gospel in the wilderness.

Although Post and his assistant John Heckewelder, who joined him the next year, failed to establish a mission among the Delawares and fled back to Pennsylvania in fear for their lives, the Moravians did not give up. In 1771, David Zeisberger met a more favorable reception when the Moravians tried again, unmindful of the political and military realities that Netawatwees attempted to balance. Nor did they understand that Netawatwees had invited them in order to use their spiritual powers secretly to end an epidemic that had taken Delaware lives and which the tribe blamed on sorcery or witchcraft. If things went right, Netawatwees reasoned, both the health and the power of the Delawares would soon be improved. Although the disease that swept among them evidently ran its course, the Delawares would soon blame these Christians for the terrible bloodshed that followed.

The Moravians and their Delaware converts quickly began building sixty log cabins and a church as well as tilling the rich soil and clearing pastures along the Tuscarawas River. The Moravians required their charges to observe Christian rituals and to work in the fields or at a craft. When the Moravians baptized an Indian, he or she gave up his or her native name and adopted a new one, preferably of biblical origin. They also stressed the sanctity of monogamous marriages, obedience to the missionaries, and the importance of Sunday as a day of rest. The Christian Delawares could not go hunting without permission, nor could they paint their faces, wear a scalp lock, shave their heads, or make war. The Moravians required all Delaware converts to settle near Schoenbrunn to avoid the distractions of the nativists and any lapse of their commitment to Christianity and their new way of life. Delaware children also went to school and learned the English language. Systematically, the Moravians worked to remake the economic, social, and political structure of Delaware society.

Despite the cultural challenges from associating with the Moravians, many Delawares were receptive to living like their relatives who had joined the "Black Coats." As the Delaware converts increased, the mission at Schoenbrunn could not meet their religious, educational, and economic needs. As a result, in 1772 the Moravians founded the sister towns of Gnadenhutten, or "Tents of Grace," about ten miles downstream, and the village of Lichtenau, or "Meadow of Light," below Coshocton four years later. These new villages were also located on the east side of the Tuscarawas to maintain a separation of at least ten miles between the missions and nativist towns. By so doing, the Moravians hoped to keep their converts from the trader's whiskey which flowed too easily and frequently in the nativist villages as well as from traditional religious practices. The Moravians preferred for their converts to sing hymns in the mission villages rather than war chants with the nativists at the other towns. Moreover, some Delaware leaders such as Killbuck, Netawatwees's eldest son, resented the presence of the Moravians and argued that each convert to the Moravian pacifists depleted the ability of the Delawares to defend themselves from an attack by Indians or whites. The Christian Delawares, then, who settled with the Moravians, divided the Delaware nation rather than united it. That division would have terrible consequences for both the Christian and nativist Delawares.

In addition to the Shawnees, Wyandots, and Delawares, several other tribes also settled in Ohio. And as many eastern tribes were forced to move west because of population pressures that ruined their food supply or by colonial government policy, several other tribes moved into the region from the west. As a result, Ohio no longer remained a great uninhabited hunting land. In 1747, a pro-English Miami of Algonquian heritage, whose traditional name, "Twaatwaa," imitated the alarm cry of the crane, founded Pickawillany or Twigthwees Town on the west bank of the Great Miami River at the mouth of Loramie Creek, near present-day Piqua. Pickawillany was the largest of the Miami towns in Ohio, with approximately four hundred families in 1751. Gist reported: "They are accounted the most powerful People to the westward of the English settlements." Although the Miamis had been in the "French Interest," they too grew tired of their price gouging and had become "well affected to the English traders." In 1750, they warned the French and their Indian allies to stay out of Miami hunting grounds or they would be taken prisoner. At that time several traders from Pennsylvania lived among them, while others operated in the general vicinity and conducted business with the Shawnees, Delawares, Ottawas, and Iroquois who also hunted in western Ohio. At midcentury, a small group of Miamis also occupied a village, known as Le Baril's [The Barrel's] Town, at the mouth of the Little Miami River. The Miamis did not stay long in Ohio, however, and about 1752 they moved back to northeastern Indiana, near present-day Fort Wayne.

By the mid-eighteenth century, the Six Nations tribes in Ohio were known as "Mingos." Along with the Loups, Moraignans, Ottawas, Abenakis of St. Francis, and Ojibwas (Chippewas), they had established villages, with a total population of about twenty-five hundred, in the Cuyahoga River region of northeastern Ohio. The hunting remained good in that area in contrast to the depleted lands to the east. The French at Detroit quickly made contact with

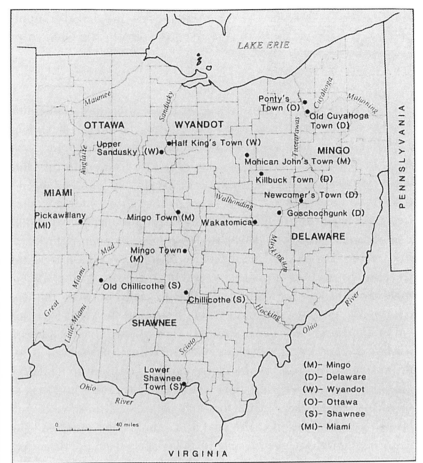

Many Indian villages nestled along the streams and rivers
in Ohio during the frontier period. Communication between
the villages became frequent, but intertribal contact was
not always friendly. From George W. Knepper, *Ohio and Its
People* (Kent, Ohio: Kent State University Press, 1989), with
permission of the Kent State University Press.

these tribes to keep them from British influence. In 1743, a French
trader brought about two hundred packs of furs to Detroit from
the Cuyahoga region, but only the Senecas proved friendly to the
French and warned the British to stay away. And when Louisbourg on Cape Breton Island fell to the British in June 1745 during

King George's War, the British temporarily strangled the supply of French trade goods to the interior. As a result, the Ohio tribes became increasingly pro-British.

* * *

Despite these new settlements and economic and diplomatic linkages with the British and French, the Shawnees, Wyandots, and Delawares depended on agriculture and hunting for their daily living. These new settlers were the first farmers in the Ohio country. They cultivated a variety of crops with skill and followed a well-developed system of land tenure. Although the Indian women had the responsibility for raising the crops, among the Wyandots and Shawnees the men participated to a greater extent in the farming process than they did among many other tribes. They cleared the trees and brush from the fields by cutting and burning. The women, however, still had the task of clearing the land between the tree stumps and grubbing the roots from the ground. Women also cultivated and harvested the traditional crops of corn, beans, squash, sunflowers, and tobacco. Among the Ohio tribes, corn served as the primary crop, and the women gave careful attention to it. Before planting time in the spring, they selected the best seeds and soaked them for several days in warm water or greased them with deer brains or tallow to soften the seed and enhance germination. The women planted several kernels in holes spaced about three feet apart. As the corn grew, they hoed up the soil around the stalks during cultivation to give the plants support. After the corn sprouted a few inches, they planted beans in the hills and pumpkins between the rows. This intercropping enabled each crop to be mutually supporting. The corn, for example, provided a pole for the beans to climb, while the leaves of the pumpkins shaded the ground and retarded the growth of weeds. Although they did not use fertilizer, the beans returned nitrogen to the soil and, when eaten with corn, provided a high-protein meal. The Ohio Indians knew that these crops provided the greatest return for their labors, and each stored for a long time. For them, corn, beans, and pumpkins became the "three sisters," which they emphasized above all other crops.

Because the women did not have horse-drawn plows to turn
the soil, their fields were relegated to the river bottoms, where the
rich alluvial soil tilled easily with bone, flint, or iron hoes. During the
1770s, David Zeisberger observed that the Delawares along the Tuscarawas River planted their corn along the river bottom. He wrote:
"This sort of land is chosen by the Indians for agricultural purposes
not only because it is easily worked, but also because it yields abundant crops for many years." He noted, however, that when "their
fields begin to grow grass, they leave them and break new land, for
they regard it as too troublesome to root out the grasses."

Sometimes the women combined their fields with the lands of
close relatives and shared the work and the harvest. Like the white
farmers who would soon come after them, they too prayed to their
Creator for rain. When the green corn was ready to harvest in
August, the women picked it to feed their families. The remainder
stayed on the stalks for harvesting and shelling and grinding into
flour in the autumn. The women stored the mature ears by stripping
the husks back and braiding them into bundles to hang from the
ceilings of their lodges; or they shelled the corn and stored the grain
in large baskets in their houses. Each family raised about one acre
of corn, and if each family had four or more people, they no doubt
consumed it before the next harvest. These corn fields were so important to Shawnee sustenance that they became military targets
when war came with the Americans.

After the harvest of the corn crop, the Ohio tribes often broke up
into small groups and left their villages for winter camps along the
streams and rivers to lessen the strain of limited food supplies on the
entire group. During the winter months the men hunted deer, bear,
and turkey for food and clothing and trapped beaver and other
fur-bearing animals which, along with deerskins, provided staples
for trade with the British. In the summer the men also trapped
and speared fish to supplement family diets. When their fields were
destroyed by white war parties, usually Kentuckians, they had little
choice but to rely on hunting, fishing, and the gathering of nuts,
wild roots, and berries to meet their food needs. At first, hunting
and fishing were not arduous tasks. The streams and lake allegedly
were "alive with fish." Passenger pigeons darkened the skies and

provided roasted fowl and squab, while turkeys, ducks, and geese were abundant.

None of the Ohio or other eastern tribes used fertilizer, but they prolonged the use of their fields by burning the stubble in addition to planting beans among the corn hills. By burning the brush from the fields before planting time, they unknowingly added magnesium, calcium, potash, and phosphorus to the soil. Burning also reduced soil acidity and thereby promoted bacterial activity and the formation of nitrogen. The prolonged practice of burning, however, decreased organic soil material. Consequently, the Ohio Indians had to relocate their fields periodically when productivity declined. Since the Ohio Indians, like the other eastern agricultural tribes, did not plant corn in straight rows, the irregularly spaced hills helped retard soil erosion. By the late eighteenth century, the Delawares living among the Moravians on the Tuscarawas obtained cattle from white settlers, but they neither made any effort to feed their livestock during the winter—a negligent practice as well among white farmers in the Old Northwest—nor used the manure for fertilizer. Instead, they let their cattle forage in the woods.

The Indian farmers in Ohio, like those throughout eastern North America, believed the land had been given to them by the "Great Spirit." Since the land was a gift from him, only he could take it from them. In contrast to colonial and American legal ownership systems, land tenure among the Ohio Indians depended on tribal sovereignty and actual use. Each tribe claimed sovereignty over an area that was fairly well recognized by other tribes. In contrast to the white farmers, Indian women rather than the men controlled the use of the agricultural lands. Although the tribe claimed the land communally, the women farmers controlled the use of the fields. Each woman claimed as much land as she needed to meet the food needs of her family. If she cleared a plot and planted crops, the woman automatically removed it from the communal domain as long as she continued to cultivate it. If she abandoned the field, it reverted to communal or tribal property, where it could be freely taken up and farmed by someone else. If the village moved, the chief allotted new lands based on family need, but usage rights passed down to the women in the lineage as long as they remained on that land, and they, not their husbands, owned the produce from their fields. Tribal lands not under cultivation could be used by all members of the tribe for hunting, fishing, berry picking, or wood gathering. Generally, land could not be sold or inherited.

Indeed, the land of the Native Americans could not be sold because it did not belong to the present generation. The present generation acted only as a trustee of the land for the generations yet unborn. Consequently, the land was in the care of the generation presently inhabiting it, but it could be loaned to other Indians in need of it, such as the Wyandots' loan to the Shawnees and Delawares, subject to their good behavior. The effect of this practice was to distribute land equitably so that each family had enough land to meet its farming needs. In this respect, then, the Indians neither accepted nor understood the white man's concept of land sales and absolute ownership.

The Ohio Indians, particularly the Shawnees, Wyandots, and Delawares, also made maple sugar. The sugar-making season usually began in February or March, when the temperature dropped below freezing during the night but warmed with the sun during the day, and it lasted about a month. Customarily, each family or group of two or three families controlled a stand of sugar trees, just as each owned or had priority over a certain plot of land. The number of "taps" on this stand of trees, called a "sugar bush," determined the capacity of the maple trees. Commonly, the Indians made two or three taps on a large tree, and about nine hundred taps on an average sugar bush. Each tap, located about three feet above the ground, consisted of a diagonal gash about three and one-half inches long. At the lower end of the cut, a four-inch-long piece of bark was removed from the trunk. A blow from a hatchet at the base of that section opened a hole, into which the Indians inserted a wooden spout. The spouts were about six inches long and two inches wide; the Indians placed a sap dish or bucket beneath each spout.

The men and women emptied the pans into larger containers each day and carried the sap back to the camp, where they poured it into the boiling kettles or troughs in front of the sugar house. Before the arrival of the Europeans, these Native Americans boiled the sap by dropping red-hot stones into wooden vessels or by heating clay pots. This task took considerable time because seven or eight gallons of sap provided only one pound of sugar. Still, large sugar maples might yield sixty gallons of sap, and David Zeisberger reported that because the Delawares had "numerous kettles and troughs they can make much sugar, for there is no lack of trees." With iron kettles the Ohio Indians could slowly boil the sap to prevent scorching until it reached the consistency of molasses. At that point, the syrup could be poured into a pot for storage; or it could be boiled further until it granulated and became "as fine as West Indian sugar." Then they formed it into cakes for storage in a kettle or basket. Because of the great abundance of maple trees, the Ohio tribes used a sugar bush for only three or four years, after which they located a new stand of trees for tapping. Zeisberger reported that a woman with only a few kettles could make several hundred pounds of sugar and a "Quantity of Molasses" each year. The Ohio Indians mixed their maple sugar with corn or bear's fat to make a garnish for roasted venison, as well as with water for a sweet, refreshing drink, and they used it for an important trade item. In these ways, the Ohio Indians drew upon the bounty of the land according to the rhythm of the seasons.

* * *

Indian culture in the Ohio country depended not only on agriculture and hunting but also on a social organization that centered in the village. Among the Shawnees, the village band was more important than the lineage. There the village chief supervised daily affairs and appointed individuals for various rituals and duties. The households of the Ohio Indians were based on the nuclear family, although the Shawnees practiced sororal polygamy. A man was required to marry the widow of his brother; thus the woman and her children gained a provider rather than became dependent on the tribe for support. Within the family, children learned respect for their elders from their parents and grandparents, as well as life skills, depending on gender, and tribal history. Families lived in individual bark-covered houses, called wigwams. Each major town had a council house for meetings and rituals. Some of these houses were quite large. The Shawnee council house at Old Chillicothe, for example, was approximately sixty feet square, while that at Lower Shawnee Town reached ninety feet long. These council houses also served as forts during emergencies. With saws and axes acquired from the white traders, the Shawnees began to build log houses. By 1771, most of the one hundred houses at Newcomerstown were log cabins.

Politically, the Ohio tribes had a loose unity. The Shawnees, whose organization was the most complex, divided into five groups—the Chillicothe, Hathawekela, Kispoko, Mequachake, and Piqua. The entire village identified with a particular group, each of which signified a special political, religious, or military division of labor. Yet each division functioned autonomously. The tribal chiefs, or "grand chiefs" or "kings," as the French and British called them, came from the Chillicothe and perhaps from the Hathawekela divisions and the Great Lynx clan, while the Mequachake provided the medicine men and the priests. The warriors primarily came from the Kispoko, while the Piqua division oversaw the rituals. The designation of chief was inherited patrilineally without consideration of age. Primogeniture, that is, inheritance by the eldest son, did not play a role in the transfer of power. Among the Ohio tribes, each band had a peace and a war chief, the latter of which had to be earned by bravery. Among the Shawnees, a man became a war chief by leading four raids in which his party took at least one scalp without the loss of a man. Tribal councils consisted of both peace and war chiefs, although the war chiefs had the most power and convened their own councils. Elderly men attended the councils and provided advice, but they could not vote. Tecumseh is the preeminent example of a war chief, while Little Turtle won that reputation among the Miamis. Women were also recognized as peace and war chiefs by the Shawnees and Miamis, but they did not sit in council with the men. Although women chiefs marshaled considerable influence, they primarily supervised ceremonial practices, directed the planting of crops, determined life or death for captives, and controlled the affairs of the women. Nevertheless, they could ask a war chief to abandon an attack.

The Delawares organized under the Turtle, Wolf, and Turkey divisions. Traditionally, a particular lineage within a village chose its chief, who served as an adviser and the first-among-equals at a council of village elders. There, the chief's powers were ceremonial rather than coercive. Matrilineal succession predominated. During the eighteenth century, tribal leadership became more effective, probably in response to the colonial officials who attempted to impose their own concepts of leadership and organization on those who represented tribal bands. In time, the Delawares recognized the chief of the Turtle clan to be preeminent, because the turtle symbolized Mother Earth, the first of all living things. Unlike the wolf, who roamed the earth, or the turkey, who could survive only on land, the turtle could live either on the land or in the water. The preeminence of the chief of the Turtle clan may have become institutionalized with Netawatwees when the Delawares moved into eastern Ohio. The Delawares recognized the hereditary and civil authority of the chiefs but, as with the Shawnees, their war leaders earned their reputations in battle and directed tribal affairs during times of conflict. The political organization of the Wyandots is not clearly understood after their migration to the Upper Great Lakes region.

The Shawnees recognized many deities under the influence of the "Great Spirit," whom the Miamis also called the "Master of Life." Prayers and communal dances served as the primary medium of worship and thanksgiving. The Wyandots believed the sun, moon, wind, and thunder had supernatural powers and that the Milky Way served as the path of souls to eternity. The nativist religious practices of the Delawares remain unclear, but they involved the use of a supernatural tutelary, such as an animal or bird, by each individual.

The cultures of the Iroquois and Algonquian tribes in Ohio permitted great personal affection and the ability to forgive one's enemies as well as terrifying violence and retribution. These attributes characterized their practice of war and peace, and each is exemplified in their treatment of prisoners. After a battle with another tribe or the French, English, or Americans, the women of the tribe determined the fate of the prisoners. Among the Shawnees, the female civil chiefs and women who wanted to adopt a prisoner to take the place of a dead husband or son could prevent their execution. If a group led by four old women, known as the Miseekwaaweekwaakee, touched the prisoners first, they would be roasted alive and eaten. Among the Miamis, prisoners who were not killed passed to the village chief, who distributed them to the children or the families of the deceased, who decided whether to accept adoption or enslavement. Although captives, both Indian and white, usually received kind treatment, physical abuse also occurred.

British and American adult prisoners seldom gained complete acceptance in the tribe. The children, however, adapted relatively quickly to Native American culture and essentially became "white Indians." In January 1751, for example, Christopher Gist met a white woman along Walhonding Creek near the Wyandot town of Conchake. Her name was Mary Harris, and Gist thought she had been captured at Deerfield, Massachusetts, in late February 1704, when she was ten years old. Gist reported that "she still remembers they used to be very religious in New England, and wonders how the White Men can be so wicked as she has seen them in these woods."

Adoption and acceptance into an Ohio tribe, however, required reciprocity by the captives, both red and white. The Ohio tribes accepted their adopted children, husbands, and wives as their own, but they expected their white captives to accept their new life. Gist reported that a woman who had been a captive at Conchake for a long time tried to escape. The Wyandots captured her and carried her about the town. Then, like a cat playing with a mouse, they cut her loose, but when she tried to run away, her executioners struck her on the side of the head with a club, stabbed her several times through the heart, scalped her, and cut off her head. On another occasion, a white female captive of a Delaware village tried to escape, for which her captors built a fire and "long made her writhe in the flames," while the other white captives watched as a deterrent to further escapes. Yet these cultural practices were neither cruel, pagan, nor silly to the Native Americans in the Ohio country. Their beliefs and practices met specific economic, religious, political, and social needs. Only an alien culture that held vastly different beliefs would deprecate those of the Ohio tribes and seek to destroy them.

* * *

The Shawnees, Wyandots, and Delawares as well as the other tribal cultures that settled in Ohio during the seventeenth century had little peace and isolation to live their lives in traditional fashion. These Indian people had been forced into the Ohio country either directly or indirectly by white civilization. Although each tribe had been influenced by white culture for a long time, in Ohio that influence had greater consequences than ever before. Far away, fashionable Europeans demanded beaver hats and deer-skin jackets and pants. When a trader demanded the payment of a "buck" for a particular item, the Indians knew what he meant. In time, bucks would mean paper money, but on the Ohio frontier the term meant "skins." The colonial legislature in Pennsylvania authorized its traders to charge a price of five bucks for a cask of whiskey in the Ohio country. If a trader tried to charge more, the Indians could legally take it from him. Bearskins for making robes and coats maintained a ready market, and traders also sought fox, otter, and muskrat skins.

The demands of the European traders brought great cultural and ecological change to the Native Americans in the Ohio country. The traders brought guns, powder, and lead that made hunting easier and more reliable than with a bow and arrow, and their metal fishhooks improved the catch. They also brought other wonderful things—iron hoes, axes, and knives that eased the burden of clearing land, cultivating crops, and skinning game. Wool blankets, shirts, dresses, and coats meant the women no longer had to make clothing from skins or use bone needles and sinews for thread. Iron and brass cooking pots improved food preparation over pottery vessels and reed baskets.

Unfortunately, the Ohio Indians did not have the skills or the technology to produce these items independent from British and French civilization. Indeed, they could pay for these trade goods only with furs and skins. Yet their wants became insatiable, and the more they demanded, the more furs and skins were required for payment. In time, they overhunted and -trapped their lands. Zeisberger reported that the Delaware men each shot between 50 and 150 deer each fall, while fellow Moravian John Heckewelder observed that a trader on the Cuyahoga once purchased twenty-three "Horseload" of peltry from the Indians in that area. With hunting and trapping such as this, the game population disappeared, and the Indians had to range farther into the interior on their hunting expeditions. The Ohio Indians also became reliant on the traders and later blacksmiths to mend their broken firearms, knives, axes, and other tools. Moreover, without powder their guns were useless. By the time tribal cultures arrived in Ohio, then, the Native Americans were already dependent on European traders for the maintenance of a lifestyle that was no longer traditional. Indeed, they had lost much of their self-sufficiency. Ultimately, the Native Americans in the Ohio country would be overwhelmed by the technology they coveted and by a new form of military and political organization and economic culture.

The traders continued to desecrate traditional tribal culture with the liberal use of liquor, which they plied to gain a trading advantage or to facilitate outright theft when bargains were struck with drunken Indians. The Moravians and the other white settlers who came after them also were convinced that agriculture offered the best opportunity for the Ohio Indians to become acculturated and assimilated into American life. Yet farming had been primarily the domain of the women, and the Indian men viewed this policy as nothing less than their emasculation. Nor did they understand the concept of land sales. Traditionally, these Indian cultures had loaned their lands to other tribal groups in need, but permanent transfer of property rights and the accumulation of property for wealth were concepts that they did not understand. Nor could many of these Indian people easily accept the necessity of learning the new religion that the missionaries preached; after all, their own religious and ceremonial practices had served them well since the formation of their societies. Tribal culture also changed in another manner. As the traders visited the villages, established trading posts, lived among the Indian people, and took native wives, they also taught them the English language, but some of the first words were profane. The Moravian missionaries were particularly shocked by the felicity with which the Indians swore, especially using the terms "God damn" and "son of a bitch."

By the mid-seventeenth century, then, the lives of the Indian settlers in the Ohio country were on the verge of great change. They had become caught in the netherland between the French on the north and west and the English on the east, both of whom wanted their lands not so much for the trade of furs and deerskins but for its own sake. Certainly, control of the fur trade remained important, because it brought influence over the friendly nations. But influence had consequences beyond the fur trade, because it meant power over the allied tribes, and power enabled control not only of peoples but also of land. Most important, the control of the land meant empire. By 1750, the Delaware chief "King Beaver" clearly sensed the danger ahead for the Ohio country, and he could not have been more prophetic when he warned the Iroquois that "a high Wind is rising." Only trouble could come from it.

2.

CLASH OF CULTURES

The Miami women busily hoed the weeds in their corn fields along the plain that rose from the west bank of the Great Miami River opposite the mouth of Loramie's Creek, where their village of Pickawillany nestled in the quiet of a late June morning. Most of the men had left the camp on a hunting expedition. This village, under the leadership of Pianguisha, whom the French called La Demoiselle and the British knew as "Old Briton," had rejected the friendly overtures and veiled threats of the French to return to the headwaters of the Maumee and the Wabash. They also had refused to join them and their Indian allies against the English who had begun to penetrate the Ohio country with Pennsylvania traders. Yet few considered the village to be in imminent danger of attack, even though George Croghan, who ranged among the "far Indians" of the Sandusky and Lake Erie region, had built a stockade there. But when the sun reached about nine o'clock high, 250 Ottawa, Ojibwa, and Potawatomi raiders, led by mixed-blood Charles Langlade from Michelimackinac, broke from the surrounding cover of the bushes and trees along the river and swept through the fields and into the village with a rush and ferocity that caught everyone by surprise. Quickly they seized the women and children, but the English traders and La Demoiselle were their goals.

When the commotion of the attack began, three traders realized that they could not make a safe dash to the stockade, where a collection of twenty Miami men and boys and several other white traders had barricaded themselves, and they sought refuge behind the locked door of a nearby cabin. The French-inspired raiders soon broke down the cabin door and seized the cowering traders, who had become so overcome with fear that they had not fired a shot. Under interrogation, these captives soon told the attackers that few men defended the stockade and that it could be easily taken.

Throughout the remainder of the morning, the Indians peppered the stockade with musket fire. In the early afternoon the raiders called to the Miamis in the stockade that they would end the siege and let them go unharmed if they would turn over the white men. Without water in the stockade and with the enemy numbered ten to one against them and holding many families, including the wife and son of La Demoiselle, the Miamis accepted these terms, hoping for mercy rather than betrayal. The Miamis then surrendered five white men, while two others chose to hide under the stockade. Upon the surrender, the raiders immediately seized one trader with a stomach wound, stabbed him in the chest, took his scalp, cut his heart out, and ate it. They then returned the captive women and children and plundered the houses of the English traders. After the attackers had taken what they wanted, they killed La Demoiselle, dismembered his body, boiled it, and ate him before the horrified Miamis and traders. With La Demoiselle's power thus transferred to themselves, the raiders departed, leaving three Miamis, including La Demoiselle, together with one Mingo, a Shawnee, and an Englishman dead as they marched five English traders north to Detroit. They had not suffered any casualties. Chastened by the attack, the Miamis, "making great protestation of fidelity," now moved back west to the Maumee as the French had desired.

With the fall of Pickawillany, the Ohio Valley belonged to the French. Like the Miamis, no Indians in the Ohio country were truly independent. All Native Americans had become dependent on European culture for a variety of trade goods, such as tools, clothing, and food, which they did not believe they could live without. The power that furnished these goods dictated the loyalty and politics of the Indians in Ohio. After Pickawillany, the British traders from Pennsylvania left, the French took their place, and the Ohio Indians adjusted to a new reality.

Although the Ottawas, Ojibwas, and Potawatomis had provided the men for the attack on the Miamis at Pickawillany, the knife had been directed by the French, with the target being Great Britain. On the morning of June 21, 1752, then, the first shots of a new French and Indian War were fired. The final clash between the French and British empires for the control of the North American continent had begun at Pickawillany on the quiet banks of the Miami River. It would not be the last violence between Native Americans, the Europeans, and their descendants for control of the Ohio country.

* * *

When King George's War began in 1744, the French quickly sought an alliance with the Native Americans in the Ohio country to block any British attempt to seize the interior. The Iroquois who lived in northeastern Ohio as well as the Shawnees and Miamis accepted these diplomatic overtures and declared support for the French, who hoped to use these tribes to drive out the English traders who were encroaching on their sovereign claims to the region. Although the French and British fought primarily on the high seas and in Europe, the English succeeded in capturing the French stronghold of Louisbourg in 1745 and thereby cut off supplies bound to French traders and military posts for the purpose of keeping the Indian trade away from the British in the Ohio country. This loss, in addition to a French reduction of trade goods as an economy measure, caused serious problems, because the Ohio Indians, that is, the Shawnees, Delawares, and Iroquois or Mingos, had become dependent on European technology, particularly guns. The Miamis also pleaded with the French for "indispensable supplies," but received little at high prices.

In the absence of trade goods and with price gouging common by the French because of supply problems, British traders quickly took advantage of a "fair Opertunity," undersold their competitors, and lured the Ohio Indians back into the English fold, where Croghan reported that they remained in "strict friendship." This achievement was not difficult because the French had demanded that their Indian allies take up the hatchet against the English. In the Ohio country, the would-be allies of the French saw that they were constantly asked to fight for France only to be gouged by French traders. By 1748, the Indians of the Ohio country believed that France had broken their alliance, and unfortunate traders began to meet their deaths at the hands of resentful Indians who thought the French cheated them and were not only ungrateful for their allegiance but also greedy.

Sporadic attacks on French traders by the Wyandots of Sandusky, the White River Iroquois of the Cuyahoga region, and the Miamis in the northwest correctly convinced the French that the British were responsible for their problems in the Ohio country. When King George's War ended in 1748, the French made the mistake of demanding that their errant Indian allies return to their protection rather than treating them magnanimously with presents and lucrative trade. For the Native Americans in the Ohio country, whose culture was founded in part on the concept of reciprocity, the French continued to be ungrateful and parsimonious. They also demanded subordination.

In order to reassert the declining influence of France in the Ohio country, Canadian Governor Marquis de la Galissonière sent Pierre-Joseph de Céloron de Blainville, with 250 French regulars, militia, and native allies, into the region during the summer of 1749 to expel the British. Céloron had the mission of forcing the Wyandots at Sandusky under Orontony (Nicholas) to settle at Detroit and to destroy the hostile camp at Sonnontio on the Scioto River. He also boasted that he would "whip home" the Miamis at Pickawillany. At Lower Shawnee Town at the mouth of the Scioto, however, Céloron could merely bury a lead plate and nail a metal sign on a nearby tree that gave France claim to the region. This action introduced the concept of European land ownership and sovereignty to Ohio. With the Shawnees less than hospitable, Céloron admonished the English traders present to leave, then bade a hasty farewell.

Céloron then traveled to the mouth of the Great Miami River, where he turned northward to Pickawillany. There he found the Miamis in an ugly mood, perhaps because he constantly referred to the Ohio country as "my territories." They also had little desire to return to the French outpost of Fort Miami on the Maumee River in present-day northeastern Indiana, where Céloron said they would "enjoy perfect peace." Upon completion of his mission at Detroit,

Céloron wrote that the Shawnees and Miamis in Ohio were "very badly disposed towards the French, and are entirely devoted to the English." To remedy this situation, the French needed a major fortified trading post in Ohio, but they did not have the financial and logistical ability to build and sustain it. At best, they could only try to persuade the Miamis at Pickawillany as well as the Shawnees and Wyandots to look to the French for friendship and support. In time, perhaps the French hoped to regain the trade they had lost to the British during King George's War; until then, they urged the Indians to attack British traders in Ohio.

In the meantime, the British continued to pay high prices for deerskins and furs while spreading the idea that the French wanted to deny the Shawnees, Wyandots, and Miamis their freedom to trade while subjecting them to slavery. With the supply line for traders back to Pennsylvania shorter than the French water route across the Great Lakes to Montreal, the British were able to maintain an economic presence that provided diplomatic and military advantages. James Hamilton, governor of Pennsylvania, also worked to prevent any rapprochement between the Indians and the French. In the spring of 1750, he authorized George Croghan to tell the Wyandots and the Ohio Iroquois that they should "resent" attempts of the French to trade with them or form alliances.

When Orontony died in 1750, La Demoiselle became the primary thorn in the French side in the Ohio country. La Demoiselle was a chief of the Piankashaw band by birth and a Miami by marriage. By the late 1740s he had broken with the French and as a war leader established the band that settled at Pickawillany in 1747. In that year he also led an attack on a French post at a Miami village on the upper Maumee. This raid marked La Demoiselle as an ally of the Wyandots at Sandusky, the White River Iroquois, and the British who operated with traders out of Pennsylvania. This perceived alliance particularly concerned the French because Orontony had considered the Wyandots and the Iroquois "one people." If the Miami rebels under La Demoiselle's leadership formed an alliance with that group, French efforts to restore their control to the Ohio country would be infinitely more difficult. When La Demoiselle's Miami delegation negotiated a treaty with the British at Lancaster, Pennsylvania, in late July 1748, he gained sufficient prestige to maintain his independence from the Miamis, who resided on the upper Maumee and who professed allegiance to France. Yet La Demoiselle's revolt from the other Miamis depended on continued support from, especially trade with, the British.

By 1750, La Demoiselle had attracted perhaps as many as four hundred families to Pickawillany, including Piankashaws and Weas, and he had made overtures to the Ottawas and Ojibwas to join them. He also made British traders welcome, and they did not disappoint the Miamis. Rather than play off the British and French against each other for his own advantage and thereby capitalize on a relative balance of power between the two European empires, La Demoiselle cast his fate with the British. He permitted British traders to build a stockade that served as a supply house and trading station, and they continued to offer goods at lower prices, paid in deerskins and furs, than the French could match. These traders promised even more goods if the Miamis would "preserve the road safe and commodious between Pickawillany & Logstown." Yet this task proved impossible for the Miamis or any other Ohio Indians. By the summer of 1750, the Ohio country was a dangerous place for both Europeans and Native Americans.

The growing influence of La Demoiselle caused the French a great deal of concern, and they began to fear a "revolution" among the villages in the Ohio country. Indeed, the Iroquois in the Cuyahoga region and the Shawnees at Sonnontio (Lower Shawnee Town) now began to act as a "sort of republic" independent of French control. While the French could tolerate, even encourage, subordinate Native American entities within New France, they could not accept independent nations that functioned with impunity. These republics particularly threatened the communication lines as well as territorial claims between French Canada and Louisiana. Moreover, by the early 1750s, both France and Great Britain realized that the political control of the villages in the Ohio country would determine the imperial control of the North American continent. William Johnson, who soon became the major architect of British Indian policy, observed that to lose the support of the Indians would be "very bad."

The French agreed. By the autumn of 1751, French officials had determined that they had "no other course to adopt than to drive from the Beautiful River any European foreigners who will happen to be there." Accordingly, Marie François Picote, Sieur de Bellestre, led an attack on Pickawillany, but most of the villagers were away hunting. As a result, these French raiders captured only two British traders and killed a Miami man and woman. Unable to storm the palisades and strike the remaining villagers, the French expedition returned to Detroit. This attack infuriated La Demoiselle, who later ordered the execution of three captured French soldiers and the ears cut off another, which he sent back to the French with a warning to leave his village alone. The Pickawillany Miamis and their Wea and Shawnee allies also increased their attacks on French traders to the west. Faced with insubordination, the French decided to forsake their policy of accommodation and alliance and determined to use military power to force the wayward tribes back into their sphere of influence. They chose Pickawillany, recently weakened by smallpox and internal dissension, for the first strike.

* * *

Great Britain did not respond to the French and Indian attack on Pickawillany with a deliberate policy, because its administrative structure did not yet function that way. Rather, the colonial governments in Pennsylvania, Virginia, and New York formulated and executed British policy. Although the Miamis, Shawnees, Delawares, and Mingos sought British military support against the French, and while the Miamis requested inclusion in the "Covenant Chain" with the Iroquois, the Pennsylvanians and the Iroquois did not respond. The Iroquois were more concerned with land problems in New York and viewed this new conflict as a personal problem between the French and British, and they professed neutrality. The Pennsylvania legislature also failed to provide funds or militia to aid the Miamis, preferring that military retaliation come from New York, because the Ohio Indians were theoretically under the control of the Iroquois. Although the Virginians could have sent aid, they were primarily interested in gaining control of the Ohio country rather than helping the Indians keep it from the grasp of the French or protecting it for the Pennsylvanians. This ambivalence clearly indicated that the French had been correct—the British wanted only land and control of the Indian peoples.

In 1753 the British finally demanded that the French leave the Ohio country. If the British fought the French, however, they would do so to claim the Ohio country as their own, rather than defend

Indian lands. With the French claiming all lands north of the Ohio River and the British all lands to the south, nothing remained for the Native Americans. If both European powers intended to deny the Ohio country to the Indian people, then it did not make sense for the Native Americans to fight either nation. Given this realization, the Ohio Indians were in a foul mood by the autumn of 1753. They stood alone against both the French and the British, and they knew it.

The French attack on Pickawillany, then, fundamentally changed the relationship between the Ohio Indians and the British. As long as the contest for empire was fought with economic weapons in the form of trade goods, the British enjoyed a considerable advantage in gaining political alliances with the Indians, because colonial craftsmen manufactured trade merchandise relatively inexpensively, and competition among Pennsylvania traders and later with the Virginians kept prices low. But when the French escalated the competition for the land by utilizing military force, the British were at a decided loss. Although British supply lines adequately provisioned traders in the Ohio country, Pickawillany and other Ohio villages, such as Sonnontio on the Scioto, lay closer to the French garrison at Detroit than to British military protection. With Fort Miami on the Maumee only 75 miles from Pickawillany and Detroit only 150 miles from La Demoiselle's village, the danger became clear, because the British had not yet built forts west of the Appalachians to protect them. The French attack on Pickawillany and the unwillingness of the British to retaliate proved the inability and unwillingness of the Crown to defend its allies.

Life in the Ohio country always remained tenuous at best for the Native Americans. Hostile military power could make that existence more difficult. In 1754, faced with the task of choosing between French muskets and British trade goods, the Shawnees, Delawares, and rebel Miamis drifted back to the French fold. Throughout the French and Indian War that followed for the next nine years, the Ohio Indians remained loyal to the French.

* * *

During the French and Indian War, which lasted from 1754 to 1763, the Ohio Indians, who lived west of the Ohio River, frequently raided with their Delaware and Shawnee relatives, who lived to the east in western Pennsylvania. After Braddock rudely rejected support from the Delawares, Shawnees, and Mingos, telling them that after he drove away the French "no Savage Should Inherit the land," Shingas, a Delaware chief, replied that if they could not live on the land, they would not fight for it. Although Braddock responded that he did not need their help, he perhaps soon regretted that decision, for he lost the battle in his attack on Fort Duquesne, and his life as well. With Braddock's defeat on July 9, 1755, the Ohio Indians believed the French would win the war and drive the British away. Nevertheless, while the Ohio Indians allied with the French as a matter of expediency, they fought more to keep their country free from British and French control.

Indeed, the Ohio Indians fought their own separate war, but divisions remained. Although Shingas, for example, whom the British recognized as the "king" of the western Delawares to simplify matters of negotiation, led raids against Pennsylvania's border settlements, Tamaqua, his brother, did not join the attacks, because he considered himself a peacemaker. Yet both understood that the war's ultimate prize would be control of the land, not just the fur trade. With military skill and necessary alliances, the Ohio Indians hoped to hold the land as their own. During that conflict, they relied on French power to offset the numerical superiority of the British, operating on the premise that once the British had been defeated, as Ackowanothic, an Ohio Delaware spokesman said, "we can drive away the French when we please." The Ohio Indians never considered themselves to be subjects of the French, only their allies. The Shawnee and Delaware attacks also showed the Iroquois that they were no longer under their control.

With war virtually over in the Ohio country by 1758, and with the French the losers, the Ohio Indians entered into a formal peace treaty with the Pennsylvanians at a meeting at Lancaster. There the Delawares negotiated on the premise that peace would not come to the Ohio country until both the French and the British withdrew from the valley. In early September 1758, Shingas told missionary Frederick Post, "We have great reason to believe you intend to drive us away, and settle the country; or else, why do you come to fight in the land that God has given us?" Then he asked, "Why do not you and the French fight in the old country, and on the sea? Why do you come to fight on our land? This makes every body believe, you want to take the land from us by force, and settle it." Tamaqua, who by 1758 was recognized by the British and the Iroquois as the leading "king" of the Delawares, wanted trade, but he also wanted the British to go "back over the mountain." Once that occurred, both Native Americans and the British could live in peace based on economic reciprocity. His view also clearly indicated that the Ohio Indians did not trust the British.

To allay the fears of the Ohio Indians, the British proclaimed that they merely wanted to drive away the French rather than seize Indian lands. Still, when Britain appropriated the lands west of the Ohio River in the Treaty of Logstown in 1758 and assumed management of Indian affairs in the Ohio country, the Indians had great cause for alarm. The British ultimately agreed to improve trade relations with the Indians but not to leave the Ohio Valley. Indeed, the British considered the Ohio country to be their land by the right of the conqueror and the Indians to be their subjects. British accommodation with the Indians based on the French presence was no longer necessary. With the French gone, the British now believed that the Ohio Indians had the obligation to obey imperial policy. The Ohio Indians, of course, did not consider themselves to have been defeated.

George Croghan, official agent of the British Indian Department, clearly understood the reality of Indian-white relations in the valley when he remarked that while the British army had defeated the French, it had "nothing to boast from the War with the natives." When Croghan held a conference at Fort Pitt in August 1760, the Wyandots, Shawnees, Delawares, Mingos, Miamis, and others eagerly sought the return of British traders. During the war their guns had fallen into disrepair, and they had exhausted most of their powder and lead. Before they could restore the fur and deerskin trade, they needed essential supplies and gunsmiths. Financial problems, however, in part prevented the British from meeting the needs of the Ohio Indians. Moreover, the return of normal relations lagged, in part, because traders could operate only at British military posts in order for the government to gain control of the process. The British planned to limit trade, that is, hold it hostage, to force the Indians, particularly the Shawnees, to return their captives and stop stealing horses from the traders.

Colonel Henry Bouquet, commander of Fort Pitt, initiated this policy early in 1761, but he was soon disappointed because the Ohio Indians considered the return of generous trading practices to be a prerequisite for the return of white captives. In late July 1761, Bouquet wrote that the Ohio Indians complained that British traders could not go to their villages. But, he observed, "when they are told that the Reasons are their not delivering the Prisoners & continuing to steal our Horses, they have nothing to say, but Repeat Promises they will not perform, till forced to it by keeping the Trade from them."

In September 1761, the Wyandots from the Sandusky area complained to Croghan and Sir William Johnson, British superintendent of Indian affairs at Detroit, that "many articles are very scarce & in particular powder is sold so sparingly & is so hard to be got that we are all apprehensive we must shortly be obliged to leave off hunting entirely, as our Young Men cannot procure sufficient to cloath themselves or provide for their Wives & Children." They again asked for guns, powder, lead, and credit. The British refused the latter request, demanding instead that for reasons of economy the Indians purchase goods by procuring furs and deerskins. But they also rejected generosity as a policy because of cultural prejudice which led them to believe that gifts fostered dependence and laziness. In contrast, the Indians believed that fathers and leaders gave presents and extended great generosity to their children and subjects. For the Ohio Indians, good relations between white and Native American cultures depended on reciprocity. They expected peace to be rewarded with trade. Indeed, gifts would "brighten the chain of friendship." In contrast, the British expected peace based not on the renewal of trade but on the fear of British military power. Between 1758 and 1762, the British used a policy of "garrison government" to hold the newly acquired empire. This policy required building or occupying a chain of forts across the Upper Great Lakes region. But most of these posts, such as Fort Sandusky, were lightly staffed and poorly supplied.

In October 1761, Lieutenant Elias Meyer, who commanded at Sandusky, reported that his detachment suffered "considerably" from the lack of an interpreter to help his men acquire food from the Wyandots. By November, however, he had solved his food problem and reported that the Indians now "supply us pretty well with venison at Moderate Rates." Reciprocity was essential for both the Wyandots and the British. Killbuck, a Delaware headman, for example, led at least one pack train of horses carrying ammunition from Fort Pitt to Sandusky for a wage of one dollar per day. Services, such as supplying venison and transporting supplies for payment in goods or money, reinforced the reciprocity that the Indians understood. But reciprocity such as this did not extend to all areas, particularly in relation to prisoners and control of the land.

Even the trade that reemerged between the two peoples was poisoned by the excessive use of whiskey and hindered from fostering good relations because of poor supplies and high prices. When the British removed knives, razors, tomahawks, gunpowder, flints, and guns from the approved list for the traders, the Indians became increasingly angry. In 1762, Croghan reported that the Ohio Indians were "very Sulkey & Ill Temper.d." Indeed, even before the ink on the Treaty of Paris had dried, the Ohio Indians nostalgically wished for the return of the French, while they sought desperately to reach accommodation with and fair treatment by the British. By 1763, the Ohio Indians interpreted British trade restrictions, particularly for powder, as an attempt to destroy them and their way of life. It was essentially an act of war.

The restriction of traders to specific locations also posed a hardship on the Ohio Indians, who now found it more difficult to acquire needed goods, which already were in scant supply and at high prices. In 1761, the Shawnees complained that the British did not "look upon them as brothers and friends." At Fort Sandusky, which became the trading center for northwestern Ohio, Pennsylvania traders earned a bad reputation. Indeed, they were a group whom George Washington called a "set of rascally Fellows divested of all faith and honor." And they kept a feeling of grievance alive among the Wyandots. By 1762, the Wyandots had not made Fort Sandusky "agreeable" for the traders and the garrison. Lieutenant H.C. Pauli, who commanded, warned Bouquet at Fort Pitt that they intended to "have it burnt." Few Ohio Indians were as blunt as the Wyandots, but despite their lack of diplomatic niceties, the British clearly understood their feelings.

The British also demanded that the Delawares, Shawnees, and Mingos return all captives. This imposition produced a cultural shock among the Indians who had adopted prisoners to replace family members who had been killed in the French and Indian War. By 1760, many of the white children taken early in the war had become thoroughly acculturated into Indian society, and their return caused hardship for both Indian parents and their adopted children. The British could not accept this cultural practice. At a council meeting at Pittsburgh in July 1759, George Croghan told the Ohio Indians that the British would "never taste true Satisfaction" until all captives had been returned.

By October 1761, 338 prisoners had been returned, but several hundred others, primarily western Pennsylvanians, remained captives of the Delawares and Shawnees. The Ohio Indians hesitated to return their hostages because they believed the British would launch an all-out attack to destroy their villages and seize their lands once the last captive had been repatriated. The Ohio Indians simply did not trust the British, who largely had given them no reason to do so.

With the British acting like conquerors and faced with the loss of their lands and adopted children, wives, and husbands, the Ohio Indians ultimately abandoned their quest for accommodation with the British, who the Shawnees said had become "too great a People." Instead, they chose war rather than diplomacy to protect their interests. In 1763, this uprising became known as Pontiac's Rebellion, and it struck the Ohio frontier.

* * *

In 1762 crop failure, famine, and smallpox swept the Ohio River valley, inflicting misery on the Native Americans. In September a Thomas Hutchins visited the Shawnee country and reported people "Sick and Dying everyday." When the Ohio Indians sought supplies and aid from the British, they met rejection. With their women and children suffering great hardship and painful death from hunger and disease, the Mingos complained that the unwillingness of the British to help them in time of dire need clearly indicated that they had "bad designs" against them. In time of crisis, fathers eagerly helped their children, and brothers aided brothers. Now British actions proved that they were neither fathers nor brothers, but rather an evil people who wished only ill on the Indians in the Ohio country. In 1763, Netawatwees (Newcomer), chief of the Turtle clan of the Delawares, reflected the general sense of betrayal when he proclaimed that the British had "grown too powerfull & seemed as if they would be too Strong for God himself."

With the military strength of the Ohio Indians diminished by restricted trade policies and by the removal of the French as a counterweight to British pressure, and with this new enemy seemingly stronger than God, only one solution offered any hope of cultural self-preservation—spiritual renewal. It came in the form of Neolin, a Delaware prophet, who called upon his kinsmen and other Native Americans to cast off all British influences, such as tools and clothes, and to return to "traditional" values by hunting with bows and arrows rather than guns, to use a bow and drill rather than flint and steel to start a fire, and for the women to make clothing from deerskins rather than wool or cotton purchased from traders. If they returned to the ways of their ancestors, they would "purify themselves of sin." The ways of Anglo civilization led only to hell, but by rejecting any association with the "White people" and by praying to an intermediary of the Great Being, they could regain the "Good Road" that would lead to a good life on earth and beyond. Separation, not accommodation, would remove the Native Americans from a position of servitude and let them enter the kingdom of heaven where no whites lived.

Neolin preached that the misfortunes and hardships of the Indian peoples resulted from their rejection of the past, when religious rituals had been faithfully followed. As a result, the Supreme Being became angry with the "evil ways" of his people and inflicted punishments upon them—hunger, disease, and the loss of their lands. Neolin, of course, had integrated the concept of sin, which the Ohio Indians had learned from Moravian and Quaker missionaries, with Native American spiritual beliefs. The Supreme Being, like the Christian God, meted out punishment, but the Great Spirit also had the capacity to forgive those who recanted and changed their ways. Neolin taught that the Delawares could regain the Supreme Being's favor and end their sickness and want as well as the loss of their adopted children and lands if they would only "purge out all that they got of ye White peoples ways & Nature." Neolin expected this goal to be achieved by peaceful means, but the result was a spiritual nationalism that brought renewed violence to the Ohio country.

Neolin's mixture of Christianity and native religion, with references to visions, heaven, hell, sin, and God, while urging a return to a lifestyle that existed prior to contact with European civilization, appealed to the Shawnees and Delawares, because peoples living under great stress and whose lives and culture hang in the balance often seek help through religion. But Neolin's message affected the British even more, because they saw this new religion as a threat to the deerskin and fur trade and their missionary work among the Ohio Indians. They also saw Neolin's religious revival as the nationalistic foundation upon which they could organize and build to drive the British from the trans-Appalachian frontier. Neolin and his followers believed this as well. The nativism that Neolin preached quickly fostered resentment against the British. The Delawares, who followed Netawatwees, welcomed Neolin's message and became particularly belligerent along the Muskingum and Tuscarawas.

Pontiac, an Ottawa war chief, whom a French contemporary called "a proud, vindictive, war-like and easily offended man," chose to combine Neolin's call for spiritual purification through prayer and a return to the old ways of living with military power that would enable the western Indians not only to reject European culture but also to drive the whites from their lands and keep them away forever—or, as General Thomas Gage put it, to "spirit up" his followers for war against the British. In 1765, Croghan wrote to William Johnson, who directed British Indian policy in the colonies, that "Pontiac is a shrewd sensible Indian of few words, & commands more respect amongst those Nations, than any Indian I ever saw could do amongst his own tribe." Pontiac was quite clear. He said the "Master of Life put Arms in our hands," a variation on the Christian concept that God helps those who help themselves. Pontiac also told his followers, "It is important for us, my brothers, that we exterminate from our lands this nation which seeks only to destroy us." By the autumn of 1762, the traders in the Ohio country expected renewed war at the very time that the British and French contemplated peace.

The traders were right. When the Ohio Indians learned of the Peace of Paris, formally announced in January 1763, which transferred all French claims in North America to the British, they were shocked. Newcomer, head of the Delawares, reportedly was "struck dumb for a considerable time." Croghan reported that the Ohio Indians insisted that the "French had no Right to give away their Country; as, they Say, they were never Conquered by any Nation." As a result, in May 1763 the Ottawas attacked Detroit in response to the urging of Pontiac, thereby beginning a new war. Although popularly known as the "conspiracy of Pontiac," this conflict should more appropriately be known as a "Defensive War" or as a war for independence by the western Indians. Other attacks quickly followed across the western frontier, which soon became a region of armed revolt. By the autumn more than six hundred Pennsylvanians had been killed or captured by the Delawares and Shawnees operating from the Ohio country. With the Shawnees, Wyandots, Delawares, Munsees, and Senecas, who called themselves the "Five Nations of Scioto," bound in an alliance, they posed a considerable obstacle to British expansion. George Croghan contended that the Shawnees had been responsible for this military union. The Shawnees, he wrote, had "More to Say with the Western Nations than any other this way."

* * *

Fort Sandusky, built in 1745 as a blockhouse from which the British operated a trading post, stood on the portage between the Sandusky River and Lake Erie. Although Nicholas destroyed the village and palisades in April 1748 to prevent the French and their Indian allies from seizing it, the British garrisoned the blockhouse on January 2, 1761, with fifteen men under the command of Ensign H. C. Pauli. By mid-February the Indians were unhappy that the parsimonious British had returned, and relations remained tense, but no serious trouble occurred until spring. On May 16, a group of Indians appeared at the gates and asked to see Pauli, who recognized them as frequent traders at the fort. Once in his headquarters they lighted pipes and began conversation, only to seize him upon a signal while the fort came under attack from their friends. Within minutes, his command lay dead about the post grounds. They set the blockhouse aflame, bound Pauli, and took him by canoe to Detroit, where he was forced to run the gauntlet and accept adoption by an old Ottawa woman who had lost her husband. In July, however, he escaped and fled to the protective custody of the British inside the fort.

Retribution for the destruction of Fort Sandusky came on July 26, when a Captain Dalyell arrived with 260 men by boat along the southern shore of Lake Erie on his way to relieve the besieged garrison at Detroit. Appalled at the decomposing bodies and charred remains, Dalyell marched against a Wyandot village at the lower falls of the Sandusky River, now present-day Fremont, where he destroyed the corn fields and burned the village.

In the autumn of 1761, other British troops under Lieutenant Elias Meyer arrived to rebuild Fort Sandusky, including blockhouse, stockade, and banquettes. Shorthanded, with forty men drawing thirty-eight rations per day, and with his troops often ill, Lieutenant Meyer made slow progress, reporting on November 15 that "the three horses belonging to the King are so fatigued by their daily work that every little while they drop to the ground exhausted." Although the troops finished the construction of the new fort in November, probably on the site of present-day Venice about three miles west of Sandusky, the British remained hard pressed to supply it. Pork and flour always remained in short supply, while beef was available only when it arrived on the hoof from Fort Pitt.

* * *

Although ill-prepared to defend against Pontiac's inspired attacks, the British military decided to launch a two-pronged attack into Ohio. In the autumn of 1764, columns led by Colonel John Bradstreet and Colonel Henry Bouquet moved toward Ohio from Presque Isle and Fort Pitt respectively. Bradstreet had the task of reaching Fort Sandusky and restoring communication along Lake Erie, while Bouquet had the assignment of destroying the hostile towns along the Tuscarawas River. When Bradstreet, however, made peace with the Indians at Detroit on September 7, because they could no longer secure powder and lead, the Delawares and

Shawnees in the Muskingum, Tuscarawas, and Scioto valleys became isolated.

On October 3, 1764, Bouquet marched from Fort Pitt with a newly recruited force of fifteen hundred Pennsylvanians, Virginians, and regulars from the Forty-second and Sixtieth regiments. Along with the soldiers and wagon drivers, Bouquet's train included two nurses for his hospital and one woman belonging to each corps, probably a prostitute or laundress or both. He ordered the other women "belonging to the camp" back to the settlements. Then, after shooting two captured deserters to ensure good discipline, the troops headed west. Three parties of Virginia volunteers led as scouts. Ax-men and two companies of light infantry followed. Behind them the regulars and Pennsylvanians, marching in single file, formed a large square with a party of light horse and another corps of Virginia volunteers forming a rear guard. Within the protection of the square, the pack-horses, laden with ammunition, officers' baggage, and tents, along with cattle and sheep for food, moved slowly forward, covering a mile and a half the first day. Bouquet's mission was not to launch a surprise attack, but rather to march to the Tuscarawas with a show of force and either overawe the Indians or inflict enough military damage to force them to accept peace.

British commander-in-chief Jeffrey Amherst had ordered Bouquet into Ohio, telling him, "I Wish to Hear of no Prisoners, should any of the villains be met with Arms." Amherst rejected gift giving to ensure peaceful relations. Instead, he said, "When men of whatsoever race behave ill, they must be punished but not bribed." Both Amherst and Bouquet wanted the villages destroyed and the Indians dispersed. Bouquet did not respect or sympathize with the Ohio Indians. He did not consider them to be independent nations that had been forced to renew war because of inequitable actions by the British. Rather, the Indians were British subjects who deserved to be treated as rebels and traitors. Bouquet did not trust the Indians to keep their word, and he believed they understood only force.

On October 13, Bouquet's troops reached the Tuscarawas River, the main branch of the Muskingum, and followed it toward the Delaware and Mingo villages. While they were camped along the river near present-day Bolivar, six Indians arrived to tell Bouquet that the villages were ready to make peace in order to avoid destruction. Bouquet agreed to a meeting the next day beyond the confines of the camp, which he now worked feverishly to secure with a stockade, because his scouts reported a large number of Indians nearby. The next day some forty warriors, mostly Delawares, along with Beaver, chief of the Turkey clan, and a few Senecas and Shawnees arrived at the designated place. After ritually smoking their pipe, they told Bouquet that the recent hostilities had been the fault of their rash young men and the "western nations," and that they would return all of their prisoners in return for peace.

Bouquet was not impressed, but he promised to think about their offer. When they met again on October 20, however, Bouquet rejected their "frivolous and unavailing" excuses, and he told the chiefs that they had the responsibility to punish their young men when they "did wrong." Then he recounted their "barbarous" attacks on whites in the Ohio country, and he told them that he could not trust them because of their past treachery and broken promises. Most important, he said, "This army shall not leave your country till you have fully complied with every condition that is to precede my treaty with you." He also told the Indians that he had brought the relatives of many whites whom the Indians had "massacred or taken prisoners," and they were "impatient for revenge." Bouquet then threatened, "It is with great difficulty that I can protect you against their just resentment." Telling the Tuscarawas villagers that the Ottawas, Ojibwas, and Wyandots had already made peace, that the Six Nations had joined the British against them, and that the French in the western country were now "subjects to the king of Great-Britain," he emphasized that they were surrounded and in danger of being destroyed as a people. "But," Bouquet told them, "the English are a merciful and generous nation, averse to shed the blood, even of their most cruel enemies; and if it was possible that you could convince us, that you sincerely repent of your past perfidy, you might yet hope for mercy and peace."

Specifically, Bouquet wanted all of their prisoners brought to Wakatomica within twelve days. He demanded everyone: "Englishmen, Frenchmen, women, children; whether adopted in your tribes, married, or living amongst you under any denomination and pretence whatsoever; together with all negroes." Bouquet also re-

quired the Delawares, Shawnees, and Senecas to furnish their prisoners with sufficient food, clothing, and horses for their return to
Fort Pitt, about 150 miles away. Once the captives had been returned, he told them, "You shall then know on what terms you may
obtain the peace you sue for."

Although the Delawares readily agreed to bring in their prisoners
and returned eighteen at that time, the Shawnees agreed to do so
only with "dejected sullenness." Bouquet, distrusting them, then
marched his force to the forks of the Muskingum, the site of present-
day Coshocton, on October 25. He decided to accept the captives
there, because this location was more central to the nearby Indian
towns. Just as important, Bouquet could "awe all the enemy's settlements and destroy their towns" if they did not meet his demands.
The Indians knew full well their danger, and during the next few
weeks they arrived at Bouquet's camp in small parties and returned
their captives.

The repatriation of the captives did not go easily. When the
bands brought Anglo children and adults to Bouquet's camp, the
white parents and family members ran to them, if they could still
recognize their sons, daughters, and wives after months and years
among the Indians. Others, desperately searching for lost children,
frantically rushed to each captive, hoping to identify a loved one or
to ask about those still missing. Mothers and fathers grasped children and tearfully hugged them while pulling them away from
their Indian parents, who also cried and grasped their adopted children, all the while trying to keep them near as long as possible.
While the Indian parents remained in camp, they visited their
adoptive children daily and brought them corn, skins, horses, and
other items just as they had while the children were a part of their
Native American families. All the time, the Indian parents showed
the marks of the "most sincere and tender affection," forgetting in
the mind of one contemporary "their usual savageness."

Not all of the children wanted to return to their birth parents
or to be cared for by Bouquet's soldiers until they could be returned
to Fort Pitt and perhaps their parents or relatives. Children who had
been captured very young and who had lived with loving Indian
parents for several years now no longer spoke English. These children had to be pulled from their Native American parents, all the

while crying and grasping for their protection. One observer wrote that some children were "so completely savage that they were brought to the camp tied hand and foot." Children "cried as if they should die when they were presented to us." Even the youngest knew that something was terribly wrong, because their parents were crying, hugging them, and pushing them away all at the same time. When Bouquet broke camp for the return to Fort Pitt on Sunday morning, November 18, with more than two hundred redeemed captives, some Indian parents received permission to travel along with their children, prolonging the final separation as long as possible.

Nor did all of the adult prisoners want to return, and the Shawnees had to "bind" several captives and forcibly take them to Bouquet's camp. Some of the adult women, who now had husbands in the native villages, escaped and fled back to the Indian towns. "Some, who could not make their escape, clung to their savage acquaintance at parting, and continued many days in bitter lamentations, even refusing sustenance," according to one report. Apparently the soldiers and the whites who accompanied Bouquet considered these adults to have been of the "lowest rank" in white society before being captured. Certainly they considered these captives to be culturally inferior, "for, easy and unconstrained as the savage life is, certainly it could never be put in competition with the blessings of improved life and the light of religion, by any persons who have had the happiness of enjoying, and the capacity of discerning, them."

White Indians, then, were as culturally inferior and depraved as red Indians. Although they might deserve pity, they could expect little more. When two of the returned captives, Rhonda Boyd and Elizabeth Studebaker, fled back to their native villages on Bouquet's return trip, their rejection of white culture could not have been more profound. When the Shawnees delivered their white captives to Fort Pitt on May 10, 1765, Lawoughqua, their spokesman, said: "Father—Here is your Flesh and Blood . . . they have been all tied to us by Adoption, although we now deliver them up to you. We will always look upon them as Relations whenever the Great Spirit is pleased that we may visit them. . . . We have taken as much Care of these Prisoners, as if they were our [own] Flesh and blood. Father we request you will use them tender & kindly, which will be a means of inducing them to live contentedly with you." The clash of cultures could not have been greater.

These scenes of separation and reunion, one contemporary observed, "should make us charitably consider the barbarities as the effects of wrong education, and false notions of bravery and heroism, while we should look on their virtues as sure marks that nature has made them fit subjects of cultivation as well as us; and that we are called by our superior advantages to yield them all the helps we can in this way." Here, then, along the banks of the Tuscarawas was an early call for acculturation and assimilation and the corresponding destruction of Native American culture.

Bouquet achieved remarkable success. Impressed with British military power and weakened by a smallpox epidemic in 1763, short on powder and lead, and knowing they could not drive the British away, the Ohio Indians accepted Bouquet's terms for peace, although the Shawnees remained "very crabby." Those terms required the Shawnees, Delawares, and Senecas each to furnish two hostages to accompany him to Fort Pitt to guarantee peace and the return of the remaining hostages, pending the conclusion of a formal treaty at that post in the spring. By accepting Bouquet's terms, the Delawares and Shawnees along the Tuscarawas River would prevent an attack on their villages and avoid any land cessions. But Bouquet also contributed to the cause of peace by ignoring General Gage's order to "deliver the Promoters of the War into your hands to be put to death." Even so, he made a list of those whom he hoped to seize, including Neolin.

Essentially, a major British problem in the Ohio country was that no Indian leader could speak for all Native Americans in the region. As a result, the British decided that Pontiac was not only responsible for the war on the frontier but also the only leader who could bring it to a conclusion. In fact, Pontiac did speak for many western villages, and he was shocked when he learned that the Shawnees along the Scioto had agreed to a truce with Bouquet. But in 1766, he too agreed to stop fighting. Peace then returned to the Ohio country. Yet the peace that the British negotiated, based on diplomacy and military strength, essentially returned the Ohio Valley to the status quo prior to Pontiac's rebellion. The British gained the return of white captives, control of French posts, and the right of passage through the region. But while the Indians became British subjects, Superintendent of Indian Affairs Sir William Johnson recognized that this designation applied only "so far as the same can be consistent with the Indians native rights," particularly regarding lands. The British, however, realized they did not have sufficient power to defeat the Ohio Indians. Accommodations by both cultures remained essential to ensure a secure peace.

* * *

The British actually embarked on a policy of recognizing Native American rights to lands as early as 1761, when the government began plans to restrict traders and settlement west of the Appalachians. Formally enunciated in the Proclamation of 1763, this policy attempted to gain British control of the West, in part by requiring the licensing of traders and restricting trading to posts in order to control pricing and limit the use of liquor in the exchange process. The British also intended to negotiate for the purchase of Indian lands to permit "fixed boundaries" and the orderly settlement of the trans-Appalachian frontier. White settlers and traders, however, aggressively pushed into that region and prevented accommodation between the British and the Ohio Indians. These "Frontier People" sought not accommodation with the Ohio Indians but rather their removal. Compromise did not enter their thoughts, and magnanimity never governed their actions. British officials in the West considered them to be the "very dregs of the people" and "lawless banditti." General Gage contended that these frontier men and women were "a Sett of People . . . near as wild as the country they go in, or the People they deal with, & by far more vicious & wicked." Respecting personal freedom more than law and advocating their right to take unused land rather than to await negotiated settlements with the trans-Appalachian Indians, these frontier people moved relentlessly into the Ohio Valley and soon cast covetous eyes to the rich lands west of the river.

By 1774 approximately fifty thousand whites lived on the trans-Appalachian frontier, and the British army could not control them, being in the words of Gage "too Numerous, too Lawless and Licentious ever to be restrained." By that time, the British Empire no longer remained the principal enemy of the Ohio Indians. Instead it was the relentlessly westward-moving Americans. The young men in the white settlements were as difficult to control as the young men in the Indian villages along the Tuscarawas, Muskingum, and Scioto rivers when grievance festered in their minds. For Gage, they were "almost out of the Reach of Law and Government; Neither the Endeavors of Government, or Fear of Indians has kept them properly within Bounds."

The young Virginia settlers were the worst. They hated Indians and preferred their extermination in the Ohio Valley. In April 1773, David McClure, a missionary, remarked that in the Ohio country the Virginians seemed "to feel themselves beyond the arm of government & freed from the restraining influence of religion." McClure observed that the frontier Virginians lived like Indians and were no better than "white Savages." Although the frontier people lived by farming and hunting, just like the Ohio Indians, when the hunt took the Virginians onto lands claimed by the Indians, they caused trouble, sometimes killing Indians on sight as if they were part of the quarry. By the autumn of 1771, George Croghan reported that the Indians did not "think themselves safe even on the West side of the Ohio." Croghan observed that the settlers in western Pennsylvania "thought it a meritorious act to kill Heathens whenever they were found." William Johnson concurred, noting that this attitude seemed to be "the opinion of all the common people."

The Indians in the Ohio country were naturally "very sulky and much disturbed" by these settlers, whom they called "long knives." However, they too were not without blame. They had killed traders, long hunters, and settlers for revenge, and every act of white retribution required a similar response. The Delawares and the Shawnees along the Muskingum and Scioto were happy to meet that obligation as they raided across the Ohio River into western Pennsylvania. By 1772 McClure observed that the Delawares of Newcomerstown exhibited "extreme resentment at the encroachments of the white people, on their hunting ground." They claimed sovereignty of their Kentucky hunting lands, and they demanded that the British and colonial Americans recognize that right.

When the British attempted to establish a permanent boundary line between Indian and white lands in 1768 to replace the Proclamation of 1763, they relied on the fiction that the Iroquois still spoke for the Ohio Indians through the Covenant Chain. When the Iroquois ceded all title to their lands east and south of the Ohio River in the Treaty of Fort Stanwix in 1768, the Ohio Shawnees, Delawares, and Mingos realized not only that they had lost a traditional hunting ground but also that now only the river stood between them and the relentlessly westering frontier people. The Shawnees rejected the Treaty of Fort Stanwix and the right of the Iroquois to make that cession. Two years later they held a host of meetings along the Scioto with various northern and southern peoples in an attempt to create an Indian alliance to stop British expansion. The Shawnee league failed to develop largely because the Indians were not united locally or regionally. Some of the villagers along the Scioto, Tuscarawas, and Muskingum chose to move west beyond the Mississippi River, while others feared British attacks on their villages if they joined. At the same time, the British worked skillfully to keep the Hurons, Miamis, and Potawatomis from joining.

When Virginia surveyors moved west of the Kanawha River, which provided the western boundary of Virginia's lands in the Treaty of Fort Stanwix, the Shawnees along the Scioto planned to drive them back. Lord Dunmore, Virginia's governor, admitted that his power was "insufficient to restrain the Americans" from settling Indian lands in Kentucky, and he did not want to do so. Without respect for law or treaties or the property rights of the Native Americans, the Virginians claimed land at will along the Ohio River across from the Shawnees and held it with their muskets. By the spring of 1774, rumors reached Pittsburgh that the Shawnees were murdering whites along the Ohio River in retaliation. Hatred and violence characterized the actions of both Indians and whites on the Ohio frontier.

On May 3, 1774, a group of Virginians coaxed two men and two women to cross the Ohio River from the Mingo village at the mouth of Yellow Creek at present-day Steubenville. With cold calculation, they plied the friendly Mingos with liquor and killed them. They also murdered eight others who came in search, one of whom was the sister and another possibly the mother of Logan, a war chief who lived in the Yellow Creek village. When the news of these murders reached the Shawnee towns, the young men demanded retribution, but the chiefs, such as Cornstalk, urged caution and sought mediation and reconciliation rather than war.

Few Shawnees responded to Logan's call for war and instead protected several Pennsylvania traders along the Hockhocking Creek, because they had guaranteed their safety. Cornstalk also sent a party from the Shawnee villages to Fort Pitt with a message that "the Traders that were amongst us were very much endangered by such doings . . . we are convinced of their Innocence. We are Determined to protect them . . . therefore we Request that you will present our good Intentions to the Governors of Virginia, and Pennsylvania, and request that a stop may be put to such Doings for the Future. . . . I have with great Trouble and pains prevailed on the foolish People amongst us to sit still and do no harm till we see whether it is the intention of the white people in general to fall on us."

Essentially, most Shawnees thought that if the British overlooked Logan's call for war, they would ignore a host of isolated killings by whites. At the same time, the Delawares had no inclination for war, and since their defeat in 1764, they had acknowledged the leadership of the Six Nations. The Iroquois also did not want war, and in May they ordered their "brethren" the Delawares out of Shawnee country so that "no evil may happen them by accident which would give us great concern." This lack of support by the Iroquois in time of need greatly displeased the militant Shawnees. The British policy of divide and conquer now proved effective in isolating the Shawnees in Ohio.

Logan, however, rejected accommodation. He wanted only vengeance for the loss of his family, friends, and relatives. Soon he traveled to Wakatomica, a mixed village of Mingos and Shawnees near the Muskingum River, where he recruited a war party for retaliation. The Shawnee and Mingo chiefs, although unable to control the passions of their young men, restricted Logan to two parties of thirteen men each and gained his promise to strike only at Virginians located west of the Monongahela. He would not attack Pennsylvanians, and upon his return he would listen to the counsel of the chiefs.

Logan and his bands of Mingos and Shawnees crossed the Ohio River and struck the Pennsylvania frontier with a bloody vengeance that sent hundreds of terror-stricken settlers fleeing from the back country. After Logan had taken thirteen scalps, he was satisfied and returned to the west bank of the Ohio River. But he did not bring peace with him. Instead, Captain John Connolly at Pittsburgh prepared for war and an attack into Ohio. Lord Dunmore, who also had the aspirations of a land speculator in the Kanawha region, in part to block Pennsylvanian expansion, offered his support. In a Kentucky cleared of Indians, land values would escalate all to the benefit of speculators such as himself, and settled lands would return important tax monies. Virtually every white man and woman in the Ohio country wanted the Indians "severly chastised" for Logan's raid.

Accordingly, by mid-August 1774, Pennsylvania militia crossed the Ohio and decimated Wakatomica and six Mingo villages, but the Mingos and Shawnees had fled before their arrival. Lord Dunmore also sent a contingent of more than a thousand militia to the mouth of the Kanawha to build a fort and to strike the Shawnees, most of whom still advocated peace. When the Virginians reached the mouth of the Kanawha, however, Cornstalk led a force of approximately one thousand Shawnees across the Ohio and struck on October 10, 1774, but they were driven back after a long and hard-fought engagement. Known as the Battle of Point Pleasant, this action was perhaps the most violent fighting ever along the Ohio River. Dunmore then sent troops in pursuit across to the north bank of the Ohio and up the Hocking Valley toward the Shawnee villages on the Pickaway Plains. There he built a temporary encampment called Camp Charolette and made contact with the Shawnees for a truce. Before these negotiations could be concluded, however, Colonel Andrew Lewis, who had remained behind at Point Pleasant, crossed the Ohio River and struck and burned several Shawnee villages nearby. With the Shawnees now terrified of the "long knives" from Virginia who were among them in force, Dunmore concluded a peace.

The peace that Dunmore negotiated required the Shawnees to yield their hunting rights in Kentucky, thereby accepting the terms of the Treaty of Fort Stanwix in 1768, which they had thus far rejected. Essentially, this was the first land cession by the Ohio Indians. The Shawnees also agreed to abide by British trade regulations, to return all white captives, and to refrain from harassing immigrant boats on the river. The Virginians promised not to hunt in Ohio, and the Shawnee agreed not to hunt south of the river. Colonel William Crawford gloated about the terms of the peace, remarking: "We have made them sensible of their villainy and weakness." Dunmore agreed, believing they had "impressed an Idea of the power of the White People, upon the minds of the Indians." With the Shawnees chastened, at least temporarily, by the military power of the Pennsylvanians and Virginians, the lands north and west of the Ohio would be their only home and hunting ground from that time on, if they could keep it.

When the Iroquois met in a grand council with the other northern nations in the autumn of 1774 to discuss the problems in Ohio, they admonished, "Quarrelsome people are dangerous." Although the Iroquois meant the Shawnees, the Americans fit that description perfectly. With the Iroquois advising the Wyandots, Ottawas, and Mingos to stay out of the Shawnee fight, Arthur St. Clair, a judge in the county court of Westmoreland, could write to the governor of Pennsylvania, "It is to be hoped the Fracas with the Shawnees will blow over without any bad Consequences."

When Dunmore and Lewis left the Shawnees on the Pickaway Plains, they built a temporary fort, which they called Fort Gower, where the Hocking River joined the Ohio. There they learned that the Continental Congress had authorized the nonimportation of British goods in the deepening crisis with Great Britain, and the Virginians voiced their support in a document known as the Fort Gower Resolutions. The "consequences" of British, American, and Indian enmity in the Ohio country loomed ominously.

3.

REVOLUTION IN THE OHIO COUNTRY

Apprehension and animosity permeated the Shawnee villages in the summer of 1775. The Ohio Indians had learned about the troubles between the British and the Americans far to the east. They could see war coming, and many did not want any part of it. The young men, particularly among the Shawnees, however, increasingly talked of war for both defense and retribution, and they found it difficult to listen to their chiefs, who counseled patience and peace. Trapped between the British at Detroit (who urged them to "take up the hatchet" against the Americans, who were a "bad" and "saucy" people) and the Pennsylvanians and Virginians, they felt caught on a middle ground that offered more danger than safety. If they did not help the British defeat the Americans, the British warned, their common enemy would not only take Indian lands but also massacre them or take them to another country as slaves.

Some Shawnee bands decided that the seemingly perpetual confrontations between whites and Indians on the frontier had become too much to bear, and they moved from their villages along the Scioto and Miami rivers to the west beyond the Ohio country. Those who stayed worried. In July 1775 several Shawnee chiefs told the Virginians: "We are often inclined to believe there is no resting place for us and that your Intentions [are] to deprive us entirely of

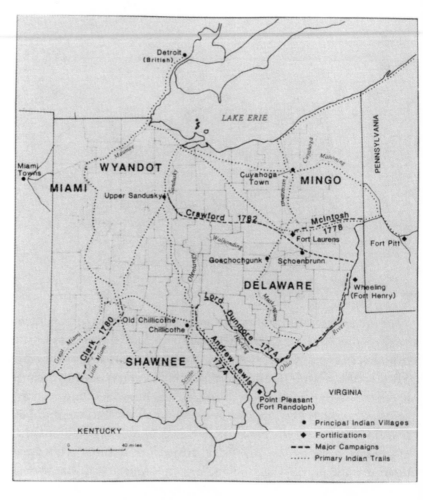

During the American Revolution, the army attempted to keep the Indians neutral or to punish those who remained loyal to the British. American military policy, however, only increased the animosity between Native and white Americans on the Ohio frontier. From George W. Knepper, *Ohio and Its People* (Kent, Ohio: Kent State University Press, 1989), with permission of the Kent State University Press.

our whole Country." As the summer wore on, the Shawnee villages were astir, with the headmen counseling as runners brought new information about the deterioration in relations between the British and Americans. Agents operating out of Fort Pitt, who attempted to keep the Ohio villagers from joining a British alliance, reported that "the Women all seemed very uneasy in Expectation that there would be War." Although the Wyandots in the Sandusky region remained hostile to the Americans from the last war, the Shawnees were divided. The Chillicothe and Piqua divisions showed increasing militancy, while the Maquachake and the Kispoko divisions sought neutrality, hoping that the British and Americans would settle their differences without harming Shawnee villages. Still, they worried about the potential for a war that would spill into the Ohio country and sweep them into it.

In an attempt to maintain the neutrality of the Ohio Indians, the Americans called a general council at Pittsburgh in the autumn of 1775. There, the Americans and the Shawnees, Wyandots, Delawares, Mingos, Senecas, and Potawatomis pledged friendship, neutrality, and peace, and reaffirmed the provisions of the Treaty of Fort Stanwix in 1768. The Americans also promised that they would not cross the Ohio River. But the proceedings did not proceed smoothly or without acrimony. The Delawares used the occasion to cast off their long-recognized subservience to the Iroquois and emphatically claimed the Ohio lands that the Wyandots had given them as their own. White Eyes spoke for them, defiantly pointing to the Allegheny River and saying, "All the country on the other side of that river is mine." If the Americans had intended to use this council to maintain the peace in the Ohio country by keeping the tribes divided, White Eyes applied the Delawares' own strategy of dividing their enemies, because the Americans needed Iroquois support in any war against Great Britain. Consequently, the Americans could not support the Delawares' claim to the lands between the Beaver River on the east and the Sandusky on the west. The danger loomed that the Delawares would ally with the British to guarantee their claims to independence from the Iroquois and their lands from the Americans. With British traders who operated out of Detroit supplying the Ohio Indians far more efficiently and lavishly than the Americans, whose newly established Congress had little organization and less money to buy their support or at least neutrality, the Ohio Indians drifted toward the British camp.

By the autumn of 1776, the Americans and the British were locked in a full-fledged war that would lead to either the consolidation of the North American empire or the creation of a new nation. While the armies maneuvered to the east, trouble came from the Mingo villages in the Ohio country. Still vengeful from their losses to white murderers before Dunmore's War and refusing to accept the cession of Kentucky in the Treaty of Fort Stanwix, the Mingos, with support from Detroit, used the opportunity created by the American Revolution to strike hard at the settlements in Kentucky. By the spring of 1777, the success of the Mingo raids had won converts from the tentatively neutral Wyandots, about half the Shawnee nation, a few Delawares, and the Iroquois, who had now joined the British cause.

The majority of the peaceful Delawares under White Eyes at Coshocton, who served as a buffer between the Pennsylvanians and the "far Indians," received increasing threats from the Wyandots to join them against the Americans. In September 1777, White Eyes reported to Colonel George Morgan, American agent for Indian affairs in the Western Department, that a war party of 210 Wyandots and Mingos had passed through the town on a raid into Virginia. The Wyandots told him that when they "struck the Virginians, they would come here & leave the Tomahawk sticking in our heads, because they said we were Virginians." Before the Wyandots left Coshocton, they killed some Delaware cattle and struck the women who tried to stop them, saying, "We only kill your Creatures, but others will Come & knock you in the Head." Neutrality, viewed as support for the Americans, clearly had a high price in the Ohio country.

The Munsees, a division of the Delawares, were "inclined to listen to the Mingoes," and in late February 1777 a Delaware Council at Coshocton reported to Morgan at Fort Pitt: "Some of our own foolish people who have been settled near the Mingo are corrupted by them." The Shawnees had the same problem. One chief lamented: "When I speak to them they will attend for a Moment & sit still whilst they are within my Sight . . . at night they steal their Blankets & run off to where the evil Spirit leads them." The Mingos who lived among the Shawnees made matters worse because they would not listen to the chiefs either and constantly urged their young friends to follow the example of the Mingos who made war on the frontier people. The Delawares, most of whom wanted peace and considered themselves mediators, requested that the Americans build a fort in their country so their villagers could be gathered nearby and given protection from the aggressive Mingos.

In 1777 the Delaware Council had reason to worry, because mixed war parties of Mingos, Shawnees, Delawares, and Wyandots struck the frontier settlements from Wheeling to Boonesborough, leaving dead settlers, burned buildings, and destroyed crops in their wake. The Virginians wanted to strike back, particularly to destroy "Pluggy's Town" near present-day Delaware, the most hostile Mingo camp located on the headwaters of the Olentangy, but feared doing so because any march across the Ohio would further alienate the Shawnees and Delawares, whose neutrality they needed to prevent a general war on the frontier. Later, when the war along the East Coast favored the Americans, the Ohio Indians could be attacked decisively.

In the meantime, the Congress called for another treaty meeting at Fort Pitt during July 1777, but this effort to avoid further animosity and bloodshed also failed. The Mingos refused to attend, and the Delawares refused to invite them, informing Colonel George Morgan that it was "useless to speak to them any more as they are determined not to listen to you or us." Moreover, when a party of Senecas arrived for the negotiations, a group of frontiersmen shot and killed several of these innocent Indians in retaliation for the loss of three whites in the surrounding area to Indian attacks. The Senecas fled and the council fell apart. One observer reported that "by this step the savages were again enraged at the white people, considered them altogether as traitors, and vowed revenge." The Delawares, who also had arrived at Fort Pitt and who still wanted accommodation and peace between Indians and whites, returned to Ohio, where the Shawnees, Wyandots, and Mingos viewed them with increasing contempt. Unless reasonable people on both sides gained control of rapidly deteriorating relations, war would be inevitable throughout the Ohio country.

* * *

Cornstalk, a chief of the Maquachake division of the Shawnees, along with several other Shawnee leaders, provided a peaceful link between the hotheads, both red and white, who talked war for the Ohio country in 1777. Cornstalk advocated peace between the two peoples and kept the Americans informed about the activities of the Mingos, who taunted the Shawnees in an "unbecoming manner" and called them "big knife People" for making peace at Pittsburgh in 1775. Unable to restrain the "foolish Young Men" among his band of Maquachake, however, Cornstalk intended to take his people and join the Delawares at Coshocton in the spring.

By September 1777 many Shawnees had become "unmanageable." With the tribe divided and General Edward Hand known to be planning an invasion of Ohio, Cornstalk attempted to maintain the peace by crossing the Ohio to meet with Captain Matthew Arbuckle, commander of Fort Randolph at the mouth of the Kanawha. During the course of the conference, Cornstalk, in the words of Captain John Stuart, attempted to "communicate the temper and disposition of the Indians." Cornstalk told Arbuckle that the British would soon pressure even the peaceful Shawnees to take up the tomahawk against the Americans, and that he could no longer control his fighting men. Although he opposed war, he would have to "run with the stream," because all of the Indians to the north were joining the British. Rather than attempt to alleviate Cornstalk's fears and convey the information as quickly as possible to Fort Pitt, Arbuckle decide to hold Cornstalk and his companion, Red Hawk, hostage to guarantee the good behavior of their villagers. Little more than a week later, Elinipsico, Cornstalk's son, crossed the river to inquire about his father, and he, too, became a captive.

Several days later a party of Virginia militia arrived at Fort Randolph and, with provisions low, sent two men across the Kanawha to hunt deer. They were attacked by unidentified Indians who shot and scalped a John Gilmore. When the militia learned of the attack, they became "pale as death with rage" and stormed Cornstalk's cabin, believing the attackers had come with Elinipsico. Captain Stuart reported that an interpreter's wife warned Cornstalk and his son that the Virginians would kill them and to flee. Elinipsico denied knowing about the attackers and "trembled exceedingly," but Cornstalk had expressed resignation about his death earlier when he told his captors, "I can die but once and it is all one to me now or at another time." Cornstalk then told his son not to be afraid because the Great Spirit had sent them to Fort Randolph to be killed.

The militia threatened to shoot the guards if they did not give way. They broke through the door, killed the Shawnee prisoners with a hail of bullets, and mutilated their bodies. Although Captain Arbuckle was "dissatisfied with this act of violence," the Virginians suffered no punishment. The governor of Virginia, however, sent a message to the Shawnees apologizing and blaming the event on "hot headed young Men" and pledged to bring the murderers to justice, "as if they had killed so many of our own People." Reaffirming the desire of Virginians for peace and friendship, the message also claimed, "We covet nothing you have." By the time this communication reached the Shawnees, White Eyes, while desiring peace and friendship with the Americans, had already warned his people that should the Americans come among them, "do not listen to them, for they lie."

The frontier people, so typified by the Virginia militia, were Indian haters first, last, and always. For them, all Indians lived by murder and deserved death on sight. Yet by killing prisoners, the Americans did not particularly differ from the Ohio Indians. Culture separated most of their actions in war, however, because the whites usually killed all Indian male prisoners and left the women and children unharmed but also unadopted. In contrast, the Indians sacrificed a ritual few and considered adoption important for perpetuating their lineages. The frontier people, while willing to kill Indians on sight or in captivity, considered themselves morally superior to the Indians because they did not torture their enemies, although exceptions, of course, occurred. When George Rogers Clark struck the Shawnee villages of Old Chillicothe and Piqua in 1780, one woman was reportedly killed by "ripping up her Belly & otherwise mangling her." The Indians sometimes also killed women captives, if they tried to escape or were in danger of being retaken by whites. The Ohio Indians noted, however, that the Americans did not kill British prisoners. Culture, then, dictated the practice of war in the Ohio country.

When word of the executions of Cornstalk and his son reached General Edward Hand at Fort Pitt, he wrote to the secretary of war, "From this event we have little reason to expect a reconciliation with the Shawnees . . . for if we had any friends among them, those unfortunate wretches were so." In time, the evidence proved that a Mingo, not a Shawnee, war party had attacked the Virginia militia and killed their man, but it made no difference to the Virginians—Shawnees and Mingos were all the same. Hand understood the intricacies of Indian and white relations, but the frontier people would not consider anything but the association of evil with all Native American peoples. Hand lamented the murder of Cornstalk and his son, noting: "If we had anything to expect from that Nation it is now Vanished." He could not have been more correct. Quickly, Shawnee war parties crossed the Ohio River and struck the settlements along the Pennsylvania and Virginia frontier.

General Hand had little means to strike the Ohio Indians from Fort Pitt. But without a post thrust deep into Indian country, from which soldiers could easily march against the hostile villagers, and with a force that consisted only of back-country militia, who had a "licentious" spirit and almost no appreciation of military discipline, and followed orders when they pleased, Hand planned an attack. Early in 1778, he learned that the British had deposited a large quantity of military supplies at the mouth of the Cuyahoga River to aid the Indians, probably the Mingos, in their attacks along the frontier. In early February, Hand led five hundred militia from Fort Pitt to the Mahoning River without finding any Indians to punish. Cold, "badly cloathed," and disheartened, they turned back, only to discover a small camp of peaceful Delawares, including Captain Pipe's mother, brother, and a few children. The militia, not wanting to return from the expedition without firing a shot, were, Hand reported, "so Impetuous that I could not prevent their Killing the Man & one of the Women," whom the soldiers repeatedly shot and scalped. They captured another woman, whom Hand with "difficulty Saved." The others escaped, but not before telling Hand that a Munsee camp lay about ten miles away. Hand detached a party to capture the Indians and bring them to his camp, but when they returned, the militia reported that the camp contained only four women and a boy, of which they were able to save only one woman.

Simon Girty served as the interpreter and guide for Hand's expedition. When the militia killed the boy at the Munsees' camp, several men argued about who should claim the credit, and to allay growing tempers they asked Girty to determine the award. After considering the evidence, Girty granted the honor to a Captain Zachariah Connell. This wanton murder of noncombatants troubled Hand, who reported, "Notwithstanding this Savage Conduct I verily believe the Party would Behave well if they had men to contend with." Despite this treachery, the Delawares maintained the peace. Captain Pipe said that he would not seek revenge but instead "keep fast hold to the chain of Friendship."

Upon the return of Hand and his ragtag militia, the failure of the mission to find and kill a significant number of hostile Indians became derisively known as the "Squaw Campaign." This embarrassing expedition proved to Hand and his fellow officers, once again, that professional soldiers, not militia, were required to secure the frontier and that a fort located in Ohio was less essential to guarantee the peace. While Hand stewed over the failure of his expedition, Blackfish planned a more successful raid at the Shawnee town of Old Chillicothe on the Little Miami River.

* * *

The winter came hard, with the privation keen in the distant and isolated village of Boonesborough, Kentucky. By January 1778, provisions ran dangerously low, however, because the Indians had burned the settlers' corn fields during the past summer. Many families were "desolate," and their hunger approached starvation. Daniel Boone reported to Virginia officials that they were "almost destitute of the necessary article of salt." This mineral not only made a monotonous diet of cornmeal and greens gathered in the forest slightly more palatable, but it also remained essential for preserving their slaughtered hogs and wild game. Although abundant quantities of salt could be boiled from the springs along the Licking River in Kentucky, the Indians had made that activity too dangerous during the past months. By the first week of January, the shortage of salt at Boonesborough had become a crisis, and Daniel Boone agreed to lead a party to the "Blue Licks" along the river to boil emergency rations. After four weeks of tending the kettles, several hundred pounds of salt had been collected, but a rise in the river temporarily submerged the spring. While the men waited for the water to recede and for a relief party to arrive, they cut wood and occupied their time as best they could. Boone served as one of the hunters who provided meat for the camp.

The morning of February 7 dawned cold with snow falling, and after checking his trap line, Boone killed a buffalo and proceeded to pack several hundred pounds of meat on his horse back to the salt camp. Before he could do so, however, four Shawnee raiders captured him after a desperate run though the woods with musket balls kicking up snow around him, one of which hit his powder horn. Realizing the foolishness of further flight because one Indian came up fast on Boone's horse and because his younger attackers had worn him out, Boone surrendered. Or, as he put it, "I was taken prisoner by a party of Shaney Indians."

The Shawnees who captured Boone were scouts ranging out from Chief Blackfish's party of more than a hundred men who had crossed the Ohio. With the brutal murder of Cornstalk and his son two months earlier on their minds, they had vengeance in their hearts and Boonesborough as their goal. At the Shawnee camp, Blackfish told Boone that he intended to kill his party along the Licking and destroy Boonesborough in retaliation for Cornstalk's death. Boone had always been able to think quickly, and he knew that Boonesborough could be easily overrun with a great loss of life. He suggested an alternative, telling Blackfish that his people were near starvation and that any march of women and children back to the Shawnee villages in Ohio would bring only misery and death, not needed captives. Boone then offered his men as hostages for the winter, if Blackfish would guarantee their safety. In the spring, he promised Blackfish they could return to Boonesborough, and he would negotiate the surrender of the Kentuckians without the loss of life on either side. Blackfish saw merit in the plan. He did not want to tax the food supply of his own people during the remainder of the winter, and he agreed.

The next morning the Shawnees surrounded the Kentuckians. Before any of his men could fire a shot, Boone called for them to surrender and trust him or they would be killed. Reluctantly they put down their weapons, and the Shawnees started them toward a crossing on the Ohio River. That night, the Shawnees made Boone run the gauntlet, from which he emerged bloodied but with no bones broken. Ten days and a hundred miles later, during which time food became so scarce that the Indians ate their dogs, the raiders and their captives reached Old Chillicothe.

Old Chillicothe, present-day Oldtown, occupied a ridge that over-looked the river. Corn fields, a spring, and a bountiful prairie and woodlands for hunting spread out from the town. Chillicothe had rows of several hundred homes, mostly log cabins without win-dows or chimneys. When the captives entered the village, with Ansel Goodman stripped naked and forced to "sing as loud as he could holler" to announce their arrival, the villagers were elated. That night they forced the Kentuckians to run the gauntlet and to "dance like the whites" in the firelight for the amusement of all. Within a few days the Shawnee women and men who were interested in adopting a white captive began to arrive from surrounding villages. With more than two dozen prospects to choose from, this was a for-tuitous and festive occasion.

Blackfish chose Boone for adoption after learning that Daniel had been in charge of a rescue party that had killed his son who had captured two white girls not long before. Upon questioning, Boone acknowledged that he possibly had fired the shot that killed Black-fish's son, but he said, "Many things happen in war" that are "best forgotten." Blackfish pondered Boone's response, then said, "Brave man! All right! When we in war you kill me, I kill you. All right!" Boone would now replace Blackfish's son. After a ritual washing in the river by family women, having his hair plucked into the Shawnee scalp lock, being decorated with feathers, and a long ritual of smoking and eating, Daniel Boone became Sheltowee or Big Turtle, a reflection of his physical strength and compact physique.

During the late winter and early spring in Old Chillicothe, Boone continued his deception, "always appearing as cheerful and satis-fied as possible." William Hancock, a fellow captive, could not understand "how Boone could be whistling and contented among the dirty Indians while he was so melancholy." After a trip to Detroit in early March, where Boone affirmed to Governor Henry Hamilton his intention to convince Boonesborough to surrender and move north of the Ohio into Indian and British territory so that they could "all live with you as one people," Blackfish began planning the spring expedition to Kentucky with the Mingos and Shawnees at the villages along the Scioto.

In the meantime, Kentuckian Andy Johnson escaped and returned to Harrodsburg, where he confirmed everyone's worst fears—Boone had become a turncoat. Johnson reported that "Boone was a Tory, and had surrendered them all up to the British, and taken the oath of allegiance to the British at Detroit." Boone, however, had kept his own counsel and did his best to win the trust of the Shawnees. Unbeknownst to the other captives, he planned his escape, hoarding powder and lead given to him for hunting, and an unstocked rifle barrel and lock from his work as a gunsmith among the Shawnees. By early June he was ready, and when he accompanied his Indian family on an expedition to boil salt along the Scioto, he took his chances.

Boone remembered his escape differently in later life, but before he recalled his Ohio captivity with nostalgia he reported, "On the sixteenth [June], before sun-rise, I departed in the most secret manner, and arrived at Boonesborough on the twentieth, after a journey of one hundred and sixty miles; during which, I had but one meal." Whether he was pursued remains unclear. Later, a Shawnee friend told Boone that on learning about his escape, "They all said let you go that you would never get home, you would Starve to death." "But," his friend said, "I told them that you would get home, for you went as Straight as a leather String."

Whether pursued or not, Boone fled south from the Shawnee villages on the Bullskin Trail along the Scioto River. He rode his horse to the ground then ran on foot, concealing his trail by following wet and rocky stream beds. One white captive in Blackfish's village later reported overhearing Boone's trackers say, "Boone is lost. Went so—so," making a zigzag motion with his fingers in the air. When Boone reached the Ohio, he placed his powder and rifle across a log and pushed it before him into the current. In time, his paddling and drift carried him across to Kentucky. On June 20, he returned to Boonesborough. Although he soon faced charges of treason, his Ohio experience was behind him—at least for now.

* * *

While Daniel Boone planned his escape from the Shawnee village of Old Chillicothe, Simon Girty, whom Moravian missionary John Heckewelder called "as brutal, depraved, and wicked a wretch as ever lived," and who had served General Hand as an interpreter in the "Squaw Campaign," plotted to flee Pittsburgh for Detroit and offer his services to the Crown. Today, Girty remains an enigma, but for the men and women, both red and white, who lived on the Ohio frontier, opinions about his character were as precise as they were divided. The Americans considered Girty a murderous traitor and a "white savage," a virtual *bête noire* of the frontier. Girty became the epitome of evil. Frontier mothers even threatened unruly children that Girty would get them if they did not behave. The Indians respected his courage, integrity, generosity, and honesty, while the British considered him a useful employee. Girty, of course, had all of these characteristics, each of which could be exhibited, depending on the particular culture that he dealt with, at any given moment.

Born in Chambers Mill, Pennsylvania, in 1741, he moved with his mother and stepfather to Sherman's Creek in 1755, only to become a refugee at Fort Granville after the French and Indians terrorized the frontier following Braddock's disastrous defeat on the Monongahela. At that time, a combined French and Indian force captured Fort Granville and took the Americans to the Delaware town of Kittanning on the Allegheny. There the Senecas from the Ohio country led Girty west for adoption. Apparently the fifteen-year-old adjusted very well to his new family and home, learning the language and customs of his new people. In 1759, following the capture of Fort Duquesne by General John Forbes the year before, the Indians agreed to peace and to bring back their captives. Accordingly, they returned Girty to his mother at Pittsburgh, where by the American Revolution he farmed and dabbled in land speculation, claiming acreage by "tomahawk right," that is, by blazing trees and claiming the land in between. He also began to serve as an interpreter for Virginia and Pennsylvania traders who dealt with the Delawares. Soon Girty gained a reputation for his ease with Indian languages as well as for "strength, agility and great endurance." The British also began to use his services. In the autumn of 1769, he served as the translator for a conference with the Six Nations at Fort Pitt. By the early 1770s, the British considered him a man who could be sent among the Indians to allay their fears and bring them to council meetings. In 1774, Girty accompanied

Lord Dunmore to the Kanawha and the Scioto country as a guide and interpreter. When Dunmore made peace at Camp Charolette, it may have been Girty who gave Logan's famous speech about the loss of his family, rather than Logan himself. At Camp Charolette, Dunmore had Girty entertain the men by doing an Indian dance, which he apparently conducted "with accompanying . . . songs, kicking fire brands about."

On February 22, 1775, Girty took the oath of allegiance to King George III at Fort Dunmore, as Fort Duquesne was temporarily called before it became Fort Pitt. He also received certification as a lieutenant in a militia unit. When the American Revolution began two months later, both the British and the Americans wanted his services, because each realized that their ability to hold the Ohio frontier depended on forming alliances with the Indians. The Iroquois specifically requested Girty for their interpreter on all matters dealing with the Americans.

At first Girty cast his fate with the Americans and provided his services. In the summer of 1775 he escorted a Captain James Wood on "almost a month of dangerous and difficult travel" to the Ohio country, where he visited the Delaware, Wyandot, Shawnee, and Seneca villages to talk peace and gain their support for the Americans. Personality clashes with his military superiors at Fort Pitt, however, led to his discharge. By August 1777, Girty had gained a reputation for being a "drunken and unfit person," although frontiersmen such as Simon Kenton thought Girty had been unfairly treated. When Girty was arrested and jailed in September 1777 for being a conspirator in an alleged plot to kill the residents and turn Fort Pitt over to the British, his sympathies for the Americans dimmed even more. Although acquitted and discharged from the militia for "ill-behavior," he would accompany Hand's Squaw Campaign in February 1778. However, he gave up his allegiance to the United States on the night of March 28, 1778, when he fled Fort Pitt with several others for Detroit, where he offered his services to British Lieutenant Governor Henry Hamilton.

The British welcomed Girty and soon sent him south to the Ohio villages to win or maintain their support. With his ability to speak Shawnee, Delaware, and Seneca as well as other Indian languages, Girty roamed the Ohio countryside and, according to one who knew him, "would live sometimes in one town, and sometimes in another—kept changing." The British Indian Department carried him in its logbooks as an interpreter for the Iroquois, with the salary of ten shillings ($2) per day, equal that of an army captain, while most interpreters earned only eight shillings. Between the summer of 1778 and 1783, Girty participated in most, if not all, of the thirty major councils held in the Sandusky-Detroit region. The British, however, relied on him not only as an interpreter but also as a scout and ranger to lead raiding parties, which took lives and scalps and saw captives burned at the stake.

After Girty raided with the Shawnees into Kentucky in 1778, he helped ambush the supply train headed for Fort Laurens in January 1779, and he would later brag about it. Early in 1781, his assignment took him to Upper Sandusky, where he lived to keep the Wyandots on the warpath. In that year, Girty also played an instrumental role in the removal of the Moravian missionaries and their "praying" Delawares from the Tuscarawas to Upper Sandusky to prevent them from giving information about British and Indian activities to the Americans at Fort Pitt. In all of these activities, Girty enhanced his reputation as someone who could deliver prisoners and scalps. When out on a raid he dressed like the Indians, but around the British at Detroit he wore American-style clothing. The Americans at Fort Pitt liked neither traitors nor chameleons and put a bounty on his head worth $800.

During the American Revolution, however, Girty saved Simon Kenton from burning at the stake in Wakatomica near the Muskingum and Henry Baker at Upper Sandusky, and he sent captive Samuel Murphy, in custody at Detroit, a pound of tea and some sugar. Murphy recalled that "Girty was good and kind to me." Margaret Handley Erskin, a captive of the Shawnees, who feared a forced marriage, was relieved one day when Girty came to her and told her not to worry about that because the Shawnees "were not the people to compel any one to such a course." And, after raiding from Sandusky to within five miles of Fort Pitt in the spring of 1783, he paid the ransom for a captive white woman and returned a boy to Major Arent Schuyler De Peyster, commander at Detroit, for release. Other captives, both men and women, reported that they had been "saved by Simon Girty."

Despite all of the good things said in Girty's favor, most Americans cared little. For all of his magnanimity, it is also true that Girty killed people without remorse—or, even worse, enjoyed watching them die by torture. Even after the Ohio frontier had been settled for more than a generation, people still talked about the Battle of the Olentangy in June 1782 and the horrible death of Colonel William Crawford.

* * *

On March 26, 1777, Henry Hamilton, lieutenant governor of Detroit, received instruction to send Britain's Indian allies against the American settlements on the Ohio frontier. With the exceptions of the Turkey and Turtle clans of the Delawares, located along the Tusacarawas and Muskingum rivers respectively, who had been influenced by the Moravians, most of the Ohio Indians now supported the British. They had joined the British because of past trade relations and a belief that the Redcoats would win, given their recent success over the French and, more important, because they believed the British would help them stop American expansion at the Ohio River. Hamilton executed his orders with alacrity. Soon he earned the reputation as a "hair buyer" among frontier men and women for sending raiding parties across the Ohio River into western Pennsylvania and Virginia. On April 1, they brought their first scalps and prisoners to Detroit and celebrated. During that summer alone, Detroit sent thirty-two raiding parties against the American frontier. Daniel Sullivan, who spied at Detroit early in 1778, disguised as a trader who had been adopted by the Delawares as a boy, reported that "Governor Hamilton did all in his Power to induce all Nations of Indians to massacre the Frontier Inhabitants of Pennsylvania and Virginia and paid very high prices in Goods for the Scalps the Indians brought in."

While the British attempted to buy the allegiance of the Ohio Indians, the Americans tried to win their neutrality by persuasion. In March 1778, Colonel George Morgan traveled to the Delaware Council at Coshocton on behalf of the governor of Pennsylvania to urge them to stay out of the war. "The Tempest," he said, "will be over in a few Months. You will then enjoy the Sweets of Peace whilst your restless Neighbors are suffering the Punishment due to their evil deeds." He asked the Delawares to "bury the Hatchet" and accept American friendship before it was too late. Morgan regretted that he could not give them any presents, especially clothing, which Governor Hamilton had used with promises that made "Fools of the wise Delawares." But, he told them, "your wants shall be all supplied by and by," provided they did not "kill Men, Women or Children, like the Governor of Detroit does," and who hired the Indians to do that dirty work. Rather, Morgan told the Delaware Council, "I do not want you to get hurt in my Quarrel. What I want of you is to live in Peace and Friendship with me as Brothers ought to do." In July, Morgan delivered a sterner message to the Shawnees through the Delawares, telling them that the United States still wished to avoid sending an army over the Ohio, and "if the foolish People who have struck us so often, will grow wise immediately they may yet avoid destruction." If the Shawnees continued their "evil deeds," the army would come into Ohio and "trample them into dust."

General Edward Hand, commander at Fort Pitt, had the responsibility of winning the support of the Ohio Indians from the British or at least gaining their neutrality. In mid-June 1778, Hand asked the Delawares to tell the Wyandots, "who have been long astray & listened only to the evil Spirit," that the Americans were "more willing to forgive an injury than to revenge it" and that the United States wanted their friendship. White Eyes, however, reported that the Wyandots would not listen and instead demanded that he take up the tomahawk against the Americans or be whipped. White Eyes pleaded for help, informing Colonel George Morgan, "If you do not assist me now as soon as possible then I shall be ruined & destroyed, but if you will assist me now at this dangerous time then nobody will be able to break our friendship." White Eyes added a desperate postscript, saying the Wyandots blamed him for betrayal of the Ohio Indians by passing messages to the Americans. "I am frightened & with my People in great danger, therefore consider & remember me for I rely now entirely on your help & assistance." David Zeisberger reported that White Eyes wanted the army sent to Coshocton immediately to protect the Delawares from the Wyandots. Zeisberger agreed. In August 1778, he reported that the Munsees, "who are the worst of them all have taken up the Tomahawk." He believed the Munsees ought to be "broken" and "deliver'd to the Delawares to be ruled by them because they are not fit to be ruled by themselves."

While White Eyes appealed for help, Hand contemplated attacking the British headquarters and stronghold at Detroit. By the summer of 1778, Washington and the Continental Congress had approved the attack to "reduce" the garrison at Detroit and "compel" the Indians to accept "terms of peace." Planning began in earnest, but with General Lachlan McIntosh now in command at Fort Pitt. McIntosh had gained experience on the Georgia frontier, and Washington considered him a soldier of "great worth and merit." Washington chose Colonel John Gibson of the Sixth Virginia to lead the two regiments of the Thirteenth Virginia and Eighth Pennsylvania into Ohio and against Detroit.

The problems of striking an entrenched and relatively well supplied enemy across more than three hundred miles of hostile Indian territory were immense. Things began to go wrong from the very beginning. A hard winter in Virginia prevented the adequate collection of food and forage for the long trip across country. Many farmers and merchants also hesitated to sell provisions to the military because the army offered low prices. In addition, Congress had to secure permission from the Shawnees and the Delawares to cross their lands on the way to Detroit. Then Virginia backed out, claiming that the expedition would endanger its frontier with so many men gone, that the distance was impossible and the season too late. In this latter fear the Virginia legislators proved painfully correct. Besides, any lands won west of the Ohio by Congress would diminish Virginia's claims to the Ohio country; success posed unacceptable economic and imperial dangers. Eventually, Virginia reluctantly agreed to participate in the expedition, but not without misgivings.

By late July 1778, few men had arrived at Fort Pitt, and the commissary still had great difficulty acquiring horses, cattle, flour, and forage for the expedition. The logistical organization of the attack had become so difficult that Congress scrapped the plan for an attack against Detroit. With the expedition "deferred," Congress then authorized McIntosh to take fifteen hundred men, including forty North Carolina dragoons and approximately one thousand militia, across the Ohio River and attack the Wyandots and other Indians in the Sandusky region in order "to chastize and terrify the savages, and to check their ravages on the frontiers of these states."

Time passed and little happened. Not until September 17 did the Delawares, represented by Chiefs White Eyes of the Turkey, John Killbuck of the Turtle, and Captain Pipe of the Wolf clans, arrive at Fort Pitt to discuss the granting of permission to the army to cross their lands. The Shawnees remained conspicuously absent. On September 19, the Delawares agreed to permit passage of the American troops provided the government would build a fort near their villages for protection and trade. In all dealings with the army, the Delawares requested that Gibson be the intermediary because "we esteem him one of ourselves, he has always acted an honest part by us and we are Convinced he will make our Common good his chief study, and not think only how he may Get Rich." They did not, however, agree to take up the hatchet alongside the American soldiers.

Nearly a month later, on October 23, the expedition set out for Ohio. The autumn weather was glorious, and the troops were exuberant, firing their weapons all too frequently as they meandered along. Killing Indians was a real lark, particularly for the militia, whose term of service expired on January 1, 1779. McIntosh got only twenty miles, to a stockade at the mouth of the Beaver River. There he awaited more supplies and decided to build a fort at Coshocton "to secure these Indians in our Interest [and], from which I may probably make excursions to some of the Hostile Towns." Not until November 4 did he break camp and march his twelve hundred men along Bouquet's route toward the Tuscarawas. That McIntosh set out at 4:00 P.M. and traveled only seven miles indicated problems to come. On November 7, unidentified Indians shot and scalped two soldiers out hunting, and the packhorses, which McIntosh called "scandalous," began collapsing from insufficient forage. Indeed, his horses could not travel more than five miles per day, even though their loads averaged only a hundred pounds. Several days later the column passed a war pole with two scalps dangling from it. The men believed the scalps were those of their two comrades, and the sign around the pole indicated Wyandots. Then winter arrived like a knife with a cold wind and snow. The jubilant mood of the men began to dampen, and the militia began to think about going home.

McIntosh reached the Tuscarawas on November 18, rendezvoused with some Delawares from the Moravian village of Lichtenau, and camped on the west side of the river at the Great Crossing about two miles north of present-day Bolivar. He was halfway to the Wyandot villages along the Sandusky, but provisions fell dangerously low and spoiled; morale plummeted, especially when the officers took the first choice from the deer, turkey, and bear meat that the Delawares occasionally provided. Given these hardships, McIntosh decided to build a fort on this site about a hundred miles from Fort Pitt. With cabins to serve as barracks for two hundred men, it would provide a staging ground for his attack on Detroit and other hostile towns as well as the post that the Delawares had been promised in the treaty that granted passage over their lands. When the work of cutting trees for the stockade and fifteen-foot palisades began, all plans for an attack on the Wyandots ended.

On November 22, McIntosh called the nearby Delawares to his camp and told them he did not intend to leave Ohio until he had captured Detroit. Then he told them to send runners to bring the Shawnees, Wyandots, Ojibwas, and others to him within fourteen days to make peace. If any refused, McIntosh pontificated, "I will never make it again nor rest or leave this Country, but pursue them While any of them remain on the face of the earth for I can fill the woods with men as the Trees, or as the Stones are on the Ground." The Delawares were amused by this bluster, because McIntosh then exposed his weakness by asking them for food. When he told them that any Indian people who did not "join us heartily by taking up the Hatchet" against the British would be considered enemies of the United States, the Delawares laughed. At the same time, the all too apparent weakness of the United States frightened them because they favored protection by and alliance with the Americans. The Delawares at Coshocton now turned cranky and made the area around Fort Laurens increasingly unsafe, occasionally attacking soldiers and killing their horses.

By December 9, the new post, which McIntosh named for his friend Henry Laurens, had been completed. Finding campaigning in wintertime Ohio with undisciplined troops more disagreeable than he had imagined, McIntosh returned to Fort Pitt, leaving 150 men under Colonel Gibson to stand guard and maintain the American presence in Ohio. Had the militia been under attack, their haste to return to Fort Pitt could only have been called a rout, some covering the distance in less than forty-eight hours. The Continentals arrived with only a little better discipline, covering the distance between Fort Laurens and Fort Pitt in four days, ten days less than their march from Fort McIntosh to the Tuscarawas. By December 21, the men who remained at Fort Laurens had attempted to mutiny, but Gibson managed to maintain control.

Fort Laurens, located about twenty feet above the Tuscarawas on a level plain, quickly attracted the attention of the British and their Indian allies. On January 6, 1779, Simon Girty left the Sandusky with a small band of Mingos to capture the Moravian missionaries at Coshocton, who he correctly believed had passed information about British and Indian activities to the Americans. He also wanted to reconnoiter Fort Laurens for a planned siege by a large force that gathered at Detroit and along the Sandusky. Several days later, Girty's band struck a party of sixteen Pennsylvania militia about three miles east of Fort Laurens, killing two and capturing one soldier. When the British learned about the desperate condition of the men at Fort Laurens from the prisoner and letters seized by Girty's raiding party, they planned their attack.

In February, Captain Henry Bird took ten men from the British Eighth Regiment to the Sandusky, where they watched the American soldier captured by Girty be tortured and killed and his head stuck on a post as the Indians prepared themselves for war. Bird then distributed power, lead, and clothing to the 180 Wyandots, Shawnees, Mingos, Munsees, and Delawares from the Wolf clan, who agreed to help besiege Fort Laurens. Half King, a Wyandot chief, sent runners to the Delaware towns asking them to forsake the Americans and join the alliance so the Ohio Indians could be of "one strong mind." If the Delawares did not join the Wyandots, they would be killed with the Virginians. Killbuck passed this information to Zeisberger, who relayed it to Gibson. The Delawares at Coshocton wanted help, but Fort Laurens was too far away and without sufficient men or supplies to protect anyone.

Upon learning about the coming attack, McIntosh responded by sending 123 Virginia militiamen with supplies to Fort Laurens and a letter by runner to the Delawares assuring them of American military support. The militia marched in February, but when they reached the Fort Laurens vicinity, they learned that the British force had arrived on February 22 and surrounded the post. Any at-

In 1772, David Zeisberger, a Moravian missionary, established a church and school at Schoenbrunn. Located on the east bank of the Tuscarawas River, the village became the first organized settlement in Ohio. Although Zeisberger came to the Ohio frontier to convert the Indians, he also passed information about British military activities that he had learned from the Indians to American military authorities. From John Heckewelder, *A Narrative of the United Brethren among the Delaware and Mohegan Indians* (Philadelphia, 1820).

tempts at relief would be disastrous, and the column turned back. The crisis worsened soon thereafter when Gibson lost a woodcutting detail of eighteen men in an ambush—all of whom were killed and scalped within sight of the garrison but just beyond rifle range.

The situation inside Fort Laurens worsened, with the men resorting to eating dried hides from the cattle they had brought with them as well as their moccasins. Unable to hunt, the men gathered roots and herbs from around the palisades, but two men died from eating poisonous plants, and others became seriously ill. When two soldiers stole out of the fort and returned with a deer, the men "devoured" it, some not waiting to cook their portion. Fort Laurens had become more farce than threat, and the men dubbed it "Fort Nonsense."

But the weather pressed as hard on the British and their Indian allies as on the men in Fort Laurens, and Ohio winters can be unforgiving. Short of food and suffering from the elements themselves, the enemy withdrew about March 20 after a month-long siege. Fortuitously, a relief party of five hundred regulars and two hundred militia with provisions arrived about March 23 after a hard four-day march from Fort Pitt. The starving garrison ate so ravenously that several soldiers made themselves sick from ingesting so much solid food when their stomachs were unaccustomed to it, and three died. With their strength restored, Colonel Gibson and his men then made the welcome journey back to Fort Pitt, while 106 Continentals from the Eighth Pennsylvania under a Major Frederick Vernon remained to garrison the fort.

Not long after McIntosh had returned to Fort Pitt, he was transferred to the south, and Colonel Daniel Brodhead, who thought Fort Laurens nothing less than a foolish mistake, assumed command. Brodhead informed Washington as forcefully as possible that Fort Laurens was "impractical to maintain," being impossible to garrison or provision adequately, and the army could not use it as a staging ground for an attack on Detroit or the Sandusky towns. It was little more than a dangerous albatross. Washington agreed, and on March 22, 1779, he authorized the abandonment of Fort Laurens, in part to use those troops in other engagements, particularly in a campaign up the Allegheny. Washington informed Brodhead that Colonel Gibson should have his men ready to go, and "when he receives his orders to march, let it be as sudden as possible." By late May the garrison had dwindled away; only twenty-six men remained in Vernon's command, because the others had been recalled to Fort Pitt. Yet, while the Americans no longer took Fort Laurens seriously in their military planning or at best used it as only a temporary decoy to tie down British forces in the West by its mere presence, the British took it very seriously. By June 9, Captain Bird had an Indian force of two hundred Wyandot, Shawnee, and Mingo raiders gathered at Upper Sandusky ready to strike.

Salvation came from an unexpected source. On May 28, 1779, Colonel John Bowman led three hundred Kentucky militiamen, armed with rifles and tomahawks, across the Ohio at present-day Cincinnati. The Kentuckians struck the Shawnees at Old Chillicothe before sunrise two days later, taking advantage of the darkness cast by a lunar eclipse to hide their movements. They burned the town, wounded Blackfish, and stole 170 horses and all the plunder in the form of blankets, kettles, and ornaments that they could carry. They lost nine men killed and one wounded before escaping back across the Ohio at the mouth of the Little Miami River. Although they inflicted little serious damage, because only about a hundred Shawnees, mostly women and children, inhabited the town, the Kentuckians distracted the Shawnees gathered at

Upper Sandusky, who ran south to protect their people. Without the Shawnees, the British did not want to attack Fort Laurens.

In the meantime, Congress, George Washington, and Colonel Brodhead finally decided to abandon Fort Laurens. On July 8, Joseph Reed, president of the Continental Congress, wrote to Brodhead, saying: "As to Fort Laurens, it has been saved more by a Miracle than any thing else; and tho' it may be kept up as a stepping Stone to Detroit, I can see no other Benefits to be derived from it. General Washington was apprehensive that the evacuation of it this Spring would have given great Encouragement to the Savages about Detroit, which was his Reason for holding it—not any Opinion of the intrinsick Worth of the Post." Accordingly, the last reinforcements under Lieutenant Colonel Richard Campbell arrived on July 16, relieving Major Vernon and his twenty-five men with seventy-five troops from the Thirteenth Virginia and the Maryland Regiment. Campbell's orders were to abandon the post as soon as his horses could carry away the supplies. Yet even the evacuation did not go well. On August 1, Indians attacked and killed two men beyond the palisades. With the danger to the post still present and adequate packhorses unavailable, Campbell burned the provisions that could not be transported and retreated from Fort Laurens on August 2. He arrived at Fort Pitt five days later. When the army finally evacuated the post, it left the Indians, particularly the Shawnees, still filled with hatred and bent on revenge for past American transgressions. Only a few Delawares under Moravian influence could be considered peaceful in the Ohio country. For the next three years, the American Revolution would be waged with vicious intensity along the northwestern frontier. But with Fort Laurens abandoned for lack of will, planning, and support, the army had neither a presence west of the river nor the capacity to defeat the Ohio Indians.

* * *

The war in Ohio dragged on with sporadic cruelty. On August 2, 1780, George Rogers Clark led a raid from Kentucky, crossing at the mouth of the Licking River with one thousand men to attack the Shawnee villages of Old Chillicothe and Piqua. The Shawnees denied Chillicothe to Clark by burning it before his arrival on

August 6, but he destroyed Piqua two days later, which he described as "composed of well built cabins located along the river each surrounded by a strip of corn." In contrast to their actions at Old Chillicothe, the Shawnees did not flee Piqua, and Clark reported that the fight reached a "savage fierceness on both sides" before his cannon and superior numbers "totally routed" the Shawnees about dark. Clark's men plundered graves and burned the corn fields for two days before withdrawing, losing fourteen men killed and thirteen wounded. Although the Shawnees suffered few casualties, the loss of their corn crop proved devastating, and they lived during the winter on wild game and British handouts. The Shawnees now turned increasingly to the British for military support.

By the spring of 1781, Colonel Daniel Brodhead expected a "general Indian War." The Moravians on the Tuscarawas had reported that the Delawares could no longer resist pressure from the other nations to join them against the Americans. A year earlier, the Delawares had informed Brodhead that the other Ohio Indians "mocked" them for giving their allegiance to the Americans, who always promised protection by their army but never delivered. Brodhead realized that the Ohio frontier would soon be swept by Indian raiding parties attempting to keep the Americans east of the river, because squatters had settled on Delaware land as early as 1779. The vast, rich lands of the Ohio country beckoned others. The Shawnees, Wyandots, and Mingos clearly saw the American Revolution as a war to defend their homelands. If the British would help keep the Americans at bay east of the Ohio River, they would accept their aid. If the British would not assist them, they would drive the Americans away themselves.

In order to prevent the violence against the settlements that Brodhead knew would soon be coming, he decided to launch a preemptive strike. He chose Coshocton for his target, where the Delawares, now under the leadership of war chief Captain Pipe, had abandoned their neutrality and joined the British alliance. On April 7, 1781, Brodhead marched from Fort Pitt with three hundred men, about evenly divided between regulars and militia, and headed for the Tuscarawas, where he burned Coshocton and destroyed Lichtenau. Overall, Brodhead set a high standard for the murder of both peaceful and hostile Indians by executing sixteen prisoners who could not prove their loyalty to the Americans, including Red Eagle, a Delaware chief, tomahawked in the head from behind while he sat negotiating with Brodhead. Overall, Brodhead's campaign made the Ohio frontier more unsafe than ever before. His Coshocton campaign made the frontier settlements in western Pennsylvania and Virginia so fearful of retaliation that the army could not recruit volunteers for further expeditions into Ohio, everyone believing that their presence at home was essential for the protection of their families.

In early August 1781, Clark floated down the Ohio with four hundred militia to strike deep in the Illinois country. William Croghan at Fort Pitt reflected at that time: "From Every Account we have the Indians Are preparing to receive him And if they should attack him in his Present Situation, either by land or Water, I dread the Consequences." Croghan had good reasons for apprehension. The militia were fainthearted, and they began to desert almost immediately and return to their homes. In addition, Colonel Archibald Lochry, who followed Clark a day later with about a hundred militia, could never catch up for an essential rendezvous to combine their forces. In the meantime, Joseph Brant, the half-blood Mohawk chief, waited in ambush with a force of thirty warriors at the mouth of the Great Miami. Unable to contest Clark's larger force, they let the militia float past. A few days later a group of Shawnees, Wyandots, and some British rangers joined Brant's raiders and waited for Lochry, who runners had reported was coming down the river. On August 24, Brant lured Lochry into a trap and killed sixty-four and captured forty-two men with the same ferocity that Brodhead had inflicted on the Delawares at Coshocton.

A few weeks later a combined party of Wyandots and Delawares attacked Wheeling. Although not strong enough to carry the fort, this attack intensified the fear among the settlements along the frontier. Pennsylvania militia under Colonel David Williamson now decided to take military matters into their own hands and strike the Delaware towns on the Tuscarawas. But when the militia arrived at Coshocton in October 1781, they found it and other Delaware towns abandoned. Yet, throughout the winter the Wyandots and some Delawares continued to raid into western Pennsylvania from Ohio. Revenge occupied the thoughts of settlers and soldiers alike.

In early March 1782, the Pennsylvanians returned to the Tuscarawas with malice in their hearts. Soon their hands would be stained with blood.

* * *

On the eve of the American Revolution, the Moravians anticipated great progress converting the Delawares along the Tuscarawas. The Delawares under Netawatwees had welcomed the arrival of the "Blackcoats" in 1772, and friendly relations prevailed. By the autumn of 1775, David Zeisberger reported that the Delaware Council had "unanimously decided to accept the word of God" and urged the Moravians to build another mission closer to their main village at Coshocton. In mid-February 1776, Zeisberger selected a site, which he called "an extraordinary piece of land," three miles below the Delaware village. On April 12, the first "Brethren and Sisters" arrived at Lichtenau, the "pasture of light," from Schoenbrunn and Gnadenhutten, some trailing cattle overland and others traveling by canoe. Zeisberger saw his fondest dreams of converting the Delawares on the verge of realization. He wrote, "A different spirit rules among the Indians. We have seen many who in times past, were our bitter enemies and would neither hear nor know anything of God's Word and now show themselves very obliging and confiding toward us." But ninety-year-old Netawatwees died in October, and the amicable relationship between the Moravians and the Delawares began to change.

Killbuck succeeded Netawatwees as chief at Coshocton, but he never commanded the respect and prestige of his grandfather. Chiefs Big Cat, Delaware George, and Captain Pipe, the latter of whom led the Munsee Delawares and lived to the north among the Wyandots, opposed the Moravian faction. When full-fledged war erupted between the Americans and the British, Lieutenant Governor Henry Hamilton at Detroit planned to strengthen British forces in the West and disrupt Washington's military strength by using the Ohio Indians to disturb the frontier. Unfortunately for the Christian Delawares, their villages and missions lay between the hostile British and their allies and the Americans.

By early 1777, Shawnee, Wyandot, Mingo, and Delaware raiders regularly headed to the Pennsylvania and Virginia frontiers from northwestern Ohio, and they made the Tuscarawas Valley a dangerous place for the Moravians. In March the Coshocton Delawares urged the Moravians at Schoenbrunn and Gnadenhutten to move to nearby Lichtenau so they could "take care of, and stand up for, the safety of the Brethren." Zeisberger welcomed the protection as well as the opportunity to consolidate his followers at a location where they could easily learn about Indian activities and forewarn Fort Pitt when trouble brewed. Hastened by news that a Mingo war party intended to kill them, the Moravians completed their move to Lichtenau by late April. Not all of the Brethren went willingly. In May, Brother J. J. Schmick complained that the hostile Indians would not have bothered them because the Brethren "love peace and want to live with others in peace," but Zeisberger made them go. Soon Schmick noted that Schoenbrunn became "a place where run-aways and partly hermits [were] living, who took possession of the houses and plantations of the Brethren." The loss of years of hard work became almost too painful to bear.

Although Zeisberger reported to General Hand at Fort Pitt on September 22, 1777, that "Capt. White Eyes and the Delaware Chiefs are yet determined to stand fast and not meddle with the War," relations became increasingly strained between the Moravians and their Christian converts at Coshocton, particularly when British agent Alexander McKee informed them that the American army had been "cut to pieces" by the Redcoats and Washington killed. In the spring of 1778, White Eyes asked the Reverend John Heckewelder at Coshocton a battery of questions. "Is there no more a Congress, and have the English hung some of them and taken the remainder to England to hang them there? Is the whole country beyond the mountains in the possession of the English, and are the few thousand Americans, who have escaped, now organizing themselves on this side of the mountains for killing all the Indians in this country, men and women and children?" Heckewelder assured the Delawares that the British had lied, but they were not convinced. Increasingly, they began to divide into groups, one supporting the Americans and the other favoring the British.

With the murder of White Eyes in the autumn of 1778, Killbuck lost his principal adviser and his support in the Delaware Council. Zeisberger now began to grow uneasy about the safety of his mission at Lichtenau as the Delawares at Coshocton showed increasing British sympathies. To gain protection, he decided to decentralize his converts and reoccupy Gnadenhutten, which had been abandoned in April 1778, and establish a new mission near Schoenbrunn. In mid-April 1779, a small group of Mohicans reoccupied Gnadenhutten while Zeisberger located a site which he called New Schoenbrunn along the Tuscarawas about two miles from the old village. The remainder of the Moravian converts under Heckewelder abandoned Licthenau in late April 1780 for a new village, called Salem, about twenty-five miles east of Coshocton on the west side of the Tuscarawas near Gnadenhutten. By the end of the year, 380 Christian Indians lived along the Tuscarawas—143 at New Schoenbrunn, 135 at Gnadenhutten, and 102 at Salem.

The Moravian missions narrowly escaped destruction by Brodhead's expedition in mid-April of 1781, when he attacked and destroyed Coshocton and burned Lichtenau. This raid and the execution of the male captives pushed the Delawares into the British camp. Those who survived the raid on Coshocton fled to the Sandusky, where they joined the Wyandots under Half King and the Munsees under Captain Pipe. In the summer, Major Arent Schuyler De Peyster, commandant at Detroit, ordered the removal of the Christian Delawares from the Tuscarawas to the Sandusky to prevent the missionaries from using them to gain information that could be sent to Fort Pitt and to consolidate British control of the Ohio Indians. The Wyandots and Munsee Delawares had responsibility for the removal.

In August Zeisberger received a message from the Wyandots to assemble the Christian Delawares at Gnadenhutten, where on August 20 they were told to accompany the three hundred warriors present back to the Sandusky. Zeisberger reported, "We felt the power of darkness, as if the air was filled with evil spirits." He argued that removal in the spring would be more convenient so that his charges could harvest their crops. Although he tried to delay, the Wyandots under the leadership of Pomoacan seized the missionaries and threatened them with death. Zeisberger recognized that not only his missionaries but also the Indian converts were in great danger, and he agreed to submit. The evacuation and long trek to the Sandusky began on September 8, with the missionaries following three days later "as if in a dream so as to hardly know our senses," Zeisberger reported, leaving three neat villages, fields of well-tended crops, and nine years of hard work behind. The refugees passed through deserted Coshocton, up the Walhonding River to the headwaters of the Kokosing, and west to the Sandusky, arriving on October 1 after a hard forced march on the trail.

The Moravians and the Christian Indians located their village on the Sandusky, probably a few miles south of present-day Upper Sandusky, where De Peyster reported, "The hindrances are out of the way . . . the birds will no longer sing in the woods and tell many lies. And now the Virginians will be in darkness and light will shine for them no more." The Moravians and their "praying Indians" would live among the Wyandots and other British allies for fifteen and a half months.

While the Moravians and the Christian Delawares lived along the Sandusky, they suffered from a constant shortage of food. Although they purchased some corn from local tribes and from Alexander Mc-Cormick, the British trader at Lower Sandusky, for the exorbitant price of eight dollars per bushel, they never acquired enough. Susan Zeisberger recalled the privation during their first winter: "Many times the Indians shared their last morsel with me, for many times I spent eight days in succession without food of my own." On December 28, David Zeisberger noted in his journal: "Many of our brethren suffer hunger, and as no corn can be had, they must subsist upon wild potatoes, which they dig up laboriously and bring from a distance." Captivity and hunger tested the faith of the Moravian missionaries. On New Year's Day 1782 Zeisberger wrote: "Satan rages, and it is as if we were given over to devils to plague us utterly, to torment us and make trials of fortune with us while we are here, not only from without, but also from within." Despite physical and mental adversity, Zeisberger proclaimed: "We are not, however, cast down nor disheartened, but oppose with might and with all our strength, to destroy and cast out of the Church the work of Satan." His converts suffered too, and Zeisberger worried about them, noting, "We pity these people, but we cannot, we know not, how to help them." Reeling from the trials akin to Job, he asked: "Why then does the Saviour let all this come upon us?"

While Zeisberger and the other Moravian missionaries pondered their fate on the Sandusky, his band of converts began to wander away. The Wyandots often took the little food the Moravians acquired. With everyone teetering on the verge of famine, the Moravians decided "to look to no other quarter for corn but to their forsaken towns." With that decision made, Zeisberger sent some of the Delawares, who had not experienced cultural reversion and abandoned their newly embraced religion, back to the Tuscarawas to collect the corn from their hastily abandoned fields. Not long thereafter, however, on March 14, 1782, the Moravians learned that their return had ended in tragedy. They prayed that the initial reports were wrong, but confirmation came on March 23. The news was horrible. In early March, a party of militia from Washington County, Pennsylvania, under Colonel David Williamson, struck the foragers at Gnadenhutten in retaliation for the loss of several lives and the capture of at least one woman and three children on the frontier.

The militia arrived at Gnadenhutten on March 8 and killed and scalped the first three Indians they discovered. When they approached the village, the Delawares did not see any reason for alarm because they recognized the horsemen as Americans, who were also Christians. The militia found many of the Delawares picking corn in the fields near Gnadenhutten and Salem and "bade them come into the town, telling them no harm should befall them." Once the Delawares had assembled, the Pennsylvanians accused them of raiding their settlements, divided them by sex, bound their hands, and placed them in separate houses. The Delawares sang hymns and prayed as the killing began. The militiamen took the Indians in groups of two or three to the two cabins that served as slaughterhouses, made them kneel, and smashed their skulls with a cooper's mallet, not unlike the way they would kill oxen or hogs. When the last body had been piled up, more than ninety men, women, and children lay in heaps. The Pennsylvanians then set fire to the killing houses. Only two Indians escaped, one scalped with blood running from his head, to tell the story. Delaware vengeance came swiftly and unmercifully.

In late March, General William Irvin, now in command at Fort Pitt, received increasing pressure from the men and women on the Pennsylvania frontier for the army to send an expedition to the Sandusky and destroy the Wyandot, Delaware, and Munsee villages. Irvin, with Washington's support, refused, arguing that he could not raise sufficient men or collect adequate supplies for such an attack. Disappointed but still angry, the Pennsylvanians decided, once again, to take matters into their own hands. By late May they had organized a frontier army of 480 mounted volunteers under the command of Colonel William Crawford, an experienced Indian fighter. David Williamson, just returned from Gnadenhutten, served as second in command. The militia departed from an area known as Mingo Bottoms on May 25, striking the trail northwest toward the Sandusky.

Crawford's army of volunteers reached the Sandusky on June 3. The next day the Wyandots attacked, and despite hard fighting the Pennsylvanians held their ground. When British reinforcements arrived on June 5 in the form of Butler's Rangers, the frontiersmen fell back before the seasoned professionals. At first the retreat was orderly, but as the Wyandots and rangers pressed the Pennsylvanians, all order broke down, and the withdrawal became a rout with Crawford's men divided. Retreating to the headwaters of the Olentangy, the Pennsylvanians made a stand before collapsing. Crawford lost fifty men killed, and the Indians took him prisoner.

Crawford became the sacrificial captive with face painted black for death. While women burned his naked body with firebrands and his head bled from the loss of his scalp, ears, and nose, he pleaded to Simon Girty, who watched, to shoot him, but Girty replied: "I have no gun." Girty's refusal to end the torture reflected not only the cruelty of war on the Ohio frontier but also his understanding of the art of the possible. The Delawares demanded revenge for the murder of their people at Gnadenhutten, and Girty could not save Crawford had he wanted or tried. If Girty had made an attempt to save Crawford, Wingenund, a Delaware leader, later remarked, he would have been killed. Girty could be a friend or enemy to both Indians and whites, and sometimes, under the most appalling circumstances, he could be neutral. At the very least, he was a hard man in a hard country.

Williamson luckily escaped Crawford's fate and skillfully led the remainder of the army back to Mingo Bottoms, where they arrived on June 13 with seventy men missing. His expedition against Gnadenhutten and the Wyandots had been disastrous for both Indians and whites, and the Ohio frontier was more dangerous than ever before.

In November 1782, George Rogers Clark made one last Ameri- can attack on the Shawnee villages in the Miami River valley. Clark crossed the Ohio at present-day Cincinnati with 1,050 men in early November. Daniel Boone accompanied the expedition, which burned five Shawnee villages along the Great Miami six days later, including Old Chillicothe and the British trading post known as Loramie's Store, located a dozen miles north of Piqua. Clark reported: "We got few scalps and Prisoners." Boone recalled that the expedition "entirely destroyed their corn and other fruits, and spread desolation through their country," but the Shawnees withdrew without a major fight. Most of the men were absent from the villages, and the Indians suffered few losses. Instead of inflicting defeat, Clark merely antagonized the Shawnees still further and kept their hatred alive for whites on the Ohio frontier.

While Clark futilely moved against the Shawnees along the Great Miami River valley, American and British officials meeting in Paris reached agreement for peace on November 30, with hostilities to stop on April 30, 1783. Although the Americans along the frontier celebrated their independence from Great Britain, the fighting between Indians and whites would continue on the Ohio frontier. Still, independence had been won, and the terms of the treaty were generous. Great Britain ceded all of its lands south of the Great Lakes to the new American nation. The British, however, had assured the Indians that the Ohio River, established as the boundary in the Treaty of Fort Stanwix, would be honored since the king had not claimed the right to Indian lands north of the Ohio. Although neither the far northern nor southern boundaries with Canada and Spain respectively had been determined, the gain of essentially the entire trans-Appalachian frontier for the Americans was fortuitous indeed. While the frontier people had been unable to defeat the Wyandots, Delawares, Munsees, and Shawnees in Ohio, they won a territorial victory with the peace, gaining possession to lands that they never held.

The Ohio Indians were "thunder Struck" by the terms of the peace. Forsaken by the British, who had pledged to protect their lands, the Indians were left to their own devices. Although the Ohio Indians had tipped the balance of power to the British in the Northwest, they had been too far from the major engagements in the East

HIO FRONTIER

ildier stood north of the Ohio when the war ended. Un-
ed in battle, the Ohio Indians now lost the war on a piece of
But culture rather than the Ohio River remained the great
divide between the Indians and the frontier people. In the end, one
Ohio Indian remarked, the American Revolution brought "all the
Noise and Miseries of War, And Blood and Murder [to] stain our
Land again." Yet with ownership of the land north of the Ohio
River unresolved, the future boded ill for both the Americans and
the Indians on the Ohio frontier.

4.

THE ROAD TO HELL

On September 29, 1785, twelve keelboats with seventy soldiers under the command of Captain Walter Finney left the docks at Fort McIntosh in Pennsylvania and drifted southward with the current of the Ohio River. They were accompanied by two flatboats carrying horses, cattle, and supplies as well as by Indian commissioner Richard Butler. The river ran low that autumn, and the company made only twelve to fifteen miles a day in the slow-moving current. But on October 22 they reached their destination, the mouth of the Great Miami River, and they began building a fort on its eastern bank. Within three weeks they had constructed a stockade about one hundred feet square, with a barracks at each corner and a magazine and supply house underway in the interior. They called their location Fort Finney.

The soldiers had been sent to protect Commissioner Butler and his party as they met with the Shawnees to gain a land concession from them that would permit peaceful settlement by whites north of the Ohio River. Earlier, on January 21, 1785, Congress had made some progress in gaining control of the Ohio lands ceded by Great Britain in the Peace of Paris in 1783. At that time, commissioners Richard Butler, Arthur Lee, and George Rogers Clark negotiated a treaty at Fort McIntosh with the Wyandots, Delawares, Ottawas, and Ojibwas (Chippewas), whom one soldier collectively called an "ugly set of devils." This treaty ceded most of the Indian lands in Ohio, south of a line from Fort Laurens to the confluence of the

St. Marys and St. Joseph rivers, which formed the Maumee, and placed the signing parties under the protection of the United States. The Shawnees and Miamis, however, had refused to participate in the treaty-making process at Fort McIntosh. They continued to demand that the United States government and its frontier people recognize their right to the land north of the Ohio, and they vowed to keep it by force.

The Shawnees distrusted the motives of the government, which wanted to negotiate, or perhaps dictate a land cession with the intimidation of its soldiers. Warily the Shawnees delayed accepting invitations to hold treaty talks at Fort Finney, and they did not arrive until mid-January 1786. Only 318 Shawnees arrived, and they did so primarily because they were hungry and short of supplies rather than because they wanted to make peace and cede a portion of their lands. Most of the Shawnees and the Miamis, under British influence, stayed away. The fears of those who attended the treaty council and those who shunned it were well founded.

When the talks began on January 28, the Shawnees quickly understood that they were being asked to accept the boundary designated by the Treaty of Fort McIntosh, the sovereignty of the United States over the ceded lands, and acceptance of American protection and law. Despite their hunger, they still had no intention of signing away most of Ohio in a treaty "leaving them no land to live or raise corn on." Richard Butler noted that the government's proposal for a land cession made the young men angry and "ready for war." Chief Kekewepellethy (Tame Hawk) spoke for all of the Shawnees, saying, "As to the lands it is all ours. You say you have goods for our women and children; you may keep your goods, and give them to the other nations, we will have none of them." Then, to show their hatred of the Americans and their rejection of the treaty, Tame Hawk gave the commissioners a belt of black wampum. Only ill could come from it, and it came immediately.

Butler threw the string of black wampum onto the table and told Tame Hawk that his people were "unwise and ungrateful." The terms for peace, Butler reminded the Shawnees, were liberal and just, and they now had the choice of peace or war. Commissioner George Rogers Clark, who had recently joined the negotiations, followed Butler, who stormed out of the council tent, pausing only to grind the belt of wampum into the ground with his boot. Cowed by this show of hostility and the presence of the soldiers, the Shawnees capitulated. After several hours of reflection, Tame Hawk told Butler, "You have everything in your power—you are great. . . . We agree to all you have proposed."

On January 31, 1786, these Shawnees signed the Treaty at the Mouth of the Great Miami. It restricted them to a small parcel of land neighboring the Wayandot and Delaware reservations in the northwestern corner of Ohio designated in the Treaty of Fort Mc-Intosh. Butler contended that the treaty gave the Shawnees "perfect satisfaction." Once again, however, the commissioners did not understand that individual chiefs did not speak for all bands and villages, and the confederacy of the northwestern tribes rejected it. The Ohio River, they contended, remained the boundary which the Americans were treaty-bound not to cross. In reality, the commissioners had not resolved the land question with the Shawnees and Miamis. Instead, they had increased the animosity of the Indians in western Ohio. Rather than light a council fire that symbolized peace and unity, they fanned the flames of war.

In the months that followed the Treaty at the Great Miami, the threats of the commissioners received a boost from the Kentuckians who believed that revenge and war, rather than magnanimity and negotiation, would bring peace to the Ohio country. For months the Kentuckians along the Ohio River had suffered attacks from Indians who struck south from the Wabash country. Unable to get adequate protection from the government of Virginia, under whose jurisdiction Kentucky remained, and with no reasonable expectation of help from the central government, the settlers south of the Ohio began to talk about a "voluntary campaign" to inflict retribution in Ohio for the lives lost and homes destroyed south of the river.

Confronted with war talk by whites, Governor Patrick Henry of Virginia authorized the Kentuckians to "concert some system for their own defense." Militia commanders met on August 2 and unanimously agreed that an attack on the Indian towns north of the Ohio was "justifiable and necessary." They appointed General George Rogers Clark to command the army of militia and ordered the men to rendezvous at Clarksville on September 10, 1786. Like most frontiersmen, Commissioner Clark preferred the sword to the pen when dealing with the Ohio Indians. He adamantly believed that the Indians understood only force. Fear instilled by the flash of rifle muzzles and the gleam of scalping knives would make them peaceful, while presents were "an Incouragement for them to make war." Clark, like many other whites, failed to understand that the Ohio Indians rejected the principle of the "right of conquest" invoked by the United States after the defeat of the British during the American Revolution. As a result, both whites and Indians claimed the land north of the Ohio. If possible, however, the government was willing to bargain for it as a cost-saving measure. George Washington clearly warned: "In a word there is nothing to be obtained by an Indian War but the soil they live on and this can be had by purchase at less expense." But both sides were prepared to guarantee their claims by force if necessary, and Indian raids into Kentucky and against settlers in Ohio made many frontier people demand retaliation.

Clark responded by planning a two-pronged attack. One group of Kentuckians would move against the Miamis under Little Turtle in the Wabash country in present-day Indiana, while another contingent would strike north into the Miami River area, where the Shawnees had a number of villages. By mid-September Clark had a 790-man army ready to cross the Ohio. Benjamin Logan, Clark's second in command, had orders to "march against the Shawnees' towns" to punish them for violating the Treaty of the Great Miami, although few had accepted it. Unfortunately, the Kentuckians had no intention or ability to distinguish between friendly and hostile Shawnees. Logan's expedition would also pressure the British to withdraw their support from the Shawnees, make concessions, or fight.

Logan's mounted column, including Colonel Daniel Boone and Major Simon Kenton, left Limestone, Kentucky, about October 1, crossed the Ohio River, and headed for the Shawnee towns along the Mad River. The peaceful town of Mackachack in present-day Logan County lay directly in their path. Mackachack, under the leadership of Molunthy, who had signed the Great Miami Treaty, and whom the commissioners had told that his people were "included among the friends of the United States," flew an American flag from a high pole. When Logan's militia arrived on October 6,

Molunthy expected to meet them as part of the American "chain of friendship." Logan, however, had prepared an attack designed to encircle Mackachack and another village on the left bank of the Mad River. The Kentuckians understood that they were only to "spare the white blood," that is, any captives in the villages. When Logan's force approached within three-quarters of a mile of the villages, the Shawnees became alarmed at the deployment of the troops and began to flee. When Logan realized that surprise was no longer possible, he ordered an immediate attack. With Boone and Kenton in the lead, the Kentuckians raced their horses toward the Shawnee towns, killing a number of women and children and ten men with both sword and shot. Lieutenant Ebenezer Denny reported: "They made no resistance; the men were literally murdered."

The fighting did not last long, and the Kentuckians rounded up their captives, including the peaceful Molunthy. Before Logan could restore order, however, Captain Hugh McGary, whom the Shawnees had previously defeated in battle with great loss of life to his Kentuckians, executed Molunthy by sinking a hatchet in his head and scalping him. Logan regained a semblance of control by threatening to kill anyone who harmed an Indian captive. Then the Kentuckians burned the villages and rode north to strike Wapakoneta. When they arrived, most of the Shawnees had fled, and the militia killed only ten defenders, including Chief Shade. Before they set fire to the village, however, they burned one captive at the stake and enjoyed the pleasure of watching him die when a bag of gunpowder exploded that had been tied around his waist.

By the time Logan's men had finished two days of raiding, the Kentuckians had burned eight Shawnee villages and destroyed fifteen thousand bushels of corn, essentially their entire food supply for the winter. On October 8 the expedition headed back to Kentucky, sporting the scalps of eleven warriors, ten chiefs, and a number of women and children. They also brought back twenty-six women and two children as prisoners and four "rescued" white captives. Yet, even by the barbaric standards of the Kentucky militia, Logan's raid had been much less than a major success.

Indeed, instead of striking enough terror into the hearts of the Shawnees to cow them from further raiding across the Ohio River and to intimidate them to accept peace, the Kentuckians merely guaranteed the continuation of war on the Ohio frontier. After Logan's raid, the Shawnees sought retribution, not reconciliation. His raid also fostered a sense of unity and common purpose that had been lacking among the Shawnees. Thereafter, the Shawnees actively supported a grand confederacy among the western Indian nations and sought British support from Detroit, particularly guns, powder, and lead. After Logan's raid, the Shawnees and their allies would accept peace only after total defeat. They would no longer agree to meet American commissioners in council. Before that defeat came, however, eight years of brutal war, in which atrocities were committed by both sides, plagued the Ohio frontier.

* * *

On November 28, 1786, the confederated tribes of the Ohio country met at Brownstown, near Detroit, where Joseph Brant, leader of the Mohawks, told them: "The interests of any one nation should be the welfare of all the others." Brant, however, spoke more for the Shawnees and Miamis, who demanded recognition of the Ohio River as the boundary with the Americans than for other tribal groups, and unity did not come easily. The Wyandots, Delawares, and Senecas had already ceded considerable lands to the government of the United States and preferred conciliation rather than war. In addition, the Shawnees contributed to division rather than unity by wanting recognition as the military leaders of the confederacy. Although the Wyandots favored peace, they resented infringement on their traditional role as military commanders. The Shawnees, however, gave them little heed, maintaining that the Wyandots and Delawares had "sold their lands and themselves with them." The Miamis were relatively few in number and had less influence than the Shawnees in demanding a confederacy, while the Ottawas, Potawatomis, and Ojibwas claimed lands not directly threatened by white settlers, and they had less need for war. Tribal ethnic differences continued to prevent political unity unless the Americans became a threat to all.

During the course of the council, Joseph Brant worked to convince the Upper Great Lakes tribes that danger was present and unity essential. The alternative to war would be the loss of Indian

lands through the cession treaty process as the government negotiated separate land cessions with individual chiefs, as it had done at
Fort Harmar and the Great Miami. Strength lay with confederation
and unified action. To use an Algonquian metaphor, if the confederated tribes would now eat out of a common dish, they would be of
"one mind and one voice." Not every tribe agreed with Chief Brant,
and when the council ended, the confederated nations could agree
only to ask Congress for a new, comprehensive treaty and the invali-
dation of all previous agreements, with the exception of recognition
of the Ohio River as the boundary between Indians and whites. The
tribes also agreed that they held the land in common and that unan-
imous approval was required for any cession and that they would
cooperate to maintain the Ohio River boundary. In the meantime,
the confederated nations hoped that the British would provide sufficient diplomatic and, if necessary, military support to keep the
Americans from establishing settlements north of the Ohio River.
The British were encouraging, if noncommittal, but their presence
in a number of forts on American soil clearly indicated to the hostile
tribes that they would provide support in a new war.

Government officials did not want war, but neither did they
intend to recognize the Ohio River as the boundary in the northwest. In 1787, Congress had provided a system for governmental
organization and the rule of law with the Northwest Ordinance. By
that time, many settlers had already crossed the river and claimed
land, and some tribes made considerable land cessions. But Arthur
St. Clair, governor of the Northwest Territory, was slow to convene
a conference to resolve the differences between the United States
and the Ohio Indians. St. Clair particularly hampered peace negotiations when he rashly blamed all of the Ohio Indians for an
isolated attack by a band of Ojibwas who struck an army detachment on July 12, 1788, about thirty miles north of Fort Harmar
at the falls of the Muskingum, where they were preparing a site for
a major treaty council. On learning of the death of two and the
wounding of three soldiers, he accused the Ohio Indians of "unpro-
voked hostility." St. Clair also angrily canceled the council. In a
letter to the tribes that had convened at Detroit, he wrote: "The flag
of the United States has been fired upon . . . when a small party of
soldiers were sent to watch the council fire, kindled at your request;

to build a council house for you to meet in, and to take care of the provisions sent there to feed you, you have fallen upon them, and killed them. . . . In the name of the United States I require an immediate explanation of these transactions, and demand satisfaction and the restitution of the prisoners. Until these are made, as there can be no confidence, it will be improper we should meet one another in council." The Shawnees and Miamis took St. Clair's letter as a clear message that the Americans would not negotiate and make concessions, and they increased their attacks on both settlers and soldiers on the Ohio frontier.

Congress, however, wanted negotiations, not war. Secretary of War Knox conveyed its wishes to St. Clair in a letter asking him to "quiet all disturbances among the Indians" by peaceful means. If St. Clair failed, Knox believed renewed war could be blamed on the Indians. Both St. Clair and General Josiah Harmar readily approved of Secretary Knox's tacit support of war, and both distrusted the Indians and believed they were "hatching a great deal of mischief," rather than seeking peace. As a result, they were both surprised by the arrival of a delegation from the Six Nations on November 7, 1788, at Fort Harmar. Captain David, one of the chiefs, presented St. Clair with a friendly message from the Indian confederacy that had recently concluded a grand council. Skillfully worded by Chief Brant, the message asked for the restoration of the treaty negotiations at the Falls of the Muskingum and indicated their willingness to recognize settlements north of the Ohio, if the Americans would negotiate a permanent boundary in good faith. St. Clair, however, would have none of it. He arrogantly informed the delegation that all negotiations would now take place at Fort Harmar, where his men could be protected from "insult" by devious and treacherous Indians.

When the Western Confederacy learned of St. Clair's rebuff of their overture for negotiations, they replied: "From the misconduct of a few individuals who live at a great distance . . . and are little concerned with a union with you, you have extinguished the council fire." These western Ohio Indians also told St. Clair: "We look upon [this] extremely hard, particularly as we have been exerting ourselves for several years past to bring the whole of the Indian nations of this country to agree to come to some terms of peace with the United States."

The chiefs of the confederacy, however, had more diplomatic skill than St. Clair. While their response was harsh, they did not discount the possibility of future negotiations, telling St. Clair, "We propose to give to the United States all the lands lying on the east side of the Muskingum." The Ohio and the Muskingum rivers then would become the boundary between the two peoples. The confederacy had offered an important compromise by agreeing to trade land for peace. Unfortunately, they had not agreed to cede enough of it. Given the cultural needs and desires of the Ohio Indians and the demands of the Americans, a long-term peace had become impossible. When St. Clair rejected the confederation's proposal as "inadmissible," the chiefs replied that events would now be decided by the "will of the Great Spirit," to whom they looked for justice. They had little doubt that the whites understood only force and that peace could be ensured only by war. St. Clair had ruined any chance for the peace that he had been instructed to obtain.

While St. Clair and Chief Brant traded barbs with pens, Secretary of War Knox informed General Harmar that war had to be avoided. "This event would at present be embarrassing beyond conception," he wrote. The government could not afford it. "It has been with the greatest difficulty that money has been obtained for the recruits, clothing, and stores which have been forwarded during the present year." Not only was the new nation in financial difficulty and unable to afford another new Indian war, but the army was virtually nonexistent. With privates paid only $6.67 per month, less deductions for their food and forage for their horses, the army had little attraction and remained far below authorized strength. Those who enlisted were often far from physically fit or mentally committed to meet their responsibilities. Without funds and an army, Knox feared, a new Indian war "might be protracted to such a length as to produce extreme distress and disgrace." His words proved prophetic as the war faction gained control of the Western Confederacy.

By the summer of 1788, Indians and whites engaged in open but undeclared war in the Ohio country. The army did not have the strength to end it, and anything less than total defeat meant victory for the Indians. In an effort to obey the directives of Congress and restore the peace, St. Clair responded by calling a council at Fort Harmar on December 13, 1788, but with the moderates now in the war camp of the confederacy, he had little hope of ensuring the peace or resolving the boundary dispute. Although twenty-seven chiefs, including Cornplanter of the Seneca, and approximately two hundred Wyandots, Delawares, and Senecas attended the treaty council, they already had reached accommodation with the Americans. Now they hoped to sign a treaty based on the proposal of Chief Brant. St. Clair and the soldiers generally treated the Indian delegation as "indolent, dirty, inanimate creatures." The Indian delegation had hoped to sign a treaty based on the proposal of Chief Brant that would make the Muskingum and the Ohio the boundary, but St. Clair insisted they sign a document that affirmed the land cessions of the Treaty of Fort McIntosh, which essentially ceded all of Ohio to the United States and required them to convince the other tribes to accept the same terms.

Cowed by St. Clair's intimidation and bribed with $3,000 in presents, the chiefs signed the Treaty of Fort Harmar on January 9, 1789, an act that convinced both St. Clair and Harmar that the Indian confederacy had been broken. Harmar contended that the treaty would have a "good tendency at least to divide the savages in their councils." The Shawnees rejected the Treaty of Fort Harmar out of hand and reminded the Americans that the Senecas, Wyandots, and Delawares did not speak for the confederacy and that its lands were "not in the power of one or two nations to dispose of it." The confederacy now believed that it had little choice but to face the "encroachers." Runners carried war pipes to the various tribes, and a delegation went to Detroit for ammunition from the British.

Quickly the Ohio Indians responded to St. Clair's mistakes. Attacks on settlers both south and north of the Ohio River increased in number and intensity. Men, women, and children were killed. Often captives were now tortured and killed rather than adopted or used for barter. In June 1789, Charles Builder, who had been the militia captain ordered to execute a group of the peaceful Delawares at the Moravian mission in 1782, was captured by the Shawnees near his farm on the north side of the Ohio River. After someone recognized him, the Shawnees gave him a painful death by systematically cutting off various body parts. Faced with increasing atrocities such as this, while discounting those of their own, the frontier people in both Kentucky and Ohio demanded that their government protect them.

* * *

On September 30, 1790, General Harmar moved out of Fort Washington and headed up the Great Miami River valley into the St. Marys watershed. He commanded 1,453 troops, including 320 regulars and 1,133 militia, of the latter of whom Harmar said, "At least 200 are good for nothing." They were bound for the principal Miami town located at present-day Fort Wayne, Indiana. Harmar had advocated a military strike for a long time, believing the Ohio Indians understood only force and that they would never agree to a lasting peace until they were compelled to submit. He had, however, wanted to lead an expedition of seasoned regulars against the hostile tribes. Instead, a ragtag contingent of Kentucky and Pennsylvania militia followed along. One question constantly worried him: When trouble came, would they stand and fight?

Although in June 1790 George Washington favored the use of the army to punish "certain banditti of Indians from the northwest side of the Ohio," and while Congress had authorized an increase in troop strength to 1,216, it also reduced the wages of privates to two dollars per month, after deductions for clothing and other necessities, while officers' salaries ranged from only eighteen to sixty dollars per month, which made recruiting more difficult than ever before. Yet, because of the considerable fear about Indian hostilities on the Ohio frontier, Congress expected the army to bring peace by force, and on September 29, 1789, it moved to facilitate that necessity by authorizing the army to use the militia to pacify the frontier.

On July 15, 1790, St. Clair and Harmar, believing that further attempts to negotiate peacefully were useless, began planning a campaign to "punish the Indians," because "gentle means" would not bring them to a peace council. The plan called for Harmar to lead approximately twelve hundred militiamen and three hundred regulars against the hostile tribes in the Ohio country, with Major John Hamtramck making a diversionary attack on the Weas along the Wabash River. Harmar's target would be the Miami, Shawnee, and Delaware towns where the Maumee River began, at present-day Fort Wayne, Indiana. The task of acquiring sufficient provisions and munitions proved difficult, but by mid-September, Harmar had assembled enough supplies to support an expedition to the north, and he was relatively pleased.

When the militia authorized by Virginia from its Kentucky district and from Pennsylvania began to arrive about that same time, however, Harmar was shocked. Even under the best of circumstances, he detested militiamen. Yet the militia who reported for duty were not seasoned frontiersmen who deftly hit what they aimed at with their rifles and who could make their way in the woods. Instead, they were raw recruits who knew little about guns and less about the rigors of campaigning on the frontier. Many carried broken weapons and exhibited a careless disregard for discipline and a propensity to argue about which officers they had elected to obey. One army officer doubted that many of them had ever fired a gun, and another observed: "Their whole object seemed nothing more than to see the country without rendering any service whatever." To make matters worse, Harmar did not have time to train them. Autumn frost would soon kill the grass on which he depended for forage to feed pack and cavalry horses.

With this army, then, Harmar was expected to "astonish" the Shawnees and Miamis and make them "smart" by destroying their villages, corn reserves, fields, and fighting men, and by this tactical maneuvering hinder their ability to make war. St. Clair recommended that Harmar not restrain the "savage ferocity about the militia." Unfortunately for Harmar and his men, Secretary Knox ordered St. Clair to send runners to the British at Detroit and to the peaceful tribes, alerting them of the planned attack and assuring them that it was not directed at them. As a result, before Harmar moved north, the Shawnees and Miamis knew he was coming.

Harmar sent his militia forward on September 26 along the old Miami Trail, followed by his regulars four days later for a rendezvous at the mouth of Turkey Creek on the Little Miami River. At that time, his column numbered nearly fifteen hundred men, but Harmar had expected the First American Regiment to have an additional four hundred men, and its understrength troubled him. He also had 578 packhorses and 175 cattle to ensure transport and a supply of fresh meat. Thirteen days out of Fort Washington, after a march that lost much time while careless packers rounded up stray horses and cattle, they reached the vicinity of present-day St. Marys, about a hundred miles north of Fort Washington, on October 13, where a patrol captured a Shawnee who evidently had been observing the expedition's progress. Upon interrogation, Harmar learned that the Miamis were preparing to destroy their villages and flee from the impending attack. With that information, on October 14 Harmar ordered a mounted column to advance and strike the Indians before they could escape. With the Miami villages only a half-day's ride away, Harmar believed that his main column could follow the mounted troops and arrive in time to provide backup if necessary. Because most of the mounted troops were Kentucky militia, Harmar ordered a six-hundred-man detachment commanded by Colonel John Hardin along with fifty regulars under Captain David Ziegler to reconnoiter and make the attack, if necessary, while the infantry advanced.

It did not go well from the beginning. Instead of leaving at dawn on the 15th, Hardin could not get his Kentucky militiamen ready to depart until mid-morning, only a half-hour before the remainder of Harmar's expedition moved out. Hardin's guides soon got lost, and the militia made little progress. While the Kentuckians floundered and the infantry plodded, war chiefs Blue Jacket of the Shawnees and Little Turtle of the Miamis waited before them. Although the Indian force numbered only about six hundred poorly armed warriors, they were determined to prevent, in the words of Blue Jacket, a "premeditated design to root us out of our land." The Shawnees and Miamis confidently believed that they were "acting in the cause of justice."

Hardin's Kentucky militia reached Kekionga (present-day Fort Wayne, Indiana), which the Americans called the Miami Village, after a hard ride on October 15. The British used Kekionga as a major trading post, and it controlled the traffic between the Wabash country and northern Ohio. It was an enemy town worth destroying, but when Hardin's column arrived, the Miamis had already burned many of the wigwams and log cabins.

With Kekionga and other Miami, Shawnee, and Delaware villages abandoned, the militia began looting, and Hardin could not bring them under control. When the main column arrived on October 17, they too joined the pillaging, and Harmar restored order only after ordering that the prizes be evenly distributed among all of the troops. Harmar believed the Indians had been cowed. Still, the disappearance of more than fifty packhorses and several cavalry mounts during the night of October 17 concerned him, and he sent a 300-man force, including 40 mounted troops, out the next day to scout the area, while his men continued burning nearby villages and destroyed twenty thousand bushels of corn. This reconnaissance accomplished little other than to discover signs that a large number of Indians had not fled the area. Consequently, Harmar ordered Hardin to scout northwest of Kekionga on October 19 with a force of 180 men, including 30 regulars.

By now, however, the militia had lost their enthusiasm. They had pillaged as much as possible, and now that danger looked imminent, the Kentuckians particularly balked. Little more than five miles beyond Harmar's camp, Hardin discovered signs which he interpreted to mean that the Indians were retreating, and he ordered a rapid advance. Several miles ahead, his men entered an empty town in a clearing, and the militia quickly went about the business of looting. When the militia were distracted and running about the wigwams of the village, Little Turtle sprang the trap. More than 150 warriors hiding in the surrounding woods leveled a fusillade into the militiamen, and panic instantly ensued.

The first reaction of the militia was to flee, retreating so rapidly that they ran through the regulars who had just arrived at the clearing and were attempting to form a battle line. The militia behind the regulars joined their colleagues in flight, leaving thirty regulars and nine militia alone. Little Turtle's combined force of Miamis, Shawnees, and Potawatomis overwhelmed them. Captain John Armstrong, who escaped, reported: "I saw my men bayonet many of them. They fought and died hard"—except for the militia, who, once back at camp, suffered Harmar's wrath for their "cowardly behavior." In a rage, he promised to "order the artillery to fire on them" if they fled again.

While the wounded received treatment, Harmar's remaining force completed burning the nearby villages and destroying Indian food supplies. On October 21, his force began its retreat, although he authorized a quick strike by his regulars the next day against

In the autumn of 1790, General Josiah Harmar marched against the Indian villages located near the headwaters of the Maumee River. Miami war chief Little Turtle, however, surprised and decisively defeated Harmar's undisciplined militia and understrength regulars. Harmar's force fled back to Fort Washington in a panic, with his career in ruin.
INDIANA HISTORICAL SOCIETY LIBRARY, C4735.

Kekionga to surprise the Miamis who reportedly had returned home. Major John Palsgrave Wyllys commanded the force of 60 regulars, while Colonel Hardin served under him with about 300 militia, 40 of whom were mounted. Near Kekionga, Wyllys divided his force to strike the village from the west with 150 Kentuckians while the remainder of the militia attacked from the east. The regulars would attack from the south. This surprise attack disintegrated when Little Turtle ambushed Wyllys's men as they waded across the Maumee River to reach Kekionga on the north bank. The initial volley left dead and wounded men and horses lying in the shallow water, but the Indians fled from the protective cover of the river bank when mounted troops arrived and made a pell-mell attack across the river, past the village, and into a corn field that they had destroyed a few days before.

Little Turtle's decoy worked. The militia and regulars now stood exposed and isolated. The Miamis launched their counterattack with a "hideous yell." The regulars once again stood their ground and died, while the Kentucky militia ran for the woods behind them. The rout ended only when the contingents that had been sent to attack the town from behind arrived, and the Indians, who did not have sufficient weapons to continue the fight, disappeared into the woods. By the time the fighting stopped, perhaps 100 Indians had died, while 75 regulars and 108 militia had been killed and 3 soldiers and 28 militia wounded. Harmar wrote in his diary: "The consolation is that the men sold themselves very dear." In the meantime, the survivors reeled back toward Harmar's camp in near-panic. Harmar learned of this second catastrophe on October 22 and sent a relief column that could do little more than help the wounded back to camp. Although Harmar proclaimed victory, his expeditionary force had been beaten, and it was saved from a complete rout, which Blue Jacket planned, only by a lunar eclipse. The Ottawas considered it an ill omen and refused to press the attack. Without the Ottawas, the Miamis, Shawnees, and Delawares did not have enough men to continue.

On October 23, Harmar began a hasty retreat, with the militia running ahead, refusing to obey orders and essentially out of control. One regimental officer reported that after the first shots, "some of them never halted until they crossed the Ohio." The regulars behaved little better, and Harmar restored some order only after he had one soldier lashed to a cannon and whipped. By the time Harmar's men reached Fort Washington on November 3, their provisions had been exhausted, and the militia were on the verge of mutiny. His expedition had been a resounding disaster, although he claimed success in the destruction of the Maumee towns and crops "without considerable loss." In retrospect no one should have expected anything but failure, because his expedition had been so poorly planned and conducted. Perhaps Harmar should have been commended for keeping his men together as a tactical unit, but instead he had to defend himself against charges of drunkenness and dereliction of duty.

Secretary Knox recommended that Harmar request a "Court of Enquiry" to investigate his conduct and, it was hoped, exonerate him. Although the court found Harmar's conduct "irreproachable" and attributed the defeat to orders that were "not properly executed," his career was finished. In mid-March he was relieved of his command and replaced by Arthur St. Clair, who had considerable military experience in the French and Indian War and the American Revolution. Planning now began in earnest to avenge Harmar's losses and secure the country north of the Ohio River by force of arms, but without application of the lessons that could have been learned from Harmar's expedition. While St. Clair planned, the Shawnees and Miamis, confident with their defeat of Harmar, saw no need for a negotiated peace.

* * *

On March 21, 1791, Secretary of War Knox ordered Governor Arthur St. Clair "to establish a strong and permanent military post in the heart of the Miami villages," which would be linked to Fort Washington by a chain of posts in order to awe and curb the Indians and establish federal authority in the region. He was to garrison it with as many as 1,200 men. To facilitate the accomplishment of this task, Knox promised to raise a second regiment of 2,000 men by enlisting "levies," that is, volunteers for six months, in order to bring the number of troops in the Ohio country to 3,000 men. St. Clair pledged to make "strong war" against the Miamis and Shawnees and to wreak "vengeance" and "utter destruction" on them. When he assumed command of Fort Washington in mid-May, however, only 85 privates reported fit for duty. Quickly he began drawing soldiers away from Forts Harmar, Steuben in Kentucky, and Knox in Indiana to bring the First Regiment up to about 300 men. By summer, however, St. Clair recognized that he would not have the full contingent of authorized troops. Only 1,674 had enlisted in the Second United States Regiment, leaving a deficiency of more than 1,000 men. Moreover, the levies were primarily social outcasts, and little better disciplined than the 1,160 militia that St. Clair drafted for three months on September 1. One contemporary observed that the levies were men "purchased from prisons, wheelbarrows and brothels at two dollars a month." From the beginning, these troops lacked leadership, training, and supplies. Adjutant General Winthrop Sargent remembered St. Clair's army as "badly clothed, badly paid and badly fed." Captain John Armstrong, who had served in the army since 1776, said St. Clair's men were "the worst and most dissatisfied troops I ever served with." No one seemed to have learned anything from the recent past.

On August 7, five weeks behind schedule, St. Clair had assembled his army, and a week later he moved it to Ludlow's Station, five miles north of Fort Washington, to improve the pasturage for his horses and cattle and enable better training once the men were beyond the lure of the taverns in Cincinnati and the temptation to desert on passing flatboats. St. Clair lingered at the station with 2,300 men until September 17, when they once again moved north. Twenty miles and two days later they camped on the Miami, where they began building Fort Hamilton to serve as a supply depot and the first link in a chain of forts that he intended to build into the Maumee country.

St. Clair lost precious time building Fort Hamilton, which he described as "a stockade fifty yards square, with four good bastions, and platforms for cannon in two of them, with barracks for about two hundred men, with some good store houses, etc." For more than a month the men worked hard with axes and saws. Some two thousand trees, cut twenty feet long and averaging about twelve inches in diameter, were set upright for the outer walls, with another two thousand set in the gaps on the inside of these palisades. The men also cleared the ground of trees and brush for approximately three hundred yards around the fort to permit a clear line of fire and to keep the enemy from approaching too closely.

The new recruits, however, showed little discipline and low morale. The expedition was also more than forty days behind schedule, and the fair-weather days of the Ohio autumn were numbered. When 300 Kentucky militia, approximately 450 fewer than planned, caught up with the army on October 5, a day after it had moved out of Fort Hamilton, the regulars treated them with disdain. The officers so distrusted them that they were not assigned regular duties. Still, St. Clair felt confident that his expedition would defeat the Indians.

His optimism, however, proved unwarranted. Rainy, cold weather slowed the march as well as St. Clair's attempt to cut two parallel roads, about 250 yards apart, through the forested country before him. Inadequate provisions contributed to poor morale and jeopardized the entire expedition, while an incompetent packmaster proved more proficient at losing horses than at finding them. At best, the army covered about five miles per day, and it held together primarily because many of the men were afraid to desert in Indian country. Sargent, whom his friend Arthur St. Clair considered "very obnoxious," made matters worse by trying to punish inappropriate military behavior by beating discipline into the troops with frequent floggings. Major General Richard Butler, second in command, resented St. Clair's power, while other jealousies pervaded the officer corps, and the competency of many remained open to question. Sargent called one officer a "damned bad soldier for peace or war." Moreover, St. Clair had not discovered the way to integrate efficiently the regulars, levies, and militia. The militia held the levies in contempt, while the regulars considered both to be unworthy of respect.

By mid-October frosts had killed the grass and made the forage problem difficult, and the Indians had stolen so many horses that not enough remained to carry the essential supplies of the army. Nearly constant rain and inadequate tents and clothing brought sickness and demands for immediate discharge by many of the men. Two executions for desertion failed to stem the tide. By that time St. Clair's army had advanced only forty-five miles north of Fort Hamilton. On October 13, St. Clair halted six miles south of present-day Greenville to build another fort to serve as a supply base and refuge, because the Miami villages were only about fifty miles away. The men laid up horizontal logs walls in a 100-foot square, but bad weather and insufficient axes prevented them from completing their work until the 23d. The men named these squalid quarters Fort Deposit, but St. Clair renamed it Fort Jefferson. By then, St. Clair's summer expedition had turned into a grueling winter campaign.

On October 24, St. Clair began his march again for the Miami villages, but he advanced only six miles before the expedition camped at the site of present-day Greenville, where they waited for supplies and suffered in the sleet and snow. Captain Armstrong wrote, "I pray God that . . . the Enemy may not be disposed to give us battle." Reconnaissance parties, however, began to report sightings of and skirmishes with the Indians. When at least sixty militia deserted on October 31, St. Clair sent his best troops from the First Regiment to bring them back and protect the supply train from being rifled by the deserters on their way home. In doing so, however, he seriously diminished the strength of his army.

On November 3, after confronting these and other problems, St. Clair made camp on the east bank of the Wabash in western Ohio. His men were hungry, exhausted, and cold as they pitched their tents in two parallel lines about 350 yards long and 70 yards apart. Forest and higher ground surrounded much of the site. Because his men were so tired, St. Clair did not order them to build breastworks or dig entrenchments. Few guards were posted as the men huddled around campfires or shivered in their tents.

St. Clair believed, however, that the Indians were neither near nor capable of standing against his army. Yet he did not know their location. Unknown to St. Clair, Little Turtle and Blue Jacket knew his position, strength, and plans, and with a force of more than a thousand men, neither was intimidated as they watched from the woods. Indeed, in late October, the Shawnees and Miamis had begun moving toward St. Clair's floundering troops with great anticipation. Their plans had been aided by a young Shawnee, called Tecumseh, and other scouts who had kept them informed about St. Clair's movements. Simon Girty reported: "The Indians were never in greater heart to meet their enemy, nor more sure of success—they [were] determined to drive them to the Ohio."

* * *

Little Turtle attacked at dawn on November 4, 1791. The Kentucky militia, approximately three hundred strong, who had been sent across the river ahead of the regulars and levies to hinder their propensity to desert, took the full brunt of the attack and immediately collapsed, retreating in chaos and terror. Little Turtle sent the Wyandots and Iroquois under Simon Girty against St. Clair's right, the Shawnees, Miamis, and Delawares into the center, and the Ottawas, Ojibwas, and Potawatomis along the left, deployed in a half-moon formation that would encircle the camp. They caught St. Clair's troops huddled around their campfires after a cold, snowy night, which increased their misery from inadequate shelter and insufficient food. Although a reconnaissance party had warned that an attack was imminent, everyone was unprepared.

A barrage of gunfire across the river at the militia camp startled everyone. Within minutes the militia began streaming through the camp of the regulars and levies, running in panic for their lives. Behind them, one officer reported, was "the damndest noise imaginable." Winthrop Sargent, who later remarked that the conduct of the militia was "cowardly in the most shameful degree," tried to gain control among the new recruits, who were beginning to panic along with the Kentuckians, by ordering a line of fire against the oncoming Indians, who had reached within fifty yards of the main camp. The artillery batteries on the high ground recovered first from the initial shock of the attack and began firing canister toward the enemy. Although the concussion momentarily slowed the attack, they shot too high, and while the battlefield was clouded with smoke, Blue Jacket rallied his men forward and breached the perimeter of the camp.

The disoriented and frightened soldiers began to concentrate near the center of the camp, while the Indians completed their surround maneuver. The constant firing of muskets, rifles, and cannon reminded one wagoner of a thunderstorm, while Robert Bradshaw, a militia ranger, remembered a nightmare of the "wildest confusion." The hard-faced, rough-handed, and tough-minded women who accompanied the army as camp followers, serving as laundresses, nurses, and cooks, as well as the wives, mistresses, and whores, perhaps two hundred in all with their children, ran for safety but found none. Some screamed, prayed, and collapsed from fright. Others yelled for the shirkers to fight. Sargent reported that many women "drove out the skulking militia and fugitives . . . from under wagons and hiding places by firebrands and the usual weapons of their sex." In the end only three women escaped. St. Clair, nearly immobilized from the pain of gout, had two horses shot before him as he prepared to mount. Musket balls tore through his clothing and clipped a lock of his hair.

St. Clair, who always contended that disciplined troops would carry the field when fighting Indians, struggled toward what appeared to be the front line and ordered a bayonet charge to drive the Indians back and gain both time and space for reorganization and defense, but it fell apart in the face of Indian muskets fired at nearly point-blank range. Further confusion prevailed because the Indians made a concerted effort to shoot the officers. In this disciplined tactic they achieved great success, in part because the officers attempted to marshal their troops from horseback. Together with their insignia, they became sitting targets. Within minutes the fighting became hand to hand and "helter-skelter." One rifleman recalled: "It seems like a wild, horrid dream in which whites and savages . . . were all mixed together in mad confusion . . . melting away in smoke, fire, and blood amid groans, shouts, yells, shrieks— the flashing of steel and crackling of firearms—all blended into one loud, continuous roar." Injured soldiers as well as the huddling women and children were tomahawked and scalped, sometimes before they were dead.

By nine o'clock, three hours after the fighting began, Lieutenant Ebenezer Denny recalled: "The ground was literally covered with the dead." The army had collapsed, with "pale and frightened" men running about searching for an escape rather than fighting. Major General Richard Butler was not one of them. Seriously wounded and propped against a tree by his two brothers, he would be dead in minutes, tomahawked in the head and his heart cut out to be eaten later by the participating tribes, a fitting end, the Shawnees believed, for a man who had humiliated them in council at the Great Miami in 1786. Colonel William Darke reported that once the artillery were breached, "the whole army ran together like a mob at a fair." At that point, running was the only sensible thing to do. Lieutenant Denny said: "There was no alternative. Delay was death."

The soldiers successfully broke through the encirclement behind a bayonet charge led by Colonel Darke, who commanded a body of levies, and reached the trace or road that they had cut on their way from the south, in part because many of their attackers paused to loot the tents in the camp and to kill and torture the wounded soldiers along with the women and children. Less a retreat than a rout, one regular observed that it was "done without form," with "every man for himself." Another likened it to a "drove of bullocks" running through the woods. The wounded were left to lie where they fell. St. Clair, who had failed to ensure that the proper precautions were taken to guard against a surprise attack and who had never gained control of his men once the fighting began, rode for the trace along with his running men. One soldier had the remarkable presence to observe that it was 9:30 A.M.

The fleeing soldiers were exhausted by the time they reached the wilderness road and headed south toward Fort Jefferson. Many had not eaten for twenty-four hours, which made their already weakened state from the stress of battle all the worse. After about five

In the autumn of 1791, Arthur St. Clair led an expedition into northwestern Ohio to punish the Indians for their attack on Harmar's soldiers. St. Clair, however, also fell into a trap laid by Little Turtle and Blue Jacket. This battle led to one of the worst military defeats of the U.S. Army by Indians in American history. INDIANA HISTORICAL SOCIETY LIBRARY, c6290.

miles, the pursuing Indians gave up the chase and returned to plunder the camp. Twenty-nine miles away, Fort Jefferson offered protection but not food or medical aid because the army and its contractors had not brought up adequate supplies. With stragglers still coming into the fort after nightfall, St. Clair put all but his most seriously wounded troops on the road to Fort Washington, escorted by the First Regiment. The men traveled the seventy miles in three and a half days, during which the officers "lost almost the shadow of command." Although a pack train met them along the way with food, they entered Fort Washington hungry, tired, and dirty, only to have the officers order them to put up tents along nearby Deer Creek, while they, Sargent reported, "quit their men" and sought rooms in Cincinnati. The consequences were a "very great disorder." Few of St. Clair's levies bothered to obey their officers or report for duty. Later, St. Clair made morale worse when he ordered the men to pay for their lost firearms and new clothing. For those who had not already left for home, desertions became the order of the day.

The condition of the men mattered less to St. Clair than the substance of his report to Secretary of War Knox on November 9. He knew that Harmar's defeat had cost him his military goals, and he was too vain and ambitious to let this disaster ruin his political career. His defeat would be difficult to explain away, with casualties of 918—623 soldiers killed and 258 wounded, and 24 civilian employees killed and 13 wounded out of approximately 1,400 men who marched with him on August 29, plus the women and children. The officer corps had been decimated, with 69 of 124 commissioned officers killed or wounded. Approximately $33,000 in supplies and equipment had been lost, including 400 horses. Little Turtle and Blue Jacket reported 21 warriors killed and 40 wounded. Never before or after did the United States Army suffer a greater defeat by the Indians. St. Clair's losses also surpassed those of any engagement during the American Revolution.

Several days after the battle, the Indians left the field unable to carry away all of the booty. They were content that they had "feasted the wolves . . . with the carcasses of enemies," and they reveled in the confidence that they could force the Americans to accept the Ohio River as the boundary as provided by the Treaty of Fort Stanwix in 1768, or, if need be, fight forever. The Wyandots and Delawares, whose support for the confederacy had wavered, now joined the hostile tribes.

While the confederated tribes celebrated, George Washington, who had masterfully prevented the destruction of his army throughout the American Revolution, exploded in rage. He had personally warned St. Clair to "beware of surprise! You know how the Indians fight us." Instead of practicing caution, Washington complained, St. Clair had allowed the army "to be cut to pieces, hacked, butchered, tomahawked, by surprise, the very thing I guarded him against." Washington insisted on St. Clair's resignation from the army, which was submitted on April 7, 1792. Although a congressional investigation exonerated St. Clair and blamed this disaster on the Quartermaster's Department, the contractors, and the militia, his military career had ended, but he would remain as governor of the Northwest Territory. Washington, however, could do little more for the army immediately and less for the men who had fallen at the

Wabash. A burying party would not collect the frozen, snow-
covered bodies and dig a mass grave until February 1, 1792.

* * *

Little Turtle, more than any Indian leader of the confederacy, knew that British support was essential for any further military action against the Americans. Only the British could feed large numbers of Indians and keep them in the field and on the attack. Only the British could provide the artillery that would be required to overcome fortifications, such as Forts Hamilton and Jefferson. Only the British could furnish the necessary powder and lead. Little Turtle knew the Americans would come again, but he was uncertain about the reliability of the British. Some whites, however, who had ventured into Indian country had no uncertainty about Ohio. Many soldiers and settlers, no doubt, would have agreed with whoever carved on a tree in the area that became Hocking County: "This is the road to hell." Perhaps so, but plans were underway by a new military commander for another journey over that road into north-western Ohio.

5.

FALLEN TIMBERS

The army did not return in force to Ohio for two years after St. Clair's defeat. In the meantime, Congress authorized an increase in the size of the army to more than five thousand men and nearly doubled the military budget to $1 million. Washington also turned to Anthony Wayne, who had experience as a brevet major general in the Pennsylvania line during the American Revolution. Wayne had a reputation for the tenacity, aggressiveness, and discipline required to lead the army, and he understood the enormity of his responsibility. The recruiting and training of an army that could return to Ohio and force the Indians to accept the boundaries established by the Fort Harmar Treaty would not be easy. In April 1792 he wrote: "I clearly foresee that it is a command which must inevitably be attended with the most anxious care, fatigue, and difficulty—and from which more may be expected than will be in my power to perform."

While Wayne prepared, the remnant of the First Regiment, whom commander Brigadier General James Wilkinson called "pedlars . . . drunkards, and nearly all of them fools," attempted to keep Forts Jefferson and St. Clair (the latter built as a supply depot north of Fort Hamilton during March 1792) provisioned and garrisoned, despite periodic Indian attacks. In late June 1792, a party of Miamis and Shawnees under the Grand Sable attacked a party of soldiers cutting hay near Fort Jefferson, killing and capturing fifteen men. Simon Girty may have been present, because Rufus Putnam reported that he had left Detroit with four hundred Indians not long before the raid. Putnam wrote that Girty "swore that he would make a strike upon the Americans immediately, and either kill or be killed on the attempt . . . may not this be the person in *red* or scarlet, who was seen with the Indians in the attack upon the Sargent's party near Fort Jefferson on the 25th of June."

These skirmishes continued into 1793. On October 17, Indians struck a "convoy of provisions" seven miles south of Fort St. Clair. The attack came at dawn, but the ninety soldiers prevented the twenty wagons from being captured, although they lost seventeen men and a number of horses. Two days later, approximately forty Indians attacked the settlement known as White's Station, located ten miles north of Cincinnati, and killed one man and two children, but they lost two killed themselves.

As Indian attacks became frequent and serious, the settlers tried to make the best of a dangerous frontier. When packet boats began a regular schedule between Pittsburgh and Cincinnati with departures spaced two weeks apart, the owner repeatedly took "great pains to render the accommodation agreeable and convenient" by keeping passengers "under cover" from rifle and musket fire and provided "convenient port holes for firing out of." Each boat had six one-pound cannon and "a number of good muskets . . . amply supplied with plenty of ammunition, strongly manned with choice hands." Because of the danger along the Ohio River, and because both men and women would be passengers, the owner of the boat line advertised that "conveniences are constructed aboard each boat, so as to render landing unnecessary, as it might at times, be attended with danger."

By 1794, the situation had not improved. About two miles south of Fort Jefferson on January 16, Indians attacked a three-wagon contractor's train carrying corn about two miles south of Fort Jefferson. The drivers either were killed or fled, and the raiders cut the harnesses and took only the horses, leaving several oxen. Unidentified Indians also fired on a white hunting party along the Scioto about this same time. In early March, two contractors' wagons were again attacked near Fort Hamilton, the drivers killed, the teams captured, and the wagons burned. One driver was "most inhumanely butchered."

Because of these and other Indian attacks and the inability of the army to prevent them, Levi Woodward, Darius C. Orcutt, and James Lyons of Cincinnati and William Brown, Ignatius Ross, and John Reily of Columbia offered a reward for Indian scalps brought in between November 5 and December 25. They promised to pay $130 for the first ten scalps and $117 for the second ten to all subscribers who had contributed to the scalp fund. Nonsubscribers who brought in scalps would be paid $100 for the first ten and $95 for the second bunch. All scalps had to have the right ear attached to permit proper identification. Federal troops, however, could not participate, perhaps because they had an unfair field advantage.

In late November 1792, however, the settlers in Ohio were happy to learn that Wayne had moved his new army of 5,120 men, now called the Legion of the United States, from its quarters near Pittsburgh to a camp twenty-two miles west near Beaver Creek for further training and equipping. Rifle practice, drill, and mock battles, with soldiers dressed like Indians attacking in a screaming frenzy, as well as full-scale drills through the nearby woods, during which his men practiced building fortified camps, were designed to discipline the men to hold their positions and think and fight rather than run. When discipline required reinforcement, the lash meted out punishment, but Wayne also worked to create pride in the newly reorganized army that had been divided into four sub-legions under a single command and each numbering 1,280 men, including infantry, cavalry, and artillery, by coloring their horses—sorrels, grays, chestnuts, and bays. Wayne also gave each sub-legion a distinctive insignia and flags. By late April 1793, Wayne believed the legionnaires were ready, and boats carried them down the Ohio to Fort Washington. He wrote, "I have a strong propensity to attend the next grand council . . . with 2500 Commissioners . . . among whom I do not wish to have a single Quaker." His movement did not go unnoticed by the Ohio Indians, but they were not afraid. In fact, they were confident in their ability to defeat the Americans once again, and that the British would give them any support that they might need.

Wayne arrived at Cincinnati on May 9 and established a camp about one mile west of Fort Washington, because the post could not adequately shelter the legion. Wayne considered the location unsatisfactory and called it "Hobson's Choice," but he continued cavalry drill and rifle practice through the early summer. There, he wrote Secretary of War Knox, "I am also endeavoring to make the riflemen believe in that arm, the Infantry in heavy buck shot & the bayonet, the Dragoons in the Sword, & the Legion in their United Prowess." Discipline, training, and confidence would help them stand firm rather than run at the moment of truth.

Although Wayne had planned to strike the Ohio Indians quickly and make them sue for peace, smallpox, influenza, and supply difficulties weakened his army from its arrival at Fort Washington. A last effort by peace commissioners Timothy Pickering, Benjamin Lincoln, and Beverly Randolph, meeting with the British at the mouth of the Detroit River, failed to reach a peaceful solution to the boundary problem and forced him to change his plans. On August 25, however, commissioners Pickering, Lincoln, and Randolph informed Wayne that their efforts had failed primarily because the Indians were divided about their demands.

Indeed, division rather than unity prevailed. The western Indians wanted any treaty to recognize the Ohio River as the boundary with the Americans. Joseph Brant and the Six Nations, however, preferred to yield southeastern Ohio to preserve most of the northwestern lands. The British hoped for the creation of a permanent Indian reserve with the Ohio or Muskingum River as the boundary. They also wanted the Indians to speak with one voice in a strong confederacy. In turn, the American negotiators were prepared to retreat from the line established by the Treaty of Fort Harmar, but not too far, because the Ohio Company had already sold some of its lands in that area. They also recognized the Indians' right of possession of the land for which they would now agree to pay for concessions, rather than continue to claim ownership of the Northwest by right of conquest from the British. The Americans also wanted to keep the Indians divided by dealing with the individual tribes.

The Shawnees, Miamis, and Delawares, with strong support from British agents, especially Alexander McKee and Matthew Elliot, insisted on the Ohio River as the boundary. With a great deal of confidence, they urged the Americans to take the money that they had intended to pay the Indians for land, and give it instead to

the whites who had illegally settled north of the Ohio in compensation for their improvements and removal. Finally, on August 13, the
confederacy told the commissioners that all cessions since 1783
were void and that "we desire you to consider Brothers that our
only demand is the peaceable possession of a small part of our once
great Country. Look back and view the lands from whence we have
been driven to this spot, we can retreat no further, because the
country behind hardly affords food for its present inhabitants. And
we have therefore resolved, to leave our bones in this small space,
to which we are now confined." All tribes except the Six Nations
signed this message, because they alone had already surrendered
their lands east of the Muskingum, and they had no hope of regain-
ing it no matter what the position of the confederacy. War now
became inevitable.

On October 7, Wayne broke camp and headed for Fort Jefferson,
which he called the "head of the line." Upon his arrival, however,
he discovered that the road he had ordered cut to the north had
not been completed and that insufficient supplies had been deposited to support his legion. Soon nearly five hundred of the
accompanying eight-hundred-man volunteer force from Kentucky
deserted. Wayne managed, however, to construct an encampment
six miles beyond Fort Jefferson, which he called Fort Greenville in
honor of his friend Nathanael Greene. There he intended to spend
the winter and let the presence of the legion intimidate the Indians
to the northwest.

By late December Wayne had solved his supply problem and
built a strong new fort. Despite these achievements and his own
troubles with gout, he did not intend to wait through a miserable
winter and let inaction destroy the already flagging morale of the
legion, caused, in part, by his "petulant" rule and command by
"insult and oppression." Instead, he decided to occupy the site of
St. Clair's defeat with a new fort. This maneuver would further
threaten the Indians and provide a base to support an attack in the
spring. With the Indians scattered in their winter camps and tied to
the food supplies in their villages, he did not believe they could
muster any resistance. Eight companies of infantry and a detachment of artillery arrived at the eerie site on December 25, 1793,
where bones still littered the field, and they began building Fort

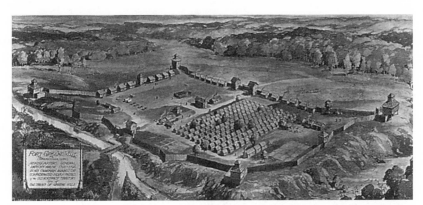

In October 1793, General Anthony Wayne established Fort
Greenville, which served as his headquarters. There Wayne
drilled his troops and prepared for an attack against Indian
and British forces along the Maumee River during the
summer of 1794. STATE HISTORICAL SOCIETY OF WISCONSIN,
Whi (x3)40386.

Recovery, which Wayne ordered them to hold at all costs. The
legion's attack on the Ohio Indians had begun.

* * *

At Detroit the British prepared for Wayne's attack. There, John
Graves Simcoe, lieutenant governor of Upper Canada, depended
upon Pennsylvania Loyalists Alexander McKee, Matthew Elliot,
and Simon Girty for advice about Indian affairs. Both McKee and
Elliot had lived with the Shawnees as traders, spoke their language,
and married Indian women, and they sympathized with the Shawnees' plight. In the autumn of 1794, McKee, a long-time employee of
the British Indian Department, after learning that Wayne's army
had begun its advance toward the Indian villages at the rapids of
the Maumee, sent Simon Girty to spy on the progress of the American army. Girty found it camped six miles north of Fort Jefferson,
and McKee took that information with him to Detroit in late November, where Elliot busily arranged for supplies for the Indians,
particularly powder, lead, and flints. Both McKee and Elliot as well
as Lieutenant Governor Simcoe were relieved to learn that Wayne
had gone into winter quarters at Fort Greenville.

On February 10, Guy Carleton, Lord Dorchester and governor of the British North American colonies, delivered a speech to the Seven Nations in Canada that led the Indians in the Maumee country to believe that the British would strongly support them in the next round of fighting with the Americans. Lord Dorchester said of the United States: "From the manner in which the People of the States push on, and act, and talk . . . I shall not be surprised if we are at war with them in the course of the present year; and if so, a Line must then be drawn by the Warriors." He told them, "You are Witness that on our parts we have acted in the most peaceable manner, and borne the Language and Conduct of the People of the United States with Patience; but I believe our Patience is almost exhausted." A week later Lord Dorchester ordered Lieutenant Governor Simcoe to reestablish the military post on the Maumee that the British had abandoned at the end of the Revolutionary War. This action would mean an overt occupation of American territory, but Dorchester believed the action warranted to protect Upper Canada, particularly Detroit, from invasion by Wayne's army as well as to protect the British fur trade from American encroachment.

Simcoe met with McKee on April 8 at the rapids of the Maumee, where they planned to build a fort on the north bank of the river about a mile downstream from McKee's camp. At the Indian encampment at the Glaize, which included seven main towns within ten miles of the mouth of the Auglaize River—three Shawnee, two Delaware, one Miami, and a British village called Trader's Town— with approximately two thousand inhabitants, Simcoe gave the assembled tribes Lord Dorchester's warmongering speech on April 14. This action led the Indians to believe not only that hostilities with the Americans were inevitable but also that the British guaranteed to provide support. By late May the Ottawas, Ojibwas, and Potawatomis had begun to arrive at the Glaize, where they joined the Shawnees, Miamis, and Delawares in anticipation and preparation for the coming fight with Wayne's army. When the Wyandots arrived on June 15, some six hundred warriors greeted them, and others were reported on the way from Michilimackinac.

Both McKee and Elliot worked to coordinate and organize the Indian army, whose ranks had expanded to fifteen hundred men by June 18. On that day the British at the Glaize donned Indian dress to ensure that no mistakes were made in the coming fight as well as to show solidarity with the tribes. Two days later, the Indian army left camp to encounter Wayne's expedition. The British officers urged the Indians to cut Wayne's supply line and starve out the garrisons at his forts, but the Indians had their minds fixed on Fort Recovery.

While the Indians organized with the aid of the British Indian Department, Lieutenant Robert Pilkington of the Royal Engineers oversaw the construction of Fort Miamis. Lieutenant Governor Simcoe and Lieutenant Pilkington had selected the site on April 10, and construction began almost immediately, with a detachment of troops cutting trees and digging entrenchments. Located about fifty-five miles south of Detroit, this post could be easily supplied by water, and Wayne could not avoid it without jeopardizing his rear if he advanced on Detroit. Several days later three companies of the Twenty-fourth Infantry and a detachment of Royal Artillery arrived from Detroit to provide protection and share the work. However, a variety of illnesses common to the frontier, collectively known as fevers, slowed their progress, and three months passed before the log walls and four bastions protected more than a dozen buildings, such as officers' quarters, a guardhouse, a bakery, and blacksmiths' and carpenters' shops. Meanwhile, the soldiers lived in tents. Beyond the walls, the soldiers cleared the land for two hundred yards. An enemy who negotiated that field of fire would then encounter an abatis (a row of stakes pointing outward) that led to a ditch about twenty-five feet deep and an elevated parapet before reaching the wall of the fort. Four nine-pound and six one-pound cannon as well as two howitzers and two swivel guns gave Fort Miamis enough firepower to make any attacking commander think twice about an assault. Major William Campbell and 120 men from the Twenty-fourth Regiment and another officer and ten soldiers of the Royal Artillery in addition to a group of Canadian militia from Detroit manned the post.

Despite the strength of Fort Miamis, which put the Indians in "great spirits," it served as a symbol of British support for the Indians more than it provided a defense against Wayne's army. Although the Indians did not know it, the British did not want war with the United States, which by this time had become Great Britain's most important trading partner. Moreover, the British had little interest in fighting an expensive war on the American frontier for lands that they had already ceded or to protect their fur trade from infringement by the Americans. And while Wayne's army advanced and while the ramparts went up at Fort Miamis, British and American negotiators were meeting to resolve the lingering problems of American pre–Revolutionary War debts and the evacuation of British troops from posts on American soil. If the Indians could inflict an injury to the Americans and slow their advance into the Northwest, the British would be happy, but they would be supportive short of war. Duplicity characterized their relations with the Indians, who would soon learn that British actions spoke louder than words.

* * *

Throughout the remainder of the winter and into the early summer, Wayne strengthened Fort Recovery with men and supplies. In mid-January, he reported to the secretary of war that the Shawnees, Miamis, and Delawares had sent him "a flag with overtures of peace" in the hand of a Delaware by the name of George White Eyes. Wayne suspected a ruse to "insidiously gain time," but he believed that the Indians would seriously consider negotiations once they learned his strength, "which they have never heretofore been able to ascertain." Wayne refused to talk peace unless all of the chiefs attended a general council and released every white prisoner. As he had suspected, the Ohio tribes were not interested in a full-scale treaty council. Instead, Blue Jacket, Little Turtle, and Buckongahelas, a Delaware chief, rejected Wayne's call for a general peace conference. The Miamis, Shawnees, and Wyandots also called upon the Ottawas, Potawatomis, Ojibwas, and other allies to rendezvous along the Maumee River near Fort Miamis to prepare for another war against the Americans. With British support, they planned to strike Wayne's supply columns, knowing that he could not keep such a large force in the field for a long time, and thereby prevent him from attacking their towns and force his withdrawal.

In the meantime, Wayne prepared for the inevitability of war with the Indians and the possibility of an armed conflict with the British at Fort Miamis. Although Wayne did not want to begin a new war with the British, Knox had authorized him to take any

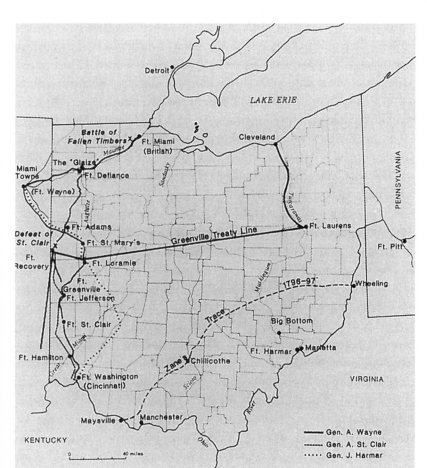

During the Indian wars that plagued the frontier from 1790
to 1795, the army built and garrisoned a host of forts in Ohio
that were designed to secure peace and lands for westward-
moving white settlers. From George W. Knepper, *Ohio and
Its People* (Kent, Ohio: Kent State University Press, 1989),
with permission of the Kent State University Press.

action that he deemed necessary to defeat the Indians, including a
strike against the British. This order had come from President
Washington himself, and Knox told Wayne: "You are hereby authorized in the name of the President of the United States to do it."
Given this freedom of action, Wayne had more confidence in his
soldiers and the outcome of the impending battle than ever before.

The Indians were confident as well, and their strategy of attrition seemed sensible, but they could not discipline themselves to refrain from attacking Fort Recovery. In both symbol and fact it presented too great a danger to their villages along the Maumee. About 7:00 A.M. on June 30, nearly fifteen hundred Shawnees, Miamis, Delawares, Ottawas, and Ojibwas, led by Little Turtle, Blue Jacket, and Simon Girty, struck a 360-horse pack train about two hundred yards from the post as it headed back toward Fort Greenville. The escort of fifty dragoons and ninety riflemen, led by Major William McMahon, rushed out to drive them away. They were quickly ambushed about a half-mile from the post in the surrounding woods. Four of the five officers in the relief force died, including a Captain Hartshorn. He had been badly wounded, and two soldiers tried to carry him back to the garrison in the hasty retreat. When the Indians nearly caught up with them, he told the soldiers to lay him down, saying, "Boys save yourselves," and they raced back to the protective cover of the fort. They suffered fifteen killed and wounded and lost three hundred horses, while the Indians left only three confirmed dead.

Emboldened by their success, the Indians could not withdraw for another strike against the supply trains. Instead, they changed their tactics and launched a night attack on the fort across approximately two hundred yards of open ground, where only tree stumps and a few fallen logs gave minimal protection. The 250 riflemen and dragoons, under Captain Alexander Gibson, who commanded the fort, put their long months of training to practical use. The fighting continued into the next morning, but the British officers, who observed from a distance, could not get them to call off the attack until the Indians recognized its futility and withdrew. Fort Recovery held, but it had lost twenty-two killed and thirty wounded. The soldiers found thirteen dead Indians, whom they promptly scalped. On August 13, an Indian prisoner reported that forty tribesmen had been killed and twenty wounded.

When the Indians returned to the villages at the confluence of the Auglaize and Maumee, known as the Grand Glaize, they began to quarrel about who bore responsibility for the failure of the attack, because their losses had been great by their own standards of warfare. The Lake Indians, who were satisfied with their success in taking a respectable number of scalps, left for home. The acrimony among the confederacy continued into July. Although Little Turtle had long been recognized as the most astute war chief among the Miamis, the Shawnees contributed greater numbers to the confederacy, and Blue Jacket and Captain Johnny increasingly dominated the debate over tactics and strategy, often substituting ardor for reflection, particularly upon learning from the British that Wayne planned an attack in early August.

Only Little Turtle among the war chiefs seemed to understand that without British military support, the confederacy could not stop Wayne's army, which had more men and supplies than either Harmar's or St. Clair's expeditionary forces. After the defeat at Fort Recovery, Little Turtle went to Detroit and asked Lieutenant Colonel Richard G. England, who commanded the post, for two cannon and twenty men to renew the attack, without which the Indians would be "obligated to desist in their plan of attempting to stop the progress of the American Army." The Wyandots also demanded that the British provide the assistance that they had promised, telling England to "rise upon your feet with your warriors and help us. If you do not, we cannot go to war any more." England, however, would offer only encouragement. Cannon and men could easily bring war with the Americans. But without substantial British military support, the Indians faced serious trouble.

Indeed, Little Turtle's fears proved well founded, because Wayne planned an attack that the Indians could neither withstand militarily nor survive culturally. Wayne intended to scorch the earth by destroying the villages and crops at the Grand Glaize. The Indians would then scatter without homes and food. They would become a burden to the British during the winter, and negotiations that would guarantee the boundaries of the treaties at Fort McIntosh and Fort Harmar would necessarily ensue.

The legion left Greenville at 8:00 A.M. on July 28. Reinforced several days earlier by 1,500 mounted volunteers from Kentucky, Wayne led 3,500 men toward the Glaize. His 2,169 legionnaires would soon put two years of hard training to practical application. To avoid the mistakes of his predecessors, Wayne halted the legion every midafternoon to build breastworks to protect the camp at night. An hour before dawn, reveille called the men to form battle lines. This army would not suffer the humiliation of a surprise attack from either Indians or British soldiers, whom he expected to join the fray. Wayne intended to engage the Indians and drive them from the field even if the battle took his life, and he reflected on the "certainty of death and the possibility that the event is not far distant."

When the legion reached the St. Marys River on August 1, Wayne halted to build a temporary fortification, called Fort Adams, to hold supplies arriving from the rear and to ensure communications with Greenville and Fort Jefferson. He did not pause long. On August 4, the legion continued toward the villages at the confluence of the Auglaize and Miami rivers, which he reached four days later. Bountiful fields of corn, squash, and beans surrounded the now-deserted villages. Wayne called the site "the grand emporium of the hostile Indians of the West." After a brief rest, a gill of whiskey per man, and congratulations all around, the men began building a fort with four blockhouses. Wayne called this place Fort Defiance. Lieutenant John Boyer said that Fort Defiance could defy "the English, Indians, and all the devils in hell," but the Indians, who had so hastily evacuated their towns, remained out of sight.

On August 13, Wayne learned from a Shawnee prisoner that seven hundred Indians had assembled down the Maumee near Fort Miamis, where they intended to make a stand. Some of the Shawnees, he reported, were apprehensive because they were not certain that the British would fight with them, even though an additional five hundred Wyandots and Ottawas were expected to join the Shawnees. Wayne responded by sending a messenger forward to inform the Indians that he possessed their villages and offered to make a "lasting peace." He also told them what many had begun to suspect: "Brothers, be no longer deceived or led astray by the false promises and language of the bad white men at the foot of the rapids; they have neither the power nor inclination to protect you." The time had come to choose another benefactor. On August 15, Fort Defiance had been essentially completed, and Wayne moved his legion across the Maumee to the north bank and toward the British stronghold of Fort Miamis.

Little Turtle understood better than any Indian leader that the balance of power had shifted to the Americans during this campaign, and he urged negotiations to establish peace. With their villages abandoned, their crops destroyed, and their fighting men outnumbered, and with little more than words of encouragement from the British, Little Turtle did not believe that the confederacy had much hope of driving the soldiers away. Blue Jacket, however, disagreed. With more than a thousand men assembled at the Maumee Rapids and more reportedly on the way as well as the arrival of an artillery squad from Detroit, the morale of the Indians remained high.

Wayne's offer of peace, however, caused so much dissension among the tribes that they held a council the night of August 14. Little Turtle spoke first, reminding his fellow war chiefs that "the trail has been long and bloody; it has no end. The pale faces come from where the sun rises, and they are many. They are like the leaves of the trees. When the frost comes they fall and are blown away. But when the sunshine comes again they come back more plentiful than ever before." The chiefs responded with silence until either Blue Jacket or Egushawa of the Ottawas said that Little Turtle wanted only to "smoke in the lodges of the Long Knives, our enemies," and that Wayne would soon "walk in a bloody path." When he asked whether they would defend the council fires and the graves of their fathers, he received a unified voice of acclamation. Faced with overwhelming opposition, Little Turtle acquiesced and supported the coming fight.

On the morning of August 18, the legion reached the rapids of the Maumee, where falls periodically broke the river as it rushed toward Lake Erie. The next day, the legion built Camp Deposit, which Wayne called the "citadel," to protect its supplies, and the soldiers prepared to confront the Indians, who now were beginning to engage Wayne's scouting patrols. Wayne expected the fight to come on the 20th. While the men rested in preparation for a 5:00 A.M. advance, one soldier wrote, "To-morrow will in all Probability produce a Victory or a Defeat—the latter we fear not, the former we flatter ourselves we are assured of. . . . Be this as it may, resolved we are of Victory or Death."

The British planned for the Indians under the leadership of Blue Jacket to ambush the legion in a tangled wooded area, which became known as the Wilderness, about five miles southwest of Fort

Miamis. On August 18, the confederated tribes moved into position, expecting to make their attack the next day. Accordingly, they fasted to prevent digesting food from making stomach wounds even more dangerous from contamination and infection. Wayne's pause to build Camp Deposit made them wait for three days, by which time they were physically weak and mentally dulled from hunger. Some Indians also had left their positions to get food from their camps about four miles to the rear. Only approximately five hundred Indians remained in position to meet one thousand legionnaires.

Wayne's army reached the Wilderness about 10:00 A.M. on the 20th. The spirits of the soldiers were high even though Wayne had told them that anyone fleeing would be shot on sight. A select group of mounted Kentucky volunteers, under Major William Price, first entered the area of fallen trees, tangled brush, and high grass, which made it difficult to see a man ten yards away. After they had gone about a hundred yards, a point-blank volley of musket and rifle fire from the Ottawas and Potawatomis decimated their ranks, and the remaining Kentuckians ran to the rear in "utmost confusion through the front guard of the regulars." Two companies of regulars tried to shoot them down, only to be confronted by a charge of the Indians as they attempted to reload their guns. Almost instantly the fighting became hand to hand and the regulars gave ground.

When the soldiers retreated beyond the woods, General James Wilkinson halted them and began to form battle lines. The Indians then withdrew to the protection of the timber for want of adequate manpower and guns to break through the lines. When Wayne got to the front lines, he saw the Indians withdrawing and quickly organized a plan of attack as well as a bayonet charge. The Wyandots and Ottawas on Wayne's left bore the brunt of the attack. When the Indians saw that they were outnumbered by the infantry with bayonets and by the saber-wielding dragoons, they did the only sensible thing—they ran. One Indian later said, "We could not stand against the sharp end of their guns. . . . Our moccasins trickled blood in the sand, and the water was red in the river. Many of our braves were killed in the river by rifle [fire]." While the Wyandots and Canadian militia provided a rear guard and slowed Wayne's attacking soldiers, the confederated tribesmen ran for the protection of Fort Miamis. The Wyandots and Canadian militia fought a stubborn rear-guard action, but Wayne's soldiers out-flanked them, and they too retreated. This fighting, which became known as the Battle of Fallen Timbers, lasted only about an hour. One soldier wrote, "This affair . . . does not deserve the name of Battle." Still, it had been bloody and intense.

Major William Campbell at Fort Miamis heard the firing from the Wilderness area and ordered his garrison to arms. As the Indian allies ran for the fort, he ordered the gates closed and locked before them. Campbell had no intention of provoking an attack by the Americans and thereby precipitating a war between Great Britain and the United States. Unable to hide, the Indians streamed passed the fort, down the Maumee River banks, and into the forest beyond. One Indian later reflected that as Little Turtle had warned, the Great Spirit would be unhappy if they did not talk peace, and he was "angry and would not help them."

The Battle of Fallen Timbers ended about noon. It had been little more than a hard-fought skirmish, although forty-four soldiers died (including eleven from wounds later) and eighty-nine were wounded. About forty Indians had been killed. The Wyandots particularly suffered, because they lost a number of chiefs. The Canadian militia, under Lieutenant Colonel William Caldwell, lost five killed and one captured, whose presence proved an embarrassment to the British, although not because the legion had him "loaded with irons." That evening the legion camped about a mile from the palisades of Fort Miamis. The 250-man garrison did not sleep that night. While the British watched the legion burn the surrounding Indian houses and destroy their fields, the Americans prepared for an attack.

On August 21, Major William Campbell sent a message to Wayne under a flag of truce asking about his intentions. Wayne responded that his motives should have been clear "from the muzzles of my small arms yesterday morning, in action against the [herd] of Savages in the Vicinity of your Post." When Wayne rode around Fort Miamis within pistol shot of the British soldiers, Campbell felt distressed and humiliated, and he dashed off another message warning Wayne to keep his troops away from the fort or he would fire on them. Wayne responded by demanding that Campbell withdraw and accused him of the "highest Aggression." Still, Wayne realized that Fort Miamis was too strong for his artillery, because a British deserter reported that it was well fortified with cannon and howitzers, and he did not have sufficient provisions for a long siege. But, like Campbell, Wayne did not want to start shooting first and provoke a new British-American war. As a result, he had little choice but to withdraw, all to the relief of Campbell and the British soldiers who watched them go. Wayne had to be content with a moral victory over Fort Miamis.

The legion began its withdrawal on August 23, and it reached Fort Defiance four days later, where it fortified the post and destroyed Indian corn fields and villages for fifty miles on both sides of the Maumee River. Wayne reveled in the "brilliant success" of his army and the "gloomy and unpleasant" prospects of the Indians. Indeed, he gloated: "The Indians to all appearances have totally Abandoned their settlements quite to the Mouth of the River, and their Villages and corn Fields being consumed and destroyed in every direction, even under the influence of the Guns of Fort Miamis. Facts which must produce a conviction to the Minds of the Savages that the British had neither the Power nor inclination to afford them that Protection they had been Taught to expect; That on the Contrary a Numberous Garrison well supplied with Artillery have been compelled to remain tacit spectators of the General Conflagration round them and their flag displayed to the Disgrace of the British, and to the Honour of the American Arms." In late September, Wayne's men began building another fort at the site of Kekionga, the principal Miami village, where Harmar's men had been defeated. A month later, they christened it Fort Wayne.

While the soldiers built Fort Wayne, the Wyandots at Sandusky sent a runner to Wayne at Greenville asking for the terms of peace. Wayne replied that peace depended on their acceptance of the Treaty of Fort Harmar. Although he remained firm on the land cessions of that treaty, he treated visiting Indian delegations who returned American prisoners as a good faith gesture to keep the peace, and who inquired about peace, with great friendliness, and he gave them gifts to win their allegiance from British traders operating out of Canada. Wayne promised to release his Indian captives at the conclusion of a general peace treaty. He was intent that the British as well as the Indians understand that the Americans now controlled the Ohio country.

In August 1794, General Anthony Wayne defeated the Indians on the Ohio frontier at the Battle of Fallen Timbers along the Maumee River northeast of the newly constructed Fort Defiance. During the fighting, the British at nearby Fort Miamis refused to aid their native allies. Soon thereafter the tribes in Ohio sought peace, and the Indian War temporarily ended. INDIANA HISTORICAL SOCIETY LIBRARY, c6289.

The Wyandots understood. They now realized that the British would not do more than encourage them against the Americans. They would not provide the weapons, supplies, and men necessary for a British-Indian coalition to defeat them on the battlefield. As a result, the Indians had little alternative but to seek accommodation with the Americans. On November 3, 1794, a delegation told Wayne: "We . . . now wish for peace, and are determined to bury the hatchet and scalping knife deep in the ground." By January 1795, the Indians who huddled outside of Fort Greenville, hoping the army would give them food, understood more than anyone the new political and military realities of the Ohio country.

Soon after Blue Jacket arrived at Greenville on February 7, 1795, and four days later accepted the terms of the Treaty of Fort Harmar, Wayne also reached a preliminary agreement with the Wyandots, Ojibwas, Ottawas, Potawatomis, Miamis, and Delawares for a cessation of hostilities, the mutual exchange of prisoners, and a permanent peace treaty to be made in mid-June. In addition, Wayne prohibited whites from entering "Indian Country" with hostile intentions, and he forbade the "killing, insulting or injury of any Indian, or Indians, belonging to the aforesaid tribes or nations . . . (unless in their own defence)." Wayne knew that the potential for peace was at hand, and he sent word to the tribes to assemble at

Greenville on June 15 to make a general peace treaty. By June 12 they were there—1,130 in all—and they agreed that the council would begin on the 16th. Everyone mingled freely and friendly under the muzzles of the loaded cannon atop the bastions.

When the treaty council began, Wayne offered peace on the basis of the Fort Harmar Treaty and gave the tribes until July 24 to consider it. When the council reconvened, Little Turtle objected, claiming that the Fort Harmar Treaty had been made by a band of pacifist Senecas who had no right or authority to give away the land of the other tribes. Dr. John Carmichael, who observed the daily council activities, wrote in his diary that Little Turtle protested the Fort Harmar Treaty because "he was not there, nor any of the Chiefs of his nation, he did not consider that the treaty of the Muskingum had anything to do with the present." Little Turtle then told Wayne that because neither he nor the other Miami chiefs were at Fort Harmar in 1789, "we know nothing of transfers of lands." Then, in an impassioned speech, he said: "The Maumee Villages, and the River is mine, the marks of my fore fathers are yet to be seen. Listen and I will tell you who has the right of soil. The Great Spirit first settled my fore fathers at Detroit and gave them all this country and told them never to part with this land. . . . My fore-fathers told me, not to sell our land, and we have never sold it." Then, in a subtle admonishment to the Senecas for their acquiescence at Fort Harmar, Little Turtle said: "The Great Spirit has not taken care of our eastern brothers—for they have always sold their land to any white man who wore a hat."

Wayne countered on the 24th by saying that the United States had paid for the land under the terms of the treaties of both Fort McIntosh and Fort Harmar and that the government magnanimously would pay for it again, even though the British had given the land away in the Peace of Paris in 1783. He also told the Indians that the recently concluded Jay's Treaty obligated the British to abandon their posts on American soil by June 1, 1796. The Indians, of course, did not understand that the British preferred peace and profitable trade with the Americans rather than the expense of maintaining posts, such as Fort Miamis, and war. Although the British would continue to use the Indians as an instrument of national policy, the expansion of American settlement and the presence of the army would increasingly make them inconsequential. The Indians, however, understood that the British would not help them now. Faced with desertion by the British, Little Turtle could not muster Indian support for a revision of the boundary between Indian and white lands, and his people wanted peace. On the 27th, Wayne asked for the approval of the treaty. The promise of peace and an annual $8,000 annuity for the confederated tribes proved too great a lure for all but the Miamis who followed Little Turtle, but in the end even the Miamis gave their voice vote to the treaty, making the approval unanimous.

On August 3, the Indians signed the Treaty of Greenville, which granted them an increased annual annuity of $9,500 and $20,000 in presents for reaching an agreement. All prisoners were to be exchanged. Little Turtle, however, refused to sign for the Miamis, and another chief made the mark. Wayne then proclaimed the treaty "a sacred pledge of the establishment of our future friendship," but he cautioned that the welfare of the Indians depended on their "faithful and strict observance" of the treaty. On August 10, Wayne closed the council and bade the Indians "an affectionate farewell," and they began to disperse, heading for their home camps. The boundaries of Ohio were nearly complete.

The Indians relinquished their land claims east and south of a line that ran up the Cuyahoga River from Lake Erie, then across the portage to the Tuscarawas River and on to Fort Laurens. Then it ran westward to Fort Loramie and northwest to Fort Recovery, then south to the Ohio River. By so doing, the treaty gained the Great Miami Valley for settlement. North of the boundary, Wayne secured sites for trading posts and defense, including tracts at Fort Miamis, at the mouth of the Maumee River, and at the head of navigation on the St. Marys River. These sites include present-day Defiance, Fremont, Toledo, and Loramie as well as Fort Wayne, Detroit, Peoria, and Chicago. The Indians, however, retained the right to hunt on their ceded lands, and they acknowledged the protection of the United States, and "no other power whatever." The Indians also guaranteed freedom of passage for white Americans on the rivers and trails through their country.

Within days after the Treaty of Greenville, the army became the benefactor rather than the enemy of the Ohio Indians at Fort Defi-

Between mid-June and early August 1795, General Anthony
Wayne met with the Indians of the Ohio country at Fort
Greenville and explained the terms by which they could have
peace. On August 3 they signed the Treaty of Greenville,
which established a new boundary between Indian and white
lands. The treaty, however, did not bring a lasting peace.
This painting was made by an unknown artist, who may
have been among Wayne's staff during the treaty
negotiations. CHICAGO HISTORICAL SOCIETY, P & S-1914.0001.

ance. There, Dr. Joseph G. Andrews observed that when a band
of Shawnees under Red Pole and four other chiefs arrived at
the post on August 23, after departing from Greenville, they had
twenty horses laden with presents. A trader by the name of Felix
saw opportunity and traded rum for their wares. As a result, the
Shawnees got drunk and lost all of their goods. Upon learning what
had happened, however, Major Thomas Hunt, who commanded,
made him return the goods to the Shawnees and to "depend on
their generosity for payment in peltry" for the rum. Felix "reluctantly restored the goods," but he would not be the last trader to
capitalize on the new relationship between the Indians and whites
in the Ohio country.

The Americans had much to celebrate with the Treaty of Greenville. The long-term implications of the peace were many, but the

short-term benefits also bolstered the spirits of the men stationed at Fort Defiance. Now this distant post was less dangerous for the men, and peace had improved the supply line. On August 20, 1795, Major Hunt ordered the artillery to fire fifteen rounds at noon to salute the anniversary of Wayne's victory. He also authorized the quartermaster to provide an extra gill of whiskey to each man. The officers and other "gentlemen" at the fort commemorated the event with a dinner of fried chicken and roasted pork. Five days later, Governor St. Clair proclaimed the Treaty of Greenville in force and reminded settlers that they were now "enjoined and required to keep and observe peace with the said Indian tribes, and individuals of the said tribes . . . and to abstain from injury or molestation to them."

Despite Wayne's victory, however, many settlers in Ohio could not easily bury the hatchet along with the Indians who sought peace. On September 8, 1794, Winthrop Sargent reported that "a party of lawless men did riotous and in a tumultuous manner, assemble in the town of Cincinnati [about noon] armed with clubs and stones and violently assault, and grievously wound a number of Choctaw Indians in the protection of the laws of the land." These Choctaws had aided Wayne as scouts during his campaign. Several days later, the editor of the *Centinel of the North-Western Territory* in Cincinnati warned that now was a good time for an Indian attack, because many settlers believed the danger had passed, and he urged the militia to arm themselves when attending church. He warned: "The practice of assembly for public worshiping without arms may be attended with the most serious consequences." And he reminded everyone that the law required the militiaman on these occasions to "arm and equip himself as though he were marching to engage the enemy," or be subject to a one dollar fine by the justice of the peace. Militia officers, he contended, had an "indispensable duty" to enforce compliance. Old fears died hard, even after the conclusion of the Treaty of Greenville, and the settlers in the Ohio country would live with them for a long time.

* * *

With the Treaty of Greenville and British accommodation of new military realities, the violence that had so characterized the Ohio frontier temporarily ended. The conflict between the Ohio Indians and the Americans had been unavoidable, because both claimed the same lands and used military force to ensure their claims. In the end the Ohio lands would go to those who had the greatest numbers, the best weaponry, and the most disciplined, organized, and supported fighting men. After Wayne's victory, the Indian policy of the United States changed as Thomas Jefferson had wished from "war to bribery." Thereafter, the government assumed that whenever it wanted more land, the Indian nations would sell it on demand, a perverse form of preemption by whites on Indian lands.

Thus, while the Indians thought the Greenville Treaty line marked the permanent boundary with the United States, the government and the white settlers saw it as merely a temporary demarcation that would change whenever the demand for additional lands warranted another acquisition. In the meantime, peace brought security and freedom for settlers to move into the interior, acquire land, establish farms, and create settlements. It would last until Tecumseh and his brother Tenskwatawa, known as the Prophet, fashioned a new Indian confederacy and, with British support, attempted to drive the frontier people from Ohio in 1813. In the meantime, settlers continued to claim Ohio lands as indeed they had been doing for a long time.

6.

OHIO FEVER

Captain Walter Finney's men worked hurriedly with their axes to build a fort that would bear his name at the mouth of the Great Miami River in the autumn of 1785. At the same time, Colonel Josiah Harmar, commandant at Fort McIntosh, sent Major John Doughty 140 miles downriver with a company each of artillery and infantry to establish another post at the mouth of the Muskingum, where it empties into the wide-flowing and tree-lined Ohio. Doughty's troops landed on the west bank and began their ax work. Soon they had constructed a pentagon-shaped fort. Each corner had a bastion that measured forty feet on each side and rose two stories high. Four-and six-pound cannon protruded from each bastion to rake the walls with grapeshot if Indians attempted to scale the walls. The stockade rose twelve feet and formed the outside of the barracks and storehouses. The roofs sloped inward to facilitate the collection of rainwater in time of siege. A main gate opened toward the river, while a sally port led to the parade ground on the land side, from which counterattacks could be launched. They called this place Fort Harmar. In time the wives of the officers would join their men at the post and plant flower and vegetable gardens around the outside log walls.

But not in the beginning. The officers and men now had a considerable task before them, and the company of wives and the enjoyment of the amenities of life on the frontier had to wait. Forts Finney and Harmar had been quickly established for a purpose.

These soldiers who had crossed into Ohio came in peace, but they had orders to exercise force. The Indians, however, were not their enemy for the moment, but their target was just as fearless, tenacious, and obstinate as the Native Americans who made the Ohio country their home. It was the squatters who had crossed the Ohio River by the hundreds and illegally settled government and sometimes Indian lands. The army would soon learn that it could repel Indians far more successfully than it could drive the squatters from the Ohio frontier.

Not long before, on May 20, 1785, Congress had passed the Land Ordinance that provided for the survey and sale of the western lands ceded by the states or acquired from the Indians. The ordinance required public lands to be surveyed and divided into townships six miles square, "by lines running due north and south, and others crossing these at right angles." The western boundary of Pennsylvania would provide the first north-south line, while the east-west line would begin where Pennsylvania's border intersected with the north bank of the Ohio River. Further subdivision would be made into sections one mile square which contained 640 acres. Each township and section would be numbered to permit easy location by anyone who bought public land. Congress also reserved section 16 in each township to support public education, and sections 8, 11, 26, and 29 to meet land bounty claims of Revolutionary War veterans. The remaining sections would be sold at public auction in New York City, with the minimum bid of one dollar per acre. Essentially, this ordinance provided for the systematic survey and sale of the public domain at a price sufficiently high to generate needed revenue for the operation of the central government.

Many land-hungry men and women chose not to wait until Congress extinguished Indian land titles or for the orderly survey and sale process mandated by Congress. Instead, they crossed the Ohio River from Pennsylvania and Virginia and settled on lands that they considered their own by right of occupancy. They had no feeling of responsibility to purchase their lands to help pay the national debt. The squatters rejected the concept of survey before sale because they believed that "Vacant Lands" should be free for the taking. Samuel Holden Parsons, an Indian commissioner, considered these frontier people "our own white Indians of no character who have their own Private Views without regard to public benefits to Serve." Government officials considered the squatters troublesome "saviges" and "worthless fellows," at best. By notching trees at each corner of their appropriated lands, they made "tomahawk" claims. Then they built a log cabin, planted a corn crop, and dared anyone, red or white, to move them off.

The squatters in the Ohio country arrived early and in great number. They were across the river soon after the beginning of the American Revolution, if not before. Some frontier people, however, believed the Ohio squatters endangered the western settlements in Pennsylvania by encroaching on Indian lands, and they became so fearful of retaliation that they sent a petition to Congress asking the government to restrain them. The petition held that the squatters "make encroachments on the Indian Territorial Rights . . . to the great imminent & manifest danger of involving the Country in a Bloody, ruinous, and destructive War with the Indians." Congress had greater concerns in 1776 than squatters on public lands in Ohio, and it did nothing about them.

In October 1779, however, Colonel Daniel Brodhead, commandant at Fort Pitt, received information that a party of squatters had crossed the Ohio River with the intent of claiming Indian lands. Accordingly, Brodhead responded to this trespass by sending sixty soldiers from the Eighth Pennsylvania Regiment, under Captain John Clark, to Wheeling with orders to cross the river, locate the squatters, and destroy their cabins. Clark found their cabins easily enough, but the squatters had disappeared into the forest by the time the troops arrived. Although Clark's men "destroyed some Hutts," he reported that the squatter problem was worse than anyone had imagined. Brodhead wrote that Clark had found that "the inhabitants have made small improvements all the way from the Muskingum River to Fort McIntosh & thirty miles up some of the Branches." Although Brodhead sent other detachments to drive the squatters away, they too met with utter failure, and Congress as well on September 22, 1783, when it issued a proclamation prohibiting "all persons from making settlements on lands inhabited or claimed by Indians, without the jurisdiction of any particular state." The squatters listened not at all.

Congress began to make some progress in gaining control of its Ohio lands on January 21, 1785, when Indian commissioners Richard Butler, Arthur Lee, and George Rogers Clark negotiated another treaty at Fort McIntosh with the Wyandots, Delawares, Ottawas, and Ojibwas. This treaty ceded most of the Indian lands in Ohio and placed the signing parties under the protection of the United States. It also proclaimed that squatters on lands allotted to the Wyandots and Delawares would not be protected by the army and that the Indians "may punish [them] as they pleased." With this cession treaty, Congress began work in earnest for a plan to regulate the survey and sale of the public domain. While Congress labored on the Land Ordinance, Colonel Harmar received orders from the Indian commissioners to "employ such force" as he judged necessary to drive off persons who attempted to settle on the lands of the United States.

Harmar moved quickly. On March 31, he sent Ensign John Armstrong and twenty infantry downriver to enter the Ohio country across from Wheeling. Armstrong soon found squatters along Little Beaver and Yellow creeks in present-day Columbiana County, at Mingo Bottom and Norristown in Jefferson County, at Hoglin's Town in Belmont County, and across from Wheeling, but his work did not go well. At Mingo Bottom, Armstrong read his eviction orders to John Ross, who refused to accept the authenticity of those instructions. Ross told Armstrong that if he destroyed his house he would "build six more within a week." Armstrong also reported that Ross "cast many reflections on the honor of Congress, the Commissioners and the commanding officer," and he considered Ross dangerous and sent him back to Wheeling under armed guard.

The situation got worse on April 4 when a party of armed men under the leadership of Charles Norris arrived at Armstrong's camp and in a "hostile manner" demanded to know his intentions. Armstrong cooled their "warmth" but told them he would treat any armed parties that he met as enemies of his country, and he would fire on them if they did not disperse. The next day when Armstrong arrived at Norristown, he wisely avoided bloodshed by reading his instructions and gaining the squatters' promise to leave their claims by April 19. Then, to the great relief of the squatters and soldiers alike, Armstrong gave the order to march to Fort McIntosh.

When Armstrong returned to Fort McIntosh on April 12, he reported his failure and disillusionment to Colonel Harmar, saying that if Congress did not "fall on some speedy method to prevent people from settling on the lands of the United States west of the Ohio, that country will soon be inhabited by a banditti whose actions are a disgrace to human nature." The squatters were, Armstrong wrote, "moving to the unsettled countries by forties and fifties." He had learned that three hundred families had already settled along the Hockhocking and an equal number along the Muskingum, while more than fifteen hundred families claimed land along the Scioto and Miami river valleys. From Wheeling to Moravian Town, he observed, "there is scarcely one bottom on the river but has one or more families living thereon."

Other military expeditions followed, each of which ordered the squatters back across the Ohio River, and each failed to have any noticeable effect. On October 4, 1785, Richard Butler, Indian commissioner, wrote from Wheeling that he had warned squatters to leave their lands but gave them permission to harvest their crops before they left. But, he noted, "I observe it is with a degree of reluctance [that they comply], and that they are fond of construing every indulgence in the most favorable and extensive manner for themselves, and seem to hint that saving their crops includes feeding their cattle on the ground the ensuing winter, and of course give them a footing in the Spring, and so on."

By the time Major Doughty arrived at the Muskingum in October 1785 with orders to "burn and destroy" any cabins between Fort McIntosh and that river and to build a fort to serve as a base of operations against the squatters and to protect his men from the Indians, the frontier people had been in Ohio for a long time. Many were relatively well established and felt at home, and Doughty soon met the same frustration as his predecessors. In November he reported to Colonel Harmar: "I destroyed by fire every house I could meet with on the Federal territory, amounting to forty in all. Notwithstanding which I am firmly of the opinion that many will be re-built, for the poor devils have nowhere to go. Many of the houses that were destroyed last spring, I found re-built and inhabited." Nearly a year later, in early August, Captain John Francis Hamtramck marched from Fort McIntosh with 160 men to Mingo

om on a search-and-destroy mission against the squatters. He
d nine houses, which he burned, and his men ruined a corn
crib, twelve hundred rails, and twenty-five acres of corn. When the
soldiers left, the squatters emerged from the woods and began
the annoying job of cleaning things up. Clearly, the army was too
small, the country too big, and the frontier people too numerous for
the government to prevent illegal settling on lands west of the Ohio
River. Only a new Indian war could drive the squatters out. That
war was already brewing, but before it broke in 1789, the federal
government began the first survey of its public lands.

* * *

The day after Captain Finney left Fort McIntosh by keelboat for
the mouth of the Great Miami River to treat with the Indians and
evict squatters, Thomas Hutchins set up his tripod and sextant over
a post that Pennsylvania's boundary commissioners had pounded
into the ground on the north bank of the Ohio a month earlier.
Hutchins took a reading from the sun and sighted to the west. While
a chainman pulled the linkages tight, Hutchins recorded the mark
of 40°38'02" north latitude. On this warm, quiet day, Hutchins and
his party established a historical precedent that would guide the location and sale of the public lands in the states that joined the
Union thereafter, with the exception of Texas. The survey of the
Ohio country had begun on September 30, 1785.

Four years earlier, Congress had gained title to most of the lands
in the Old Northwest when, on March 1, Virginia ceded all but a portion of its western lands to Congress to gain approval of the Articles
of Confederation by the states that did not have land claims on the
frontier. Maryland had been particularly obstinate about not approving the Articles until Virginia and Connecticut ceded their
lands, arguing that those states could sell their western lands to pay
their war debts but that the smaller states without such claims
would need to tax their people to meet these obligations. Moreover,
the states without land claims contended that the Indian country
had been won by a joint effort and that it should belong to the
people as represented by Congress.

By early 1781, Maryland was convinced that the states with western claims would cede those lands to the central government for the

"common benefit," and it signed the Articles of Confederation on March 1, 1781. Before Congress could deal with the western lands, however, the Revolutionary War had to be successfully concluded and legislation provided to establish the guidelines for its disposition. Peace in 1783 and the Land Ordinance of 1785 cleared two of the three remaining obstacles to the orderly survey, sale, and settlement of the Ohio country. Although the Treaty of Fort McIntosh in January 1785 attempted to gain title to Indian lands, only bitter fighting and a protracted war culminating in the Treaty of Greenville in 1795 would alienate most Indian lands and bring a temporary peace.

In the meantime, Hutchins, the geographer of the United States, had the responsibility to survey the newly acquired public lands. Congress directed him to employ a surveyor from each of the thirteen states and to begin his work immediately west of the Ohio River, where the title to Indian lands had been acquired and the western boundary of Pennsylvania determined. If need be, the troops at Fort McIntosh would provide protection. George Washington, who knew the region firsthand from his explorations in 1770 as a land speculator, believed: "This is the tract which, from local position and peculiar advantages, ought to be first settled in preference to any other whatever." Washington thought that the settlers in eastern Ohio would have easy access to Pittsburgh on the Ohio River and that this area would help meet the bounty claims of Revolutionary War veterans. Hutchins and his men would soon learn that Washington and others with a bent for land speculation had been too optimistic. The Allegheny Plateau extended beyond the Ohio River, often making the land too rugged for farming. The military support at Fort McIntosh also proved insufficient to provide adequate protection for the surveyors to proceed with confidence. And the Wyandots and Delawares, who had ceded this area in January, soon found that their actions were not supported by the hostile and increasingly defensive Shawnees and Miamis to the west.

Although only eight states sent surveyors to help Hutchins in September, the group included New Englanders Benjamin Tupper, Isaac Sherman, and Absalom Martin. Tupper would use his experience to gather information for the Ohio Company of Associates, who soon sought a large land grant in Ohio from Congress. Sherman used this opportunity to help Connecticut ensure its claim to a strip of land that became known as the Western Reserve. Martin's appointment showed an early interest in the Ohio country by speculators in New Jersey that would culminate in the Miami Purchase of John Cleves Symmes. These men, together with the other five surveyors and thirty helpers, then, began to run the east-west base line that would extend forty-two miles and enable the survey of seven ranges of townships running south to the Ohio River.

Hutchins proved a timid surveyor constantly worried about Indian attack and threatened to "instantly quit the business" if trouble occurred. It did, or at least Hutchins thought so, when he received word on October 8 that two traders had been attacked along the Tuscarawas about fifty miles to the west. By that time, Hutchins had surveyed only about four miles of the base line. But on receiving this "disagreeable intelligence," and knowing that his promised military support had already floated downriver to establish posts at the Muskingum and Great Miami, he ordered everyone to make a hasty departure back for Pennsylvania. With that retreat, the first year of surveying came to an end.

By the summer of 1786 Fort Harmar had been well established, a treaty had been concluded with the Shawnees at Fort Finney, and Congress had authorized Hutchins to begin the survey again. Winthrop Sargent and Ebenezer Sproat were among the new party of twelve surveyors. Representing New Hampshire, Sargent came from Massachusetts, where he would soon be elected secretary of the Ohio Company of Associates. Sproat, Rhode Island's designated surveyor, would become a major stockholder and surveyor for the Ohio Company. Israel Ludlow from New Jersey, but representing South Carolina, would later make his fortune as a land speculator in the Miami Purchase. The surveyors began their work on August 9, 1786. Two days later, Absalom Martin, representing New Jersey, began running a line south from the first six-mile marker on the base line. The other surveyors turned their chainmen south at the other six-mile intervals, with each surveyor responsible for a range of townships, but not for further subdivision into sections. This part of the original plan had been dropped to speed their work.

Trouble came on September 13, when the surveyors reached the area for the seventh range. Hutchins received word that the Wyandots and Delawares would not guarantee the safety of his party. Captain Pipe, speaking for the Delawares, wrote that he was caught "between two fires." He said, "I am afraid of you, and likewise of the back Nations." Peace as well as war threatened to bring his people only hardship. Several days later, the surveyors learned that the Shawnees were gathering along the Scioto and planning "to cut off Hutchins and all his men." With most of his military support back at the Ohio and unable to move for lack of supplies, Hutchins believed that his men were in grave danger, and he again ordered them to abandon the field. Everyone eventually left, but not willingly. Winthrop Sargent, surveying the fifth range, reported that "the Geographer had run away and all the surveyors after him," and he retreated back across the Ohio with great scorn for Hutchins. Colonel Harmar at the post on the Muskingum, however, believed that Hutchins's fear was justified, writing to Secretary of War Henry Knox in October about the surveyors that "the intelligence received from the Indian country is of so serious a nature as to excite in them very just apprehensions of danger."

In early October, Hutchins renewed the survey, intent on completing four ranges, but this time with adequate military protection. Hutchins, however, did not want to commit his surveyors beyond range 4, which prompted Sargent to write that the Geographer was *"fond of council and . . . wanting in decision,"* which together with his lack of confidence sometimes caused *"disagreeable altercations and disputes about modes and forms and the more essentials of our duties."* At the same time, Colonel Benjamin Logan's raid with the Kentucky militia against the Shawnees in southwestern Ohio ended the threat against the surveyors, and their work proceeded smoothly. Cold weather and inadequate supplies for the soldiers, however, many of whom were "barefoot and miserably off for clothing, particularly woolen overalls," ended the surveying for 1786 with the completion of four ranges. In mid-November the troops left for winter quarters at Fort Harmar, and the surveyors crossed the Ohio to Virginia and temporary quarters at the home of William McMahon, where they began platting, that is, mapping their work. In February 1787, Hutchins completed the plats and descriptions of four ranges and seven townships in range 5, totaling 800,000 acres, and "flattered himself that he had performed his duties to the entire satisfaction of Congress."

Hutchins had deceived himself with that latter observation. Congress was displeased that only four ranges had been surveyed during two years, and at considerable expense. Since the intent of Congress had been to survey quickly seven ranges in order to begin sales and generate critical revenue for the government, Hutchins's work fell far short of its expectations. Now Congress would commit to the completion of the survey only by authorizing additional protection from a newly established Fort Steuben within the survey area and with an escort from Fort Harmar, but it would not authorize the survey of additional ranges. The entire process of survey, sale, and settlement had to be rethought. By this time Colonel Harmar too had become annoyed with the surveyors. "They are extravagant in their demands," he wrote. "The whole regiment would scarcely suffice them." With general unhappiness on the part of Congress, the army, and the surveyors, then, the work continued, and by midsummer it had been completed, with the plats submitted to the Board of Treasury on July 26, 1788.

Without question, Hutchins and his surveyors significantly improved the manner by which settlers could claim and locate lands. Prior to the Land Act of 1785 and their work, settlers claimed land in a haphazard fashion by "metes and bounds"; that is, they chose lands by noting such features of the landscape as trees, creeks, and boulders for boundaries, not invisible lines determined by the mathematical accuracy of the surveyors' instruments. The result was a hodgepodge of field shapes, sizes, and overlapping claims. Creek beds could change, trees could blow down, and rocks could roll away. Systematic survey promised to open the Ohio frontier to an orderly settlement process by enabling anyone who wanted to acquire public lands to locate them without difficulty and know precisely where the boundaries lay.

But not at first. Hutchins and his surveyors had made a number of mistakes. When he determined the latitude for the base line by taking a "great number" of readings with his sextant using the sun and North Star, he missed his mark by twenty-five seconds, or

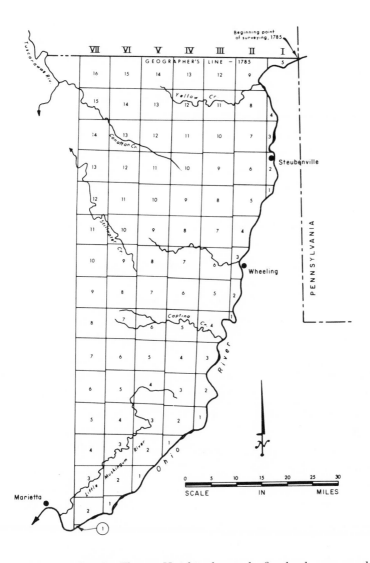

In 1785, Thomas Hutchins began the first land survey on the Ohio frontier. Known as the Seven Ranges, this area proved too hilly to merit extensive settlement for agriculture. Moreover, with the price of government land set by Congress at $1 per acre and with a minimum purchase of 640 acres required, few settlers could afford to purchase land in the Seven Ranges. COURTESY DEPARTMENT OF THE INTERIOR.

about half a mile. He also failed to run the base line as a parallel of latitude; that is, he did not allow for the curvature of the earth. With the straight line that he ran, the western end fell fifteen hundred feet south of his starting point. Although the surveyors used a circumferentor, that is, a compass that gave readings in degrees, to run the township lines south from the base line, Congress, in its haste to sell these public lands, did not require the surveyors to determine true meridians, which would have slowed their work. Instead of correcting the north-south township boundaries for the convergence of lines of longitude to the north, they merely took compass readings to determine their general location. Range lines that began six miles apart at the base line should have been forty feet wider six miles to the south, but because the surveyors did not make corrections, the north and south borders of the ranges were kept roughly parallel. Invariably the common corners of the townships established by one surveyor did not match those of his neighbor. Rather than coordinate the location of a single post marked by "witness trees" at the corners, each surveyor left his own corner post or the corners unmarked to be precisely located later. In addition, the Ohio River did not provide a stable southern boundary for the survey of the Seven Ranges. As it changed, so did the later attempts to correct past surveying errors.

Rough terrain also made their work even more difficult and often inaccurate, and the decision to number each range of townships, beginning with number one at the Ohio River, proved cumbersome and confusing. Still, the surveying problems in the Seven Ranges stemmed more from the inadequacy of standards and procedures than from technology and geography, because speed rather than accuracy mattered the most. In time, Congress and the General Land Office would tighten procedures, end the practice of hiring "gentlemen surveyors" based on state quotas, and return to the use of the "true meridian" for land surveys. Even so, more rigorous oversight would not come for another twenty years.

When the surveyors had completed their work on four ranges, Congress decided to offer these lands for sale, because it could not determine when the survey would be completed, and it needed the revenue from the lands in Ohio. It authorized advertisements in at least one newspaper in each state to run four months prior to the sale, which began in New York City on September 21 and lasted until October 9, 1787. The lands bordering the river sold quickly, but the rough interior lured few settlers, and Congress closed the auction after only 108,431 acres had been sold for $176,090. With the minimum bid of $1 per acre, one-third paid down and the remainder due in three months for a section of land, the terms proved prohibitive. Moreover, the purchaser then had to have his specific acreage surveyed. Soon buyers forfeited 35,457 acres, leaving a net sale of 72,974 acres or about two-thirds of the area sold, bringing a loss of $60,000. These problems, together with a $14,876 bill for surveying, prompted Congress to end this work during the Confederation period. And with the inability of small-scale farmers to purchase, let alone use, 640 acres of forested land, many people thought there had to be a better way to survey, distribute, and settle the Ohio country for the benefit of both government and individuals.

Five of the surveyors who worked in the Seven Ranges thought so, and one, Winthrop Sargent, who had explored to the south, sent back glowing reports about the Ohio country. By so doing he helped to stimulate the great influx of settlers during the last dozen years of the eighteenth century. The primary beneficiaries of the survey work in the Seven Ranges were a group of speculators in Massachusetts. In the early spring of 1786, five surveyors joined other Massachusetts investors and formed the Ohio Company of Associates for the purpose of acquiring a large land grant southwest of the Seven Ranges from Congress. The Associates intended to survey those lands and divide the grant into smaller lots so that small-scale farmers could afford to buy land. By providing this service, they would also earn their fortunes.

While Congress, then, had viewed the Ohio lands as a source of revenue for the government, land speculators saw the Ohio country as a means of economic gain by 1788. Most of those who came considered the Ohio country a place to profit. Although class pretensions would undeniably be built on property in lands, the acquisition of the Ohio lands by small-scale farmers, whether from speculators or from the federal government, created an economic democracy based on profit, not class. And with the exceptions of the Miami Purchase and the Virginia Military District, the survey of the

Seven Ranges established the precedent for the further division and orderly sale of the Ohio frontier.

* * *

In 1787, Congress not only approved the Northwest Ordinance, which provided for a governmental system in that western territory, but it also sought some viable way to pay the war veterans and boost land sales in the Ohio country. The Ohio Company of Associates, organized in Boston on March 1, 1786, had a plan to help achieve both goals, and the members did not hesitate to press Congress for approval. With the Reverend Manasseh Cutler serving as director and Winthrop Sargent as secretary, the Ohio Company offered to purchase 1.5 million acres southwest of the Seven Ranges for $1 million, half to be paid immediately and the remainder on completion of the surveying.

Essentially, the Ohio Company of Associates had been founded for speculation in western lands. Yet, just as the forefathers of these New Englanders had attempted to build a "City on the Hill" during the early seventeenth century in the Massachusetts Bay colony, Manasseh Cutler wrote that the Associates intended to settle the Ohio country in a "regular and judicious manner," and their colony would "serve as a wise model for the future settlement of all the federal lands." The Associates believed their proposed land grant would show the logical progression of settlement beyond the Seven Ranges, and with proper supervision it would ensure stability and order in the political, social, and economic affairs of the Ohio frontier. It would also provide an escape for men of property, education, and breeding who worried about the decline of civilization in Massachusetts because of outrages such as Shays's Rebellion and the lack of social discipline of the men and women in the countryside.

In October 1786, Cutler wrote to Winthrop Sargent about Massachusetts, saying, "Who would wish to live under a Government subject to such tumults and confusions." Instead, the Associates described themselves as "reputable, industrious, well-informed men" with considerable "wealth, education, and virtue," and they had a strong dislike for social disorder. Joseph Barker, an early settler in the Ohio Company's town of Marietta, said of the Associates that during the Revolutionary War its members "had been disciplined to obey, and learned the Advantages of subordination to Law and good order in promoting the prosperity and happiness of themselves and the rest of Mankind." In Ohio the Associates and company subscribers would set things right, and make their fortunes in lands at the same time. Indeed, their land acquisition and settlement scheme was a sophisticated combination of social planning and economic speculation.

The "adventurers" of the Ohio Company based their organization on the principles of a joint-stock company. Each subscriber could purchase a maximum of five shares, with the price per share $125 in gold or $1,000 in continentals, that is, inflated paper money. Each share entitled the holder to a city lot and acreage in proportion to the investment. After considerable maneuvering and less than honest or ethical dealings by many congressmen, Congress granted the Associates their requested 1.5 million acres on October 27, 1787. Congress set the price at $1 per acre, with $500,000 down and the balance due upon the survey of the "outlines" of the grant, all payable in gold, silver, or securities, with a cost reduction of one-third to compensate for "bad" lands. Because Congress permitted the Associates to pay for their lands with depreciated government securities and land warrants, they acquired the grant for about eight and a half cents an acre.

Ultimately, the Associates purchased 964,225 acres, and the shareholders enjoyed an egalitarianism in land because most did not own more than one share, but it still made them large-scale landowners on the Ohio frontier. Considering that a farmer could not cultivate more than about 50 acres except after clearing the land with great difficulty because of technological problems and inadequate labor, by holding nearly two sections each, the company members owned considerable acreage for speculation. Only the availability of other rich lands in central and southern Ohio kept prices from escalating beyond reason.

The Associates chose the country adjacent to the Ohio River southwest of the Seven Ranges, including Fort Harmar, for their grant, because the Indian towns that might cause trouble were relatively far away, and the grant gave them access to a hundred miles of river as well as protection by the soldiers. Congress required the Ohio Company to survey its lands and to reserve sections 16 and 29

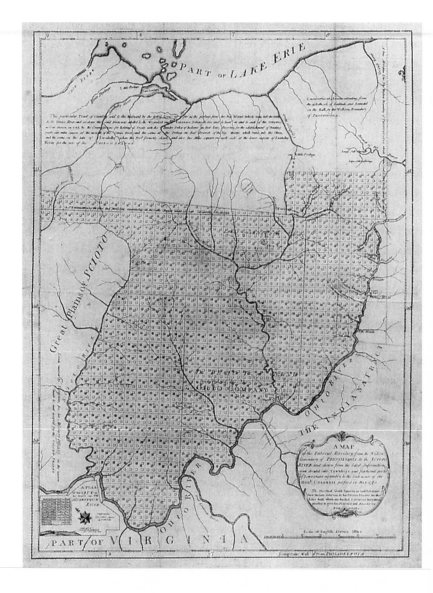

In 1787 Congress approved the sale of 1.5 million acres to the Ohio Company. By accepting payment in depreciated government securities, Congress encouraged the rapid settlement of the frontier and the sale of public lands near the Ohio River. THE CLEMENTS LIBRARY, UNIVERSITY OF MICHIGAN.

in each township for the support of the schools and "purposes of religion." In addition, Congress reserved two townships to support a university, and sections 8, 11, and 26 in each township for disbursement at a later date, with purchase by Revolutionary War land warrants in mind.

The Associates of the Ohio Company emphasized equality in the distribution of lands to the investors. Rather than give each subscriber a large tract of land that might be located away from the river, they allocated small plots to keep the settlement in the "most compact manner," with the property holders equally situated from the river. By surveying the townships, they divided 822 shares with 1,173 acres each into lots ranging from .37 of an acre to 640 acres. Although Rufus Putnam had been instrumental in the organization of the Ohio Company, the leaders overruled him when he argued that "the first actual Settlers should take their choice of the best land on the Ohio and other navigable streams." Instead, the Associates planned to establish as many as a dozen towns up the Muskingum, while others would be established along the Ohio, all of which would enable them to give "handsome farms to every right in the Propriety." An egalitarianism among landholders, guided by the elite, would create an agrarian democracy that would ensure public tranquility and private prosperity. James M. Varnum believed the Ohio Company's lands would prove "a safe, an honorable asylum" where "the labor of the industrious [would] find the reward of peace, plenty, and virtuous contentment." Yet it would not become an isolated paradise but rather a vibrant commercial enterprise based on social and economic planning and the fertile soil.

Congress believed that the plan of the Ohio Associates would encourage the settlement of the West more quickly than its own efforts in the Seven Ranges as well as transfer the administrative costs of land sales from the government to the Ohio Company. Settlement also meant that developed lands would be subject to taxation. Moreover, that settlement would be led by men whose interests in property, law, and order boded well for the expansion of the new nation. Indeed, Manasseh Cutler had promised that the colony of the Ohio Company of Associates would "be a continuation of the old settlements, leaving no vacant lands exposed to be seized by such lawless banditti as usually invest the frontier countries distant from the seat of government." The Ohio Company, then, promised to bring to the Ohio frontier an ordered liberty based on the equal opportunity for profit.

On August 29, 1787, John Cleves Symmes, a judge on the New Jersey Supreme Court, encouraged by the favorable treatment of the Ohio Company's petition, also asked Congress for a large tract of land between the Great and Little Miami rivers. Little more than a month later, on October 3, Congress responded favorably and authorized the Board of Treasury to prepare a contract for the 2 million acres that Symmes requested. The board provided that the government would survey the east and west boundaries of the tract, but that Symmes had the responsibility of surveying the townships according to the Land Act of 1785, reserving the designated townships for education, religion, and Congress, within seven years, unless "Indian irruptions" made that work impractical.

Congress granted the tract to Symmes provided he paid $1 per acre in specie or government certificates. Military bounty warrants could not be applied to more than one-seventh of the amount due, but Congress granted a price reduction of one-third to compensate for lands that could not be farmed. Congress required Symmes to pay $200,000 when the contract became final and a similar amount in semi-annual installments after the boundary had been surveyed. Symmes could begin selling 300,000 acres after he made the first payment. Thereafter, he would receive deeds to additional lands when he made the other payments.

Trouble began almost immediately. Symmes could not raise the required amount for the first payment even though he had planned to purchase land bounties at a discount from New Jersey's war veterans. By July 1788 he had deposited only $83,330, but he had asked Congress to reduce his grant to 1 million acres between the two Miami rivers. Congress agreed but arbitrarily provided that the eastern boundary would run north from the Ohio twenty miles east of the Great Miami. This dictate considerably shifted Symmes's purchase, but the Treasury Board had the right to make this adjustment because the original contract had not been closed since Symmes had failed to meet his original payment obligations. Symmes, however, had proceeded to sell lands based on a grant of 2 million acres. He sold some of this land beyond his actual grant to speculators, such as Benjamin Stites, who in turn sold portions to other settlers. Symmes had been in a hurry to make money from his land grant, particularly because he had difficulty raising money to complete the purchase. By doing so, however, he transferred land to Stites and others that they had purchased but technically did not own. Governor Arthur St. Clair considered those settlers "outsiders" on federal lands and subject to removal.

On October 15, 1788, Symmes's representatives signed a contract that gave him immediate access to 123,297 acres for his first payment. When he deposited $82,198 for his second payment, Symmes would receive a patent for 246,594 acres. This acreage expanded somewhat on September 30, 1792, when the Treasury issued him a patent, that is, title to 311,682 acres, of which he had purchased 248,540 acres with $165,963 in military warrants and other certificates, Congress waiving its rule that no more than one-seventh of those lands could be purchased by that means. The amount of specie that Symmes paid probably averaged about fifteen cents per acre for the warrants and twenty-two and a half cents per acre for the certificates. Symmes had five years to locate the northern boundary of latitude of his grant or lose it.

Although the lands that Symmes had already sold along the Little Miami were not included in his grant, Symmes did not care. He believed that if he could settle even more people on the lands that he contested with the government, he could win congressional approval of a larger tract. In the meantime, Congress authorized the survey of the external boundaries of his purchase, which surveyor Israel Ludlow reported to Secretary of the Treasury Alexander Hamilton on July 10, 1793. However, the thirteen surveyors that Symmes hired in the autumn of 1778 to run the lines for ranges of townships made many mistakes, which compounded his problems because settlers who purchased these lands had to survey their own east-west boundaries. In contrast to the orderly process of survey and sale by the Ohio Company, Symmes's buyers operated on the principle of every man for himself.

With Symmes selling lands that he did not own and refusing to return the money as well as improperly surveying lands in his own tract, settlers entered the Miami country risking more than Indian attack. Many settlers faced with the possibility of paying for their

In 1788 John Cleves Symmes, together with New Jersey associates Elias Boudinot and Jonathan Dayton, acquired a million acres of public lands in southwestern Ohio. Symmes, however, could not pay for the land that he received, and Congress substantially limited his claim. Symmes never kept adequate records, and he died in poverty despite having been one of the last great proprietors on the American frontier. Miami University Art Museum, Miami University, Gift of the Board of Trustees and Friends, including John H. Rowe.

lands twice, since they were on public lands but had paid Symmes for their acreage, soon considered armed resistance. Territorial Governor Arthur St. Clair observed that some settlers in the Miami country "talk plainly of holding their possession by force of arms, and it has been hinted to me that they are stimulated to it by the Judge."

Eventually, on March 2, 1799, Congress, following St. Clair's advice not to "increase the evil," authorized settlers who had purchased public lands from Symmes the right of preemption at two dollars per acre. In addition to this avenue to secure their lands, many settlers who thought they had legally purchased acreage from Symmes sued him, and he had considerable property seized to satisfy a host of judgments against him. Instead of gaining great wealth from Ohio lands, Symmes suffered poverty by the time of his death on February 26, 1814. In time the Miami country would support a strong commercial agricultural economy, with Cincinnati its chief domestic and export market, but before that occurred, attorneys, not farmers, earned considerable income from Symmes's haste to speculate in Ohio lands.

Most important, Symmes's failure prevented further attempts to apply a proprietary system of land development to the Ohio

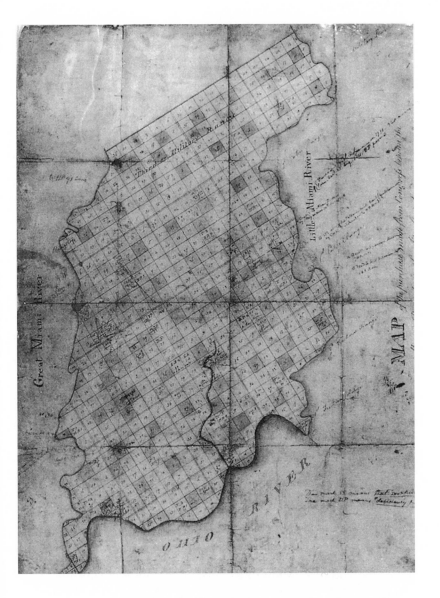

Ultimately, John Cleves Symmes received a title to 311,682
acres in 1792. This tract, also known as the Miami Purchase,
ran from the Ohio River to the Bellefontaine area and
occupied the region between the Little and Great Miami
rivers. Symmes did not provide for the adequate survey of
these lands prior to sale, and he often sold the same lands
more than once. Overlapping claims and legal battles
hindered the settlement of this area into the nineteenth
century. CINCINNATI HISTORICAL SOCIETY.

frontier. Although Symmes had rights only over the land, not over government, and while he sold land in fee simple, he could dispose of his lands as he pleased subject only to the laws of the nation. Symmes required buyers to purchase at least 160 acres, to settle their land within two years, and to remain on their property for seven years or risk forfeiture of one-sixth of the purchased acreage, unless Indian hostilities interrupted that process. Forfeited land would be available free to any settler who agreed to live on it for three years and pay a small fee. The Land Act of 1796, which raised the minimum bid to two dollars per acre for public lands, increased the value of his lands, and he charged various fees to cover the costs of surveying and administration. Symmes also reserved an entire township for himself at the junction of the Great Miami and the Ohio River as well as portions of other townships. Yet, even if a portion of the grant was acquired with depreciated government securities and land warrants, such a large undertaking was beyond the financial means of one man. Moreover, the job of overseeing the survey and sales of his lands also proved too much for an individual to administer efficiently without mistakes.

As a result, Symmes sometimes sold his own lands to more than one settler, some even before they had been surveyed. Usually the boundaries of farms in his Miami Purchase did not match, and deeds that overlapped boundaries prevailed. All too often Symmes sold lands on credit, then neglected to pursue payment. His responsibilities as a territorial judge also took him away from his land business. All of these problems proved that land speculation on a proprietary colonial scale exceeded the capabilities of one man. Thereafter, the Ohio lands would be sold by either the federal government, small-scale speculators, or land companies. After the fiasco of Symmes's Miami Purchase, the federal government never contracted with private interests again for the transfer of its lands in Ohio, and it confirmed the need for the federal government to provide accurate surveys of its lands.

One land company, operating on a smaller scale than the Ohio Company of Associates, gained control of the Connecticut Western Reserve. On September 13, 1786, Connecticut ceded most of its western lands to Congress, with the exception of a "reservation" of about 5,000 square miles lying south of Lake Erie and extending

120 miles west of the Pennsylvania border, the sale of which would support the schools in Connecticut. But Connecticut did nothing with the Western Reserve until 1795, when the state legislature authorized a committee to sell it to any group or individual for a minimum of $1 million. In September, thirty-five speculators, led by Oliver Phillips, organized the Connecticut Land Company and offered $1.2 million, payable in five years with 6 percent interest after two years from the receipt of the deeds for the Western Reserve. The speculators thought their purchase would total nearly 3 million acres, although no one knew for certain. Eventually the surveyors documented 3.2 million acres in the Reserve. In 1792, however, Connecticut reserved 500,000 acres for grants to its people who had suffered property losses from the British during the American Revolution. This remote western area (essentially present-day Huron and Erie counties) became known as the "Sufferers' Lands" or the "Firelands," the sale of which would support the communities that had petitioned for aid. It would not be settled until after the War of 1812 and the threat of Indian attacks ended in northern Ohio, and the Firelands were not part of the Connecticut Land Company's purchase.

The Indians also made the Western Reserve unsafe for settlement prior to the Greenville Treaty in 1795, and surveying on lands east of the Cuyahoga River did not begin until the following year. Led by General Moses Cleaveland, the surveyors platted the area in a rectilinear pattern as provided by the Land Ordinance of 1785, but they made the townships five miles square instead of six. The investors in the Connecticut Land Company received their lands by drawing lots according to their investment to ensure equity, and the Reserve opened for settlement in July 1796. With the Ohio River far away and the linkage of Lake Erie with the Hudson River nearly thirty years in the future, however, the Western Reserve remained isolated and settlement slow until after 1825. Moreover, Congress did not consider the Western Reserve part of the Northwest Territory, because the Connecticut Land Company acquired the "judicial and territorial right"—that is, Connecticut relinquished to the land company its right to govern the area. Many speculators from Pennsylvania also claimed land in the Western Reserve, and settlers hesitated to purchase land from the company because titles could not be guaranteed or their property protected by law and an organized government. These problems were not resolved until 1800, when Congress gained control of the Western Reserve and transferred it to the Northwest Territory as Ohio's Trumbull County on July 10.

By the turn of the nineteenth century, only about one thousand people lived in the Western Reserve, and the company had paid a mere $100,000 to Connecticut. With renewed hostilities with the Indians and the British continuing to slow settlement, the company could not meet its obligations by selling land, and it dissolved on January 5, 1809. Jefferson's Embargo of 1807 limited the ability of settlers to purchase Ohio lands with specie, and the economic situation soon became worse, with land agent Seth Tracy reporting that the War of 1812 "much retarded emigration from the Eastward" to the Western Reserve. Land speculators such as Pierpont Edwards maintained title to their lands after the company collapsed but found that settlers paid their installments only reluctantly, often with local bank currency that eastern financial institutions discounted heavily or refused to accept, and that lands valued from only $2.50 to $3.00 per acre to the south prevented them from selling at $4.00 per acre. A combination of problems, then, hindered much of the Western Reserve from being settled until after the frontier period in Ohio.

While the Connecticut Land Company struggled and disintegrated, Virginia on August 10, 1790, opened its military district, located between the Scioto and Little Miami rivers and the Ohio River and present-day Auglaize, Hardin, and Marion counties, containing 42 million acres. By that time, Virginia had granted nearly all of its lands allocated for veterans in Kentucky, but more land warrants remained outstanding. Because Virginia had reserved these lands from its western cession to Congress, the Land Ordinance of 1785 did not apply to this reserve. As a result, veterans, and after 1794 speculators and others who had purchased land warrants, often for as little as $.20 to $1.00 per acre, claimed land anywhere in the district by the southern custom of "metes and bounds"; that is, Virginia did not require rectilinear survey. Instead, "indiscriminate surveys" enabled the land to be platted and patents received, a process that also encouraged litigation well beyond the frontier period. Because surveys overlapped, corners could not be precisely located, and gaps occurred. One survey, for example, had 118 sides and left a tract of unclaimed land within it. Often settlers who claimed acreage in the Virginia Military District paid a surveyor, such as Nathaniel Massie, who located the claims, with a portion of their land, usually one-quarter to one-half of the acreage. Because of their expertise, surveyors usually located and kept the best lands for themselves. This payment procedure created many small-scale capitalists in land.

As a result, Virginia extended its land policy to the Ohio frontier. The Virginia system encouraged speculation and isolated settlements. Soldiers who needed cash and speculators who wanted land both profited from the Virginia system and the Military District. On August 1, 1787, the land superintendents for both Virginia and the army authorized Richard Anderson, Virginia's principal surveyor for the military district, to begin "enter'g lands on the North West side of the Ohio."

Most of this land, however, went to someone besides a soldier. Indeed, only 35.1 percent of those men who received warrants for their military service had their lands surveyed. And only 15.4 percent received a patent, that is, title to all of the lands that had been warranted. For the most part, these patents went to single owners who claimed lots ranging from 100 to 1,000 acres, with the smallest patent for 5 and the largest for 5,333 acres. Speculators bought up most of the land warrants for the Virginia Military District. Nathaniel Massie eventually owned 28,400 acres, or 7.2 percent of the district, while Duncan McArthur held 21,132 acres, for 4 percent of the area. Usually, the more acres for which an individual received warrants, the more likely he was to have it surveyed and patented.

The remaining lands in Ohio belonged to the federal government after the Treaty of Greenville, although some lands were later set aside for Indian reservations or to compensate people for various services or misfortunes. One area, known as the United States Military District, consisted of 2.5 million acres located east of the Scioto River in central Ohio. On June 1, 1796, Congress created this district to cover land warrants from the American Revolution. The surveyors began their work early in 1797 and completed it three years later. The federal government accepted claims until 1803, when it transferred unsold lands in the district to the status of congressional lands that were open to general acquisition and settlement. Congress provided for the U.S. Military District to be divided into quarter townships that included about 4,000 acres, but few settlers other than speculators could afford such purchases. As a result, in 1800, Congress approved sales in 320- and 640-acre tracts. This reduction helped smaller-scale buyers, but the price remained at two dollars per acre; surveyors' fees of three dollars per mile added to the total cost. Although Congress mandated that its military district be surveyed and divided into townships five miles square, other congressional lands, that is, public domain, were surveyed and divided into townships six miles square. By approving two private land purchases by the Ohio Company of Associates and Symmes, who usually sold lands cheaper than two dollars per acre over time at 6 percent interest, Congress created stiff competition for its own sale of the public domain.

* * *

The public and private lands in Ohio had great appeal for the westward-moving frontier people. Although the Seven Ranges and southeastern Ohio were too hilly to permit relatively easy clearing and cultivation, most of the frontier lands proved a compelling lure, particularly Symmes's Miami Purchase and the Virginia and U.S. military districts, and later the Connecticut Western Reserve and Congress Lands. In 1788, an immigrant in the Ohio Company area confirmed the observations of the early traders who reported the fertility of the land. The soil near the Muskingum River, he wrote, "exceeded any thing I ever saw east of the Allegheny Mountains."

Yet, while the frontier people sought rich lands for settlement, few had sufficient capital to purchase public lands. Although many settlers simply ignored congressional regulations by squatting on public lands and hoping for the right of preemption later, others preferred to buy smaller tracts from speculators. Land speculators provided an essential service by helping men and women acquire land and settle on the frontier. By purchasing land at less than $1 per acre, the Ohio Company of Associates, Symmes, the Connecticut Land Company, and speculators in the Virginia Military District could still make considerable money by selling uncleared or under-developed lands for $1.50 per acre. These speculators divided their extensive holdings into tracts for sale to small-scale farmers. Many settlers could afford to purchase 50 or 100 acres at the price of $75 or $100 respectively but not pay $1,280 for 640 acres of public land after 1796. Indeed, by 1800, less than 50,000 acres of Ohio's public lands had been sold under the Land Act of 1796. Most settlement occurred on privately held lands, because settlers could afford it.

In November 1793, for example, Stewart Wilkins, a speculator in Cincinnati, advertised to sell four tracts as small as 200 acres along the East Fork of the Little Miami River in the Virginia Military District. Wilkins stressed the "luxuriance" of the soil, and the opportunity for commercial not subsistence agriculture. Because of the nearness of his lands to Cincinnati, he noted, "every article will find a ready sale, [and] make it of immediate consequence." Wilkins did not list the price, because he, like other speculators, wanted to bargain for the best offer possible, but he promised that settlers could buy on credit and that the "terms of payment [would] be made easy."

At that same time, D. C. Orcutt, another land speculator in Cincinnati, offered a 230-acre tract lying seven miles from the mouth of Licking Creek which gave access to Cincinnati down the Little Miami River. The shortage of cash on the Ohio frontier forced Orcutt to take corn, whiskey, poultry, cattle, horses, pork, and beef in payment, because these agricultural commodities could be sent downriver for sale or sold or traded in Cincinnati. Still, cash was the preferred "object of sale." In August 1801 John McDougal in Chillicothe offered 200 acres along Paint Creek about fifteen miles from Chillicothe for two dollars per acre, with the payment divided between cash and pork. Fellow speculator John S. Willis sold 1,000 acres in the same area for cash, horses, cattle, and pork.

Other speculators offered particular advantages for dealing with them. In December 1793, a Captain James Henry advertised his lands along the Great Miami River and promised to give 10-acre "Out Lots" to the first settlers who bought from him; the next spring, a John Armstrong also offered to give favorable terms to "any number of families" who would form a settlement on his lands near Fort Hamilton along the Great Miami River. In January 1796,

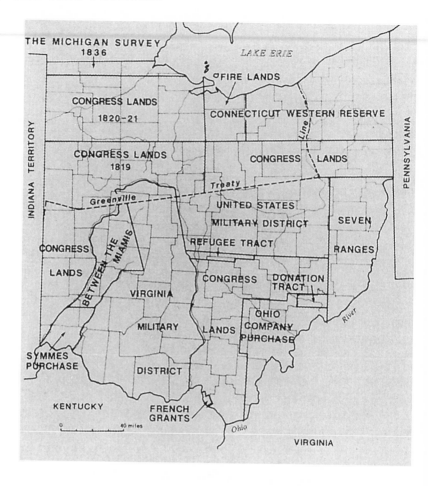

The division, survey, and sale of Ohio's lands became
complex. Entrepreneurs acting in groups or as individuals
obtained vast tracts of land. Speculators and settlers often
acquired lands with warrants for military service. Others
purchased lands from speculators and the federal
government. From George W. Knepper, *Ohio and Its Peoples*
(Kent, Ohio: Kent State University Press, 1989), with
permission of the Kent State University Press.

Samuel Robins sold 300 acres located three miles north of Cincinnati. This property had 9 acres cleared and 4 acres planted in
timothy, and it included a good cabin. Whether Robins was a large-
scale land speculator or a pioneer entrepreneur who had acquired a
tract and improved it remains uncertain. In August 1800, an agent

working on behalf of four speculators who held lands in the Virginia
Military District also offered the opportunity for buyers to make
money from their lands in addition to farming when he advertised
5,000 acres of "good oak land" near New Market. Clearing land was
a difficult task at best, but the possibility of selling hardwood during
the process provided an additional economic benefit and lure.

Some speculators such as Joseph Kerr near Chillicothe attempted
to make their lands more attractive to settlers by hiring "industrious young men" to cut trees and split rails for fences. Kerr offered
"generous wages in cash," but he preferred to employ men who
would take their pay in land or horses based on cash values. As
late as November 1809, he still accepted horses, cattle, sheep, and
hogs as well as a "few good wagons" in partial payment for his
lands. Samuel Smith, who sold land in the U.S. Military District,
also offered to pay for clearing and fencing with acreage. In addition, Edward Tiffin, who held considerable lands along the Scioto
River, tried to make the acquisition of land easy for either settlers or
speculators who operated on a smaller scale than himself. In late
November 1803, he advertised 1,000 acres either as a whole or divided into "small farms, so as to suit purchasers."

Speculators also stressed the commercial and social advantages of their holdings. In April 1795, James Taylor owned 3,000
acres along the Little Miami in the Virginia Military District.
Creeks, such as Clough, which ran through his land, afforded
good mill sites with access to the Cincinnati market and Ohio
River trade. Moreover, people who bought his lands could be certain that they would not be isolated in the wilderness. Rather, he
noted, they would enjoy the social interaction and benefits of community because "settlements are already made almost all round the
land."

Some speculators, such as Thomas Worthington near Chillicothe,
who had acquired large holdings by taking lands in payment for
surveying in the Virginia Military District, often sold acreage to
other speculators who operated on a scale above the settler but
below themselves. In July 1800, for example, Worthington offered to
sell 12,000 acres in tracts of 1,000 to 1,200 acres along the Little
Miami River and Paint Creek. He had located and surveyed these
lands in 1787 and had "indisputable title" in the form of patents

from the federal government. Given the problems of settlers and speculators in the Miami Purchase, the buyers of Worthington's lands appreciated peace of mind, knowing that they could acquire land from him free from claims by others.

In the early autumn of 1800, Lucas Sullivant, a large-scale speculator who held lands in the U.S. Military District, also offered acreage with secure patents. In September, Sullivant advertised 30,000 acres, divided into 50-acre lots, for sale along the Scioto River and Alum Creek. For settlers who could pay cash, he offered terms of one-third down and four years' credit on the amount due, of which half could be paid in goods, that is, various kinds of property. Sullivant improved his lands and increased their price per acre by hiring settlers to clear several hundred acres at the rate of four dollars per acre with the right to farm it for three years, after which they could purchase the land or move on. By April 1801, Sullivant had changed his terms slightly. He now accepted only one-fourth of the money down, with the balance due in five years, but he agreed to take two-thirds of the balance in property. He also offered to rent lands for seven years, with the lease renewable for a maximum of ten years. While settlers rented his land, of course, they would improve it by clearing trees, plowing fields, and building cabins and fences. After a decade, it would be worth far more than before.

Duncan McArthur, a land speculator who had been a chainman for Nathaniel Massie and later succeeded William Henry Harrison as commander of the Army of the Northwest and became governor of Ohio, also acquired large tracts of land, often by purchasing acreage that reverted to the federal government because a buyer could not meet his obligations. In addition to selling in 1801, McArthur also rented land in the Virginia Military District for ten bushels of corn and two pounds of sugar per acre. Unless speculators advertised cleared land with improvements, they could not command much more than the two dollars per acre charged for government land, but their credit and rental terms proved attractive. In August 1800, for example, four speculators offered 10,475 acres for sale along the Scioto and Little Miami rivers with "reasonable credit" for half the purchase price and the price per acre dependent on the amount of cash put down. Speculators such as Samuel Smith in Chillicothe also adopted "Congress payments," that is, payments scheduled over time, with three months of credit from the date of purchase for the first payment and the final payment due at the end of twelve months. Although these terms were not as generous as the four-year payment period provided by the Harrison Frontier Land Act of 1800, the price was less because he did not require 320-acre minimum purchases.

Despite the advantages that speculators advertised for dealing with them, immigrants continued to settle illegally on federal lands, and on May 12, 1796, a group of squatters in Ohio petitioned Congress for preemption rights, that is, the first right to purchase the property on which they resided upon survey. Congress, however, refused, contending, "Inasmuch as illegal settlements on the lands of the United States ought not to be encouraged, and, as yielding to the said claims would interfere with the general provisions for the sale of the said lands . . . the . . . petitions ought not to be granted." The squatters never gave up, though, and on February 25, 1801, Congress addressed their preemption requests once again, arguing that "granting the indulgence prayed for, would operate as an encouragement to intrusions on the public lands, and would be an unjustifiable sacrifice of the public interest."

Yet while the Harrison Frontier Land Act of May 10, 1800, permitted settlers to purchase public lands on credit, the price remained at two dollars per acre, beyond the means of many potential squatters. In 1804, Congress amended the land act to permit a settler to buy 160 acres for eighty dollars down and equal annual payments of eighty dollars the following three years. This federal policy enabled settlers to purchase small tracts on credit and made legal access to Ohio's public domain relatively easy for small-scale farmers and their families. Moreover, the buyer had the guarantee of clear title when purchasing government land, compared to uncertain titles acquired from a speculator. One observer wrote: "What a contrast between occupying land by a doubtful title [in Kentucky] and purchasing from the United States."

Still, by 1805, with lands selling at $6.50 per acre along the Great Miami River by private dealers, settlers needed credit, and speculators often met their needs better than the federal government. William Ruffin offered 3,000 acres along Bear Creek near Springfield in the Miami Purchase for cash or "extensive credit." These wooded and prairie lands already had several farms with fences, cabins, and other improvements and supported a nearby tannery and distillery that turned cowhides and corn into value-added products of leather and whiskey. Heavily wooded and unsurveyed tracts, however, brought only $1.50 per acre along the Scioto. In December 1805, for example, Joseph Kerr sold 200 acres for $300, with $100 down and equal payments due thereafter, with the first required within two months following the survey and the last due in 1807. John Wilkins also sold several tracts ranging from 150 to 400 acres for $1.50 per acre, with two-thirds due within one year of the date of sale and the remainder in two years. Terms such as these were still cheaper than from the government and made land acquisition relatively easy for the settler without substantial capital. The cheaper prices for uncleared land and the credit policies of the speculators significantly contributed to the rapid settlement of the Ohio frontier.

The speculators' terms remained preferable because cash continued in short supply and most speculators sold some of their lands for goods. In May 1807, Fielding Loury, agent for John Smith in Cincinnati, advertised 50,000 acres of "first rate land" between the Great and Little Miami and Mad rivers. He offered credit if buyers paid most of the purchase price in cash, but otherwise accepted flour, whiskey, pork, beef, wheat, rye, corn, iron nails, and castings. The federal government accepted only cash or land warrants. As late as May 1816, S. H. Smith offered 4,000 acres in the U.S. Military District near Mount Vernon, most of which had been divided into 100- to 300-acre tracts to "accommodate actual settlers," for one-third down and the remainder over the next two years, with a "liberal discount" for anyone who paid the entire agreed-upon price in cash.

Soon after the War of 1812, improved lands in settled areas brought considerably more than the two dollars per acre for public lands. In April 1816, Nahum Ward sold land with "very decent cabins" thirty miles below Gallipolis along the Ohio River for fifteen dollars per acre, but he and other land agents usually offered lots in different quantities and qualities on terms "calculated to suit purchasers." Some even attempted to soothe hard feelings when squatters had to be removed from private lands. In June 1815,

Joseph Kerr sold Jacob Grundy a tract in Franklin County, but the contract stipulated that Grundy would "make to John Compton or his family a reasonable compensation for any work him or his family has done on the place."

Despite the efforts of speculators to make their lands readily available at an affordable price, however, by 1810 less than half of the 34,730 males twenty-six years of age or older owned land. If those settlers who occupied federal lands on a credit plan are included, the percentage of landowners in Ohio increases only from 45 to 50 percent. The top 10 percent averaged 480 acres each and collectively held 50 percent of all acreage. Put differently, 1 out of every 100 owners held approximately 25 percent of the resident lands in their county or township. During the settlement period on the Ohio frontier, then, speculators, that is, large-scale owners, owned half of the land, with the top 10 percent owning one-third of the property listed on the tax rolls. Lucas Sullivant, who resided in Franklin County, was the largest-scale speculator, owning 41,459 acres distributed among eighty-six properties, or one-tenth of the state's acres, with a tax valuation of $340,582. At that same time, a T. Spencer was the smallest-scale property holder of the 15,750 men who owned land, holding only .3 of an acre in Butler County.

In 1810, 90 percent of the population who owned land held fewer than 480 acres, with the median holding being 150 acres, but this group owned 50 percent of the land. Overall, half the adult male population averaged 271 acres, and only about 2 percent held less than 40 acres, with much of that land being town property. Although inequality characterized landholding, it did not jeopardize individual agricultural development and economic gain because most farmers could not clear and cultivate more than 40 acres during the frontier period. Almost all property holders, excluding those in the towns, held 40 acres or more and easily met their immediate needs while they attempted to produce for a market economy. There would be no demands by "levellers" for the redistribution of land on the Ohio frontier.

Instead, the little opposition to the large-scale landowners that did occur came from small-scale businessmen early in the settlement period. One such individual, who signed his name as "Manlius," resented paying taxes while the land speculators avoided it. "If we let the great land holders go exempt from taxes," he charged, "they will keep their lands until their avarice is satisfied in the sales of them." If their property was taxed with that of the "trader and poor tavern keeper," however, they would be "obliged to sell their great tracts in small parcels to such people as [would] make immediate settlements, and who [would] be more terrible to the savage enemies of this country than all three dollar soldiers that can be collected from the Continent." Still, demand for the equitable and timely payment of taxes was far different from a cry for the redistribution of land. With land cheap or temporarily free for use by squatters, inequitable distribution never became an issue on the Ohio frontier.

Moreover, those who owned property were highly mobile. Both speculators and small-scale farmers recognized that land brought wealth as well as independence and security, but it was not something that a settler often wanted to keep forever. As land values rose with improvements as well as from greater demands created by population increases in an area, many settlers chose to sell out and take their capital gains for investment in other lands or endeavors. Out of 188 property owners studied in 1800, only 82 remained on their lands a decade later. Although the ownership of land provided security and economic gain, it did not guarantee or even encourage stability of residence. Indeed, the Ohio frontier families who owned land usually did not put down roots. They treated land as a commodity to be acquired, used, and sold. Although some farmers failed and moved on, mobility indicated opportunity.

In addition to the inequitable distribution of lands in Ohio from the beginning of settlement, the largest-scale landowners wielded the economic and political power in the state. In 1810, the four largest landowners in Ohio included Lucas Sullivant in Franklin County with 41,459 acres, William Lytle in Clermont County with 38,998 acres, Duncan McArthur in Ross County with 35,341 acres, and John Kinsman in Trumbull County with 33,986 acres. Each was middle-aged and, with the exception of McArthur, had had personal wealth before investing in Ohio lands. All had been surveyors before making their purchases in the Virginia and U.S. military districts and the Western Reserve. Large-scale holdings, however, brought more than wealth; they also provided the social recognition and opportunity for leadership that could be parlayed into political gain. Surveyors-speculators were well and widely known. If they conducted their work honestly and fairly while they gained title to large acreages, they gained considerable prestige and influence that could be parlayed into political power. In 1810, for example, Thomas Worthington held 5,442 acres and John Smith 1,940. Both served as Ohio's first U.S. senators, while Jonathan Meigs with 1,630 acres held a position on the state supreme court, and Edward Tiffin, who had served as the state's first governor, owned 720 acres.

While speculators divided and sold their holdings, the federal government conducted a modest business in Ohio. By September 30, 1811, the land offices at Marietta, Zanesville, Steubenville, Canton, Chillicothe, and Cincinnati had sold 3 million acres, but 6.9 million acres remained untaken from those jurisdictions. Sales increased substantially during the next year at the Canton, Steubenville, Zanesville, and Cincinnati offices.

Of course, not everyone who bought lands from the government, private land companies, or individual speculators profited. Many settlers fell into arrears on their payments and taxes. In 1800, for example, so many settlers had become delinquent on their property taxes in Ross County that they were assessed a 10 percent penalty. A year later, many settlers in the Virginia Military District lost their lands because of tax delinquency even though Ohio assessed taxes at only fifty-five cents per hundred acres. Some who could not meet their obligations sold out with "utmost reluctance" and moved on. Both private sellers and the federal government sometimes foreclosed on buyers. In January 1814, Thomas Gibson, register in the federal land office at Canton, announced that he would sell the lands of all defaulters who were five years past due, unless they made payment by February 24.

In addition, many wanted to emigrate to the "new country," but not everyone considered the Ohio frontier to their liking once they arrived. In August 1809, a John Fuller, passing through Chillicothe from Vermont on his way to Mississippi, reported that a three-week stay had convinced him the country was given to idleness, dissipation, and expense, with brandy selling for "six dollars per gallon and all kind of spirits in proportion." He wrote, "Nothing will grow here that will not grow in Vermont that is required to support life." About 1812, a Daniel Mott from Massachusetts visited Ohio and had much the same opinion. In the words of Quaker John Williams to Thomas Rotch near Steubenville, Mott would not move there "if thou would give him thy settlement."

Still, most settlers found the Ohio frontier to their liking, with land readily available for purchase or rent at favorable prices and terms. While the population increased fivefold from 51,006 in 1800 to 269,407 by 1810, land values also rose, despite the two dollars per acre price for public lands, which held constant until 1820. In 1789, for example, Symmes sold land near Cincinnati for eighty-three and a third cents per acre, but in 1805 those lands were valued at two dollars per acre for unimproved acreage and from forty to fifty dollars per acre for developed farms. Although Manasseh Cutler spoke of the Ohio Company's grant when he called it the "garden of the world," few men and women would have hesitated to apply that term to all of Ohio as they pressed hard to settle the frontier at a pace that some called "Ohio fever."

7.

Early Settlements

On November 21, 1786, the Associates of the Ohio Company met at Brackett's Tavern in Boston to plan the settlement of their pending land grant in Ohio. Although Congress would not extend a contract for a million acres of land until October 27 of the next year, the directors and agents of the company were optimistic and eager to plant a colony on the Ohio frontier. At this meeting the directors and agents, that is, those who had the responsibility for twenty or more shares of stock entrusted by the shareholders, resolved to send four surveyors and twenty-two men to begin preliminary work as soon as possible. The party would include six boat builders, four carpenters, one blacksmith, and nine common laborers, all of whom were to be proprietors, that is, investors in the company. Each man would take an ax, hoe, musket, bayonet, powder, and lead. And, "in case of interruption from an enemy," they were subject to military command, with the penalty of forfeiture of wages for those who refused to obey. The Associates placed General Rufus Putnam in charge, with a notice to all that he was to be "Obeyed & respected accordingly."

Delays in Congress that slowed approval of a grant to the Ohio Company prevented Putnam's party from leaving Hartford, Connecticut, until January 1, 1788. On January 23, after difficult travel in heavy snow through the Allegheny Mountains, Putnam's group reached an advance party at Sumrill Ferry (present-day West Newton, Pennsylvania), on the Youghiogheny River. They remained there, dragging logs and hewing and sawing timbers for boats to carry them down the Ohio to the Muskingum. Captain Jonathan Devol, a shipbuilder from Rhode Island, directed the work, which resulted in the construction of two "Kentucky boats," that is, flatboats, the largest forty-five by twelve feet with a roof. To mark their resolve, they christened it the *Mayflower*. On April 1 they set out; six days later they were off the shore of Kerr's Island, and Fort Harmar soon came into sight. After missing the mouth of the Muskingum because it was covered by overhanging trees, the party poled the flatboats back and landed on a point across from the fort, where a party of Wyandots and Delawares waited and watched, hoping to trade furs for whatever useful things the white people carried in the flatboats and the three accompanying canoes.

The men of the Ohio Company were not interested in trade on that 7th of April, but quickly went about their work setting up a tent for Putnam's headquarters and nailing board huts for temporary shelters, while surveying and scouting parties explored the area. Putnam assigned the men who were unneeded for surveying to begin work on a stockade because he believed "the Indians would not be peacible very Long." "Thus," he wrote, "were all hands employed until the 5th of May," when he permitted anyone who desired to plant 2 acres within the town and to make up their time to the company after July 1. Most of the men accepted his offer, and soon 130 acres of corn had been planted. The directors of the Ohio Company had allocated 5,760 acres for their settlement, which they planned to divide into sixty rectangular blocks, ten wide and six deep, divided by streets 100 feet wide, except for the main avenue, which had a width of 150 feet. All but four of the squares would be subdivided for "in-lots," that is, house lots of 90 by 100 feet, and nearby "out-lots" of 8 acres for agriculture. The remaining acres would serve as a town commons, thereby transplanting the New England practice of orderly, compact settlement.

Although skeptics back home in Massachusetts had dubbed the Ohio Company's plans for a colony "Putnam's Paradise," the forty-eight inhabitants called the first legal settlement in Ohio under the government of the United States "Adelphia," meaning brotherhood. On July 2, 1788, however, at the first meeting of the company in Ohio, they changed the name to Marietta, in honor of Marie Antoinette of France, to recognize French aid during the American Revolution. They also honored the ancient Romans, naming their stockade Campus Martius, the town squares Quadranou, Capitolium, Conus, and Cecilia, and a road Via Sacra, which led up from the banks of the Muskingum.

Campus Martius, the main storage area and place of safety for the company's members, took the form of a "very ancient and very extraordinary fortification." It included four blockhouses of hewed and sawed timber on each corner of a square. Log walls formed the outside of the perimeter and served as the exterior wall of private homes, leaving a "cleane area within of 144 feet square." One resident called Campus Martius "the handsomest pile of buildings on this side of the Allegheny mountains." The Ohio Company's plans, worked out in the winter of 1787, called for the planting of mulberry trees along the sides of each street, about ten or fifteen feet from the houses, which, according to Manasseh Cutler, would "make an agreeable shade, increase the salubrity of the air, and add to the beauty of the streets." It would also create natural walkways while leaving the streets an ample seventy feet wide. These New Englanders named their streets after the company's founders and their contemporaries to transfer a sense of public responsibility, marking the streets perpendicular to the Muskingum with signs bearing the names of Knox, Cutler, Putnam, Greene, and St. Clair, while they applied Washington's name to the main thoroughfare. They then gave numerical designations to the streets that paralleled the Muskingum. By so doing, the founders gave Marietta a "perfect harmony" in design as well as predictability and regularity.

Although the Ohio Company created a new town, it transferred the physical and social culture of New England town building to the Ohio frontier. At Campus Martius, the New Englanders agreed to use one blockhouse as a school and another as a church, where their values and traditions would be nourished and perpetuated. In an August 1788 sermon, Manasseh Cutler reminded the New Englanders to give proper attention to the "cultivation of the principles of religion and virtue" to ensure "civil and social happiness." The perpetuation of the New England tradition and the classical age, then, mandated support for education and religion to achieve an ordered liberty.

But not for everyone. Although Cutler believed that "men of property" should naturally control the economic, social, and political life of Marietta, and while associate Thomas Wallcut contended, "Our people will be the means of introducing more ambition and better taste to the West," other settlers, primarily back-country Virginians and Pennsylvanians, soon came to Marietta and upset all hopes and plans for the creation of a uniformly cultured society based on good breeding, high education, and honest piety. The founders, for example, built Campus Martius on high ground almost a mile from the Ohio River to avoid perennial flooding, but settlers not associated with the Ohio Company erected cabins along the banks where the Muskingum converged with the Ohio and called it "Picketed Point." Soon a store and tavern lured the river traffic and the rabble of society that the associates had fled in New England and which they believed jeopardized the peace and tranquility of Marietta.

The Associates at Campus Martius and the frontier people did not socialize and willfully snubbed each other. In March 1791, David Barker, who had lived at Marietta since November 1, 1789, reported that a dozen "Indian Chiefs" had arrived at the Point by canoe and "received from the people at the Point such attention & hospitality as was due to friendly sovereigns who pass through the Territory of a Republic." Upon learning of their presence, the Associates at Campus Martius invited the Indians to dine and treated them to a drum roll, the presentation of arms, and a cannon salute when they entered the compound. But the frontier people at the Point were absent. Barker wrote, "As the Point folks did not invite Campus Martius, they did not invite the Point." Social and cultural differences between the New Englanders and the frontier people often proved as divisive as those between whites and Indians.

To contend with the rabble drifting into the Ohio Company's settlement, who had little respect for the customs of New England, the city founders adopted a code of laws in July 1788. But while Governor Arthur St. Clair, who arrived via a twelve-oared flatboat flying an American flag on July 15 and who created Washington County by proclamation, personified the law, he did little to ensure the order that the New Englanders desired. The problem, of course, did not involve the flagrant violation of law by the frontier people at

Although the settlers who lived in the Ohio country were no strangers to violence, easterners usually assumed that only the dregs of society lived on the frontier. This early nineteenth-century engraving emphasized the worst aspects of frontier life. Violence such as this prompted Congress to provide for a territorial government under the Northwest Ordinance of 1787. OHIO HISTORICAL SOCIETY.

Marietta but rather their propensity to follow whim rather than conform to the forms of behavior expected by the New Englanders. The frontier people drank, argued, and fought, and their children created a noisy nuisance playing on the ceremonial mounds left by an ancient people within the confines of the town, but they were not a band of thieves. In fact, when the first court held proceedings at Campus Martius on September 2, it quickly adjourned because it did had not have any business. Even so, in early February 1790, Thomas Wallcut reached the limits of his tolerance for these common people and complained to Governor St. Clair that he wanted the "passions of oppressive, cruel and avaricious men" controlled. He also charged that the tavern of Isaac Mixer at the Point was "destructive of peace, good order, and exemplary morals upon which not only the well-being but the very existence of society so much depends." Wallcut and the other members of the Ohio Company wanted system and order, and they got it with a law that authorized the licensing and regulation of taverns.

In time the court had ample business and usually identified the convicted as "Virginians" and "hunters" who had a propensity to steal horses and who conducted themselves with "riotous behavior" in Marietta. Most cases involved assault and battery, the failure to perform public responsibilities, and fighting. The social tensions created by the settlement and mutual habitation of the New Englanders and frontier people made Marietta a town of order, culture, and education as well as a place where the unchurched, undisciplined, and illiterate made their daily lives. From the beginning, cultural heterogeneity, not homogeneity, characterized the frontier settlement of Marietta.

Despite cultural differences and the preference of the New Englanders for everyone else to conform to their own standards, they found the frontier people useful as a buffer between Marietta and the Indians. In 1789, the Ohio Company began offering a limited number of 100-acre tracts to non-shareholders to attract settlers, whose presence would help build the settlement's economy and attract others who would buy land. At the same time, they would help defend the settlement. Within five years, however, these settlers had to build a house that measured at least twenty-four by eighteen feet, with a cellar ten feet square and six feet deep, and lay up a brick or stone chimney. They also had to plant fifty apple and twenty peach trees within three years and clear fifteen acres for pasture and five acres for corn and other crops within five years. With these terms met, the settler would receive a deed to the tract, which the Ohio Company called a "donation" lot. Because these lots were located to the north of the company's original grant for the purpose of providing advance warning and protection from an Indian attack, the heads of each household were obligated to five years of service in the local militia.

In April 1790, about forty settlers took advantage of this opportunity and established the town of Belpre to the south along the Ohio River. The next year, thirty-six frontier people traveled about thirty miles up the Muskingum and founded the settlement of Big Bottom on the north bank. In the frontier tradition, they built a blockhouse as the Ohio Company had intended. Unfortunately, they did not chink the gaps between the logs because the ground remained too frozen to dig and mix the required clay and stone, and they took a remarkably careless attitude about defense, not posting guards or building a picket wall around their buildings. As a result, on January 2 a band of Wyandots and Delawares struck the settlement at twilight, first feigning friendship, then breaking down the blockhouse door and firing between the logs, killing eight, including a "stout, backwoods, Virginia woman" who had injured one of the attackers with a tomahawk before being killed. The raiders set fire to a cabin and blockhouse and attempted to burn the bodies before taking their five captives northward.

The attack at Big Bottom brought a new Indian war, but it also temporarily halted the attempt of the Ohio Company to expand its foothold and build "proper Defenses." Only the army could provide the necessary protection. As a result, the outlying settlements beyond the protection of Fort Harmar and the troops stationed at Belpre and at the newly established palisade down the Muskingum from Big Bottom at Waterford were abandoned until after Wayne's victory in 1794.

After the Treaty of Greenville ended the Indian wars in 1795, Marietta began to gain social control with the aid of a capable police, which enforced the code of 1788 that required newcomers to register with the officials within twenty-four hours of their arrival and which included a law that limited the movement of the settlers outside of Marietta. The New Englanders also prohibited unlawful assembly, punished drunkenness and swearing, and authorized public whippings for a host of offenses. Morality would be achieved in the New England way.

Even so, Marietta remained less a New England town than a backwoods frontier settlement, despite institutional transfers of law, education, and religion as well as immigration from the Northeast. By 1810, for example, of 627 heads of household whose origins can be identified from a total of 1,001, only 367 came from New England. Moreover, in surrounding Washington County only an estimated 2,202 heads of household out of 5,991 had been born in New England at that same time. Because the New Englanders were more literate and less mobile than other immigrants in the Ohio Company's colony, many of the 374 heads of families who cannot be identified by place of birth probably came from Pennsylvania, Virginia, Maryland, and New York. In time, travelers would see Marietta as "New England in miniature," but not during the early frontier period.

* * *

Although the New Englanders believed that Marietta would "serve as a wide model for the future settlement of all federal lands," in Cincinnati speculators and profit-oriented merchants ruled rather than New England patricians; they made the settlement the center of trade and culture in the Ohio Valley. On December 28, 1788, twenty-six men under the leadership of Colonel Robert Patterson and Israel Ludlow, who with absentee speculator Matthias Denman purchased eight hundred acres from John Cleves Symmes opposite the mouth of the Licking on the Ohio River, founded Cincinnati. Denman had put up the money, and Patterson agreed to furnish the settlers; Ludlow would survey the tract and establish a town. The party arrived by flatboats from Limestone, Kentucky, and busily went about tearing them apart to build a blockhouse with the lumber. They called their settlement Losantiville.

By January 7, 1789, Ludlow had surveyed and platted the town site, laying off four-acre out-lots and half-acre in-lots. The three proprietors promised a free in- and out-lot to the first thirty settlers to lure land buyers. Settlement lagged, however, because the proprietors were not present to encourage business. In mid-May, Symmes complained that Losantiville "would have been much more important by this time if Colonel Patterson or Mr. Denman had resided in the town." The owners responded by giving away another fifty lots. Although these grants theoretically meant that at least eighty adult males occupied Losantiville at that time, few actually lived in this struggling frontier settlement. In early February only three log cabins with dirt floors occupied the site, but the settlement had expanded to twenty cabins and one frame house giving shelter to eleven families and twenty-four single men by the end of the year.

The fortunes of the early settlers at Losantiville improved in August 1789, when General Harmar selected the site for a new fort to protect the settlers in the Miami Purchase and across the river in Kentucky. Located just outside of Denman's tract, the site consisted of fifteen acres which the federal government had acquired from

Symmes. In late September, Harmar had more than two hundred soldiers at the site hewing timbers and putting up two-story block-houses 20 feet square and 180 feet apart at the four corners. Barracks occupied the middle of each side, which a palisade of pick-ets linked with the blockhouses. The soldiers completed enough work to enable General Harmar to establish his headquarters there on December 28, one year after the founding of Losantiville. Harmar christened the new post Fort Washington, "on account of its superior excellence."

Fort Washington usually had a complement of 320 men until after the Treaty of Greenville, but the general traffic of officers, sol-diers, and civilians on military business increased the population of Losantiville to about 500. Contract hunters provided Fort Wash-ington with meat, and they sold their deer, bear, and buffalo skins to a local tanner. On January 2, 1790, Governor Arthur St. Clair ar-rived and found "small cabins, and the inhabitants of the poorer class of people." St. Clair soon organized Hamilton County and proclaimed Losantiville the county seat. The governor, however, apparently disliked the name of the settlement and rechristened it Cincinnati to honor the organization by the same name composed of officers who had served in the American Revolution.

Although the settlers organized a court and appointed a sheriff, they often quarreled with the military authorities and fought with the soldiers. The army officers usually intervened when order broke down and imprisoned the civilians involved in the disturbances. But the community began to expand with the arrival of forty new fami-lies by late 1790, bringing the civilian population to about 250, who lived in approximately sixty cabins. When more than 800 militia from Kentucky and Pennsylvania rendezvoused at Fort Washington in September, the population increased to about 1,500. Harmar's defeat slowed the expansion of Cincinnati, and the Indians made the countryside and even the streets unsafe. But the population doubled between May and September 1791, when more than 3,000 men, mostly militia, arrived for training at Fort Washington in preparation for a new campaign to the north.

The settlers took advantage of economic opportunity by raising corn, which they distilled into whiskey and sold to taverns that catered to the soldiers. Drunkenness became such a problem that

St. Clair moved his soldiers to Ludlow's Station, located several miles north of Cincinnati, to keep them out of town. Winthrop Sargent, who moved from Marietta to Cincinnati in 1791, despaired that the citizenry was "very licentious and too great a portion indolent and extremely debauched." When St. Clair moved against the Indians on September 17, 1791, only to meet disaster, however, prospective settlers continued to question the safety of Cincinnati, and many left the community, although three new taverns, a mill for grinding corn, and a general store opened by the end of the year. In 1792, spring flooding drove many from their cabins, and a riot between the settlers and soldiers kept life hard and everyone alert in Cincinnati.

The river and military trade, however, drew the most adventuresome frontier people, who saw risk as opportunity. By July 1792, 354 lots had been surveyed in Cincinnati, with the selling price ranging from thirty to sixty dollars. Thirty warehouses met the needs of merchants, prompting one observer to remark that Cincinnati was "overrun with merchants and overstocked with goods." By the end of 1792, the lure of opportunity brought fifty new immigrants, swelling the population to about nine hundred, which necessitated the opening of the first school and encouraged the proprietors of two new general stores.

General Anthony Wayne arrived at Cincinnati with a thousand men in the spring of 1793. In August he began building a series of forts to the north for a new campaign against the Indians. This military activity stimulated the economy of Cincinnati and encouraged settlement because people felt more secure migrating to the Ohio frontier, where a large contingent of soldiers were stationed. The army needed packhorse masters, food, and other essentials, and the people at Cincinnati were more than happy to contract for these services and supplies. Despite an epidemic of smallpox that killed one-third of the population, by 1793 Cincinnatians could measure progress with the establishment of a newspaper on November 9, followed by a post office and jail. In December a commercial packet boat went upriver to Pittsburgh, and lots that had been purchased for two dollars in 1789 now brought one hundred dollars.

As settlers and military traffic increased, business opportunities also expanded in Cincinnati. On August 1, 1794, regular keelboat service began between Cincinnati and Marietta. The first lawyer arrived, a French pastry shop opened, and a hairdresser advertised for an apprentice. Although the presence of these professionals and tradesmen along with blacksmiths and merchants marked the economic success of a new settlement, the cultural traditions, prejudices, and sympathies of these frontier people prevailed, particularly evidenced by an advertisement in the local newspaper soliciting subscriptions to pay bounty hunters for the delivery of Indian scalps.

With the defeat of the Indians at Fallen Timbers in August 1794, immigration to the Ohio frontier rapidly increased, and a "considerable number of flatbottom boats," bearing men, women, and children, arrived at the landing in Cincinnati the following spring. Opportunities seemed to abound. In May the local editor reported: "Three Kentucky boats have lately arrived with a fresh assortment of attorneys at law." By spring 1795, a new butcher shop, brewery, pottery, Windsor chair and spinning wheel manufacturer, and parchment maker had recently opened for business. As the population increased with the end of the Indian wars, the price of in-lots rose rapidly to three hundred dollars in 1796 and to five hundred dollars a year later. Even so, a decade passed before Cincinnati regained its population of 1793. When the army abandoned Fort Washington in 1803, Cincinnati had only about 1,000 inhabitants. Thereafter, it grew steadily based on the marketing of agricultural commodities from the Little Miami River valley down the Ohio River to New Orleans. By 1810, the population had increased to 2,320. At the end of the War of 1812, Cincinnati no longer remained a frontier town, and it boasted a population of 6,000, which rapidly increased to 9,642 by 1820.

* * *

In the summer of 1790, while the New Englanders and frontier people worked to make Marietta and Cincinnati a success, approximately five hundred French men, women, and children left Alexandria, Virginia, by wagon bound for lands located along the western bank of the Ohio about three miles below the mouth of the Kanawha River. In mid-October, after a grueling overland trip to Pennsylvania, then downstream by flatboat, they reached their destination—a wilderness clearing with rough log cabins huddled behind a stockade and breastwork. Dense forest fringed the settlement on three sides, and the Ohio River bounded it on the fourth. At best, this new settlement provided little more than temporary shelter and protection for these adventuresome immigrants on the Ohio frontier. Nevertheless, the "French Five Hundred" were optimistic about their future and pridefully named their new settlement Gallipolis, "City of the Gauls."

Their optimism proved ill founded, because they did not have title to the lands that they purchased. Instead, their site belonged to the Ohio Company, not the Scioto Company, from whom they thought they had bought it. The Scioto Company, with Manasseh Cutler and Winthrop Sargent as shareholders, had been organized to secure 4.5 millon acres from Congress at the time of the Ohio Company's grant. Led by Colonel William Duer, secretary of the Board of Treasury, and a group of "associates" bent on speculative gain in Ohio lands, the Scioto Company set aside approximately 3 million acres for sale in Europe. Congress required six payments before transfer of title to these lands, but the Scioto Company began selling these tracts in an indirect fashion before any of the payments had been made.

It did so by authorizing Joel Barlow to serve as the agent for the Scioto Company in Paris. Barlow soon solicited the aid of William Playfair, an English businessman who understood French customs and business practices. Playfair, whose ethics betrayed his name, along with a small group of French speculators, established the Compagnie de Scioto on August 3, 1789, for the purpose of purchasing the land from the American Scioto Company for $1.14 per acre and selling it to French investors in 100-acre tracts. They apparently planned to use the money generated from these sales to pay the Scioto Company in America, which, in turn, would pay Congress. In time, they would receive deeds for transfer to French buyers. The first payment was due to the Scioto Company on December 31, 1789, and the last on April 4, 1794. No one would be harmed in the process, a few would earn handsome profits, and the French buyers eventually would receive clear titles to their lands.

Playfair accepted cash or American securities at 90 percent of their value for these lands, which he priced at six livres per acre, approximately six francs. He required only half of the purchase price as a down payment. The remainder could be paid two years later after the French settlers sold bountiful crops of cotton, tobacco, and wheat and sent thousands of hogsheads of pork down the Ohio River to New Orleans. As more immigrants arrived, land values would increase, thereby earning more money for the Scioto Company in Ohio. Playfair's offer proved doubly attractive in revolutionary France, especially for the middle class, which had little hope for social, political, and economic stability after the fall of the Bastille. But French geographer C. F. Volney, who visited Gallipolis in 1796, wrote: "The offers of so many benefits did not say that these fine forests were a preliminary obstacle to every sort of cultivation, that all provisions must be secured from a distance for at least a year, that these excellent lands were in the neighborhood of a species of ferocious animal worse than wolves and tigers, the man called savage, then at war with the United States." Moreover, Playfair did not tell the French that he really sold only preemption rights, not the land itself, because title depended on payment to Congress for the grant. Those who wanted to escape revolutionary France did not press Playfair for the details, and like many Americans, they got caught up in the quest for land and profits through speculation. The promotional literature also promised French investors and potential immigrants that the Scioto Company would supply them with provisions for six months, after which their crops would make them self-supporting.

The first party of French immigrants who thought they had bought Scioto Company lands left Havre in January 1790. They did not know, however, that although Playfair had sold more than 100,000 acres along the Ohio River, he had not forwarded the money to the American Scioto Company. Consequently, when more than six hundred French citizens arrived at Alexandria in May 1790, they were disappointed to learn that they did not have the right to claim the western lands that they had purchased before leaving home, because the Scioto Company had not gained title for lack of payment to Congress. Still, they had some reason for optimism, because the Scioto Company hoped to plant a settlement and gain title to those lands. Earlier, in March 1790, Rufus Putnam had arranged for a group of Massachusetts woodsmen to clear a site and build shelters for the French immigrants on Ohio Company land. Those workmen soon erected four blockhouses, each containing twenty single rooms, but these quarters had only dirt floors and clay chimneys. At best, the Ohio Company provided temporary shelter for the first group of French immigrants, who arrived on October 20, 1790.

Those French citizens who made the journey primarily were lawyers, doctors, merchants, watchmakers, goldsmiths, milliners, noblemen, and army officers. Some indentured servants, who had been promised fifty acres, a cabin, and a cow after three years of work clearing land and planting crops, also came along. They all spent a hard winter on the Ohio frontier, where life was far different from that in Paris. When spring arrived, they set about the task of becoming farmers, but they had great difficulty because of inexperience, even though the promotional literature hailed Ohio as "the most salubrious, the most advantageous, the most fertile land . . . known to any people in Europe." Their settlement hardly looked like "the garden of the universe, the center of wealth, a place destined to be the heart of a great Empire" that they had been led to believe it was.

During the first two years on the Ohio frontier, the French settlers at Gallipolis nearly starved, because they had few agricultural skills. Several Frenchmen even lost their lives when they were crushed by trees they were chopping down. Although Duer established a store at Gallipolis to provide the immigrants with essential supplies, the resources of the Scioto Company were insufficient, and it closed after a few months. Duer soon ended up in a debtors' prison in New York. At first, the French immigrants planted formal gardens, rice, artichokes, and almond trees. Later they achieved more practical results by raising grapes and peaches, which they exchanged for bread and pork with flatboat traders as well as distilled into brandy. Hunters hired by the Scioto Company kept them in fresh meat. Without valid title to the land on which they resided, however, they had little interest in making major improvements, such as clearing trees, planting fields, and building better log houses. Essentially, the Scioto Company left the French to their own resources. Their choice was either to survive or to perish on the Ohio frontier.

Although the distance, both physical and cultural, between Paris and Ohio proved great and life in the wilderness hard and depressing, the frontier did not create an insurmountable cultural shock for all members of the party. One Frenchman, who arrived on October 20, 1790, felt great satisfaction with the settlement. He wrote: "To some the surrounding woods might appear frightful deserts; to me they are the paradise of nature; no hosts of greedy priests; no seas of blood to wade through; all is quiet, and the savages themselves shall soon be taught the art of cultivating the earth, refinement of manners, the duties of genuine devotion. Under this free and enlightened asylum, our language and customs will here be preserved in their original purity for ages to come, and France shall find herself renovated in the Western World, without being disgraced by the frippery of kings or seeing the best blood wasted in gratyfing [sic] the ambition of knaves and sycophants."

Despite this optimism, however, many left to seek their fortunes elsewhere. Although approximately four hundred had settled at Gallipolis by late 1790, two years later only three hundred settlers remained, and another one hundred planned to leave at the earliest convenience. Even so, missionary John Heckewelder observed that Gallipolis had gained a reputation because of its craftsmen, who made watches, compasses, and sundials "finer than any I had ever beheld," and who cut and "artistically carved" stone for fireplace mantels.

Problems, of course, abounded. In 1792, Bishop John Carroll, who had obtained information from Dom Didier, the priest at Gallipolis, wrote that "many of them are refugees from Paris who have brought with them the vices of the large cities, and a hatred for religion." He hoped that Father Didier would be "able to apply a remedy to this evil and to encourage labor and simplicity of morals." Father Didier, however, had already fled Gallipolis for Upper Louisiana, leaving much spiritual work behind. When two priests later stopped at Gallipolis for three days during a journey downriver, they received a hearty welcome, delivered a High Mass, and baptized forty children. One contemporary observed that "the good French colonists were delighted; and shed tears on their departure."

By June 1794, about ninety-five men and forty-five women composed the settlement, but a General Victor Collot, who passed through Gallipolis, reported that "the appearance of the place is dirty, and it seems to be the abode of wretchedness." During the summer of 1796, French traveler Constantin-François Volney visited Gallipolis and had much the same opinion. He reported that at his first sight of Gallipolis he "was struck with its forlorn appearance; with the thin pale faces, sickly looks and anxious air of its inhabitants." No doubt malaria plagued the settlement, but Volney also believed that the "damp, unwholesome and uncomfortable" cabins contributed to their misery. He facetiously wrote that the French settlers lived in "whitewashed log cabins . . . built contiguous, no doubt that they might all be burnt up at once." In November, Thomas Chapman, another traveler, reported much the same, noting that Gallipolis was "a Small miserable looking Village of upwards of 100 little wreatched [*sic*] Log Cabbins, all Occupied by poor starved sickly looking Frenchmen. . . . The whole of the Inhabitants of this Town . . . have Starvation and Sickness strongly pictured in their faces." Chapman left "this wreached [*sic*] place" as soon as the baker made him a dozen loaves of bread. Given these conditions, many French settlers abandoned Gallipolis to acquire lands elsewhere in Ohio or downriver. Indeed, they soon discovered that the lands of the Ohio Company were not as fertile as tracts offered by speculators in the Miami Purchase, and like other frontier people, they took advantage of the opportunities presented and moved on. The bitter winters, illness, hunger, hostile Indians, and uncertainty were burdens too great for many settlers to bear.

But life was not grim for everyone in Gallipolis. On September 24, 1795, for example, a Mrs. Marest wrote to a friend in Paris, "Poverty doesn't exist here." Although wine was not common, settlers could obtain imported Madeira easily if they were "willing to pay." Some colonists made apple and peach brandy and wine, the latter of which sold for four shillings a gallon. She also noted that "clothes are expensive here, but it doesn't bother us, because people dress informally here." Clearly the settlers at Gallipolis did not starve or go threadbare. Moreover, not all of the French were willing to abandon Gallipolis, because they anticipated favorable treatment on their petition to Congress asking for land.

In the autumn of 1793, the residents petitioned Congress through their agent Jean Baptiste Gervais to grant them lands of their own. On March 3, 1795, Congress responded favorably and awarded them 24,000 acres, known as the "French Grant," forty miles downriver, near present-day Portsmouth. Gervais received 4,000 acres of the tract for his efforts in Philadelphia, while ninety-two males over the age of eighteen and the widows of the original settlers who still resided in Gallipolis divided the remainder into equal portions of 217.4 acres. Few French families, however, chose to move to their new grant; instead their lands were sold for speculative gain, and they soon became settled by American frontier people.

Gallipolis, however, still belonged to the Ohio Company, which had title to the lands along this portion of the Ohio River. Although the Ohio Company would not give the French the land on which they lived, in December 1795 it agreed to sell the town site and the four-acre surrounding out-lots, totaling nine hundred acres, for $1.25 per acre. These settlers then purchased their lands twice, but at Gallipolis as well as at the French Grant, they had ample land to claim as their own. The Ohio frontier certainly created hardships, but after a difficult beginning, the French settlers had the opportunity to use their lands for economic gain and security like the other frontier people.

At the turn of the nineteenth century, however, Gallipolis continued to struggle. In 1802, François André Michaux, an amateur botanist and professional traveler, stopped in Gallipolis. He reported that the settlement was composed of about sixty log houses, most of which were uninhabited and falling down. The French residents "breathe[d] out a miserable existence." Only two of them enjoyed any comfort. One kept an inn and distilled brandy from peaches, which he sent to Kentucky or sold at a "tolerable advantage." The other individual also earned a comfortable living as a distiller. The settlement still did not have a priest, which meant that children could not be baptized or people married in a Catholic church. In 1805, Jean Dilhet, a visitor, noted that "rationalism and humanitarianism" prevailed in Gallipolis. Instead of learning Catholicism, the settlers practiced "infidelity, deism and other such abominations." The settlement was no longer French but had become "entirely American owing to the influx of Americans there who occup[ied] first place in everything." By July 1806, only sixteen French families remained. English traveler Thomas Ashe reported that were it not for the peach brandy trade on the Ohio River, the settlement would be "entirely abandoned."

Despite this pessimism, Gallipolis consisted of more than fifty houses by 1807. Four years later, the economic fortunes of Gallipolis had improved. About seventy houses provided homes for approximately three hundred people, mostly "Americans," who had drained surrounding marshes, improved the orchards, and constructed new buildings. Town lots sold for as much as two hundred dollars. A brick courthouse, an academy, and a Masonic lodge gave the community the appearance of stability and permanence, while a tavernkeeper, two blacksmiths, two tanners, three storekeepers, three master masons, and a half-dozen carpenters kept busy about the town. English traveler John Melish now reported that Gallipolis was "quite healthy" and enjoyed a "beautiful situation." By 1817, its citizens boasted of a community with a hundred homes. By that time, however, most of the "poor starved sickly looking Frenchmen" had left Gallipolis. Moreover, Yankee settlers and land speculators had purchased all but 912 acres of the French Grant to the south. Only eight or ten French families still resided at Gallipolis.

By the turn of the nineteenth century, then, Gallipolis was in transition from a French- to an English-speaking community because it did not have a consistent or sufficient influx of French immigrants and because so few wanted to stay and preserve French culture in a frontier enclave. Ultimately, the frontier rather than French culture determined the fate of Gallipolis. There, life proved difficult, the amenities few, and social graces were seldom practiced. Those who adapted to their physical and cultural environment adjusted the best and even prospered. But societal distinctiveness, without support or will, could not long endure, and Gallipolis gave way to American culture. Moreover, the river trade brought ruffians to the settlement, whom town authorities tried to control by teaching them proper respect for law and order at the whipping post, which did little for the perpetuation of French culture. By the end of the frontier period, however, Gallipolis had become an important trading and banking center for Gallia County, and the local economy was firmly tied to agriculture, mining, lumbering, and the river trade. But poor lands nearby, better opportunities elsewhere, and absorption by the American frontier people prevented the recreation of French society and the perpetuation of French culture. The settlement of Gallipolis would endure and modestly prosper, but it would do so as an American rather than a Gallic community on the Ohio frontier.

* * *

Far to the north of the Ohio River settlements, on July 4, 1796, General Moses Cleaveland reached the eastern border of the Western Reserve. His party of fifty-two included two women and several children. The men had signed on "as in the army, for two years, providing it took so long." That evening the group camped at Conneaut and prepared to survey six townships of the Western Reserve. One township would provide the site for a settlement or "capital," at which the company would locate a sawmill and gristmill. The other township lands would be allotted to the shareholders for sale to actual settlers. Cleaveland, the agent of the Connecticut Land Company in charge of surveying, had invested $32,600 in the enterprise and therefore had considerable interest in the settlement of the Western Reserve.

On his way to Ohio, Cleaveland met with the Massasagas who lived near the Pennsylvania border, and once more the clash of cultures became readily apparent. The Massasagas, a small, poor, and weak band of Indians, expected the stronger and richer Americans to give them presents, because generosity reflected the concern and consideration of leaders for those who were less fortunate and under their power. Cleaveland, however, merely dispensed a few trinkets and whiskey. Later he arrogantly reflected that he had informed them that "to be liberal of others property was no evidence of true friendship; those people I represented lived by industry, and to give away their property lavishly, to those who live in indolence and by begging, would be no deed of charity." The Massasagas did not trouble Cleaveland's party after that admonishment, and the surveying proceeded as planned.

Cleaveland's group had given "three cheers" when they reached the Ohio frontier, where a surveyor's post marked the northwest corner of Pennsylvania, after a hard journey from eastern New York. They had begun on April 28. But now, Cleaveland wrote, the "difficulties, perplexities and hardships" of the trail were behind, and they were on "the good and promised land." They could hardly contain their exuberance. To celebrate, the men fired fifteen rounds in honor of the United States and another to pay tribute to Connecticut, after which they began drinking. They toasted the president, "New Connecticut," the Connecticut Land Company, and procreation, with Cleaveland lifting his cup and saying: "May these sons and daughters multiply in sixteen years sixteen times fifty." Then they drank some more, "several pails of grog" in all, christened their site Port Independence, ate supper, and "retired in remarkable good order." The party then spent the next two days where Conneaut Creek empties into Lake Erie, building a cabin for their supplies and putting the camp in order, and on July 7 the surveyors, axmen, chainmen, and rodmen began their work in earnest.

It did not go well. The axmen had considerable work cutting down trees to enable the surveyors to make their sightings. The marsh lands proved difficult to negotiate and the mosquitoes insufferable. Their supplies ran low, and packers from their commissary of Port Independence had difficulty locating the four surveying teams; the men often ate wild berries and broiled rattlesnake, which they washed down with rum. The berries gave them cramps, and the water caused dysentery and the mosquitoes malaria. For a time they endured with remarkable good cheer, returning to their camp at night to "push about the bottle."

Before Cleaveland had left Connecticut, his employers had determined that a settlement be laid out in the center of the Reserve on Lake Erie to provide a base of operations for land sales and trade. On July 22, Cleaveland was off the mouth of the Cuyahoga River in a boat with a scouting party, and the surrounding land looked as favorable for a settlement to him as it had to Major Robert Rogers, who had met Pontiac there in 1760, and to the Moravians who had sought temporary shelter along the river's banks in 1786. Several dilapidated log cabins built by French fur traders marked the site. Here the Muskingum-Cuyahoga Indian trail from the Ohio River reached Lake Erie and the Lake Shore Trail. Cleaveland believed that this location had great potential for a settlement and that immigrant land buyers would find "a lean, but dry and pleasant soil." Quickly, Cleaveland's party built cabins for the surveyors, the commissary, and Job Stiles and his wife Tabitha Cumi, aged seventeen, who would manage the stores. By October 1, they had surveyed and platted a square mile at the mouth of the Cuyahoga River, 220 lots, and two major streets. The mapmaker, however, who perhaps had never seen Cleaveland's name written, designated the site "Cleveland." The error went undetected until it was too late.

By mid-October, Cleaveland's supplies were exhausted, and the chill autumn air and cold, rainy weather hinted of worse to come. His men were tired, and their morale was so low that they threatened to quit. Cleaveland understood, and apparently took issue with those at home who wanted quicker results. On August 5 he had made his first report to the Connecticut Land Company, in which he complained: "Those who are meanly envying the compensation and sitting at their ease and see their prosperity increasing at the loss of health, ease, and comfort of others, I wish might experience the hardships for one month; if not then satisfied their grumbling would give me no pain." On September 30 Cleaveland attempted to prevent a mutiny by giving each man a stake in his work by preparing a contract that granted the forty-one who signed the right to purchase a township for one dollar per acre. For this privilege, however, they had to remain with the company for the remainder of the year and agree to help settle eleven families in 1797, eighteen a year later, and twelve in 1799, as well as build cabins, clear land, and each plant eight acres of wheat. This benefit temporarily buoyed their spirits, but it did not prove long-lasting. On the 18th, Cleaveland had his crew pack up and return to Connecticut. At that time, only four ranges had been surveyed from the southern base line and the eastern border of the Reserve.

John Milton Holley, one of the surveyors who worked on the layout of Cleveland, wrote in his journal that they "left Cuyahoga at 3 o'clock 17 minutes for HOME." John Stiles, Tabitha, and Edward Paine agreed to stay as caretakers until Cleaveland returned with another party the next spring. Then Holley wrote that fourteen men boarded a boat and ran east with the wind in the sail. Holley noted that "never . . . were fourteen men more anxious to pursue an object than they were to get forward." Elijah and Anna Gun together with James and Eunice Kingsbury and their three children, one of whom would not live through the winter, stayed at Conneaut.

Although disappointed that not more lands had been surveyed for sale, the directors of the Connecticut Land Company were not discouraged and authorized the work to continue. In the spring of

1797, a new surveying party of sixty-three returned to the Western Reserve, but Cleaveland did not go with them. Seth Pease led this party, which made Cleveland their base of operations on June 1. This time they planned better. The surveyors were amply fed from the supply house, and they planted a garden to supplement their diet. Although the surveyors ate better, malaria and dysentery still plagued them. Amzi Atwater, a member of one surveying party, wrote in his journal that "these were days and nights of sorrow and affliction." The crewmen treated themselves with quinine extracted from Peruvian bark and tartar emetic and endured.

By mid-September they completed the township lines east of the Cuyahoga River and laid off the lots and major streets of Cleveland, which they marked with stakes. The surveyors also had laid out 160-acre farms in four townships. They did not, however, reserve sections for the support of the schools or churches. In contrast to the Ohio Company at Marietta, the Connecticut Land Company cared only about selling the lands. The settlers could solve the problems of education and religion as they saw fit. In December, when Seth Pease reported the completion of their work, the directors of the Connecticut Land Company began allocating the lands among shareholders, by holding a drawing for lots with the order determined by the amount of an individual's investment. After this distribution, each shareholder was responsible for his own lands. Some chose to sell for a profit, while others moved to the Western Reserve and Cleveland. With no unified group organized to come at once to the Western Reserve as at Marietta and Gallipolis, and with the best access to this isolated region by boat on Lake Erie, people could not easily move into the area as they did at Cincinnati. As a result, the settlements of the Western Reserve, particularly Cleveland, grew slowly, even though the directors offered town lots free to blacksmiths and mechanics.

At Cleveland, the proprietors asked $50 per lot, but potential settlers considered $25 per lot overpriced. The proprietors also fixed the price for 10-acre out-lots at $3 per acre; they priced 20-acre tracts at $2 per acre and 100-acre tracts at $1.50 per acre. Town lots required the full amount paid in cash, while the proprietors accepted 20 percent down for the out-lots, with three annual installments plus interest. Lands often could be purchased more

cheaply in areas more healthful than the mosquito-ridden Cuyahoga River valley. As a result, settlement lagged so severely that on
July 17, 1800, Turhand Kirtland, an agent for the Connecticut Land
Company, wrote to Moses Cleaveland that only three men inhabited the settlement of Cleveland, and two planned to leave because
the lots were too expensive. With 2-acre town lots selling for a reduced price of $25, he believed that he would "never expect to see it
settled." Because the "universal scarcity of cash" made land sales
extremely difficult, Kirtland wanted authorization to sell land for
horses, cattle, and provisions, or on credit, but he did not get it.

Cleveland's location, however, made it impossible to ignore. By
the turn of the nineteenth century, a distillery and a gristmill provided a market for nearby farmers, and a merchant carried basic
necessities for home and farm. By 1800, approximately one thousand settlers lived east of the Cuyahoga. To the west, the land claims
of the Delawares, Shawnees, and Wyandots were not resolved until
July 4, 1805. Until Indian lands were alienated, many potential immigrants hesitated to purchase acreage west of the Cuyahoga in the
Western Reserve. Cheaper lands to the south continued to hamper
quick sales and settlement by the Connecticut Land Company.

Cleveland also continued to languish because the harbor needed
improvement and dredging so that larger boats could negotiate the
channel of the Cuyahoga River. In November 1801, Samuel Huntington, a proprietor of the Connecticut Land Company, claimed that if
the people of Cleveland had a harbor, they could "supply the Ohio
Country . . . cheaper than they can be supplied from Pitt." At that
time, Cleveland still proved too difficult to reach by land or Lake
Erie to make it an attractive settlement. As a result, by 1810, Cleveland had a population of only fifty-seven people, who lived in sixteen houses and supported two taverns, two stores, and one school.
The settlers on the nearby farms still struggled to produce a surplus,
and local trade remained confined to flour, pork, and whiskey, but
not in sufficient quantities to stimulate the local market. Moreover,
because Cleveland remained isolated, a merchant class could not
stimulate settlement and economic development. In October 1811,
John Melish, who visited Cleveland, observed that some of the
mills were "idle and appeared to be going to decay." The inhabitants
looked "pale and sickly," and the surrounding area appeared grim

"without a single object to exhilarate the imagination, or cheer the spirits." With wheat bringing one dollar per bushel, flour seven dollars per barrel, horses and cows one hundred dollars and twenty-five dollars each respectively, and board at the tavern three dollars per week, Cleveland was a pricey settlement.

Cleveland would not prosper until after the War of 1812, when peace and safety enabled the federal government to open northwestern Ohio for settlement and until road and harbor improvements along with cheap water transportation helped make the settlement a major market town. Although the Connecticut Land Company financed road construction from Buffalo to the Reserve along the Lake Trail in 1801 to link Cleveland with Albany and the Mohawk Valley via the Genesee Road, little economic improvement resulted. Another road ran from Pittsburgh to the Mahoning River valley by the early nineteenth century. Other roads linked Cleveland with towns along the Ohio River. The roads leading to Cleveland, however, remained poor. As late as 1819, Seth Tracy, a land agent, complained that he had great difficulty selling land east of Cleveland because the roads were "extremely bad." Without improved transportation and harbor facilities, then, settlement lagged. Even so, the immigrants who came usually stayed. Although homesickness for New England caused some Yankees to leave "with the determination never to see the Reserve again," others remained. Perhaps they did so, as immigrant Margaret Dwight observed, because "it is not that the . . . country is so good, but because the journey is so bad."

* * *

While Cleveland struggled, settlers drifted into the Reserve from Pennsylvania and established communities, such as Youngstown in 1796, in the Mahoning River valley. Others came from New England. On June 10, 1799, for example, with two months' travel from the Connecticut town of Goshen behind them, David Hudson's little band of settlers arrived on the site of their new home, via Lake Erie and Cleveland. On the plat maps of the Western Reserve it was designated as township 4 of range 10. Hudson and five others had acquired title to the tract of 16,000 acres the previous year from the Connecticut Land Company at a price of thirty-four cents per acre.

Hudson claimed that he had "got religion" and intended to establish a colony in the Western Reserve "based on moral and religious principles." Repenting his life as a freethinker and follower of Thomas Paine and David Hume, he decided to remove "to the solitary wilds of the Connecticut Western Reserve," which he considered to be a "howling wilderness." There, with his "former sins" unknown, he would make an "atonement" for his transgressions by founding a town and administering it on Christian principles, emphasizing law, order, morality, and education. Hudson, however, was less than honest about his motives. In January 1798 he had purchased the township, and as early as 1794 he had invested $1,500 in Western Reserve lands. If his soul now felt better, it was because he had the opportunity to make his fortune in western lands.

During the summer of 1799, Hudson's party surveyed town lots, built cabins, and cleared fields to attract other newcomers. Hudson returned to Connecticut in the autumn, and the following spring he brought his wife and five children and others to the Ohio settlement. Hudson and his colleagues had their tract surveyed and began selling land for $1.00 to $2.50 per acre, a price that had greater appeal than the lots in and near Cleveland or elsewhere in the Reserve, where speculators asked $5.00 per acre. Two years later, the Trumbull County commissioners bestowed the name of its founder on the thriving settlement. In 1802, a Congregational church, school, and sawmill provided services, and by 1806 a merchant, who brought his supplies through Cleveland, had opened for business.

With a well-organized founding, Hudson grew rapidly. The malodorous pits of a tanyard and the whine and rumble of lumber and flour mills proclaimed the prosperity of the community to travelers along the roads that linked Hudson with Cleveland, Pittsburgh, and the state capital in Chillicothe. More settlers arrived, and by the mid-1820s, at the end of the frontier period, Hudson had become a regular stagecoach stop between Cleveland and Pittsburgh and a mail distribution center for the surrounding area. Here, Yankee immigrants transferred New England culture to the Western Reserve. In Hudson, their architectural legacy remained visual evidence of their cultural heritage around the town square. Moreover, the spirit of New England and the old Puritan reverence for education flickered bright as David Hudson helped lay the cornerstone for the Presbyterian-oriented Western Reserve College, whose purpose was to "prepare competent men to fill the cabinet, the bench, the bar and the pulpit." In January 1825, the commissioners of the Presbytery of the Western Reserve selected the town for the site of Western Reserve College, largely as the result of an outpouring of public support. David Hudson raised more than $7,000 and personally donated 160 acres for its location. The dedication address, delivered in Latin on April 26, 1826, by the Reverend Caleb Pitkin, brought forth an outpouring of community pride in the new school and marked as well as anything the end of the Ohio frontier.

To the south of the Western Reserve during the 1790s, speculators, farmers, and craftsmen founded other settlements, often called "stations." On December 1, 1790, for example, Nathaniel Massie contracted with nineteen men to settle in the Virginia Military District. Massie intended his settlement, which was located about one-third of the way between the mouth of the Scioto River and Cincinnati on the Ohio, to lure others into the area to buy land. He gave each man an in-lot, a 4-acre out lot, and a 100-acre tract, provided they built cabins, cleared land, and planted crops. By March, Massie's Station, later called Manchester, had been tenuously established. Massie used the settlement as a base of operations for his surveys in the interior.

In March 1790, Israel Ludlow, a speculator at Cincinnati, established a settlement known as Ludlow's Station about five miles up Mill Creek in the Miami Purchase. Ten men built a blockhouse and began clearing the nearby lands. A month later, Ludlow wrote to Jonathan Dayton, one of Symmes's associates, that the settlement was "flourishing well," despite the capture by Indians of a boy who had gone to drive the family's cows home. About this same time, twelve miles up the Great Miami River, John Dunlap established a station with thirty settlers, including women and children, who had bought land from Symmes. Renewed war with the Indians, however, restricted the expansion of settlements in the interior until after the Treaty of Greenville in 1795. Even so, between 1788 and 1795, some thirty settlements had been planted in Hamilton County alone. Fourteen of these settlements had been founded by loosely organized family-related groups. Only four settlements originated from the location of a single person, while five sprang from the location of single families. Family ties and informal social and community relationships were more important for the establishment of settlements on the Ohio frontier than individual action—although fourteen towns laid out by surveyor James Kilbourne to the north provide an exception.

These stations often remained for only a short time. Indeed, the founders considered them temporary until they could establish farms and, once the army brought peace with the Indians, move beyond blockhouses and palisades. Then individuals and single families would settle the land. By 1800, twelve of the thirty settlements in Hamilton County established by 1795 had ceased to exist. In contrast to the settlements of Marietta, Gallipolis, and Hudson, for example, many of the early communities established in Ohio were not highly organized affairs. Most were designed to place families on the land for the purpose of luring other buyers into an area. But as the frontier people located more appealing and distant lands, lost their claims for want of payment to speculators or the government, or just moved on for a host of private reasons, the settlements struggled, remained small and nondescript, or returned to nature. Ludlow's Station, for example, apparently had been abandoned by the time General Wayne moved north in 1794, although settlers had drifted back to the site by spring 1795. Dunlap's Station had an even briefer existence. By the summer of 1790, Dunlap had failed to gain title to the one thousand acres that he had purchased, and the settlers who had paid him money for smaller tracts of land near the settlement began giving him trouble. Indian attacks made matters worse. After St. Clair's defeat, the settlers abandoned the station in November 1791. Transition, then, rather than permanence characterized the settlement of the Ohio frontier, where people were always in a state of becoming rather than stability.

Some settlements developed not because of economic motives but because of religious unity. In 1812, for example, Jesse Thomas and Robert Carothers laid off a town site about fifteen miles southwest of Steubenville, with the intent of making money from the sale of lands. But it really amounted to very little until an influx of North Carolina Quakers, members of the Society of Friends, vitalized the community, stamping upon it a character that is discernible today. By 1807 it was their town, and they named it Mount Pleasant. Within a few years, the vigorous and thrifty Quaker community sought to organize a yearly meeting of elders. In 1814 they began the construction of the first permanent Yearly Meeting House west of the Appalachians. Completed in 1815, it seated two thousand Friends.

To the south on the Ohio River, James Poage had more success than Jesse Thomas and Robert Carothers. In 1812 he laid out a town in the Virginia Military District with an eye to the commercial potential of the passing river traffic. He called the site Staunton. Four years later, in 1816, residents of the village changed its name to Ripley in honor of Eleazer Wheelock Ripley, a general in the War of 1812. Although the town gained prosperity as a river port and shipping point for the produce of the country, its chief notoriety derived from its characterization by sympathizers of slavery as a "damned abolitionist hell-hole." Although escaped slaves from Kentucky crossed the river at Ripley as early as 1815, the town did not become an important destination for fugitive slaves until the end of the frontier period during the mid-1820s.

In the spring of 1815, another individual acting alone established a settlement to the north on Congress Lands. Abraham Trux erected a log cabin along the Wyandot Trail near the headwaters of the Huron River. Trux may have passed through that country as a sutler during the late war, when, following the fall of Detroit, several hundred militia under General Reasin Beall widened the path which led from Fort Pitt to the mouth of the Sandusky River into a wagon road to improve the movement of supplies. In any event, Trux liked the land, and he settled there. If this adventuresome pioneer staked his claim to a piece of land on the edge of the Western Reserve to find solitude in the wilderness, he did not have it for long. Soon other frontiersmen and their families were hewing logs for houses which they erected nearby, probably lured to the site by hopes for mutual security and companionship.

Unknowingly, perhaps, they built their town near the Richland and Huron county line. As the village grew, it expanded across the boundary, thereafter giving the village the dubious distinction of being located in two counties. As they went about the task of town building, no one realized the problems that this accident of geogra-

phy and enterprise would create for future generations. With an optimistic eye toward an as yet entirely imaginary importance, they
called their settlement Paris.

The work of cutting timber, removing stumps, and clearing land
for agriculture was hard, but it brought acknowledgment and
reward. About 1817, the federal government, during the administration of James Monroe, initiated postal service. The citizens built a
school the next year, and in 1819 a Presbyterian church. Not to be
outdone, the Methodists followed with one of their own in 1821.
As the town and the Western Reserve increased in population, the
settlers built new roads, and communication and transportation improved. Beginning in the early 1820s, a stage line linked Paris with
Columbus and Portland (Sandusky).

As the town and countryside prospered, more New Englanders
arrived with land warrants in their pockets and claimed farms in
the surrounding area. During the early 1820s, village expansion was
haphazard. Apparently, no one gave much thought to platting, that
is, to laying out the town in a consistent form and fashion, until
1825. On May 17 of that year, Trux and two other real estate devel-
opers surveyed the town and divided it into forty-seven lots, all of
which sold within two years. Additional surveys followed as more
immigrants arrived, and the town prospered from agriculture, but
it would not change its name to Plymouth until 1838, after learning
that another Ohio town had taken the same name.

Other settlements, such as Steubenville, have their origin in military posts. In 1786, the government authorized the army to establish
Fort Steuben on the Ohio River to provide protection for the survey
of the Seven Ranges. Although the fort burned in 1790 and the soldiers went to other locations where the need was greater, the
squatters whom the army also had intended to drive away used the
location for a settlement, and in time the town grew up on the old
fort site.

To the west, Fort Loramie became located by accident as much as
by design. This settlement had its origin in 1769, six years after the
Peace of Paris ended the French and Indian War, when Pierre
Loramie drifted into the back country of Ohio. Loramie probably
entered from Canada, perhaps passing through Detroit or Vincennes. He may have been a Jesuit priest intent on inciting the

Indians against the British as well as converting nonbelievers and saving souls. Or he may have been a mere trader who preferred the solitude of the frontier to community life. Later, however, Colonel John Johnston, the Indian agent at Piqua, referred to Loramie as the "French Father," but without the appropriate historical records, no one can be certain of his origin or personal motives other than his desire to establish a trading post among the Indians.

Loramie chose his site well. He located on the southern end of the portage between present-day Loramie Creek and the St. Marys River. This well-traveled twelve-mile portage was a major pathway that various tribes used as they moved between the Great Lakes and the Ohio River. Loramie conducted a thriving business, particularly for raiding parties of Shawnees who made their way to strike settlements in Kentucky. Loramie's trading post offered the last opportunity for those tribesmen to acquire needed items before embarking by canoe down the creek and into the Great Miami River as they made their way south. Loramie's source of supply, however, remains a mystery.

By the beginning of the American Revolution, Loramie's trading post was well known among the Indians, British, and Americans on the Ohio frontier. Although the British did not control him, they were content to use the tribesmen against the Americans whenever possible, and Loramie's store became not only an important source of military supply for the Indians, but also a staging ground for their raiding activities throughout the area. Loramie's trading post became so notorious for its link with the hostile tribes that General George Rogers Clark moved against it in his 1782 campaign against the Shawnees. At that time a mounted contingent of 150 men, commanded by Colonel Benjamin Logan, overwhelmed, sacked, and burned the trading post.

The ashes of Loramie's store remained undisturbed for a dozen years, although Indians and backwoodsmen continued to use the portage. Peace, however, did not come easily to the region. In March 1794, General Anthony Wayne was at Fort Greenville planning his strategy, which included building a fort at the site of Loramie's store. In August, Wayne's victory over the Indians at Fallen Timbers temporarily delayed that construction and changed his plans. Instead of erecting a full-fledged military post at the site of Loramie's trading post, Wayne had decided by mid-October 1794 to build only a blockhouse and storage facilities. This supply depot would serve the northern garrisons at Forts Adams, Wayne, and Defiance, provide a base for the distribution of annuities to the Indians, and establish a postal point between Cincinnati and Fort Wayne. Construction began in September 1795, and by mid-December the work had been completed. Wayne appointed Captain Edward M. Butler post commandant and ordered that it be named Fort Loramie. The garrison, consisting of one officer, two noncommissioned officers, and eighteen enlisted men, settled down to the task of managing a major supply post in the Old Northwest as well as giving protection to travelers over the portage and to settlers who might venture into the area.

Fort Loramie continued to serve as a supply depot through the War of 1812. When the war ended in 1815, however, the army abandoned the post and turned the storehouse over to James E. Furrow, who operated it as a trading post, tavern, and post office. By 1820, when Furrow gave up his business, a few settlers had built cabins about a half-mile south of the fort site, and a town was in the making. With the Indian and British problems solved, immigrants moved into western Ohio, and the land around Fort Loramie proved bountiful. As the population in the countryside increased, the town also expanded. Some people called it Fort Loramie, but not all. In fact, most of the new settlers were of German heritage, and a substantial number moved into the region from the New Berlin area of Stark County at the close of the frontier period. These settlers called the village "Berlin" to remind them of their previous home. They were a tightly knit group of hard-working farmers and devout Catholics, who cleared the fields, reaped abundant harvests, and kept to themselves. They tolerated immigrants of non-German stock, but bought them out whenever possible. Soon Fort Loramie became a solidly entrenched settlement that perpetuated German culture for the remainder of the nineteenth century.

The early settlements in Ohio, then, were established in many ways. Organized groups from New England bent on profiting from the sale of lands that they purchased cheaply from the federal government or Connecticut created well-defined communities over time. Other settlements were founded by loose associations of family groups or by individuals, usually for the purpose of developing nearby lands for agriculture, which they had acquired from a specu-lator or the government. Some settlements grew from the sites of military and trading posts. In each case, however, the people who established the settlements brought their cultural characteristics to the Ohio frontier. In some areas, New England customs prevailed, while Virginia and Pennsylvania backwoods or even French and German characteristics or religious practices gave identity to these new settlements.

In September 1790, a traveler who passed through Marietta noted the "industry, sobriety and good order of the Newenglanders." But in the Virginia Military District and the Miami Purchase, moccasins were perfectly acceptable forms of attire, while settlers in Gallipolis and Mount Pleasant gave spoken English a peculiar sound that marked their heritage. In every case, the lure of the land and oppor-tunity brought men, women, and children to the settlements on the Ohio frontier, no matter their cultural origin. Some sought profit through land speculation or trade. Others sought economic gain, se-curity, and independence that only the ownership of land could provide. The manner in which these early settlements developed, however, ultimately depended on the frontier people in town and country.

8.

FARM COUNTRY

The Ohio settlers were a profit-minded people. The acquisition of land, of course, enabled freedom and independence within a social and political system that honored the accumulation of property and granted status and power to those who acquired it. Beyond the realm of the speculators, however, frontier lands had little value unless a settler could use them to earn a profit. On the Ohio frontier, livestock raising provided the best way to make money quickly. After the Treaty of Greenville in 1795, most of Ohio became relatively safe from Indian attack. New settlers now streamed into the rich lands of southern and central Ohio, and they brought hogs with them. Indeed, hogs became the chief livestock on the Ohio frontier, and the hog crop provided the basis for one of the state's earliest industries—meat packing.

At first, though, frontier farm families gave very little attention to the feeding, sheltering, or breeding of their hogs. Instead, early Buckeye families were primarily concerned with clearing land, planting seed, and building log cabins to have both bread and shelter for their first winter on the new land. They allowed their hogs to run free in the woods, fend for themselves, and root for beechnuts, grubs, or anything else edible. These long-legged, narrow-bodied frontier pigs became fiercely independent with unfriendly dispositions, and they were commonly known by a variety of names, including razorbacks, elmpeelers, land sharks, alligators, and prairie rooters. When butchering time came in the late autumn, farmers drove their hogs into the corn fields to fatten for a month; or, if the hogs were too wild, they hunted them with a rifle, because rounding up the herd was nearly impossible. The razorback was poorly suited for commercial pork packing because it yielded small hams and only a little lard, but it provided the frontier family's meat supply for the coming year. Bacon, smoked hams, salted pork, sausage, and lard were basic staples for the frontier family's diet, while lard oil fueled their lamps.

Virtually all farm families raised hogs for their own use and for sale, but farmers had great difficulty identifying their swine among the others that roamed about the neighborhood, and few farmers could afford the time or labor to build wooden fences to confine their hogs. To solve the problem of identification, they resorted to the practice of notching the ears with a specific pattern which they then registered with a local official. In 1796, Patrick Fagan in Cuyahoga County's Anderson Township recorded his mark as "a crop off the left Ear." At the turn of the nineteenth century, Samuel Dunn, a farmer near Hamilton, advertised that he held five hogs that had wandered onto his property. Each had a crop off the left ear and a slit in the right. The owner could claim them by customarily paying the cost of the newspaper notice. By January 1806, Duncan McArthur near Chillicothe apparently was having trouble keeping his hogs from being collected by others, either intentionally or accidentally. He reported in the local newspaper that his registered mark in the townships of Scioto, Union, and Concord was a crop and a slit in each ear, and he warned buyers to beware of purchasing hogs with that mark without his permission. Earmarks, of course, helped farmers identify their hogs, but those like McArthur who let their swine roam about several townships continued to have problems locating their hogs that only proper fencing and better management could solve. The territorial and state legislature authorized township clerks to register a farmer's earmark to avoid as much duplication as possible and to aid identification of swine. Anyone convicted of altering an earmark could be fined fifty dollars. Hogs, like other livestock, however, were liquid capital on the hoof. Once they were sold out of the neighborhood and butchered, ownership could not be proven. Still, earmarks provided some legal protection for frontier farmers.

Ohio frontiersmen, however, lacked an adequate means for transporting their corn to markets over the mountains. Consequently, they chose to sell their corn in the form of pork or whiskey, since more corn could be taken in a pig or whiskey jug than in grain sacks strapped over a mule or loaded in a wagon. Before the construction of a railroad network in the 1850s, which would transport the corn crop to market cheaply and efficiently, about half of the annual crop was converted into pork or whiskey, which brought fifty cents per gallon during the later frontier period. The remainder was consumed locally or shipped down the Ohio and Mississippi rivers to New Orleans. In addition, bumper corn harvests decreased the market price and encouraged farmers to feed even more hogs, and if hog prices increased, they sold less corn.

Buckeye farmers sold their hog crop either on the hoof or already dressed. As early as 1810, Ohio farmers drove an estimated forty thousand hogs over the Appalachians to the eastern markets, and during the War of 1812, "vast numbers" of northern Ohio hogs were driven to Detroit and other military garrisons in that region. Later, some of those hogs were driven to Detroit from northern Ohio, then slaughtered and shipped to Montreal by the Great Lakes and to New York City via the Erie Canal, which opened in 1825. Through the 1840s, however, thousands of hogs would be driven eastward each year. Even though the first steamboat traveled down the Ohio River from Pittsburgh to New Orleans in 1811, the river trade would not become important until the steamboats began plying the waters upstream in 1817, bringing salt for pork packing.

In the meantime, Ohio farmers packed their pork as best they could at home and drove additional animals to market. The most important swine route eastward followed the present-day thoroughfares of U.S. highways 35 and 66 through Gallipolis and the Kanawha Valley. Although the distance to market was long, hogs were frequently driven with cattle and allowed to forage on the wasted feed. Hogs were driven at the rate of eight to fifteen miles per day, and two months or more might pass before the drive terminated at the eastern market. If fed and driven properly, these swine would maintain and even gain weight over the long trail drive. There, farmers frequently bought the pigs for five to six cents per pound and fattened them for slaughter. Others were sold directly to the packers at Philadelphia, Baltimore, and New York City, where they soon became common fare in the mess of the navy or merchant marine, or on the family dinner table. Although drovers who took their swine eastward over the major routes had difficulty enough, these routes were easy compared to those encountered by drovers who tried to supply the Detroit market. During the winter of 1819, for example, Jeremiah Butterfield drove a large number of hogs from Butler County to Detroit in hopes of earning a greater profit than from the Cincinnati packers. At best he had only a trail to follow, and after a heavy snowstorm he had to use his horse to break a path for his hogs to follow.

Although hog droving was an important annual event, the home pork-packing business also brought money or goods of exchange into the home. Merchants dealt in a wide variety of goods, including farm produce, and they provided a limited but significant market for frontier farmers. In early December 1793, for example, A. Hunt & Co. at Cincinnati advertised to purchase a "quantity of corn-fed pork." It offered to pay cash at the store, but probably not for the purchase of live hogs. Rather, the company sought smoked, salted, or pickled pork that men and women had prepared on the farms. With specie always in short supply on the frontier, pork became a form of currency for daily trade. In 1800, because of an insufficient amount of currency in circulation, the editor of the *Scioto Gazette* announced that he would take pork for subscription payments. From the beginning of settlement, merchants accepted pork in exchange for dry goods, groceries, and salt. Indeed, if they wanted to make a sale, they had little choice. After they received pork for payments, they had to find a market, usually down the Ohio River. These frontier merchants quickly learned that southern and eastern markets could be reached by making shipments downriver on flat-boats or keelboats to New Orleans, where the pork could be sold in the southern trade to planters who preferred to raise cotton and to feed Ohio pork to their slaves. Or it could be transshipped by ocean vessel to eastern, Caribbean, European, or South American markets.

By 1800, the provisioning trade in pork provided an important market for frontier farmers. In February, Rice Bulloch promised to pay cash for 20,000 pounds of pork delivered to his premises in

Hamilton by March 1. In October of that year, John McDougal in Chillicothe advertised to buy 150,000 pounds of "good corn fed pork" at two dollars per hundredweight, payable in merchandise with delivery contracted between December 15 and January 15. For any farmer who could furnish a "considerable quantity" of that amount, McDougal promised to pay "part cash." McDougal intended to send this pork down the Scioto and Ohio rivers to New Orleans in time to capitalize on high springtime prices. Money could be made by frontier farmers and merchants alike, and McDougal did not want to miss this opportunity. As a result, he required the farmers who wanted to sell pork to him to sign contracts, which he considered "bonds of compliance," and he warned those farmers who failed to deliver their pork on time that he would sue them for breach of contract.

Some merchants apparently preferred to slaughter the frontiersmen's hogs themselves. In November 1801, for example, W. Stanley in Hamilton offered to purchase "large corn fed pork," for which he agreed to pay $2.50 per hundredweight, half in cash and half in merchandise. In January 1803, Abner Ammidon, who also operated along the Miami River in Hamilton, wanted to buy hogs that weighed at least two hundred pounds for packing. Other merchants, such as those in Cincinnati and Chillicothe, also began buying live hogs. These early packers preferred "really fat" hogs, for which they paid as much as $3 per hundredweight in 1809. The farmers who delivered their swine on the hoof could watch as they were weighed and killed at Joseph Kerr's slaughterhouse in Chillicothe to guarantee that they received a fair payment.

Farm-packed pork, however, varied greatly in quality, and the "flabby, oily stuff" which reached either the local or the eastern markets was often nearly inedible. Consequently, to regulate pork packing, in 1802 the territorial legislature required inspection for all hog products exported. The meat had to be uniformly packed in properly marked white oak barrels that held 200 to 225 pounds of pork. Lard had to be packed tightly in 50-pound kegs and certified that it was mold-free before it could enter the export trade. Although this regulation helped improve the quality of pork sold beyond the boundary, the product did not approach any degree of standardization until the packing industry moved from the frontier farm to the city. This move occurred largely because the packers preferred to handle live hogs themselves rather than the spoiled farm-packed pork or tainted carcasses which many farmers delivered to them. The packers in Cincinnati, Chillicothe, and Hamilton bought hogs from a number of producers and processed the animals in a uniform manner suitable for the demands of various markets.

Temperature, in the pre-refrigeration age of commercial pork packing, was the critical factor that relegated meat packing to wintertime. Since the carcass had to be thoroughly chilled before cutting, the packing season could not begin before the first frost, and generally not until consistently cold weather assured the prevention of spoilage. Since the slaughtering and butchering activity was conducted in open buildings, in order to take advantage of the cold, the pork-packing industry tended to locate along the Ohio River, where the water helped moderate the cold as well as provided transportation of the product to market. Because of the packing industry's location, most Ohio pork reached the eastern market by way of New Orleans during the frontier period rather than overland on the hoof.

During the early developmental stages of the pork-packing industry, slaughterhouses and packinghouses were usually separate establishments. The slaughterhouses were located outside the residential areas in Cincinnati along Deer Creek and later along Mill Creek to keep the smell from the holding pens as far away from the public as possible. The packinghouses, in turn, were located along the wharves or as close to the river as possible in order to facilitate easy movement of the pork barrels down to the docks and the waiting steamboats. The division between the slaughterhouses and packinghouses may have been the result of European influence, because slaughter- and packinghouses on the continent remained separate well into the twentieth century. Certainly it indicated that the packers, at least at first, had no use for the heart, liver, and offal, since the slaughterers kept those parts of the hog in payment for doing the killing. In any event, the slaughterhouses were owned by only a few entrepreneurs. If the streets were not clogged with hogs on their way to the slaughterhouses, they were jammed with the draymen's wagons hauling carcasses to the packers.

Clearly, pigs meant profits to Ohio farmers, and swine were an essential part of daily life in the countryside and towns. In December 1805, an exhibit billed as the "Learned Pig" also provided entertainment for those who thought of hogs only as moneymakers for frontier farmers. For the residents of Chillicothe who wanted to pay twenty-five cents for the pleasure of being fooled, several hucksters exhibited a pig that could spell "common christian names," read printed or written words, tell time, and distinguish colors as well as add, subtract, multiply, and divide. He also could tell the name of the president of the United States, all to the accompaniment of a variety of music. Groups of "any number exceeding eight" could schedule a performance any time between 9:00 A.M. and 9:00 P.M. during a three-week stay.

Most farmers, however, concerned themselves with more practical matters. Farmers preferred contracting the sale of their hogs, because it relieved them of the trouble of driving their stock to market or packing the pork themselves. It also gave them a guaranteed price, often during the summer months, thereby enabling better planning and management of the farm. Almost all of the hogs for which the packers contracted were delivered live to the slaughterhouses, and Cincinnati soon became known as a "city of pigs" during the winter months.

* * *

In the decade following 1790, the frontier people occupied the Scioto Valley in present-day Ross, Pickaway, and Franklin counties, and moved up the Miami Valley to the Greenville Treaty Line, and they brought cattle with them. Perhaps as early as 1790, cattle had been driven to Marietta from Clarksburg, Virginia, and Kentucky farmers sold beeves in Cincinnati to local butchers and to St. Clair's army. In 1791, John Cleves Symmes wrote that the need for cattle was so great in the Ohio country that "people emigrating hither will do well to bring out their luggage by the labor of oxen . . . in lieu of horses." Ohio's frontier farmers raised cattle to meet their family's food needs for beef, and because surplus livestock brought cash to the pocketbook. As early as December 1793, cattle raising had became important on the Ohio frontier, and Obediah Scott near Cincinnati advertised that he would winter cattle on his property.

By so doing, he earned money and enabled frontier farmers to purchase several head of livestock on speculation in hope of selling them for a profit later when their own lands could support the fattening of cattle for sale. With a yoke of oxen valued at ten dollars and beef cattle at twenty dollars per head, Ohio's frontier farmers could earn needed income by selling cattle. If they lived sufficiently close to a town, local butchers provided a limited but important market. In April 1794, for example, John Miller established a butchering business in Cincinnati, buying cattle from nearby farmers.

Beef, however, did not preserve as well as pork with the use of traditional methods of salting and smoking, and in the absence of refrigeration, other than natural ice, preservation became a problem after the winter season. As a result, butchers and merchants who sold fresh beef could not purchase more than a few cattle at any one time. Although William McCluney advertised in March 1796 that he offered a "quantity of well saved beef" at his store in Cincinnati, consumers preferred fresh beef whenever possible. Spoilage, however, always remained a problem, and butchers tried to gauge their purchases to the local demand. With money "extremely scarce in this part of the country" by the turn of the nineteenth century, beef cattle brought as much as two dollars per hundredweight in Chillicothe. Although merchant John McDougal preferred to buy live beef after mid-October in 1802, butcher John Odle purchased beef throughout the year. When John McDougal began buying and packing beef in 1800, he hoped the trade would be of "considerable advantage to the farmers in Ross County," and with more than a little self-confidence he billed himself as the "Farmer's Perfect Friend." By selling fresh beef to "actual inhabitants" on Tuesdays, Thursdays, and Saturdays, he could plan his purchases from area farmers and reduce spoilage to a minimum. Local butchers, however, could purchase only a few cattle each week, and farmers who sought economic gain could meet disappointment. In 1807, for example, a farmer near Marietta complained that while John Clark advertised that he would give a "generous price" for fat cattle, anyone driving livestock to his business would receive neither a good price nor cash, and his advertisement was "wholly unworthy of notice."

Although a frontier farmer could occasionally sell a steer or heifer to a reasonably close butcher or merchant for either cash or goods, they soon raised more cattle than their families or the local population could consume, and they began thinking about driving cattle to eastern markets. As early as 1800, Scioto Valley cattlemen pastured livestock on the Darby Plains of west-central Ohio, and Ephraim Cutler, a merchant and land speculator at Amesville in Athens County, drove a herd of cattle that he had collected for payment of land and store bills to the east. Two years later he sent another herd to the South Branch of the Potomac River in Virginia to be fattened for later sale in the eastern cities. Quickly merchants and farmers realized that considerable profits could be made by trailing cattle to urban markets far from the Ohio frontier. In December 1803, John Ludwing advertised in Chillicothe that he would sell ninety to a hundred cattle for "ready money," apparently to anyone willing to take the speculative risk of making the purchase and driving them to market. The next autumn Jonathan Fowler drove the first herd from the Western Reserve to the Philadelphia market, and John McDougal soon advertised for "good fat steers" that weighed a minimum of four hundred pounds to be delivered to him at Chillicothe in early August 1805, for which he would cancel old debts or exchange for iron, glass, and other merchandise at "moderate prices." These purchases and traffic of live cattle from west to east helped establish agriculture on a commercial basis on the Ohio frontier almost from the beginning of settlement.

Yet Ohio became important frontier cattle country not because local land speculators and merchants began buying surplus cattle or taking beef in exchange for debts, but rather because some settlers came to Ohio specifically for the purpose of raising cattle. George and Felix Renick exemplify this breed of cattlemen. Felix Renick, of Irish descent and Virginia birth, first came to the Ohio frontier in the autumn of 1798 after hearing about the beauty and fertility of the western country from neighbors who had served in Lord Dunmore's campaign. Renick arrived at Marietta on horseback with two friends and obtained maps at the land office run by General Putnam. After deciding on the areas that merited a personal look, they traveled up the Muskingum River to Zane's Trace, where, at the current site of Zanesville, they found one log cabin and a "kind of excuse for a tavern," where the landlord busily traded whiskey to a group of Indians for their furs and skins. After spending the night, only to learn well into breakfast that they had been fed "panther meat," they departed in "pretty short order" up the Licking River above present-day Newark and headed west by compass and the sun until they struck Whetstone Creek and turned south.

Renick and his party reached Franklinton, near the site of present-day Columbus, which consisted of a "considerable number of log cabins, most of which had recently been put up, and were without chinking, daubing or doors." After resting for a few days, they proceeded down the Scioto River valley to the Ohio River. Along the Scioto, they found a cabin every six to ten miles. They crossed the Ohio River near the mouth of the Little Kanawha and proceeded home. Renick clearly liked what he saw along the Scioto. In May 1801 he returned to Chillicothe and purchased a large tract of land for $2.50 per acre. This land was located about four miles south of Chillicothe and became known as his Indian Creek farm. His brother George arrived a year later, opened a store in Chillicothe, and joined him in the cattle business.

Although Renick began raising corn and hogs like other frontier farmers, he and George quickly set their sights on becoming cattlemen. Using the experience that they had gained in the cattle country along the South Branch of the Potomac River, especially in Hardy County, Virginia, where stockmen fattened their cattle on unhusked corn in ten-acre lots during the autumn and winter before driving them to market, the Renicks built a herd constituted of their own cattle and those that they purchased from neighborhood farmers. Although the eastern markets were far away, Renick was convinced that he could take a herd of corn-fattened cattle overland and sell it for a profit. Until this time, the only cattle that had been trailed eastward to market had been grass-fattened beeves that allegedly not only were hardier than corn-fed animals but also could withstand the long drive without the significant loss of weight.

In the spring of 1805, George Renick drove sixty-eight head of corn-fattened cattle from the Scioto Valley to Baltimore and sold them for $32 per head, a price that justified driving corn-fed beef cattle to distant markets. Other cattlemen soon followed. In June 1808, Joseph Kerr advertised in Chillicothe that he would drive cattle east in August. He offered to take cattle for debts that farmers owed him, provided they were "fit for beef," lean, and aged two to five years. He also offered to buy cattle for cash at a "generous price," with payment made on his return at collection points in New Market and Sinking Spring. Cutler also drove cattle to York, Pennsylvania, and Allegheny County, Maryland, for fattening between 1809 and 1812. By the autumn of 1810, the cattle country had expanded northwest into Clark and Champaign counties near Springfield and Urbana. There, along the eastern fork of the Mad River, drovers from Lancaster, Philadelphia, and Baltimore visited the farmers each year to purchase cattle. This aspect of commercial agriculture on the Ohio frontier thrived, and the drovers brought the market to the door of the farmer.

In 1810, Felix Renick began buying stockers from outside the area to fatten on Scioto Valley corn. By 1811, the range cattle industry had spread across the grasslands or "barrens" between the Scioto and Little Miami river valleys, where one observer reported that the numbers of cattle "would be almost incredible could we tell them." Although the War of 1812 temporarily halted the improvement and expansion of the cattle industry on the Ohio frontier, Renick soon revived the driving of corn-fattened cattle to market when peace came in 1815. By that time, the number of cattle fattened in the Scioto Valley had doubled since 1810. Thereafter, farmers also began to expand the cattle business. Within a few years, herds as large as five hundred head fattened on the grass in Champaign County alone in 1815. There, farmers earned an estimated $100,000 for fat cattle, while they sold still more as feeders to cattlemen in the Miami and Scioto river valleys. During the summer of 1817, A. M. Drenning took six hundred cattle from Chillicothe to Baltimore, Philadelphia, and New York City. A butcher in New York reported that he had never seen "finer cattle" and predicted that on slaughter the beef would be equal or superior to that fattened near the city. Indeed, the cattle appeared "as fresh as if just taken off one of our Long Island farms." When the New York butchers offered $12 per hundredweight, Drenning refused, but he apparently sold when the bids reached $12.50 per hundred pounds.

Droving, of course, was no easy task. With the Atlantic markets more than four hundred miles or about forty days from the Scioto

River valley and with the Alleghenies and streams to cross, the task proved long and arduous. The routes of the drovers essentially were the same ones used by those who drove hogs to market, often along with the cattle that they had acquired. The most important trail for the Ohio drovers that led to the Baltimore market passed through Gallipolis and up the Great Kanawha River valley to Charleston, then on east to Maryland. A second route led though central Ohio that soon became known as the National Road, while northern cattlemen often sent their livestock along the Lake Erie shore to Buffalo and beyond. In 1805 George Renick followed an earlier portion of the central route when he drove his herd out of the Scioto Valley over Zane's Trace to Wheeling, where he struck the National Road that led to Cumberland, Frederick, and Baltimore, Maryland. This route drew the cattle from the upper Great Miami River valley as well as from the cattle counties of Ross, Pickaway, Licking, and Fairfield and eastern Ohio. Drovers preferred the National Road once out of Ohio because it had more bridges to facilitate the crossing of streams and rivers than any other road.

Drovers bound for the New York and Philadelphia markets turned northeast off the National Road at Cambridge and headed for Steubenville, where a ferry took the lead cattle across while the others swam for continuation on to Pittsburgh and beyond, where packers paid as much as seven cents per pound in 1814. No matter which fork in the road a drover took at Cambridge, the route was steep, hard, and slow going. Drovers on the National Road also could reach Philadelphia by turning north at Cumberland or Frederick, Maryland. Drovers from central and northern Ohio, who assembled their herds at Mt. Vernon, Wooster, Cleveland, Zanesville, Akron, and Ashtabula, used a trail that led along the lake though Erie, Pennsylvania, to Utica, New York, before it branched toward either Boston or New York City.

The Ohio drovers started their herds toward market any time between mid-February and June and reached the eastern buyers from mid-April to August. After that latter date, Ohio's corn-fattened cattle had to compete with grass-fed livestock from New York State, and the price usually fell. Drovers often sent other herds eastward, particularly to Philadelphia in the autumn, with arrival at the stockyards scheduled for December. The trails out of Ohio and beyond gave the drovers considerable problems, depending on the time of year. In the spring, swollen rivers and muddy roads slowed travel, but a dry summer meant fighting dust and tending lame cattle, particularly on macadam roads where the stones injured hooves. Always the drovers worried about the "drift" or "shrink" of the herd, that is, the loss of weight on the way to market. Cattle sent east from the Ohio frontier averaged about 900 to 1,000 pounds. Drovers believed that heavier cattle lost more weight on the trail. Usually they could expect a steer to lose 100 to 150 pounds. Along the way, the drovers depended on feeding and watering their cattle at stations, called "drove stands," where a farmer or local entrepreneur provided pens, forage, and corn for the livestock, at about twenty-five cents per bushel or thirty-eight cents per shock during the early 1820s, and provided food and lodging for his crew. With adequate feed, water, and a leisurely pace, they could get their cattle to market in good shape and earn a substantial profit, despite the distance and hardship.

Some Ohio cattlemen, such as the Renicks, often drove their own cattle to market. Others used a hired man or a freelance professional drover. The professional drovers circulated through the Ohio frontier during the winter for the purpose of buying cattle that they would collect for the spring drive. Although Ohio's cattlemen treated them with a wary eye, they appreciated the cash sales and relief from the responsibility of taking their cattle to market by themselves. The drovers then reappeared at collection points near towns, such as Chillicothe in Ross County or South Charleston in Clark County, the major cattle towns in Ohio, at a certain date. At that time, the cattle would be delivered and the herd assembled for the drive eastward.

Drovers on the Ohio frontier, whether owners or hired agents, did not resemble the cowboys of the Great Plains. Rather, they handled their herds more in the British tradition as practiced in colonial Carolina. They might use two riders, but their hired "drove hands" usually walked alongside and used a long "black snake" or "Centerville" whip from Belmont County, which had a linen or silk cracker that the drover could pop like the sound of a rifle shot, rather than a lariat to keep the cattle under control. The herds from the Ohio country averaged between one hundred and two hundred head, although in late June 1816, a traveler between Zanesville and Lancaster met a herd of three hundred. No matter the size of the herd, the drovers moved them at a rate of about ten miles per day, or as few as five miles if a herd of hogs followed along. Along the route they hired "pike boys," young men from the neighborhood who would travel along and help herd for one or two days, then return home. Late in the frontier period a drove hand, who acted as an assistant in charge of the herd in the absence of the drover, could earn fifteen dollars per month. The drovers usually used a five-man crew, including a boy to walk along with the "lead" ox tied to a rope at the head of the herd, while the others followed, either on foot or on horseback. The drovers returned home by the same route and collected the cattle that had been left behind because of illness or lameness and to pay the keepers of the drove stands for their care.

The cattlemen and professional drovers always faced an uncertain market and price, because each depended on the supply and demand. If an Ohio drover purchased his cattle for two to five cents per pound, he could take them to market and earn a profit. In 1805, George Renick sold his cattle for an average of $31.77 per head in Baltimore. This return meant a profit of nearly 53 percent for one hundred head. This profit margin generally held. Years later, in 1817, Renick averaged $133 per head for a herd that he sold in Philadelphia. At the average cost of $45 for feeding the steer to market weight and $11 for trailing it to Philadelphia, Renick earned $77 per head, or a gross return of $7,700 for one hundred head. Low prices, however, occasionally offset the good years. The next year, Renick earned only $17 per head on a herd sold in New York City, and he reported that his drive in 1824 had been only "reasonably profitable." Year in and year out the drovers, whether Ohio cattlemen or professionals, usually made money, often a "handsome sum," which in time became "comfortable fortunes." Despite the risks, then, cattle raising remained the most lucrative commercial agricultural activity on the Ohio frontier.

* * *

Although no one can say with certainty when the first sheep were brought to Ohio, the early settlers on the frontier kept them for wool, which they carded, spun, dyed, wove, and made into clothing. By the late 1790s, however, farmers near Belpre had imported sheep from western Pennsylvania. Most of the sheep on the Ohio frontier were "native" or nondescript animals and probably entered the Ohio country along the various immigrant routes from Connecticut, New Jersey, and Virginia. The wool and mutton quality of native sheep was poor, as farmers seldom provided adequate shelter or supplementary feeding for their animals.

The first attempt to improve the quality of Ohio's sheep came in 1807 when Seth Adams of Dorchester, Massachusetts, sent some twenty-five to thirty Merino grades to the state. Those animals, a cross between native sheep and purebred or blooded Merinos, which Adams had imported from Spain in 1803, were driven from Massachusetts to Pittsburgh and shipped to Marietta by boat. The flock was then driven to Adams's farm on Wakatomaka Creek near Zanesville. Adams's sheep were the first fine-wooled animals to cross the Appalachians, and the editor of the *Scioto Gazette* reported that he intended to rent the rams to anyone with an "inclination to improve their stock." His fee ranged from one-third to one-half of the lambs produced by the breeding service. In 1811, a Scioto Valley farmer also advertised to breed his Merino ram at the rate of five dollars per ewe or one-half of the lambs. Still, they were insufficient in number to improve immediately the quantity or quality of Ohio's wool. Moreover, in the summer of 1811, Adams lost thirty-five head to marauding wolves, an event that discouraged him. Most important, no economic stimulus existed to encourage farmers to improve their flocks, and frontiersmen kept only enough sheep to meet their household needs.

Thomas Rotch, who settled in Stark County, also worked to establish a Merino flock in northeastern Ohio. In 1811, Rotch arrived by boat at Cincinnati and traveled up the Little Miami and Scioto river valleys in search of land. Soon he selected a site near Kendal and with six men drove a flock of 410 sheep from Connecticut. Rotch built his flocks by contracting their care to Quaker farmers, who had recently settled near Mount Pleasant, and to others in Stark County. This practice of letting sheep on shares proved moderately successful until he had his lands sufficiently cleared for hay and grain to enable wintering a large flock. Rotch offered contracts to the Quakers that required stock keepers to feed, wash, shear, and care for the health of a certain number of sheep for four years. Rotch would receive all of the wool free from expense from the full-blooded Merinos and five-sixths for the grades. Rotch agreed to furnish a full-blooded ram for the keeper's use to upbreed his own flock, although Rotch maintained the right to half of the increase. Upon completion of the contract, the keeper was obliged to return as many ewes with the "same degree of blood" as he originally had received.

Although a keeper could increase his flock in number and quality, Rotch struck a hard bargain among these frontier settlers, but the potential for profits seemed worth the trouble at first to several Quakers. And, while Rotch clearly had the best of the bargain by gaining an increase in his flocks and much of the wool over the contract period, the Quakers were hardly frontier rubes. A friend of Rotch warned him to beware of the Quakers when he entered into agreements for the care of his sheep. A farmer by the name of Arvine Wales, who served as an agent for Rotch, cautioned him that the Quakers appeared as "harmless as doves" but that they were as "wise as serpents." The Quakers did not reject Rotch's agreement as too taxing because they desperately wanted to upbreed their flocks with Merino rams. In the early summer of 1813, they worked to fence their pastures to keep "runagate," that is, common rams, from breeding with their ewes. With fences up and Merino blood or part-blooded stock from Rotch's rams, they intended to make sheep raising profitable as well as to clothe their families.

Still, the best-laid plans and intentions could not always over-come problems of climate and disease on the Ohio frontier. By spring 1814, the Quakers who had agreed to keep sheep for Rotch had serious problems with lambs dying during raw, wet weather, and rot and distemper took even more, the latter of which the Quakers believed infected their pastures. Some at Mount Pleasant asked to be relieved from their contracts. Indeed, the Quakers who had contracted with Rotch felt pressured by the other brethren to send their sheep back. In June, Jesse Parker wrote that the further shepherding of his sheep would cause "discord" and that he would find it a "very bad task" to fulfill his obligation. "I am almost abused," he wrote, "for complying to such terms and I believe if thee will consider the thing and wishes peace and quietness abroad as well at home thee will take them back." Parker's Quaker neighbors, fearing the spread of disease, put extreme social pressure on him to quit this economic venture. He told Rotch: "I am willing to give up summering and wintering of the others to get clear of such a bargain that threatens disunion and ruin of what little we have in the world."

Rotch agreed and sent drovers to collect his sheep and to pay the expenses for their keep among three Quakers. Rotch, however, continued to put his sheep out on shares and developed a sound reputation for producing quality stock. As early as June 1813, W. R. Dickinson, a sheep and woolen mill owner in Steubenville, tried to purchase a Merino ewe from Arvine Wales, who also kept sheep for Rotch. Wales reported that Dickinson "used every art he was master of to get her, some of which were beneath the gentleman." He went away vexed that he did not succeed. Rotch's sheep remained in demand, even though he complained that wool sold for only one dollar per pound in 1816, after trade resumed with Great Britain. Even so, he contracted with nearby farmers to take his sheep for three years and to return half of the annual clip and two-thirds of the lambs and as many of the original flock as possible, including one-half of the number of full-bloods lost by the end of the period.

Rotch continued to use his "endeavors" to convince farmers to raise sheep to be self-sufficient in clothing and for sale. In December 1816, Rotch wrote that Stark County flockmasters sent wool fifty miles for manufacturing at a cost of $1 to $2 per head, and "it is very pleasing to customers." Rotch thought that Ohio would be a "fine country for sheep when the cultivated grasses are introduced." Two years later, he spent $300 for grass seed and $6,618 for driving more sheep over the mountains to his pastures. By October 1821, Rotch had established a woolen mill at Kendal. He continued to let out sheep for a four-year period, taking one-half of the wool and lambs.

An economic stimulus to produce more wool came in December 1807 as a result of the Napoleonic Wars. At that time, Congress passed the Embargo Act in an attempt to apply economic pressure on the belligerents and to prevent further losses of American ships to the British and French navies. The embargo effectively stopped the bulk of American foreign trade; European wool, particularly

British woolens, could not be imported, and the price of domestic wool rose quickly. Sheep men, in turn, gave increased attention to upgrading their flocks, particularly Seth Adams, who continued his "unwearied exertions" to expand the number of Merinos. In September 1811, E. Hutchinson reopened his fulling mills, which operated by horse power to ensure against any "want of water" in the Ohio. He offered to receive woolen cloth for fulling and to take payment in wheat, rye, whiskey, maple sugar, linen, wool, hemp, flax, tallow, and beeswax at cash prices. In February 1813, Adams also confidently professed that soon the "din of war and the confused noise of battle will be exchanged for the music of the spinning wheel, and the harmony of the flying shuttle."

Still Adams worked to improve the quality of Ohio's sheep and fleece. In January 1812, he wrote that if farmers wanted to "increase and improve the internal resources of the country," then the "improvement of our sheep is of the first importance to the country at large, and more especially to the western portion of it." Accordingly, Adams offered some full-blooded Merino rams and ewes as well as grades for sale from his farm near Zanesville. Profits as well as patriotism influenced Adams and other Ohio farmers. He offered to sell his grades at prices ranging from ten to twenty-five dollars per head on six months' credit or in "neat stock," that is, in common sheep. Or he would take a certain number of lambs produced by either the rams or the ewes. Adams offered to send wool samples to potential buyers and to deliver the sheep to any farmer in Ohio unless he lived on some "extreme part" of the frontier.

In 1812, the year in which the United States became embroiled in war with Great Britain, the Wells-Dickinson woolen mill opened at Steubenville to provide a market for Ohio's raw wool. Two years later pure Merino wool sold for $2.75 per pound, and Ohio farmers began producing even more sheep. Robert Marshall also opened a wool-carding mill on Buffalo Creek near Charleston, where he charged ten cents per pound for wool that he carded and put in rolls. For colors "handsomely mixed," he charged twelve cents per pound. In addition, he required payment of one pound of "clean hog lard" or "fresh butter" for every eight pounds of wool carded, because manufacturers commonly mixed one pint of "sweet oil" into every twelve pounds of wool to improve its spinning and weaving characteristics. Often early flockmasters gave little attention to cleaning their fleeces before sale, and wool mill owners constantly complained about the burrs, chips, sticks, and dirt in the wool brought to them for processing, all of which they contended reduced their price by 20 percent, if a farmer chose to sell it. Despite complaints, carding mills cleaned up the wool, and made spinning easier at home. Frontier women preferred machine-carded wool because the mills relieved them of that task and because it made better yarn, enabling a tighter weave and "handsomer" and "more durable" cloth, blankets, stockings, and linsey-woolsey. Near Marietta, flocks were reported to be "multiplying abundantly," and carding and fulling mills were built as far west as Worthington.

* * *

Properly speaking, Ohio dairying began when a farmer milked the first cow on the frontier. Commercial dairying, however, came later, largely as a result of the influence of New Englanders who had experience raising dairy cows for the production of cheese and butter. During the late 1790s, A. W. Putnam operated a prosperous dairy near Belpre. At least as early as 1802, Washington County dairymen shipped cheese down the Ohio River to southern markets. Traders docked their boats at the landings of these dairy farms and bought cheese at high prices. Soon a "good dairy farm" comprised about eighteen cows, and farmers profited from the demand for cheese by well-settled and frontier areas. In 1802, Matthew Nimmo, a Cincinnati merchant, advertised to buy as much as three thousand pounds of cheese. A year later, George Stillson, a Trumbull County trader, sold eight hundred pounds of cheese in Pittsburgh. At that time, however, dairying remained only a sideline because most frontier farmers kept cattle primarily for beef. Still, farm women converted large quantities of milk which could not be used at the family table into cheese and butter for sale.

By the War of 1812, with the exception of the "Connecticut farmers" in the Western Reserve, Ohio dairying still languished even though the price of cheese rose in the western country from 33 to 50 percent above eastern prices. Except for the New England settlers, few Ohio farm women knew how to make cheese, and the demand exceeded the supply. To try to improve the situation, one Ohioan noted that dairying was women's work and stressed that "there is nothing so healthy for young ladies, in particular, as to be engaged at milking a few minutes each morning before sunrise." Cheese and butter money would enable their husbands or fathers to buy them "genteel clothing." When Ohio farm women realized this, he believed, they would readily "embrace this opportunity of making themselves useful." Whether Ohio dairying substantially increased after that urging is unknown, because cheese and butter records for much of the frontier period are nonexistent. Nevertheless, dairying began to expand gradually.

Ohio cheese played an important role in the Pittsburgh market by 1815, and by 1820 Western Reserve dairymen shipped their first load of cheese down the Ohio River. Western Reserve cheese was soon in great demand from Wheeling to New Orleans. As the river trade increased, the Western Reserve became the center of Ohio dairying. There, soil and climatic conditions made crop farming a risky business; but the area gained the nickname "Cheesedom" because of the lush grass and immigrant population (composed primarily of New Englanders already skilled in dairy practices). Western Reserve cheese monopolized the southern markets until the end of the frontier period, when former New Englanders in the Darby Plains of central Ohio began competing in Cincinnati and Louisville. Darby Plains cheese equaled the quality of the Western Reserve product and sold for less because its dairymen incurred lower transportation costs. Nevertheless, Darby Plains dairymen could not produce enough cheese to meet the demand in the southern markets; so Western Reserve dairymen were not adversely affected.

In addition to cheesemaking, Ohio's frontier women also made butter. Unfortunately for the state's agricultural reputation for dairying, almost all of the butter processed was notoriously bad. As had been true with cheese, butter sold in the Ohio River trade and on the New Orleans market early in the nineteenth century. In 1805, the legislature attempted to regulate that product by requiring all butter sold to be clear of mold and free from a rancid or musty taste. Butter could not be sold unless it was well packed and its grade of quality labeled on the outside, but that legislation was insufficient to improve Ohio butter. Because butter making was considered women's work, many believed that it gave them an opportunity to show their skill. At the same time, if the butter turned rancid, they received the blame. Indeed, much of the butter on the Ohio frontier turned out bad because farm women made it during the winter and held it for sale in the spring or summer. Dairymen, however, were partly responsible as well because they improperly fed and sheltered their cows during the winter. Better care produced more and better-quality milk, but farmers were slow to accept changes. Until they did, Ohio's butter remained inferior. Still, the fault did not entirely lie with farm women. They made good butter, but merchants often mixed it with rancid butter, or it spoiled on the way to market. This problem occurred because country merchants bought farm-churned butter of all grades, paid one price for it, and mixed it all together. When the merchant obtained a sufficient quantity to merit shipment, he graded and packed it. The result was a "streaked, speckled, rancid mass" which sold as "Ohio butter." As a result, Ohio gained a bad reputation for making all of the poor butter that reached the New York market.

In addition to the importance of dairying for the production of cheese and butter for household use and for family income, it also reflected the migrant pattern and social structure of the Ohio frontier. Anyone knowledgeable about American regionalism and culture could have traveled through the frontier areas of Ohio and without talking to the people yet tell generally where they came from merely by watching them milk cows. Among the New England migrants in the Western Reserve and in the Marietta and Belpre areas, for example, the men traditionally did the milking. In contrast, among the migrants from Virginia, who settled below the Reserve, the women customarily milked the cows in the southern tradition. In each case, however, the women had the responsibility for making butter for home use and sale.

Overall, then, the Ohio frontier became important livestock country, and farm families relied on pork, beef, wool, cheese, and butter for important income. Livestock raising enabled them to both diversify and specialize as their needs and interests dictated. It helped farm families to meet food needs, but subsistence agriculture did not mean complete self-sufficiency on the Ohio frontier. Ohio farm families used livestock as an important form of insurance against crop failure for food and income, but livestock raising also enabled farmers to earn money for the purchase of the material things of life, both necessities and luxuries. As a result, they sought markets with great success. Indeed, livestock formed the backbone of Ohio's frontier agricultural economy. But livestock raising was not the only agricultural interest of Ohio's frontier farm families.

* * *

Dreams of well-cultivated fields, bountiful harvests, and access to markets down the Ohio River, together with the security and independence that only the ownership of land can bring, created a *mentalité* that the immigrants called "Ohio fever," and it could be assuaged only by moving to that frontier. In October 1787, the reports of Manasseh Cutler and others like him willingly fed that fever. Cutler, who toured the Ohio country from the Scioto to Lake Erie in the mid-1780s, reported that the river bottoms were "as rich a soil as can be imagined, and may be reduced to proper cultivation with very little labour." Although he admitted that his evidence was secondhand, Cutler noted that in "many of these bottoms a man may clear an acre a day, fit for planting with Indian corn; there being no underwood; and the trees growing very high and large, but not thick together, need nothing but girdling."

Cutler certainly ranked among the best boomers of Ohio. Like other land speculators who hoped to make a fortune, he did not hesitate to misrepresent the facts about the Ohio country, reporting, "Cotton is the natural production of this country, and grows in great perfection." The only settlers Cutler saw on his trips were squatters, and they invariably raised corn, not cotton, although some immigrants from the Upper South tried to bring that culture with them. But Cutler also described Ohio as a land of excellent springs, plentiful millstreams, and "gentle and swelling" hills that were "no where high nor incapable of tillage." He reported "deep, rich soil, covered with a heavy growth of timber, and well adapted to the production of wheat, rye, indigo, and tobacco." And, he wrote, Ohio had little "waste land."

Other immigrants, who were not speculators, often agreed with Cutler's assessment of Ohio's land and its potential for commercial agriculture. As early as 1793, Joseph Barker, an early settler at Marietta, recalled that travelers on the Ohio River and immigrants in the

town "furnished a ready market & demand for all the surplus produce that Could be spared from home consumption." In February
1796, settlers near Cincinnati also expected the army to be a good
customer for "country produce," except whiskey, and they believed
the contractors would pay a "generous price in cash" for farm products. Two years later, a settler reported from Cincinnati that the
Mad River country was "checkerboarded with Prairies well calculated for the raising of stock for which a ready market can be
had at Detroit." "But yesterday," he wrote, "that country was a
waste, the range of savages . . . today we see stations formed, towns
building and population spreading." This settlement meant the development of local markets. In 1796, Dayton already had "upwards
of forty cabins and houses," and a mill would soon be built at
the site of Tourneville, twenty miles north at the forks of the Mad
River, to provide a service and give farmers a market for their wheat
and corn.

In April 1810, Roswell Caulkin, who had settled near Berkshire,
Ohio, wrote to a friend in Connecticut that his land was "superior"
to what he had expected to find. It lacked nothing, he wrote, but cultivation to make it a "delightful spot." Like other immigrants,
Caulkin met the subsistence needs of his family first, noting that
they lived "comfortably" with "good beef and pork, turnips and
potatoes, wheat, rie and indian corn, [and] tallow for candles."
They also had made 120 pounds of sugar from their maple trees.
Although the agricultural attention of the settlers in his vicinity
had been "almost entirely on Indian corn and hogs," once the
subsistence needs of his family had been met, he looked forward
to making money by raising wheat, which sold at three dollars
per hundredweight. While subsistence agriculture, then, always
remained important during the early settlement stage, an all-
pervading desire for self-sufficiency had little appeal. The streams
that led to the Ohio and the river towns brought markets within
reach of farm families. Markets meant financial gain, which in turn
meant profits to invest in additional lands, to hire labor for clearing
trees, and to improve the family's standard of living. Caulkin as-
tutely observed that "people here are verry [*sic*] industrious."

In the spring of 1790, a Virginian bound for Kentucky on a flatbottom boat made that same observation, although a bit more

crassly. At Marietta, a farmer who owned land along the river near Belpre boarded for a ride home, during which time he told the Virginian about the work that had been required to raise the corn along the river. "Well," said the Virginian, "I know one thing—you must have been G—D—poor or you would not have worked so hard." David Barker, who recorded this exchange, wrote, "When that crop was matured, plenty, Commenced, & want has never lookd Industry in the face since."

Although almost every immigrant hoped for economic opportunity and dreamed of financial gain, however, the Ohio frontier was not a land of milk and honey. Life on the frontier could be harsh and disappointments keen. In January 1796, the Reverend John Heckewelder wrote to Rufus Putnam that he would soon discover that the hills were "much broken and barren." The Ohio country was considerably less than a fertile plain. Moreover, not every immigrant could be considered a friendly neighbor. In May 1817, the Western Emigrant Society in Cincinnati, allegedly composed of the most respectable citizens of the town, urged caution. Although the society existed to help immigrants settle in Ohio, it warned, "A very great proportion of those who cross the Allegheny mountains are far from being in affluent circumstances, and very few have sufficient knowledge of these western regions, to enable them to fix at once on a residence the most advantageous to their pursuits." The society cautioned that "extravagant descriptions" of the land had been spread by land speculators whose motives for capital gains had caused "great disappointment and loss to thousands." Because the "rudest spot in the wilderness [would] always have one to recommend it," the society urged immigrants to seek "disinterested advice" about the quality and price of lands. Those who came to Ohio without means, the society warned, usually failed and either returned home or moved somewhere else on the frontier.

Those who stayed and who had the capital to buy or rent land as well as the ability to farm often prospered. When they arrived in Ohio, however, they confronted an area that was approximately 95 percent forested with hardwoods, with beech and maple trees covering much of the land from the northeast to the southwest. Oak and hickory held the soil in the southeast, while elm and ash sheltered the river valleys. As a result, Ohio's extensive forest dictated that the ax became the most common tool on that frontier, no matter whether the settler had little wealth or held vast lands for speculation. The thump of the woodsman's ax and the pungent smell of wood smoke became common and comforting on the Ohio frontier. Both meant that the frontier people were at work reshaping the land for purposes far different from those when it had accommodated both Native and white Americans and served as a middle ground for intercultural associations.

* * *

Frontier farmers who could afford a plow commonly used a wooden moldboard that had a wrought-iron share. Local blacksmiths or plowwrights crafted these implements, and standardization remained impossible until the moldboard and share could be cast or wrought in one piece and until interchangeable parts permitted easy repairs. In the spring of 1818, Ohio farmers could acquire David Peacock's plows through their local merchants, who purchased these implements from the manufacturer in Pittsburgh. A year later, Cincinnati merchant Cyrus Coffin sold Wood and Swan's Improved Patent Plow. The light, one-horse model, suitable for cultivating corn, cost sixteen dollars, while the two-horse plow brought eighteen dollars. Farmers paid two dollars more for a steel share and a coulter. Coffin serviced the back-country merchants as well as nearby farmers because he advertised a 10 percent discount for anyone who purchased at least ten plows. Robert Thompson also sold plows in Steubenville that had been manufactured by William and Robert Leckye in Pittsburgh. These plows had either cast- or wrought-iron moldboards that had been ground smooth to cut through the soil and turn a furrow without clogging. By the autumn of 1822, the foundry in Columbus crafted Jethro Wood's Improved Patent Plough. Wood's plow had interchangeable parts so that the share could be replaced when it wore out, usually after one or two years. This change could be made by the farmer in the field, "thereby saving much time and expense."

Once the frontier farmer plowed his field, he invariably planted corn, either by dropping seeds in an opening chopped with a hoe or in a furrow which he covered with a harrow. Corn served as the universal crop on the Ohio frontier as it had on other frontiers as settlers moved west from the Atlantic coast. Frontier farmers fed most of their corn to the hogs and ground the remainder into meal for cornbread and distilled it into whiskey. When converted into pork or whiskey, the corn crop had a market demand, particularly in the towns that bordered the major rivers. There, merchants sent barrels of pork, whiskey, and cornmeal downstream and into the Ohio River trade as far south as New Orleans for transshipment to the East Coast or international markets.

Occasionally, shelled corn also brought cash into the frontier farmer's household. In October 1799 John Armstrong in Cincinnati advertised to buy a thousand bushels of corn at twenty-five cents per bushel. Four years later corn brought seventy-five cents per barrel on the ear in New Orleans, while cornmeal commanded a price ranging between two and three dollars per barrel. In 1800, merchants such as Hugh Rankins in Chillicothe often accepted corn at the exchange rate of one shilling per bushel to pay debts, but Ohio's frontier farmers usually marketed corn as pork and whiskey and ground enough to meet daily needs. Throughout the frontier period, corn remained the most important crop.

As soon as the frontier farmers met the subsistence needs of their families, they cleared land to plant wheat, which would give them a cash grain crop that had a ready market via export through the middlemen on the Ohio River. Frontier farmers broadcast seed in the spring over newly plowed ground and covered it with a harrow. In July it ripened and the harvest began. If a farmer had sons, he often wielded the heavy cradle scythe and cut about three acres per day. In this age of hand power, agricultural tools could be purchased from local craftsmen. In 1807, for example, Edward Scott Degin advertised in Marietta that he sold "grass, cradle and briar sithes and cutting knives," all made with the benefit of forty years' experience in Europe, Virginia, and Pennsylvania. If a farmer read the *Western Herald and Steubenville Gazette* in June 1817, he knew that the newest technique for sharpening the blade required a file rather than only a whet- or grindstone.

When a farmer began to cut the ripened grain, his helpers followed, one to rake the cut stalks into a windrow and another to bind the sheaves for later collection and shocking. When the grain had thoroughly dried in the heads, the farmers collected the sheaves for threshing, which they conducted on the barn floor or outside on flat, hard-packed ground. Small-scale farmers threshed with a flail. If they had help, they customarily paid every tenth bushel in wages. Then they cleaned the chaff from the grain with a sieve or riddle by tossing it into the air while the breeze, or two people using a sheet, blew or fanned the chaff away. When the cleaned grain fell to the ground, it was ready for bagging or storage loose in the barn. Ohio's farmers did not use hand- or horse-powered threshing machines until the mid-1820s, the first being introduced in Richland and Wayne counties.

As farmers planted more wheat, merchants began to build mills to convert the grain into flour, thereby adding value to the product for the export trade and creating greater market demand, which in turn encouraged more wheat production. In 1801, John Symmes offered to take wheat for debts at the rate of five shillings per bushel at the gristmill of Jacob White along the Miami River in order to convert it into flour and sell it downriver. Flour soon reached the price of fifteen dollars per barrel in New Orleans, but a new European war brought the British blockade of that French port, and the price fell to three dollars per barrel. Ohio's farmers quickly learned that while they might be isolated on the frontier, their lives were inextricably linked to the world beyond.

In late April 1801, a new brig left Marietta with eight hundred barrels of flour bound for the West Indies, but the editor of the *Scioto Gazette* was not optimistic that it would reach the market. He wrote, "The prospects of the enterprising citizens of the western country [are] blasted in the bud—their only avenue to foreign markets obstructed by an arbitrary and unfeeling nation, whose subjects are *starving* for the very article which they have prevented from proceeding; perhaps to their own markets." The sentiment of Ohio's frontier farmers would soon coalesce and hold Great Britain responsible for any economic hardship suffered from its maritime policy designed to defeat France. When war came between the United States and Great Britain little more than a decade later over that maritime policy, few Ohio farmers were surprised. They had suffered in their pocketbooks for a long time, and they favored war for economic reasons as well as matters of security.

Still, with merchants such as John and Matthew Nimmo buying wheat with goods at cash prices at the rate of fifty cents per bushel paid at Hamilton in July 1803, and with others, such as Bezaleel

Wells, paying four shillings per bushel in cash at Steubenville in December 1806, and Thomas Moore paying sixty cents per bushel a year later at Little Beaver for two thousand bushels, frontier farmers could reap sufficient reward to merit continuation of wheat production. Soon Cincinnati became the major wheat market and shipping point for Ohio's farmers. In August 1808, Samuel and Josiah Halley, for example, advertised to purchase five thousand bushels of wheat from farmers along the Little Miami River between September and November, for which they would pay fifty cents per bushel. They also wanted five hundred barrels of flour.

Other towns also provided markets for wheat. In October 1810, William Green worked to set up a steam mill with an elevator in Marietta. He planned to use a twenty-horsepower Evans steam engine to turn two pair of five-foot burr millstones. At the same time, an I. Gilman formed a company with several others in Marietta to establish a wheat and wool mill, a distillery, and a cotton manufactory. Then, the local editor contended, Ohioans could say to Great Britain, "We can do without your manufacturers, but you cannot live without our bread." The editor of the *Western Spy* in Cincinnati agreed with this "noble and independent example." He wrote, "Farmers lay aside that old threadbare word of 'HARD TIMES' and turn to industry, raise Wheat, and you will then get cash." When war finally came, wheat reached $1.50 and corn $1.00 per bushel in the Firelands by mid-January 1813. The wheat market became so important by 1815 that the Cincinnati Steam Mill operated two pair of six-foot millstones capable of grinding nearly twenty bushels into flour per hour. Three years later, a flour mill in Steubenville used six pair of millstones to grind a thousand barrels of flour each week.

The farmers on the Ohio frontier, then, entered the market economy by producing for a "settlers' market" created by the newcomers on the farms and in the fledgling towns as well as by immigrants on the Ohio River. They also sold agricultural commodities to the army. In 1792, for example, the farmers near Marietta sold ten thousand bushels of corn to the commissary department. The next autumn, the settlers in the vicinities of Belpre and Waterford sent several boatloads of corn to Fort Washington at Cincinnati. When the immigrants were able to meet their subsistence needs,

Ohio's farmers then turned to the river trade, particularly sending agricultural produce down to New Orleans. By 1800, the commission business had been well established at Cincinnati for the shipment of farm products to the Crescent City. Moreover, flatboats laden with pork, whiskey, and cornmeal also headed downriver from docks on the Muskingum at Marietta and on the Scioto at Chillicothe. In 1801, 514 flatboats carrying agricultural commodities arrived in New Orleans from Ohio.

At New Orleans, Ohio shippers paid Spanish import and export duties before transshipment to East Coast or foreign markets. In 1795, Pinckney's Treaty provided westerners the right of navigation and deposit at New Orleans free from customs duties. The Louisiana Purchase in 1803, however, ensured freedom of access to the Gulf of Mexico and the export of Ohio's agricultural products unhindered by a foreign power at the mouth of the Mississippi River, and Ohio's agricultural trade flourished. In late February 1811 alone, after the ice had broken up on the rivers, between forty and fifty boats "richly laden with the products of the Scioto country" had embarked from Chillicothe for the Ohio River and the markets beyond.

After the turn of the nineteenth century, the market towns developed quickly. By December 1812, Cincinnati had two market days per week. John Force, who traveled through the town from New Jersey, observed: "I could scarcely believe my own eyes to see the number of people and wagons and saddle horses and the quantities of meat, flour, corn, fish, fowl and sauce of all kinds [jams and jellies] that were offered and . . . actually sold." Other towns also became important agricultural centers. In April 1814, the owner of Alexander's Store in Zanesville paid twelve and a half cents per pound for unhackled flax of good quality and twenty-five cents per pound for well-hackled and cleaned flax, while the William Marshall Brewery, which produced thirty barrels of beer per week, advertised to buy five hundred bushels of barley and a large quantity of hops. At the same time, Jacob Crooks wanted to buy corn, oats, rye, and whiskey for cash, while Joseph Hawkins paid between thirty-seven and a half cents and sixty-two and a half cents per pound for clean, dry hog bristles, depending on their length. In Marietta, John H. Piott advertised for five thousand bushels of flour and two hundred barrels of whiskey to be delivered to Fort Meigs between June and September, "or at any convenient place on the Lake Shore to some transportation by land."

In northwest Ohio, where the War of 1812 had the greatest effect on agricultural production and marketing, prices increased rapidly. In May 1814, a contemporary reported "a general scarcity of provisions" for the settlers in the Western Reserve, who often had to travel eighty miles to procure grain and flour for the subsistence of their families. When flour could be purchased, it cost $6.50 per barrel. This food shortage resulted in part from "incessant rains" that ruined the crops in 1813 and from the market for agricultural produce created by the army on the frontier. One observer noted that "many people who had plenty of produce in the fall were so completely bewitched to find a market that they hurried it off to the army on the frontier in order to get a great price." The army contractors, however, were slow to pay, and these farmers soon found themselves in a difficult position. They had forsaken safety-first agriculture, that is, production to ensure their subsistence needs, for commercial gain. Now they had no money and scant food reserves. As a result, many settlers were "obliged to buy of other persons for their own consumption, and at a greater price than they sold theirs for last fall—a very proper reward for their avaricious dispositions."

* * *

From the beginning of settlement by whites, Joseph Barker at Marietta wrote, "there were no Arts absolutely necessary but the Art of handling a narrow ax, & no imployment [sic] but clearing Land." The early settlers in Ohio cleared land by both the southern and New England methods. The southern method, also called "deadening," involved girdling the trees and clearing away the underbrush. When the trees died, they let them stand, but continued to burn the fallen branches until they eventually cut them down. In the meantime, they plowed between the stumps and trunks, because they did not have sufficient capital to hire the labor needed to dig out the stumps and chop down all of the dead trees. Farmers who were "weak handed" and who could not afford hired labor for clearing usually girdled their trees rather than spend time cutting them down. Girdled trees died after two years and could be felled and burned more easily than cut green trees. Frontiersmen also believed that the stumps of girdled trees rotted more quickly than those of cut green trees. As a result, the fields of frontier farmers remained pocked with stumps and decaying trees for a generation. The New England method involved cutting down trees and burning them in heaps on the spot. The stumps, however, usually remained. During the spring, William Cooper Howells, who settled with his family near Mount Pleasant in Jefferson County in 1813, reported: "It was a very common thing for the fire to get into the dead trees in the spring time, where it would burn for several days and nights together." Howells reflected that "the sight of a field of these burning trees was always beautiful—usually a little more so in your neighbor's field than your own; you had the advantage of distance and safety."

The farmers on the Ohio frontier always had a pressing need for labor, particularly for clearing land. Plowing, planting, and harvesting took time, and the frontier farmer did well to clear several acres by himself during a year. Young men without sufficient capital to buy or rent land, however, could work as agricultural laborers and, in time, acquire sufficient funds to purchase or lease a farm of their own. In order to do so, they needed only a strong back, calloused hands, and a good ax. The first requisites could be acquired on the job, while a quality ax cost about two dollars. At the rate of fifty cents per day, however, several years of hard work and parsimonious saving were required to buy 160 acres of public domain or land from a speculator.

Land speculators often advertised to employ men to clear land and split rails for fences. Early in the frontier period they paid their workers in land or gave them the right to use a certain number of acres for a specific period of time. The best axmen could clear an acre of trees in three to seven days. The men who worked at this pace obviously regarded themselves as experts. Most workers, however, could not maintain that speed. During the 1820s, for example, Plin Smith, who migrated to northeastern Ohio from Vermont, bought a first-rate ax for seven dollars and offered his services to cut timber and pile brush. One landowner hired him to clear a hundred acres, a task that wore out his ax and left him incapacitated.

Although some who cleared land were itinerant workers, many were local settlers who cut timber on a part-time basis to earn money working for their neighbors. In 1817, for example, Ephraim Brown, a large landowner in Trumbull County in northern Ohio, used both itinerant workers and his own tenants to clear land. In October, he credited the account of a tenant named Enos Mann with $100.14 for clearing and fencing ten acres. This high rate of pay reflected the extra work for splitting rails and fencing the acreage. Similarly, Frederick Udell arrived in Ohio from Pennsylvania in 1823 and bought eighty acres of wooded land. With the aid of a hired man, Udell cleared ten acres, then hired himself to a neighbor for $10 per month for more work cutting trees. He also took employment cutting trees for road survey and construction crews. Until a farmer could produce enough corn, pork, or wheat to bring money into the household, tree-clearing jobs that earned a man $8 to $10 dollars per month or fifty cents per day served as a reliable source of income on the frontier.

After the initial clearing of ten or twelve acres, farmers and their hired hands usually cut timber during the winter months after the corn had been harvested, the ground plowed, the hogs slaughtered, and the pork packed. When spring brought more plowing and planting time, they put away their axes and returned to their fields, although the smell of wood smoke from windrows of tree trunks and branches drifted through the air during most of the year. Besides the seasons, cost also determined how much land a farmer cleared during a year. Working alone, he could clear only about ten acres, but if the settler had capital, he could hire the work for between five and twenty dollars per acre, the cost determined by the thickness of the trees. Without question, land clearing became the greatest expense for settlers, even though frontiersmen considered this work to be a poor man's employment.

Land clearing just involved girdling or felling the trees and piling the brush for burning. Usually, the landowner also cut cordwood and split rails, both of which met needs for heating and fencing and enabled the removal of as much wood as possible before he set fire to the smaller branches or trunks too large to handle easily. Land clearing, however, did not include removing the stumps. Usually, farmers let the stumps dry from five to ten years, then burned them out. In the meantime, they planted corn and wheat between the

stumps, a technique that made plowing and harvesting incon-
venient and often difficult.

Farm families could also sell ashes from their cleared lands to
businessmen, such as Eben Meriam in Zanesville. At the rate of
twelve and a half cents per bushel, a hundred bushels would pay
for their labor. Meriam exchanged pot ashes for their wood ashes
and thereby saved women the task of leaching ashes for the making
of soap. Meriam contended that women could use his services and
"make as much soap with one dollar of pot ashes in one day as
from the same quantity of common ashes in three weeks." Many
farmers also crafted barrel staves, which had a ready market
among the coopers in the nearby towns, as well as split shingles for
roofing from suitable timber.

Workers on Ohio's agricultural frontier also earned money cutting wood for the heating of homes and the powering of steamboats. If a farmer had wood to sell, the standard measurement
was a cord, that is, a stack eight feet long, four feet high, and four
feet wide. Local and itinerant wood choppers earned twenty-five to
seventy-five cents per day or a set wage per cord. Wood choppers
could cut from one to two cords per day. In 1815, Daniel Drake in
Cincinnati noted, "Many teams are constantly employed in hauling
wood into town from the surrounding hills; but the principal part is
rafted and boated down the Ohio and Licking Rivers." During the
winter of 1816–17, Elnathan Kemper, who farmed near Cincinnati,
used hired hands to cut cordwood. He paid them from sixty-two
and a half to seventy-five cents per cord, less two dollars per week
for board. In 1817, when steamboats became sufficiently powerful to
travel upriver, the demand for cordwood substantially increased,
because most steamboats burned one and a half to two cords per
hour. Woodcutters and retailers who sold to steamboat operators
charged $1.25 to $1.50 per cord.

* * *

In 1796, Israel and Rufus Putnam brought a wagonload of Rox-
bury Russets and some forty or fifty other apple varieties from
Connecticut. These trees provided the basis for the Putnam nursery near the Muskingum River a few miles north of Marietta. This

nursery was the first west of the Alleghenies, and it supplied farmers with apple trees until 1821. Other settlers frequently brought apple seeds and young trees to remind them of their former homes as well as to furnish beauty, shade, food, and drink on their new lands. As a result, the most common apple varieties in Ohio during the early nineteenth century reflected migration patterns. In the Western Reserve, New England varieties dominated the orchards, while Pennsylvania and Maryland varieties prevailed to the south. In time, other varieties from New Jersey, New York, and Virginia—Early June, Carolina Red, Pryor's Red, Fall Queen, Milan—came to Ohio, giving the state a host of apples of varying size, shape, and color. Ohioans who occasionally returned to the East for business or pleasure also brought back shoots of the best varieties. Grafts of these scions helped expand Ohio's apple orchards before enough nurseries were established to meet the demand. In mid-November 1808, for example, John Johnston, Indian agent at Piqua, planted 180 grafted apple trees, some of which he obtained from the Detroit area.

Most apple orchards on the Ohio frontier, however, grew from seedling trees. Grafting and budding, which guarantee the reproduction of a specific variety, were not unknown, but most farmers did not understand that process or were unable to acquire the appropriate grafts for their rootstocks. As a result, most of the apple production was fit only for drinking. This suited Ohio farmers, who raised apples primarily for cider—the cooking and keeping qualities were of secondary importance. Cider offered an alternative to water as a thirst-quenching beverage. When fermented into hard cider or made into apple brandy, commonly called "apple jack" or "Jersey lightning," it provided a potent and salable libation. Consequently, most farms had cider presses, and few apples were wasted. Those unsuitable for cider, immediate eating, storage, or vinegar were fed to the livestock. By 1800, most farms along the Ohio River between Beverly and Marietta had apple orchards ranging in size from two to thirty acres. Although some apples reached Pittsburgh by canoe and flatboats carried others to New Orleans, production above that needed for home consumption lacked a ready and reachable market.

As the country grew up, entrepreneurs such as the Putnams planted nurseries to meet the increasing demand for fruit trees.

About 1803, Thomas Worthington established a nursery and orchard at his "Adena" estate near Chillicothe, furnishing central Ohio farmers with many varieties. In late July 1806, a large nursery along Mill Creek near Cincinnati, bowing to the West's chronic shortage of cash, offered to trade apple trees for corn at the rate of thirty cents per bushel for corn and seven cents apiece for the trees. Six years later, a Chillicothe nursery advertised a wide selection along with a nursery established in Dayton in 1824, which served southwestern Ohio.

By 1813, Ohio's apple harvest reached bountiful proportions. The Ohio Company, for example, required each settler to plant at least fifty apple trees, and managed to ship several thousand barrels of apples annually to markets in Pittsburgh, Wheeling, and Cincinnati. Ohio apples also reached the New Orleans market each autumn and spring. The apple orchards in Ohio continued to expand and blossom until farmers had more fruit than they could sell or use. In October 1818, a traveler on the road between St. Clairsville and Morristown in Belmont County noted that because of a bountiful crop, "it is no crime for either man or beast to rob orchards."

As farmers cut trees and broke ground across the state, they realized that some apple varieties grew better than others. In northern Ohio, green and yellow varieties prospered, while those of red color dominated in the south. In southern Ohio, Bellflower and the Vandervere Pippin were excellent fruits, but in northern Ohio the Belmont, Fameuse, and Esopus Spitzenburg developed the "finest fruits." Despite rapid expansion of the orchards and abundant harvests, most Ohio farmers were not skilled and careful horticulturists. While the apple crop was economical and profitable when the trees were selected judiciously, no other aspect of Ohio's agriculture was more neglected. All too frequently, farmers cultivated other crops between the trees, pastured livestock in the orchards, and failed to cultivate, fertilize, prune, or graft their trees, and the niggling problem of apple blight became increasingly serious. While apple growers disputed the cause, they did not know how to combat it, other than to use a host of home remedies which acknowledged their ignorance and faith in superstition. Still, apples soon became the "main crop" in the Marietta area, and in other towns nurseries continued to expand to meet the demand for apple and other fruit trees.

Without doubt, however, John Chapman was the most eccentric, if not the most well-known, nurseryman who raised apple trees on the Ohio frontier. Chapman, alias Johnny Appleseed, arrived in the Ohio country about 1800 from Pennsylvania, where he had acquired apple seeds from the cider mills in the western part of the state. Chapman quickly planted his apple seeds on lands that he claimed for his primitive but successful nursery business. By planting his nurseries on the frontier, he planned to have apple trees ready for sale whenever settlements overtook his holdings. Although his simple manner and dress clearly identified him as one who marched to the beat of a different drummer, his horticultural practices were not unusual for the early nineteenth century. Many people commonly collected apple seeds from cider presses in order to expand their orchards. Chapman's trees, of course, were suitable only for cider apples, but that did not matter to his customers. Moreover, Chapman, and many others like him, did not believe in grafting.

Chapman's first nursery was near the town of Carrolton, Ohio. He planted other nurseries along the Muskingum and Licking river valleys. In time his nurseries could be found across central Ohio from Zanesville to Newark to Lake Erie—an area which today is marked by the towns of Coshocton, Mount Vernon, Mansfield, Bucyrus, Ashland, and Wooster. Chapman knew that this area had great potential for farming. Indeed, it contains some of the best agricultural land in the country, and Chapman capitalized on the wants of the frontier people for apple trees to plant in this rich land. By the War of 1812, Chapman had nurseries on the most northerly branches of the Muskingum River system, and he had pushed across the divide into the Lake Erie watershed. Soon his nurseries grew along the Blanchard, Maumee, Auglaize, and St. Marys rivers in northwestern Ohio. Sometimes he planted apple trees on lands that he owned or leased, but more often than not he cultivated his trees on the lands of others. In short, John Chapman was a squatter who roamed about cultivating and selling apple trees. Then, as the surrounding lands were settled for other agricultural purposes, he abandoned his nurseries and moved on. Still, Chapman was a good businessman. He visited new settlers as soon as possible and told them about his apple trees as well as about the Swedenborgian faith, if they so desired. In time, his reputation spread throughout the Ohio country. By 1822 people referred to him as "John Appleseed." The diminutive "Johnny" came with old age and the creation of a bountiful folklore about this gentle but enterprising man.

Although Mansfield became Chapman's home, to the extent that this roamer ever had a permanent one, by 1830 he had extended his work into the area of Fort Wayne, Indiana. At the time of his death at the age of seventy in 1845, few people in Ohio actually remembered him. As early as 1846, however, tales of Johnny Appleseed began to circulate, and within a generation, his legend became permanently etched in American folklore. Apart from the Johnny Appleseed mythology and his own remarkable history, John Chapman's greatest legacy can be seen at apple-blossom time in Ohio.

* * *

The rivers in Ohio provided access to markets for frontier farmers, and markets meant profit, which encouraged greater production. And with the increasing importance of commercial agriculture, farmers began to organize agricultural societies to encourage agricultural improvement. In 1795, for example, prominent farmers in Washington County organized an agricultural society, but it soon failed for lack of practical importance. In April 1803, however, farmers and merchants organized the Miami Exporting Company to reduce costs and increase profits by purchasing and selling collectively. The company sold shares for $100 each, requiring $5 down and the remainder paid in produce during the next two years. The company would then sell the cattle, pork, lard, flour, cornmeal, hemp, tobacco, pot ashes, and other commodities and add the returns to its coffers and dividends. It also used this money to support the creation of a bank to provide credit to farmers. The Miami Exporting Company probably raised about $200,000, and it engaged exclusively in banking activities from 1807 until it temporarily suspended operations in 1822. In June 1823, the editor in the Queen City clearly recognized the significance of the close relationship between the town and country for merchants and farmers, fostered in part by the bank of the Miami Exporting Company, when he wrote: "The pride and support of Cincinnati is her rich and extensive back country—and the people of that country, should never forget how much the value of their lands and the profits of their industry depend upon her welfare and commercial relations."

In 1810, the sheep men in northeast Ohio also organized the Canton Company for Encouraging the Raising and Improving the Breed of Sheep. Fifty shares had been subscribed by late June, with the election of officers scheduled for July 4 at the home of Samuel Coulter. At the same time, agriculturists in Butler County organized the Farmers' and Mechanics' Exporting Company of Hamilton to "provide a market for produce and the manufacturers of the country, and secure to the farmers and mechanics safe, speedy and effective returns." Shares cost five dollars each, payable in twenty equal installments, with the company to become operational when three hundred shares had been sold. Investors were limited to fifty shares until one thousand were sold to ensure widespread inclusion. The results of these efforts are unknown.

* * *

Overall, Ohio's frontier farm families practiced extensive agriculture, and they gave little thought to crop rotation. When crop productivity declined to unacceptable levels of profit, they seeded their lands with clover and let them rest for several years. Corn and wheat prices rose as immigration increased and as farmers improved their land, that is, cleared it for crops. In 1810, Ohio's farmers had improved 225,675 acres. Rapid settlement of the frontier, however, increased that area to 2,892,456 acres by 1820. After the Treaty of Greenville in 1795, then, agriculture became the defining characteristic of the Ohio frontier. The Louisiana Purchase, the Embargo of 1807, and the War of 1812 tied Ohio's agriculturists to international events and made farmers increasingly dependent on governmental policy. At the same time, Cincinnati became the chief regional market for Ohio and the Old Northwest, while other towns along the rivers and major roadways in the interior provided similar services only on a smaller scale. The countryside, then, gave the frontier people in Ohio freedom, independence, and economic opportunity. It also shaped all aspects of their lives.

9.

THE FRONTIER PEOPLE

The men, women, and children who migrated to the Ohio frontier were a country people, hailing from the Piedmont, Blue Ridge Mountains, and Shenandoah Valley as well as from the Appalachian and Interior Low plateaus of the Upland South. Others migrated from New England and the Midlands of the Delaware and the Susquehanna valleys. At first the uplanders from the Virginia Panhandle and Kentucky who settled in southern Ohio became the most important cultural group to migrate to the Ohio frontier. Soon, Scots-Irish immigrants from southwestern Pennsylvania occupied portions of eastern and central Ohio, such as present-day Licking and Knox counties, settling Utica and Wilmington about 1803. The land office in Steubenville served the eastern Ohio counties of Belmont, Carroll, Columbiana, Guernsey, Harrison, Jefferson, Mahoning, Stark, Summit, and Tuscarawas. There, during the first two decades of the nineteenth century, most of the immigrants came from the Middle Atlantic and Upland South, especially Pennsylvania and Virginia and to a lesser extent Maryland and New Jersey. New Englanders and immigrants from the Lower South seldom bought land in this area. Appalachian roots, then, dominated both the geographic and cultural inheritance of most settlers in this area and elsewhere in Ohio, with the exception of the Western Reserve.

Most settlers arrived on flatboats via the Ohio River, except those in northern Ohio who traveled from New England. There, Yankee immigrants had passed through upstate New York and along Lake

Erie to reach their lands in the Connecticut Western Reserve, where they formed the most homogeneous settlement of New Englanders in the Old Northwest. Because these Yankees were better educated and more wealthy than the settlers from Pennsylvania, Kentucky, and Virginia, and because they lived in a relatively small region of Ohio, they formed and perpetuated a cultural and political influence that exceeded strength through numbers alone. Above all, however, the immigrants to the Ohio frontier were native-born. The fertile lands and deep forests of Ohio did not draw large numbers of foreigners until after the frontier period had ended.

Families that moved to Ohio early in the settlement period, often along a line relatively parallel to their point of origin, sent letters home to kith and kin urging them to come to Ohio and enjoy its bounty as well as to provide the comfort of family and friends on the frontier. Although thousands of immigrants had traveled down the Ohio River from Pennsylvania or had crossed over from Virginia and Kentucky, the Treaty of Greenville promised the peace and security that they needed to move up the Scioto and Miami rivers or to cross into the uplands in order to claim land, build homes, and establish farms. Once that immigration began in earnest, it did not slacken until the Panic of 1819 and the financial policy of the federal government brought the acquisition of the public domain to a temporary near-halt. By that time, however, the Ohio frontier as a borderland had essentially ceased to exist.

In late April 1795, a "considerable number of flatbottom boats" arrived in Cincinnati. The *Centinel of the North-Western Territory* reported that they were "loaded with families for the purpose of settling this country." By early December 1800, more than 1,500 immigrants alone of Ohio's approximately 42,000 people had settled between Le Tart Falls and the upper end of the French Grant along the Ohio River to the mouth of the Scioto, a distance of only 104 miles. Two years later, French traveler François André Michaux reported that a "great number" of immigrants came from the continuous areas of Pennsylvania and Virginia. In the autumn of 1805, one frontiersman at Wheeling observed that "not less than eighty wagons with families from various quarters of the Atlantic states" awaited ferrying across the river to Ohio. "The emigration to the state of Ohio the present season," he wrote, "exceeds all reasonable bounds of calculation." Five years later, a resident of Chillicothe proudly, and not entirely inaccurately, reflected on the rapid increase of the population in Ohio, which not long before had been a "howling wilderness, inhabited only by savages and beasts of prey." But in late December 1810, he contended that "the strong and nervous arm of the industrious husbandman has subdued the forest, and converted it into plowed and well cultivated fields." Roswell Caulkin, who farmed near Berkshire, also reported the steady arrival of new immigrants, and he mused that "with the smiles of heaven we shall be very populous."

In southwestern Ohio, Hamilton County provides a particularly good example of the social and cultural effects of migration. Less than one-fourth (271 out of 1,425) of the people living in Hamilton County between 1788 and 1795 whose names can be identified (not counting soldiers) were adult women, while 27 females were under sixteen years old. An additional 169 women also immigrated with their husbands, but their names are not known, making a total of 440 women out of a population of 1,594. If 3 children are added to each of these 169 families, which was the average number of children for families on the New England frontier, then the population of Hamilton County increases by 507 to a total of 2,101 settlers. This number, of course, is not precise because the names of women often were not recorded. Still, of the 25 settlers who founded Columbia in 1788, 5 were women, while all 26 founders of Losantiville were men. This ratio of men to women (or the lack of it) remained typical throughout the frontier period where new stations or settlements were founded in Hamilton County. After men established the stations, however, women and their children soon joined them.

These settlers were a restless people. In Hamilton County, for example, 288 of 1,085 male settlers who lived in Hamilton County before 1796 had lived in more than one settlement in the county. Forty-four left the county between 1788 and 1795, while 22 remained at their original stations. Sixty-seven died, but the residency or movement of the other 664 remains unknown. Put differently, 93 percent or 288 of the 310 immigrants who remained in Hamilton County lived in more than one settlement during that period. Usually these immigrants settled at one of the three larger stations of Cincinnati, Columbia, or North Bend, then they moved up the Little and Great Miami river valleys or north along Mill Creek. Of the 38 adult males who left Hamilton County, 10 went to Kentucky, New Jersey, and Pennsylvania, apparently after forfeiting their lands. The destination of the others remains unknown, but they too probably moved to other locations on the Ohio frontier or to Kentucky, the Illinois country, or Louisiana.

Those who stayed in Hamilton County usually left their stations to establish farms. Between 1795 and 1800, 80 percent of the adult males who can be identified became full-time farmers, while 10 percent practiced agriculture on a part-time basis, a percentage comparable to the number of Americans overall who were engaged in agriculture in 1800. During this same period, of the 457 adult males who can be traced, less than 5 percent remained at their original settlement, while 25 percent left the county. The population in Hamilton County, then, was rural, agricultural, and located on individual farms rather than at stations or towns. Surveyors, army contractors, physicians, tailors, cobblers, and tavernkeepers, who catered to the needs of the army and the river trade, also served in important trades or professions on the Ohio frontier in Hamilton County. By 1795 only one woman can be identified as having an occupation, and she was a laundress at her home for the army. Generally, the women can be identified only as being wives or widows.

So far as origin is concerned, the birthplace for only 264 of 1,425 settlers, that is, 18.5 percent, can be identified. If the spouse and children are included, then an estimate can be made for 55 percent of the settlers. This estimation, of course, is imprecise, but it is suggestive. Of those for whom a birthplace can be identified, 93 percent were born in America. The middle colonies furnished 76 percent of that population, of which 95 percent were born in Pennsylvania and New Jersey. Only 19 percent were born in the southern states, but 75 percent of that group came from Virginia and Kentucky, the latter of which remained a part of Virginia until 1792. Only 4 percent of these identifiable immigrants to Hamilton County were born in New England, while 6 percent were born abroad. Those born in Virginia, Kentucky, and Pennsylvania almost always had frontier experience before moving to Hamilton County. Southern origins apparently increased by 1805, when the *Liberty Hall and Cincinnati Mercury* published the log of local ferry operator Joseph Kennedy.

During April 1805, Kennedy tallied 2,639 immigrants who used his ferry to arrive in Ohio. South Carolina led with 669, followed by Kentucky with 568, while Virginia and North Carolina contributed 465 and 463 settlers respectively. He also transported 264 Georgians, 200 Tennesseeans, and 10 Illinois settlers across to Cincinnati from the mouth of the Licking River.

The immigrants to Hamilton County between 1788 and 1795, then, were an ethnically homogeneous group, with 1,306 of the 1,425 settlers having British surnames, while 99 had German and 20 French surnames, for 92, 7, and 1 percent of the population respectively. British heritage, a Pennsylvania or New Jersey birthplace, prior frontier experience, and at least one move already behind them characterized these early settlers on the Ohio frontier. Collectively these characteristics made these settlers as homogeneous as those in the Western Reserve or in the Ohio Company's purchase.

Single males and young families made up the largest portion of the early settlers. By the end of 1788 and within three months of the arrival of the first settlers with the Ohio Company, nineteen women lived with their families in Marietta. In 1820, for example, in Geauga County's Claridon Township, the ratio of men to women was 125 to 100. Most of those women in Claridon Township and elsewhere on the Ohio frontier were of childbearing age. Many women brought children with them and had large families after their arrival. After the first decade of settlement, beginning in 1810, the declining availability of land and the out-migration of males in the township, both of which affected the opportunity of women to have more children, caused fertility rates to decrease by the close of the frontier period.

Some women, such as Rowena Tupper at Marietta, called the Ohio country a "savage land," but it answered "every expectation," and she and most other women on the frontier adjusted quickly, although some returned to their former homes. The essential roles of wife, housekeeper, and mother occupied their time, especially child raising. Women could marry with parental consent at the age of fourteen, while boys could marry at the age of seventeen. The physical ability to support a family and to bear children became an important determinant for marriage. Hard work and frequent childbearing reduced the raw average for life expectancy to about thirty-four years for males and thirty-six years for females.

During this same period, of the 691 individuals who first settled in Cincinnati, most came alone or as part of an individual family. None immigrated as part of extended families, and only a few arrived as members of a group. The six groups that attempted settlement all quickly failed because the settlers abandoned them in favor of owning their own farms. At best the organized group that founded stations did so only as a temporary expediency until the members acquired land of their own. They had no intention of retaining group solidarity and certainly did not plan any form of communal association. Throughout the frontier period, then, virtually all of Ohio remained mobile and rural. Only Cincinnati, with 9,642 of the state's 581,434 people in 1820, could be considered urban, but that total accounted for less than 2 percent of the state's population.

* * *

Pittsburgh served as the chief point of embarkation for immigrants to Ohio via the river. There, sawmillers ripped lumber for flat-bottomed "Kentucky boats." Commonly fifty to one hundred feet long and fifteen to twenty-five feet wide, with square ends and sides that rose about five feet above the water, these boats had roofed cabins at the sterns, cost only $1 to $1.25 per running foot, and provided cheap transportation. As early as 1792, keelboats also provided transportation for passengers and mail between Pittsburgh and Cincinnati. Keelboats could be rowed, poled, or pulled through the water. These boats also had a square sail to catch the wind. Keelboats averaged thirty tons in capacity and ran forty to eighty feet long and seven to nine feet wide, with a running foot cost of $2 to $3. One keelboat operator advertised that he supplied passengers with "provisions and liquors of all kinds" at a reasonable price. Immigrants who were worried about their baggage could insure it for an additional "moderate" rate.

Others crossed the Ohio at Wheeling and opposite Cincinnati by ferry. On December 28, 1789, Absalom Martin received the first license from the territorial governor to operate a ferry across from Wheeling. In early February 1792, Robert Benham received the second license to establish a ferry at Cincinnati. Benham's license limited his charges to six cents per person, eighteen cents for a man and horse, and one dollar for a team and wagon. In 1799, the territorial legislature authorized county courts to grant licenses and regulate charges to enable local authorities and entrepreneurs to meet the transportation needs of the frontier people more quickly and efficiently. Rates remained about the same throughout the frontier period for individuals transported across the Ohio. In 1807, Ruffin's Ferry charged six and a quarter cents per person, while a team and wagon were assessed fifty cents and a man and a horse twelve and a half cents to cross the Ohio at Cincinnati.

Zane's Trace, however, became the only major overland route into Ohio away from the river between 1797 and 1812. Indeed, until the War of 1812 essentially ended immigration to the Ohio frontier, Zane's Trace served as the chief overland route through southeastern Ohio, linking Wheeling with Zanesville, Chillicothe, and indirectly Cincinnati with its terminus on the Ohio River across from Limestone, Kentucky.

In 1796, Ebenezer Zane, a speculator from the West Branch of the Potomac, who had claimed the land where Wheeling now stands, petitioned Congress for permission to carve a wagon road through the Northwest Territory from Wheeling southwest to the Scioto River then south to the Ohio and Fort Washington. Because the road would necessarily cross the Muskingum, Hockhocking, and Scioto rivers, ferries would be necessary, which required the permission of Congress since the route would traverse federal lands. In order to earn a satisfactory compensation for his efforts, Zane asked Congress to grant him military bounty warrants for land at the river crossings and to pay his surveying expenses.

Zane impressed Congress with the importance and cost-effectiveness of a wagon road from Wheeling to Fort Washington, contending that his route would shave 380 miles off the usual 980-mile route from Philadelphia to the military post. He also contended that his proposed all-weather road would enable the government to send mail for $1,000 or less per year from Wheeling to Frankfort, Kentucky, a savings of $3,000 from the fee charged by the boatmen who floated at the mercy of the sometimes flooded and ice-filled Ohio River. Congress agreed and on May 17, 1796, authorized Zane to build a road and granted him a section of land at the three river crossings. Congress, however, stipulated that the road was to be open and ferries were to be operating by January 1, 1797.

Upon receipt of congressional approval, Zane quickly began the task of laying out a route through the wilderness, aided by his brother Jonathan, who had become familiar with Ohio while serving as a scout for Colonel Brodhead's expedition and for General Crawford. The Zane brothers, along with John McIntire, Ebenezer's brother-in-law, and an Indian guide by the name of Tomepomehala, began blazing trees with an ax and removing fallen limbs and underbrush to mark the trail. Whenever possible they followed Indian trails or paths opened by military expeditions. From Wheeling, for example, to the mouth of the Licking River they followed the Mingo Trail, passing through present-day St. Clairsville, Morristown, Washington, and Cambridge. After crossing the Muskingum below the mouth of the Licking, they blazed southwesterly along the Moxahala Trail into the Hocking Valley and through present-day Lancaster.

The party crossed the Pickaway Plains, striking the north bank of the Scioto opposite Chillicothe. Then they continued southwest, passing through present-day Sinking Spring, Locust Grove, Dunkinsville, West Union, and Bentonville, aiming for the Ohio and Limestone. Zane, however, made no effort to survey the most direct route. Rather, he avoided marshlands and hills, favoring a relatively easy but circuitous course rather than a more direct but difficult route. Even so, his road proved to be challenge enough, especially during foul weather. Indeed, when he had finished, his road was no more than a path with blazed trees showing the way. Riders with packhorses could negotiate their way on this bridle path, but it would not be a wagon road for a long time. Moreover, Zane did not complete even this rudimentary work until the summer of 1797, and the first ferry, consisting of two canoes lashed together, did not become operational at the mouth of the Licking until that autumn. Two years later this site became the fledgling village of Westbourn, subsequently known as Zanesville.

Improvement of the road, which everyone called Zane's Trace, did not come until statehood in 1803, when the legislature provided that 3 percent of the returns from the sale of public lands would be used for road building. The physical work for the improvement of Zane's trace and much of the financing came from county taxes and local farmers who worked under the direction of township road supervisors. Eventually they widened the route to twenty feet by cutting down trees and removing stumps, corduroying the road with logs over marshy ground, and building bridges, all of which helped facilitate wagon travel. As a result, by 1804 a wagon road linked Wheeling with Chillicothe, and the frontier people began to call it other names, such as the Wheeling Road, Wheeling-Limestone Road, or Limestone Road.

Immigrants from the Mid-Atlantic States and New England as well as from the Upland South soon created considerable traffic with ox carts, wagons, and packhorses along Zane's Trace as they headed for lands in Ohio from both ends of the road. The road also quickly developed into a trade route for the merchants in the newly forming towns, such as Chillicothe, where, for example, John McDougal made four trips annually by 1800 to Philadelphia to re-supply his store via pack train. Drovers soon used the Trace to take their cattle to eastern markets, and later freighters would follow the road with their giant Conestoga wagons pulled by six teams of horses.

The immigrants who used Zane's Trace to reach the Ohio frontier needed food and shelter for themselves and their horses, and entrepreneurs soon began establishing taverns along the road to provide for those needs. Accommodations varied in these hewn log houses, ranging from Andy C. Rooks's tavern west of Zanesville, where weary travelers slept on a puncheon floor, to John Treber's tavern in Adams County near West Union, where guests were treated to clean bedding and hearty frontier cooking. Some tavern-keepers even provided rudimentary entertainment. In November 1800, a traveler who stopped at a tavern near Chillicothe com-plained that the operators "had two shocking bad violins, one of which was of their own manufacture, on which they scraped away without mercy." Whether these taverns provided good or bad ac-commodations, however, fifty-four served the frontier people who traveled over Zane's Trace, or who lived near it, at six-mile intervals by the War of 1812.

Many of the early immigrants who followed Zane's Trace to the Ohio frontier were Germans from Pennsylvania, who settled in Fair-field and Perry counties. From the time that the town of Lancaster was laid out in 1800, it became a distinctively German community with store signs printed in both German and English. By 1809 enough immigrants of German heritage had moved to the Lancaster area to support a newspaper called *Der Ohio Adler*, and nearby Somerset became the center of Roman Catholicism in Ohio. In this region along Zane's Trace the settlers commonly spoke German and English. During the early nineteenth century, Zane's Trace also provided the route for Welsh immigrants bound for Licking County. There, Theophilus Rees and Thomas Phillips, who lived in the Welsh settlement of Beulah in western Pennsylvania, purchased approximately eighteen hundred acres in Licking County, which became the settlement of Welsh Hills. Although the first party of Welsh settlers traveled down the Ohio and up the Muskingum River to Zanesville in 1802, those who came later followed Zane's Trace before striking northwest from Zanesville for Licking County. In addition, French settlers from the island of Guernsey used Zane's Trace to reach the Ohio frontier in 1806. Partly because of exhaustion, they selected lands where the Trace crossed Wills Creek. These twenty-six men, women, and children were pleased with the land and the newly laid-out town of Cambridge. Soon they were writing letters home urging kith and kin to join them on the Ohio frontier. A year later, a second party of Guernseyites arrived and took up residence in Cambridge or on nearby farms. Three years later, the state legislature organized the county of Guernsey to honor them. Other settlers also came to Ohio over Zane's Trace. By 1807, homesteads had been located approximately every mile along the road, with the exception of the "wet prairies" west of Lancaster and the hilly ridges near Washington (Beyerstown). Fortescue Cuming, who traveled over the road at that time, reported that the land west of Zanesville was "so thickly inhabited, that was it not for the dead, girdled trees everywhere in the corn and wheat fields and meadows, it would have the appearance of an old settlement."

The farmers who settled along the Trace had a ready market for their crops and livestock in the form of vegetables, bread, and meat. Although this "settlers' market" was limited, it brought cash into the frontier farmer's home. At the same time, farmers located near Zane's Trace used the road to haul wheat to river towns, such as Zanesville on the Muskingum and Chillicothe on the Scioto, for export to New Orleans to reap high prices stimulated by the Napoleonic Wars. In 1802, François André Michaux reported that "the Americans of the interior cultivate wheat rather for speculation, in order to send the flour made from it to the seaports, than for their private consumption, because nine-tenths of them use bread made of corn." A year after Michaux made that observation, the first boat built in Chillicothe left its dock in February, laden with flour and barrels of pork, much of which farmers had taken to commission men over Zane's Trace bound for the Crescent City. Similarly, in 1807, James Van Zandt loaded his flatboat with flour, packed pork and beef, and casks of whiskey produced by farmers along the Trace, and floated down the Muskingum bound for New Orleans. Money earned from the sale of agricultural commodities along the Trace and over it to more distant markets provided the wealth for consumption and further encouraged the development of commercial agriculture. Prior to the War of 1812, which redirected the agricultural trade to the army, the wealth earned by agricultural exports brought keelboats up the Ohio River with coffee, tea, wine, and other luxuries which could be purchased in the stores and taverns along Zane's Trace.

Along Zane's Trace, land speculators often laid out tracts for towns, hoping to profit from the sale of lots on the arrival of settlers, particularly after the Treaty of Greenville in 1795. Chillicothe provides an example. Nathaniel Massie, one of the largest-scale land speculators on the Ohio frontier, laid out the town in 1796. He located the land on which Chillicothe rose while a surveyor in the Virginia Military District. In the spring of 1796, he left Massie's Station (Manchester) on the Ohio River, accompanied by a congregation of Presbyterians, with the intent of founding a town near the mouth of Paint Creek on the Scioto River.

Massie laid out the streets in a grid to give easy access to the river. He also laid off 456 lots and promised 100 free to the first settlers. Immigrants quickly claimed Massie's lots, and by winter several merchants, artisans, and tavernkeepers conducted business. In 1800, Chillicothe's politicians succeeded in moving the territorial capital to the town, allegedly to be nearer to the center of population. In 1806, Englishman Thomas Ashe, who passed through Chillicothe, reported that is was a "flourishing little town, containing about 150 houses neat and well kept," but he did not believe that

This building in Chillicothe became Ohio's first capitol in 1803. There settlers from Virginia created a political cadre that supported the Jeffersonian Republicans while opposing Federalist policies. Although Zanesville served as the capital from 1810 to 1812, Columbus became the permanent site of the state government in 1816. OHIO HISTORICAL SOCIETY.

it would survive for long. By the War of 1812, however, Chillicothe boasted a population of 1,360 and an additional 100 houses, and businessmen operated a cotton and woolen mill, rope walk, pottery, distillery, and tanning yard. Six taverns, including the Red Lion, which advertised private rooms with "good clean beds" and a "supply of the best liquor," served weary travelers. Nineteen stores provided a market for agricultural goods produced on the nearby farms, which commission men sent down the Scioto and Ohio rivers to New Orleans on flatboats built in the Chillicothe boat yard. The credit and cash earned financed the shipment of daily necessities as well as luxuries upriver by keelboat for the town's shopkeepers.

Similarly, in 1800 Ebenezer Zane had a surveyor lay out the town of Lancaster where his trace crossed the Hocking River. Lots went on sale on November 14. Depending on the location, the price ranged from five to fifty dollars per lot, with one-fourth paid in two weeks and the remainder in two years. Zane, like other real estate promoters, understood the necessity to attract merchants and artisans to ensure success, and he reserved free lots for a blacksmith, carpenter, and tanner in order to provide essential frontier services and lure other settlers to Lancaster who would buy his lots. Each favored craftsman had to live on his lot for four years, then Zane promised a deed. Several merchants and craftsmen would create a town nucleus that would attract doctors, lawyers, and ministers as well as other businessmen. As a result, Lancaster grew rapidly. In 1807, however, Fortescue Cuming reported 60 houses and 9 taverns that provided guests with the "roughest style of conviviality" as well as challenged them to a good night's sleep with bedbugs. By the War of 1812, lots brought three hundred dollars, and a population of 350 lived in 100 houses. Lancaster, like Chillicothe, had become an agricultural marketing and service center, where residents of the town and country received their mail and conducted business at the county courthouse.

In 1800 Zanesville was also laid out. Four years later it became the seat of Muskingum County. By the War of 1812, Zanesville had a population of 1,200 and 250 houses, for a growth rate of about 140 people per year over the previous eight years. Town lots ranged from one hundred to one thousand dollars, and the village included a saw- and gristmill and soap and candle manufacturer along with a cabinetmaker, saddler, cobbler, distiller, brickmaker, milliner, tin- and coppersmiths, and eleven taverns. The pottery, which began in 1808, soon became a major industry. Merchants received their goods over Zane's Trace by packhorses or freight wagons or by keelboats that plied the water up the Muskingum.

Additional towns such as Somerset, St. Clairsville, and Washington sprang up along Zane's Trace, but others, such as Smithtown and Hanover, failed to match the dreams of their founders. Poor soil or problems with land titles usually ended the hopes of their founder speculators. Of the towns that remained, however, each had been developed to meet not only the needs of the countryside but also the desires of land speculators to make a profit. They acquired land, built a ferry or tavern, surveyed lots, and lured settlers, particularly artisans, with free land. Soon the towns became service and marketing centers, especially the county seats located on the Muskingum and the Scioto, which, in turn, lured others to both the towns and the nearby countryside.

Zane's Trace, then, provided an all-weather road into the interior and served speculators, merchants, and farmers alike. In 1798, postal riders used the Trace to carry mail between Wheeling and Cincinnati. Other mail routes soon branched off so that by 1807, Ohio had sixty-four post offices. Zane's Trace would also serve as a road for the movement of troops when a new Indian war occurred. Most important, Zane's Trace served as the route for a heavy and rapid flow of immigrants from the Ohio River to available lands in southeastern and central Ohio, and it fostered the establishment of towns and encouraged commercial agriculture in this part of the frontier. Indeed, while Ohio's population totaled only an estimated 3,000 in 1790, by 1800 it numbered approximately 45,365 whites living north of the Ohio River. Many of those immigrants arrived at the river towns, and Zane's Trace served as the only major overland route to Ohio's interior from both east and south. Moreover, while the Ohio River brought settlers and provided access to the Miami and Little Miami valleys, Zane's Trace provided the route for many immigrants who settled in the Muskingum, Hocking, and Scioto river valleys by 1800.

Zane's Trace and the Ohio River, then, enabled the rapid settlement of the frontier after 1800. At the turn of the century more than 75 percent of the population resided in the counties that bordered the Ohio River. A decade later that concentration had decreased by approximately 30 percent. During that same time, the population of the interior increased from about 25 percent to almost 52 percent of the total. Most of those people lived on the Congress lands that bordered Zane's Trace, or in the Virginia Military District that the Trace and its branches helped link with the outside world.

* * *

In the towns that grew up along Zane's Trace and elsewhere on the Ohio frontier, merchants exchanged goods for agricultural commodities, which they then sold on the local market or shipped down the river systems of the interior to the Ohio and more lucrative centers in Cincinnati, Louisville, St. Louis, and New Orleans. They served as necessary commission men by extending credit or paying in cash, when possible, both of which stimulated consumerism and encouraged commercial agricultural production.

In the villages, merchants often served as bankers until proper banks became established. They kept the earnings of farmers and other merchants in their safes, and they lent money at interest. By so doing, these frontier merchants profited from their sales as well as from using money placed in their care as operating capital. These banking services also generated more trade for the merchant because depositors usually gave him their business that they might have taken elsewhere. The merchant's stores also served as gathering places where men could visit and take a drink of whiskey from the communal cask, while women talked with friends and neighbors, whom, in the case of farm women, they saw at best only on weekly trips to town. By creating an amiable gathering place, merchants increased their business. Merchants also provided mail services by collecting letters for the postal rider and by holding letters for pickup by residents and nearby farmers, and they used the local newspaper to notify people who had letters waiting for them. Merchants wrote letters and served as subscription agents for newspapers printed beyond their immediate areas. They also stocked at least a few books on their shelves, particularly histories, British literature, and Bibles.

Frontier merchants, however, did not exist merely to provide necessary services, such as building towns and serving as bankers and postal clerks. They operated to make a profit by wholesaling and retailing, as did Cincinnati merchant Thomas Gibson, who in November 1793 advertised to sell dry goods, Madeira, sherry, brandy, brown sugar, allspice, pepper, and other groceries. Ohio's frontier merchants could begin business with a few hundred dollars, and they charged based on cash or barter prices. Although merchants preferred cash, they often accepted agricultural commodities because their customers had little money. Perishable commodities could be resold through the store, while staple and relatively nonperishable products, such as pork, butter, and cheese, could be collected for sale to other commission men down the Ohio River. In January 1801, for example, John McDougal and William

Neblach in Chillicothe advertised to buy five hundred bushels of corn at one dollar per barrel in merchandise or to settle outstanding debts. A year later, the mercantile store of Ferguson and McFarland advertised groceries, dry goods, iron, and Queen's ware for cash, furs, maple sugar, salt, and ginseng.

Local commission men also advanced credit and cash (if they were prosperous) and helped expand the circulating currency on the Ohio frontier. By so doing, merchants helped Ohio's frontier economy pass from agricultural subsistence to a market economy. By the end of the frontier period, successful merchants could expect to conduct about forty dollars' worth of business per day, or from one hundred to three hundred dollars' worth per week. Bad weather and muddy roads, however, could bring business to a halt, but merchants in the river towns, such as Zanesville, Chillicothe, and Hamilton, had the best access to the wholesale markets and commission men in Cincinnati. Even so, low water on the Ohio could increase shipping rates as much as 20 percent for new goods, which merchants then passed on to their customers.

Even when the Ohio River ran at bank-full, however, the frontier merchant had a difficult job restocking his shelves. In 1811, for example, Joseph Hough, who operated a general merchandise store in Hamilton on the Miami River, traveled six hundred miles to Philadelphia to purchase new goods and wares. He then hired wagons and drivers to haul goods three hundred miles to Pittsburgh at a cost of $6 to $10 per hundredweight, depending on the merchandise. At Pittsburgh he transferred these goods to a flatboat for transport to Cincinnati, then he hauled them to Hamilton. This trip took Hough three months. Similarly, in 1806, Dayton merchants Henry Brown, John Compton, Jr., and Joseph Pierce had to freight goods overland from Cincinnati at the rate of $2.50 per hundredweight, because the Miami River was too difficult to navigate upstream.

Merchants often had to plead with their customers to settle their accounts, because businessmen had made their purchases on credit, usually at 6 to 12 percent interest, with accounts payable in twelve months to eastern wholesalers. In mid-November 1793, for example, John Armstrong, a merchant in Cincinnati, placed a newspaper notice in which he demanded "immediate payment" of all bills in corn, beef, pork, butter, cheese, potatoes, and "furr and skins" at market prices. At the same time, he announced a "fresh assortment" of merchandise and groceries, and he obviously needed his customers to pay their debts so that he could pay his creditors. Several years later, in the autumn of 1800, mercantilers by the name of McLandburg and Candlish in Chillicothe notified their customers in the local newspaper that they would soon make a buying trip to the East and that they needed payment. Those who met their obligations would continue to receive credit, but those who did not pay would be visited by "collection officials." With these problems, the turnover rate among frontier merchants always remained high, with constant failures and reorganizations under new partnerships. Like the frontier in general, social and economic mobility kept the stores small, and merchants chronically lacked the capital to support large inventories. In June 1826, for example, eleven merchants applied for operating licenses in Hamilton. Mercantilists Andrew McCleary and Caleb Decamp had the largest stock, valued at five thousand dollars, while the business of Clinton Stockhouse opened with only one hundred dollars' worth of inventory.

The frontier merchants in Ohio did not sell brand names. Rather, products such as coffee, tea, and dry goods bore trade names that they bought in bulk from wholesalers. Patent medicines were the only exception. With few doctors on the frontier and medical practice still based on considerable superstition, patent medicines provided a cheaper and less painful remedy for a medical problem than a trip to the doctor, and often the results were the same. In January 1796, the store of Hatch and Barns in Cincinnati advertised medicines "suited to the disorders incident to the climate," such as Dragon's Blood, Bateman's drops, Godfey's cordial, essence of peppermint, Anderson's and Cooper's pills, oil of pennyroyal, camphor, and Peruvian bark. In the absence of a doctor to make a diagnosis and write a prescription, the label on the bottle noted the illnesses that it treated and the dosage necessary. Parents with a sick child hastened to the merchant who sold these medicines. As a result, patent medicines made a considerable contribution to the frontier merchant's sales.

Frontier merchants also sometimes served as contractors for the army. The merchants in Hamilton conducted a particularly profitable trade with the military, which, combined with their location on the Miami River and the bountiful countryside for agricultural products, helped make them the economic and social leaders of the community. Joseph Kerr in Chillicothe also bought agricultural produce from area farmers for delivery at Upper Sandusky between December 1812 and July 1813. Kerr advertised to employ "sober men and good drivers." If they owned their own horses, he paid them $4 per day to make the sixteen-day haul with wagons loaded with flour, soap, candles, and whiskey. By March 1, 1813, Kerr had earned $13,048 from his government contract. Commission men in Cincinnati provisioned army posts as far west as Jefferson Barracks, Missouri, by the late 1820s.

Despite the level of capital investment, the towns which the merchants helped create quickly became more than commercial centers for the sale and exchange of agricultural products and merchandise of local or eastern manufacture. They served as important social and cultural centers, particularly as the frontier transcended from borderland to settled community. The towns often supported literary and debating societies, dedicated to spirited discussion and intellectual improvement as well as social interaction.

Although the Northwest Ordinance provided that "religion, morality and knowledge being necessary to good government and the happiness of mankind, Schools and the means of education shall forever be encouraged," it did not provide a system for establishing or funding them. In the absence of territorial taxation for the support of education, citizens who commanded wealth often founded private schools, called academies, where both boys and girls gained rudimentary training in the classics as well as reading, writing, and arithmetic. Tuition met the teacher's salary and other school expenditures. In February 1801, the citizens of Franklinton advertised for a "gentleman" schoolmaster, and they assured that a well-recommended individual would get a "large school," that is, a profitable enrollment. In March 1802, for example, John Hutt opened an academy for girls where they learned reading and writing as well as basic arithmetic. They were also taught "plain and open tambouring and embroidery." Hutt also planned to provide coursework in double- and single-entry bookkeeping. Four years later the Reverend Robert W. Finley opened the Farmers' Academy, where he taught basic education for $6 per year and English, Latin, and Greek for $12 per year. In July, a Mrs. Williams in Cincinnati advertised in the newspaper that she planned to open a school for young ladies at the home of a Mr. Newman. Her charges were: "Reading 250 cents; Reading and Sewing $3.00; Reading, Sewing, and Writing 350 cents per quarter." A year later, residents in Chillicothe advertised for a schoolmaster who could teach reading, writing, and arithmetic.

Upon statehood in 1803, the constitution provided that "no law shall be passed to prevent the poor . . . from an equal participation in the schools, academies, colleges, and universities of this State, which are endowed, from the revenues arising from the donations made by the United States." The state legislature did not provide taxation for the support of public schools, but approved the incorporation of private schools.

Technical schools also opened at the turn of the nineteenth century in Cincinnati, where students could learn the fine points of surveying and navigation. Less technical and academic schools provided other training. In November 1806, Garret Lane opened a dance school in Cincinnati. The following spring, Sarah Browne and Eliza Heighway also established a school for women in Cincinnati, where they taught "various branches of polite education," including embroidery and painting. Although women had limited educational opportunities on the Ohio frontier, men and women supported female education because they believed it would help them fulfill their roles as homemakers and mothers. Moreover, educated women would help improve home and community life. The schools, then, particularly in the Western Reserve towns, played an important role in helping ensure and preserve social order.

Still, public schools were not established until the population became sufficiently large and dense to support them, especially beyond the towns. In 1818, one traveler reported that the schools in Ohio were "very few" in number and "wretched" in condition. Where schools provided at least adequate educational training, such as those in Marietta, Warren, Hudson, Cincinnati, Cleveland, and Zanesville, private not public funding met the necessary expenditures. In the meantime, one-room schools, usually a log house, provided the setting for basic educational instruction, especially reading, spelling, arithmetic, and writing, with memorization the key to success, and with the work conducted with chalk on slate boards. As a result, in 1818 a letter to the Cincinnati *Inquisitor* signed "Lycurgus" complained that "in many places the robust native sons of Ohio . . . [were] growing up to manhood, with scarcely more intelligence than can be gleaned from the bare light of nature."

Public education came primarily with the development of libraries in the towns and villages. Belpre, Cincinnati, and Dayton had circulating libraries by the late 1790s, while the residents of Amesville created a library in 1803 by selling coonskins and other pelts. An annual fee of $2.50 for borrowing privileges also could be paid in coonskins. Newspapers, however, provided the most information to the literate public.

* * *

Although women in the towns as well as the countryside lived lives dedicated to homes and families, some women shrugged off all bonds to their husbands and filed for divorce. Unhappy husbands turned to the newspapers in their towns to notify all concerned that they had been wronged for no cause and that they would not be responsible for any bills that their unloving and former partners might charge to them. As early as March 1794, John Meeker in Columbia posted notice in the Cincinnati newspaper that he would not pay the debts of his wife because she had "absconded from [his] bed and board without provocation." Several months later Peter Davis in Cincinnati made the same proclamation because his wife had "taken up with another man." In March 1796, the general court in Cincinnati granted two divorces, and more followed in increasing frequency for a number of reasons. In August 1807, for example, Samuel Logue of Gallipolis sued his wife for divorce on the grounds that she had committed adultery with a "number of other persons" and because she had been gone for more than five years. Life on the frontier was always hard, and emotional, physical, and financial support among spouses proved essential, but on the frontier many women were not intimidated by the fear of being alone in a hostile environment. They filed for divorce or fled their husbands and began life anew. Indeed, many women sought personal freedom and took advantage of the opportunities for independent action on the Ohio frontier.

Women, however, had few occupational opportunities other than teaching, and they also primarily accepted the responsibility for teaching Bible lessons, thereby applying their learning and moral authority to the settlements on the Ohio frontier. Always, however, their lives were controlled by social and cultural boundaries that relegated them to the roles of wives, mothers, and housekeepers. But their lives were not always filled with days of drudgery. On July 4, 1801, for example, Alexander C. Elliot outside of Cleveland made arrangements to take a Miss Doan to a dance. When he arrived at her home on his mare, she was waiting on a stump. As he rode up, she lifted her calico dress and swung onto the horse behind him. They danced to a violin on a puncheon floor. Periodic stops to refresh themselves with drinks of whiskey laced with maple sugar made the scamperdown, double-shuffle, western swing, and half-moon easier to dance as the evening wore on. Elliot reported that they had a "fine time."

* * *

Women also had the responsibility for family health care in an age when medical science had not yet shrugged off the bonds of superstition. On the frontier a variety of illnesses commonly called fevers, agues, or "miasmas" brought misery and debilitation. "Bilious fever," probably typhoid, dysentery, or flu, plagued adults on the frontier throughout the year, while cholera infantum and croup killed many children. Measles and diphtheria remained common, while mosquitoes spread malaria. The frontier people often attributed these and other afflictions to "bad air" near marshes and along the river bottoms, "whence deleterious exhultations arise."

Most fevers were not fatal, but other illnesses brought death. In 1792 an epidemic of scarlet fever, called "putrid throat," swept the Ohio frontier. The children of the settlers of the Ohio Company particularly suffered, and one report claimed that "five or six in some cases died out of a single family." In November 1793 a Cincinnati resident reported that smallpox, also known as cowpox, "now prevails with great virulence in this place," with many children dying.

Although smallpox threatened anyone who had not submitted to the discomforts of inoculation, it was not a major problem for the white population after the early years of the nineteenth century. The first inoculation for smallpox may have been by Dr. Jabez True in Marietta as early as 1793, while William Goforth in Cincinnati first vaccinated for the disease in 1801. A year later vaccination was common in many Ohio settlements by doctors, such as P. S. Mason in Steubenville, who advertised this service in local newspapers. In 1824, an outbreak of smallpox in Cincinnati encouraged the city council to locate a doctor who would vaccinate anyone for fifty cents, while those who could not pay would be vaccinated free of charge, and he planned to supply the vaccination to country doctors through an agent in Philadelphia.

Drafty, damp cabins provided little comfort for anyone afflicted with "Hooping Cough," pneumonia, or fever. During February and March 1807, the people in the towns along the Ohio River, such as Belpre, suffered "catarrhal fevers of great severity and obstinacy." And in August "scarcely a family in the township was free of disease of some form or other." This illness, probably yellow fever, "appeared in various grades of intensity"; it struck Marietta hard during the summer, and fifty people died. The worst form of this fever caused a "billious remittent," and the disease ended only with the first frost.

Influenza also struck the Ohio frontier during the autumn of 1807. Doctors such as Walter Buell in Chillicothe, who advertised that he had been "longer acquainted with the diseases of this settlement than any other physician," prescribed a host of drugs, such as quinine and opium, and other medicines, such as arsenic, calomel, and borax, to alleviate the fever that accompanied flu and malaria. "Sub-carbonate of soda" became another favorite remedy. Doctors theorized that it neutralized "septic acid in the stomach and bowels . . . rendering the fever mild and more manageable." Although bicarbonate of soda worked best when taken internally, some doctors preferred to wrap their patients in sheets wet with a mixture of bicarbonate of soda, alcohol, and capsicum to cool the patient and break the fever. Others preferred administering a mixture of powdered charcoal and yeast every two or three hours.

If a patient had a particularly bad case of any diagnosed disease or illness, frontier doctors believed that "bleeding was useful early in the attack, followed by evacuants," both of which left the patient far weaker than before. Medical care by physicians did not differ in many respects from that practiced by self-proclaimed horse doctors, who also quickly resorted to bleeding and purging. Usually frontier doctors had too many lancets and too little training. Most doctors on the frontier did not have a medical degree and learned their profession under tutelage, that is, by apprenticeship. Often doctors practiced dentistry on the side. Given the common medical training and treatments of the day, it is little wonder that the frontier people sent for the doctor only in time of dire emergency. By that time it was often too late, a situation that led to the axiom that doctors "healed slow" but "killed quick." For the most part the frontier people were better off letting an illness run its course, if possible, rather than submitting to the torture and suffering usually caused by doctors, who probably contributed as much to the graveyards as to good health on the frontier.

Often home remedies, rather than a call for the doctor, improved the chances of recovery for the sick. One such cure for ague or flu was a mixture of cloves, cinnamon, quinine, whiskey, and a "small lump of alloways," of which the afflicted took three drams per day until cured. Mustard and onion poultices allegedly helped sore throats, and a mixture of flaxseed, licorice, raisins, sugar, and white vinegar fought colds. A teaspoon of brandy soothed a cough, while whiskey served as the common remedy for almost any ailment. A folk remedy for consumption or tuberculosis was a diet of white bread and buttermilk.

No matter the cure for any disease or sickness, the immigrants invariably suffered poor health during their first year on the frontier, a time known as "seasoning." James Kilbourne, a journalist and legislator, wrote during the latter part of the frontier period: "Respecting the healthfulness of this country, I have to repeat that it is in fact sickly to a considerable degree." In March 1820, the *Scioto Telegraph* reported, "The angel of disease and death, ascending from his oozy bed, along the marshy margin of the bottom grounds . . . floats in his aerial chariot, and in seasons favorable to his prowess spreads mortal desolation as he flies." Three years later in September, more than half of the 165,000 people who lived in the seventeen counties within a fifty-mile radius of Columbus were ill, which caused some politicians to advocate moving the capital to Zanesville.

Sicknesses and diseases that could not be prevented or cured by contemporary medical knowledge brought suffering, stress, anxiety, and all too frequently death to many frontier homes, particularly for children. On the frontier the mortality rate for children remained high; perhaps as many as 25 percent died before their first birthday. The key to survival was to live through the first year. Then the next challenge became surviving until about the age of twenty, by which time another 25 percent of the children and young adult population may have died. Those who could endure the host of diseases and illnesses that plagued the frontier until adulthood had a reasonably good chance of living into their sixties. Most families, however, had the heartbreaking experience of burying their children. Speculators and land companies made no mention of the problems of disease on the frontier. Instead they continually reported only the "healthfulness of the country."

* * *

While the frontier people went about their daily lives, Congress dallied in creating a governmental structure for the Ohio country after the Peace of Paris ended the Revolutionary War in 1783. It did so largely because so few white settlers lived on the frontier. By 1787, however, Congress acted and passed the Northwest Ordinance, which created a territorial system of government. The Northwest Ordinance provided for a governor with wide-ranging powers, including command of the militia, and three judges with whom he would consult. Yet the governor as chief executive officer essentially exercised the combined powers of the executive and legislative branches of government because he had the power to enforce, adopt, and administer laws from other states, appoint all judges and civil officials, purchase Indian lands, and sell federal lands to settlers and speculators. When the population of the Northwest Territory reached five thousand, however, he had to share power with an elected assembly. Since the first territorial legislature did not meet until 1799, St. Clair wielded almost total political, economic, and military power in Ohio for a decade. And when the time came to share political power, he could not give it up easily. Although the Ordinance imposed a governmental system on the Northwest Territory, including Ohio, and created a colony of the United States, it provided the order necessary to govern and administer a vast area undergoing rapid settlement. The Northwest Ordinance also created the framework for often bitter political maneuvering.

Upon passage of the Northwest Ordinance, Congress appointed Arthur St. Clair governor of the Northwest Territory. St. Clair held this position until 1802, during which time he became the most important figure in Ohio's politics. St. Clair saw both economic and political opportunity in Ohio. It offered a chance to build an estate in frontier lands as well as enhance his reputation in politics on a national level. The Northwest Ordinance did not provide for democracy, and St. Clair arrived as a proconsul appointed from afar. He intended to rule with authority and establish a system of territorial government that would ensure stability, peace, and prosperity on the Ohio frontier.

St. Clair arrived at Marietta on July 15, 1788. Almost immediately territorial judges Samuel H. Parsons, James M. Varnum, and John Cleves Symmes charged that St. Clair attempted to exercise too much power. Although obliged to consult with the territorial judges over the adoption of laws, St. Clair drew up a legal code during his first six months in Ohio, largely on his own initiative. He also organized the militia, laid off Washington County, created a county judicial system, established county offices, banned unlawful assembly, prohibited swearing, and required the observance of the Sabbath. Property and morality would be protected in Ohio by political fiat. When he finished, St. Clair reported to Congress that the government had been "put in motion."

The judges, however, disagreed with St. Clair about the nature of the governmental process in the Northwest Territory. The Ordinance had authorized the governor and the three judges "to adopt and publish . . . such laws of the original states, criminal and civil, as may be necessary, and best suited to the circumstances of the district." St. Clair interpreted that section to mean that they could adopt laws only from the thirteen states. We must "take them as we find them," he wrote, and reminded the judges that the adoption of any law required the governor's approval, even if the three judges favored it. In contrast, the judges contended that they could enact new laws and revise various state laws to meet the conditions of life in the Northwest Territory. St. Clair reflected that "the point was battled, both verbally and in writing, for a considerable time." In the end, St. Clair and the judges both adopted and enacted laws because of necessity, even though Congress had not authorized the latter action.

St. Clair believed that order must come before liberty and that the frontier people could not be trusted to govern themselves or live peacefully and civilly without firm control and guidance from the territorial government. The early politicians in Ohio were prepared to mold this frontier society for the better. On May 29, 1795, St. Clair and territorial judges John Cleves Symmes and George Turner met in Cincinnati and adopted thirty-seven laws, mostly from Pennsylvania, which became known as "Maxwell's Code." Essentially, it was a summary of all territorial laws in effect, with considerable alteration to meet the needs of the Northwest Territory. Maxwell's Code met immediate needs on the Ohio frontier, while the common law provided a legal institutional framework for the future, and by so doing created a stable system of government in which power began with the governor and passed down through various offices by the appointive process. Until the first territorial legislature met, St. Clair continued to create new counties, determined the county seats, authorized local militia units, and appointed most of the officers. St. Clair essentially operated on the premise that the Northwest Territory served as an independent political entity and that congressional acts did not apply to it unless Congress specifically designated. St. Clair believed that the Northwest Territory was a colony under his jurisdiction. It was a contention that quickly brought political trouble.

St. Clair turned to the New Englanders, whose conservatism and political ideology he respected, to administer his colonial government. In Marietta, for example, he appointed Rufus Putnam and Benjamin Tupper justices of the peace. If New Englanders were not present, he chose men who were well respected in their communities, such as William McMillan, William Goforth, and Benjamin Stites, who became judges, and Israel Ludlow, clerk of the court in

Hamilton County. Essentially, St. Clair's appointees ran local governmental affairs and kept the governor informed. Although Congress had the power to veto the laws adopted by St. Clair and to remove his appointees from office, it seldom intervened in Ohio's frontier politics.

Yet despite St. Clair's good intentions, his firm control of territorial government began to wane almost from the very beginning. As immigration began to swell, Ohio qualified for the next phase of territorial government, which provided for an elected legislature. By the late eighteenth century, most of the new immigrants did not hail from New England, but instead migrated from Pennsylvania, Virginia, and the Carolinas, and they had different ideas about the nature of government and society than the New Englanders. Indeed, they sympathized with the political views of the newly emerging Jeffersonian Republicans, who soon formed the Republican party. For them, limited government was the key to good government. They opposed strong central authority and instead favored freedom that would enable settlers to create order through state and local governmental systems. For these Jeffersonian Republicans, individualism rather than national authority should dictate life on the Ohio frontier. This world view clashed hard with St. Clair's philosophy of government and human nature. As a result, leadership elites began to emerge, and political divisions based on cultural origin politicized Ohio's governmental process. Indeed, differences between the assembly and the governor created factions that had crystallized into the Federalist and Republican parties in Ohio by 1800.

A considerable part of St. Clair's political troubles in Ohio lay with the Northwest Ordinance, which provided that as soon as five thousand adult males lived in the territory, it could create an assembly through the electoral process. And upon reaching sixty thousand residents, it could apply for statehood. Accordingly, as early as February 1, 1796, a movement began in Cincinnati that called for an assembly to counter St. Clair's authoritarian ways. Indeed, Judge John Cleves Symmes and other non-Federalists in the Scioto and Miami valleys had concluded by the late 1790s that the Northwest Ordinance was "inadequate to the wants of the people." The governor delayed until October 29, 1798, when calls for a census encouraged him to face the inevitable, and he proclaimed that the

Northwest Territory now had more than five thousand adult males. As required by the law, he called for a territorial election in December to create a twenty-two-member assembly. This lower house would then meet in Cincinnati on January 24, 1799, and nominate ten men for the upper house, and President John Adams would choose five from that list. St. Clair required that all delegates to the assembly be American citizens and residents of their county. In addition, all voters had to own fifty acres or have made a hundred dollars' worth of improvements on their farms or their town lots that had the equivalent value. Those who ran for office in the lower house had to freehold two hundred acres, while the council or upper house required ownership of at least five hundred acres to qualify. Only men who had a stake in society could participate in Ohio's frontier politics. At the same time, however, St. Clair ruled that all voting had to take place at the county courthouses, an edict that prevented many frontier farmers from reaching the polling stations. As a result, only the more prosperous farmers who lived near county seats and the residents of those towns voted. St. Clair hoped that wealth and community ties, particularly those that extended to New England and Federalism, would carry the day.

St. Clair was disappointed, however, because partisan politics did not enter into the election process in 1798. Instead, the frontier people voted for the most respected and best-known leaders who stood for election to the assembly. Still, four blocs emerged among the newly elected assemblymen—the pro-statehood Cincinnati advocates, the Virginians from Chillicothe and the Scioto Valley, the Federalists from Marietta and Washington County, and a group from the French counties. At first these divisions were primarily geographical, but soon two blocks solidified—the New England Federalists and the Scioto Jeffersonians.

The first legislative assembly met on September 16, 1799, and eight days later elected Edward Tiffin to the post of speaker. On October 3, the two houses elected William Henry Harrison to be the nonvoting delegate to Congress. Harrison had strong support from the Scioto Valley delegates, particularly Nathaniel Massie and Thomas Worthington and their fellow Chillicotheans who opposed the election of Arthur St. Clair, Jr. Harrison's election indicated early opposition to the governor and his supporters. Even so, the territorial legislature increased St. Clair's authority by granting him veto power and the ability to call or prorogue the assembly. When St. Clair vetoed several bills that attempted to restrict his power, particularly those that created counties by assembly rather than executive action, partisan political lines became increasingly clear and fixed. In fact, Worthington and Massie began a campaign to have St. Clair removed from office or not reappointed when his term expired in 1801, an action that further alienated the Ohio Federalists.

St. Clair contributed to further political partisanship by advocating the division of the Northwest Territory at the Scioto and Wabash rivers. Publicly, his intent was to improve administration of the far western settlements, but in reality he hoped to isolate the Virginians in the Scioto Valley and politically control the eastern division with Federalist appointees from Steubenville and Marietta, who would form a "counterpoise" to the Scioto Virginians. In addition, he believed that "sober industrious" easterners who had settled in Cincinnati would dominate the Virginians who had settled on military lands west of the Scioto River in the central division. At the same time, St. Clair rejected the growing demands for statehood by the Scioto faction, because he did not believe that Ohioans had the capacity for statehood. St. Clair contended, "A multitude of indigent and ignorant people are but ill qualified to form a constitution and government for themselves." More important, "They are too far removed from the seat of government to be much impressed with the power of the United States." The Ohioans, he argued, were a pack of debtors who wanted nothing more than to fleece their eastern creditors. So far as fixed political principles were concerned, St. Clair wrote, "they have none." By dividing the Northwest Territory, he could keep Ohio under colonial rule and protect his own position and power. The Jeffersonian Republicans, however, increasingly argued that the source of political power should come from the "people" who were "fully competent to govern themselves."

When the Scioto Virginians succeeded in gaining congressional approval to move the capital to Chillicothe from Cincinnati, St. Clair began building a coalition with politicians to ensure that when statehood occurred he could preserve Federalist control of the assembly and relocate the capital in Cincinnati. When the assembly convened for a second session on November 3, 1800, St. Clair complained that "the vilest calumnies and the grossest falsehoods are assiduously circulated among the people," all intended to prevent his reappointment. Soon the assembly divided over the governor's power to veto bills, particularly its creation of counties. It also went about the business of addressing the needs of a frontier society by passing legislation that ranged from the encouragement of the killing of wolves to the care of illegitimate children.

At the end of 1800, then, the Scioto Virginians favored a Republican government, that is, the election of officials by a qualified group of voters, as opposed to the Federalists, who supported the colonial, appointive power of the governor. Neither the Federalists nor the Republicans, however, could control the legislature on all matters. Yet each party had developed a program for Ohio, attempted to enlist supporters, and sought affiliation with the Federalist or Republican parties on the national level.

The election of Thomas Jefferson to the presidency in 1800, and with it the Republican party on the national level, had an immediate influence on Ohio's politics, largely because of the appointive power of the presidency, and because the Ohio Republicans now had champions in Congress and the executive branch who favored statehood. On January 12, 1801, the Federalists in Marietta met and opposed statehood because they would lose considerable political power and offices, but they argued that the world suffered too much "turmoil" for the people of Ohio to form a state government. In contrast, the Scioto Virginians saw their opportunity to get rid of St. Clair and his abusive veto power once and for all. Worthington spoke angrily of the need to "curb the tyrant," while St. Clair raved that the Ohio Jeffersonians were "ambitious, designing, and envious men" bent on destroying order and society in their territory.

Statehood remained the chief political issue throughout 1801. When the assembly convened at the governor's request on November 4, the Republicans held a slight edge. St. Clair anticipated a "stormy" session, and he planned to prorogue the assembly if it called for statehood and a constitutional convention. Indeed, St. Clair and his Federalist supporters in Marietta feared the worst. For them, the situation was clear. As long as Ohio remained "a mixed mass of people, scattered over an immense wilderness" without any "connecting principle," statehood remained dangerous, if not impossible.

Quickly, the delegates from Marietta and Cincinnati developed a plan to divide the Territory at the Scioto River. Thereby, they reasoned, each division would take longer to acquire the sixty thousand residents needed to apply for statehood. This delay would not only preserve Federalist power in the territorial governmental system but also delay the necessity of new taxation. A division would also fragment Chillicothe's power and end its bid to serve as the new state capital by removing the locus of power and government offices to Marietta and Cincinnati. The Scioto delegates, of course, vociferously opposed this plan. Nathaniel Massie argued that the Northwest Ordinance guaranteed Ohio's boundaries and that division would created undue administrative expenses. Nevertheless, the Marietta and Cincinnati coalition passed the bill in the lower house by a 12 to 8 vote, and unanimously in the council or upper house.

The matter of territorial division was not merely an issue to be argued in the assembly, governed by rules of order and accustomed civil niceties. On Christmas Eve a group of thugs called the "Bloodhounds" assembled to burn St. Clair in effigy before a flaming barrel of tar at Gregg House, which served as quarters for the governor. The leader, Michael Baldwin, threatened to horsewhip anyone who got in his way. Although Worthington bitterly opposed St. Clair and championed statehood, he met the crowd and convinced it to disperse. He also threatened to kill Baldwin if the mob continued with its plan. The mob reappeared on Christmas night intent on harming William R. Putnam, who was also staying at Gregg House, because he had made a toast to the division of Ohio at the Scioto. A confrontation ensued, with "warm words" exchanged between the Bloodhounds and the Federalists and Republicans who attempted to maintain order. When an assemblyman drew a knife and attacked one of the rioters, the crowd dissolved into the darkness. With the exception of a fistfight between two delegates to the assembly, the remainder of the session proved uneventful, because some of the leaders left Chillicothe to present their case to Congress.

Worthington and his Jeffersonian supporters favored division of the Northwest Territory, but at the Great Miami River, with the

Thomas Worthington acquired a fortune by purchasing bounty warrants for lands in the Virginia Military District and United States Military District. He also played an active role in territorial politics by seeking statehood, opposing the policies of Governor Arthur St. Clair, and serving as one of Ohio's first two senators.
OHIO HISTORICAL SOCIETY, SC 4120.

creation of a new state to the east. Accordingly, he lobbied Congress, telling his Republican colleagues that statehood would bring two Republican senators, a representative, and three electoral votes to the Jefferson administration and Congress, and he did his best to denigrate St. Clair as a tyrant bent on fulfilling his own "pecuniary interests" and stifling the will of the people. Even though a census had not been conducted to determine whether sixty thousand people resided in the Territory, he urged an immediate declaration of statehood. William Goforth of Cincinnati aided the Republican cause by writing President Jefferson that St. Clair had "all the power of a British Nabob," and that he appointed only Federalists, relatives, and friends to governmental offices. He also charged that St. Clair arbitrarily created counties in order to build his political base through patronage. Worthington also agreed and sent a letter to Jefferson calling St. Clair "an open and avowed enemy of the republican form of government."

Jefferson agreed, and promised to seek statehood for Ohio and block the Federalist scheme for redivision of the Territory. St. Clair, however, used Paul Fearing, territorial delegate to Congress, to press the Federalist cause and create fear of statehood by arguing that the frontier people would seize federal lands as soon as national control ended. This warning fell on deaf Republican ears, and Congress passed an Enabling Act for statehood which the president signed on April 30, 1802, to make Ohio the seventeenth state. When the announcement of the statehood enactment, along with news that Congress had repealed internal taxes, reached Chillicothe in early July, a town celebration became so exuberant that one traveler was convinced that St. Clair had died. In contrast, congressional delegate Paul Fearing urged the Ohio Federalists east of the Scioto River to break away and form their own state, no matter what Congress decreed. Fortunately for Ohio, cooler Federalist heads rejected that suggestion and instead considered strategy to elect as many Federalists as possible to a constitutional convention.

Although the Federalists campaigned by appealing to public fears that the Republicans would increase the cost of government, levy taxes, and extend slavery to Ohio, the Republicans carried the October elections for delegates to a constitutional convention, relying on "hand bills and long tavern harangues" to convince an already favorable public to support them on election day. When the constitutional convention met on November 1, thirty-five delegates elected Edward Tiffin as its president. Although twenty-six delegates favored the Scioto Republicans, St. Clair attempted to take control of the convention by naming a secretary and demanding that the delegates give him their certificates of election for his approval. He also addressed the delegates, arguing that only the Chillicotheans wanted statehood and that Congress could not force it on any people. He believed the Virginia Republicans wanted statehood merely to extend slavery into Ohio. Desperately and pathetically St. Clair pleaded, "We have the means in our hands to bring Congress to reason, if we should be forced to bring Congress to reason, if we should be forced to use them. If we submit . . . we should be trodden upon, and what is worse, we should deserve to be trodden upon." Evidently he wanted Ohio to govern itself independently as a renegade, as Vermont had done before admission to the Union. The delegates, however, simply ignored him and went about the business of drafting a constitution for the approval of Congress, which under the terms of the Northwest Ordinance was the last step before gaining statehood.

Worthington listened to St. Clair's harangue and predicted that "the poor old man . . . will very soon die politically." To ensure his prophecy, he sent a copy of St. Clair's speech to Jefferson. The president reacted angrily at this test of national authority. Secretary of the Treasury Gallatin called it "indecent" and "outrageous," while James Madison remarked that the president thought it a "very evil example." Quickly, Jefferson removed St. Clair from office on November 22, and appointed Charles Byrd to the office of governor until statehood could be achieved. When St. Clair had arrived in Marietta in 1788, he was saluted by fourteen cannon and an excited public that referred to him as "Excellency." Now he departed a bitter and broken man.

The delegates to the constitutional convention operated on the premise that the Republican party knew best for the people of Ohio, and blocked most Federalist proposals. Significantly, the delegates provided the vote for any white male who paid taxes or worked on the roads, a provision that essentially meant universal white manhood suffrage. They also denied the governor the veto power, required legislative approval for all executive appointments, and required the chief executive to stand for election every two years. They also gave the assembly the authority to appoint all judges. The constitution thoroughly replaced the colonialism and arbitrary authority of St. Clair's government. At the same time, it placed governmental power under the control of the people, that is, the legislature. Federalist delegates succeeded only in gaining approval of provisions that required representatives to the assembly to be at least twenty-five years of age, as well as traveling circuit courts and a ban on slavery.

Thomas Worthington presented the new constitution to Congress on December 22; it was approved on February 19, 1803. With victory within their grasp, the Jeffersonians at the constitutional convention called for an election in January. Although statehood had not been formally approved, the voters elected Edward Tiffin governor and Jeremiah Morrow to the House of Representatives. The legislature also sent Thomas Worthington and James Smith to the United States Senate. Soon after, on March 1, the General Assembly met for the first time. Ohio had now passed from a frontier territory to a frontier state. During the next half-dozen years, increased migration from Pennsylvania and Virginia further spread Scots-Irish culture and brought adherents to the Republican party. By 1810, Ohio had become a homogeneous frontier state, with the exception of the Yankee Western Reserve. Twenty-nine counties provided a host of offices for which local leaders competed. As the population grew and the political structure expanded, faction occurred in the Republican party, largely over personal and geographical rather than ideological or philosophical issues, and Ohio became more like other states with political jockeying for power.

In time, Ohio's political concerns became similar to those of the older states, particularly after the Indian threat had passed following the War of 1812. During the remainder of the frontier period, Ohio's political system was basically honest, with politicians relying on patronage to win friends rather than to line their pockets. For the remainder of the frontier period, the Republicans dominated Ohio's politics and government. After statehood, the Federalists returned to private life; their days of influence on the Ohio frontier lay in the receding past.

In time, a new Indian uprising and war with Great Britain gave the Federalists a brief flicker of hope for a political revival. The War of 1812, however, destroyed the Federalist party in Ohio as well as the last semblance of Indian resistance to white settlement on that frontier. Most important, the governmental procedures established by the Northwest Ordinance had been observed. Both Federalists and Republicans had contributed to the delicate political balance of order and liberty in the Old Northwest. Although the relatively homogeneous interests of the Ohio people would soon dissolve into contentiousness and faction, they made Ohio the crucible of Republican government on the frontier.

10.

THE RELIGIOUS FRONTIER

Evangelicalism, Pentecostalism, and communalism characterized religious life on the Ohio frontier. But Ohio was also a frontier of the unchurched, given the migration of its settlers from the
woods and mountains of Pennsylvania, Virginia, and Kentucky.
Even so, or perhaps because of their origins, many of the men,
women, and children on the Ohio frontier would be particularly
receptive to the evangelical message and style of Methodist circuit
riders and the Pentecostal expression of faith characteristic at revival camp meetings.

In 1798, the Methodists established a circuit in Ohio and sent
John Kobler from Kentucky to preach on it. Known as the Miami
circuit, it ran up the Little Miami and Mad rivers from the Ohio
to present-day Dayton, then down the Big Miami to Cincinnati.
In 1800, the Methodists organized the second circuit in Ohio among
the settlements along the Scioto River. By 1811, eleven circuits
had been organized in two districts, the Miami and Muskingum.
The Methodists also organized the Western Conference beyond
the Alleghenies, which provided an organizational structure until
1812, when the leadership divided it into the Ohio and Tennessee
conferences.

Unlike the soldiers who moved across the frontier in armies or
the surveyors who worked the frontier in crews, itinerant ministers
called circuit riders were sent by the Methodist church into Ohio,
where they traveled alone, fighting the ever-tempting devil, multi-

tudes of hungry mosquitoes, and often a cantankerous horse. With the frontier settlers often unable to attend organized worship services because of time and distance, the Methodists took their church to the people. They stopped at isolated cabins to offer a prayer, collect neighbors for worship, and hope for food and lodging before riding to the next opportunity to spread the word of God and perhaps save a soul. The circuit riders provided necessary services by conducting weddings and funerals, and they sold prayer books, hymnals, and Bibles from their saddlebags and delivered letters and messages from across the frontier.

A circuit was measured by the time it took a preacher to complete it rather than by miles, which often numbered several hundred. Circuits usually followed the streams where most settlers built their cabins, running from the mouth to headwaters on one side and back down the other. The Miami, Scioto, Hockhocking, and Muskingum were typical early circuits and indicated the practice of naming circuits after the rivers and streams. A circuit rider might have as many as thirty stops and take as much as six weeks to complete his route before starting back over the trail. If the circuit rider discovered a young man with the proper spirit who showed some ability for public speaking, the preacher recommended him for the position of "exhorter," which meant that he could serve as the local minister until the circuit rider returned on his next round. Exhorters might soon become circuit riders themselves.

Between 1800 and 1816, the circuit rider's pay tallied only eighty dollars per year plus modest traveling expenses, although he received an additional eighty dollars if he had a wife. Most circuits could not pay even the minimal amount, and provisions rather than cash sustained these preachers. Because the circuit riders rotated after one- or two-year assignments, and ministered to three or four congregations, they did not have time to settle down and supplement their income by farming or to form local attachments. Between 1817 and 1825, for example, the Le Tart Falls Circuit, which included Gallipolis, had eleven traveling ministers. Conference officials believed that after a year, people grew tired of the circuit rider, and he probably had exhausted his material by that time and thereafter risked putting people to sleep instead of putting the fear of God into them. Moreover, conference officials warned their circuit riders to "converse sparingly, and conduct yourselves prudently with women," because marriage would prevent them from doing their job. Circuit rider James B. Finley reported that traveling ministers were not "exactly obliged to take the Popish vow of celibacy, but it almost amounted to the same thing . . . if a preacher married he was looked upon almost as a heretic who had denied the faith." Those who married often found that their names had been dropped from the "Traveling List" when they attended the annual conference. Although conference officials contended that married preachers could not properly attend to their circuits, wedded ministers were also denied circuits because the leadership knew that the circuits remained too poor to support a single preacher, let alone a married one. If an itinerant minister decided to marry, however, he needed the approval of his parishioners, and woe to anyone who did not marry a Methodist.

Whether single or married, however, David S. Stanley, born in the village of Congress in Wayne County in 1828, recalled that "the Methodists were more aggressive, sending ministers to the people rather than await their call." As a result, the Methodist organization usually enabled its circuit riders to contact the frontier settlers before representatives of any other denomination. Indeed, they conducted the first baptisms and burials and won converts in the competition for souls. The Methodist circuit riders were ignorant, but they had great influence on the common sinner and operated on the premise that individuals had to be called by God rather than be educated to preach. For evidence that a college education was not necessary, they offered Jesus and the Apostles as examples. Stanley recalled not long after the end of the frontier period that "the sermon of the average Methodist preacher in those days was a wonder. . . . He launched out in the loudest and most violent tone, threatening his hearers with hellfire, then came around to deceased mothers, sisters, brothers, or baby, and if in the course of an hour he could set the women crying and the men to yelling 'Amen!' he set down a very well-satisfied creature."

In 1820, Dr. Zerah Hawley, an easterner who traveled through Ashtabula County, wrote that "at least eleven months in twelve, the great body of people have no better oral instruction than what they receive from the most uninformed and fanatical Methodist preachers." He complained that the Western Reserve needed learned Presbyterian and Episcopal missionaries because the sermons of the Methodists were "without plan or system, beginning with *ignorance* and ending with *nonsense*, blasphemy in many cases." The Methodist ministers got their training in the school of experience, and their Harvard, Yale, and Princeton competitors castigated them for it, while the circuit riders won most of the converts. The frontier people needed ministers who could preach; they were not readers or interested in the fine points of theological argument, and the Methodist circuit riders met their needs.

Invariably the settlers received the circuit riders with kindness and often joy, except at isolated taverns where they were less than welcome, given their propensity to blame personal, national, and world problems on drinking. Many frontier people no doubt enjoyed the opportunity to sing a hymn, repeating the lines after the circuit rider and listening to him offer prayers for their blessing and sermons about repentance and salvation. But they also welcomed these itinerant ministers because they brought news from the outside world and served as an informational link to the settlements in the East. The circuit riders often first spread the news about the location of a new gristmill, the beginning of another settlement, or the well-being of friends who made their lives elsewhere on the Ohio frontier. For the frontier people, then, the circuit rider bridged the gaps that separated them from both heaven and civilization.

By preaching that individuals had control over their own salvation or damnation, the Methodist circuit riders also enunciated a doctrine that appealed to the frontier people. The Methodist doctrine of free will and individual responsibility had greater meaning for these independent settlers who relished their liberty. Calvinist orthodoxy ordained that a person had to take what came, but free will meant that people could control their spiritual as well as secular lives. It also gave sinners hope, in contrast to the orthodox Presbyterians, who preached predestination. Certainly the Methodists tried to reduce the propensity of the frontier people to swear, drink, fight, and accumulate wealth, but they also advocated civility and the living of life based on the Golden Rule, the Ten Commandments, and the Sermon on the Mount. By so doing, they advocated a doctrine that complemented the growing political democracy on the frontier, emphasizing the equality of all men and women. They also personalized religion by appealing to the emotions and emphasized the direct relationship between God and man. The frontier was dangerous and death always near. God, however, was always present, watching, and ready to help during adversity—all anyone had to do was ask.

Moreover, the Methodists prided themselves on their Wesleyan system of church government, established in the United States by Francis Asbury. Respect for the strict laws of Methodism not only made the church an efficient institution, but it also transferred the concepts of daily moral order to social life on the frontier. In addition, the Methodist ministers had conviction and "bought out many of the pioneer Presbyterians." By 1815, Methodism was the prevailing denomination in Cincinnati. In many respects, then, Methodism became the church of the West.

Although the circuit riders brought the gospel to sinners, however, it was not an efficient way to reach the depraved on the frontier. Scattered stations and isolated farms meant that only a relative few heard the minister at any one stop. Long circuits and many preachers were required to reach even a few frontier people. The learned Presbyterians first discovered how to reach sinners more efficiently by inaugurating the concept of the revival camp meeting in Kentucky during the spring of 1800. This technique involved sending out word that a great meeting would take place at a certain location at a specific time. Everyone would be welcome, and the camp meeting would be interdenominational, with ministers of various churches invited to preach. Although the conceptualization for the camp meeting must be credited to the Presbyterians, who had largely discarded it by 1805, the Methodists, who conducted their first camp meeting in Ohio at Eagle Creek in Adams County on June 5, 1801, made it a major Pentecostal experience on the frontier. They also used it to double their membership in the Western Conference.

The camp meetings were held during the late summer and early autumn, after the corn crop had been cultivated for the last time and while mild weather prevailed. With farm work lessened until the crop matured for harvesting, the frontier people had time to socialize. When they received word about a camp meeting, they loaded family, cooking utensils, and camping equipment into a wagon and left home for both celebration and devotions. A cross-roads site with ample shade and a good, convenient water supply served as the annual meeting ground for a revival. By the end of the frontier period, many of these sites had become permanent and were named after the benefactors on whose land they were located, such as Windell's Camp Ground and Turner's Camp Ground.

At the camp meetings the ministers preached the evangelical message of sin and salvation to their congregation with such fervor that many often lost control of their emotions. These "religious awakenings" caused them to fall into a Pentecostal communion with God characterized by uncontrollable jerking and shouting. Collapse often followed, after which they were carried to a "glory pen" or altar, depending on whether one was a scoffer or a believer, located before the preaching platform, where they lay until they re-gained their senses. The "deeply affected" were carried to separate tents, where women sang "melodiously" to them or a man prayed aloud over them. Usually the women experienced this physical emotionalism, although many of those who attended considered it "evidence of great piety" by either women or men. Indeed, some compared the emotionalism of the camp meetings to standing at the gates of heaven, while others likened it to peering through the gates of hell. Certainly, many people questioned these emotional conversions, but they were afraid to make too much "fuss" with the Methodists for fear that the minister might afflict them with the jerks in retaliation.

Many frontier people attended the camp meetings, not only for the religious experience but also to renew acquaintances, visit with friends and relatives, and catch up on local happenings. Others who were less devout attended to harass the preachers and their congre-gations, get drunk, and steal the horses and belongings of those who attended, usually after dark during the evening service. In 1806, at a camp meeting near Marietta, a group of "rabble and rowdies" ap-peared intent on making trouble. Peter Cartwright, who preached at the Sunday morning service, reported that they were "armed with dirks, clubs, knives, and horsewhips, and swore they would break up the meeting." Cartwright ordered them to leave, but they contin-ued to harangue the worshipers. Although temporarily cowed, the prayerful gained confidence when Cartwright attacked one of the rowdies. A general fight ensued, with thirty of the troublemakers captured and placed in the custody of the local magistrates. Heckling, however, remained a problem for both camp meetings and circuit riders. In 1817, for example, rowdies broke up a worship service held at the log home of Ahaz S. Morehouse in Gallipolis by the Reverend Henry Baker. As a result, Baker refused to stop there on his circuit unless a more secure site could be located. Whiskey, which troubled Methodists more than anything, often caused these problems, particularly when individuals either brought it to or tried to sell it at the camp meetings.

Those who attended camp meetings followed a rigorous schedule, with the first sermon often delivered at 8 A.M. and the last after nightfall. The Presbyterians were accustomed to such discipline because their Sunday services customarily involved two-hour sermons in the morning, a ninety-minute sermon in the afternoon, and sometimes a night service, all devoted to the fine points of Calvinist theology. At the camp meetings the various denominations shared the preaching. Three or four sermons separated by time for personal prayer filled most of the day. The night prayer meeting usually lasted until midnight and provided a forum for "intense religious excitement." The Methodists tallied the number of converts at each camp meeting and gave the lists to the circuit rider responsible for their areas. In Marietta, two hundred converts were counted at a camp meeting during the summer of 1806. Whether in the church or at a camp meeting, however, the audience expected the preachers to deliver their messages without notes, relying instead on enthusiasm rather than itemized points of fact.

As the country grew up and as the population increased, the various congregations built churches and employed a settled minister, and the need for camp meetings ended. When the bell rang at the crossroads church, it symbolized both spiritual and secular community, thereby ending much of the interdenominational rivalry fostered by the camp meetings. Throughout the frontier period, however, many settlers, particularly young men and women, attended the camp meetings for social opportunities, rather than to seek conversion or to cause trouble, and perhaps as many souls were made in the bushes as saved before the speaker's platforms and candle-lit pulpits.

* * *

The United Society of Believers in Christ's Second Appearing, commonly called Shakers, arrived in 1805. These Believers expressed their communion with God in a less physical manner than the evangelical and Pentecostal Methodists. Yet without a clearly defined Christian doctrine, the Shakers became even more upsetting to many settlers on the frontier. Established at New Lebanon, New York, in 1774 by British immigrant "Mother" Ann Lee, who believed herself to be the embodiment of Christ and the minister of the spiritual family, the Shakers looked to the Ohio frontier after the initial success of the camp meetings as an area to recruit members. Called Shakers, or less politely "Jerkers," because of their propensity to tremble during worship services, they capitalized on a schism among the New Light Presbyterians in southern Ohio, who opposed the strict Calvinism preached by the Synod of Kentucky. These Presbyterians favored a "theological Arminianism"; that is, they rejected predestination and believed the Holy Scriptures were the "only rule of faith and practice, the only standard of doctrine and discipline." They also believed in visions and the unifying spirit of Christ. The New Lights made Turtle Creek, located northeast of Cincinnati and three miles west of Lebanon, the center of a newly formed and short-lived Springfield Presbytery.

In early spring of 1805, Shaker "witnesses" or missionaries John Meacham, Issachar Bates, and Benjamin Seth Youngs left New Lebanon and arrived at Turtle Creek in Warren County, after a stop in Kentucky. They stayed with Presbyterian Malcolm Worley, who believed that "his heavenly Father had promised to send help from Zion," and he believed the missionaries fulfilled that prophecy. Worley converted on March 27. Soon Richard McNemar, the leader of the New Light Presbyterians, and his entire church accepted Shaker beliefs. By late April, thirty people had "opened their minds" and joined the Shakers.

The Shaker missionaries often participated in camp meetings and took their turn behind the pulpit, and they traveled through the countryside much like the Methodist circuit riders, introducing the frontier people to the Shaker gospel. They professed that the second coming of Christ had already occurred in Ann Lee, whom God had given "the same gifts of the Holy Spirit." Beyond this contention, their theology was unremarkable, advocating the need for believers to confess their sins, accept salvation through Christ, and embrace the "cross against the flesh, the world, and all evil" in order to be saved. Their formalized singing and dancing, the former noted for its simplicity and melody and the latter for its ritualistic shuffle by the men and women who marched in ranks and unison around the room, set them apart from other Protestant churches.

In July 1811, James McBride of Hamilton observed a Shaker worship service at Turtle Creek and reported that they danced and paraded about the room while they sang "brisk lively airs . . . such as often heard played on the violin at a country dance." He wrote, "At certain times during their dance some of them would jump up, clap their hands, whirl around on their toes or heels like a top, cutting all kinds of extraordinary capers, and shouting sometimes so loud that I thought beyond all doubt they would bring the house down about our ears." This dancing lasted about two hours, and during the summer, McBride observed, "their cloathes [sic] were as wet with sweat as if they had been engaged in a harvest field."

The Shaker belief in celibacy, self-denial, repression of passion, communal living and ownership of property, withdrawal from the secular world, and pacifism, however, caused them problems on the Ohio frontier, where most settlers typified anything but model believers in the Shaker context, if judged by their love of liberty, pursuit of wealth, aggressiveness, and propensity to father and bear a host of children. Celibacy no doubt made the Shakers attractive to some frontier women, whose bodies wore out from bearing and rearing children. Indeed, most women would not live to see their grandchildren.

For the Presbyterians and other frontier people who were dissatisfied with the dry intellectualism of their own church or who needed emotional support, the Shakers offered an attractive alternative theology that emphasized intellectual freedom and a physical participation that involved more than singing hymns and bowing heads for prayer among these highly independent settlers. Moreover, where conflict and uncertainty prevailed, frontier people often sought peace and order in religion, and the Shakers provided an opportunity for them to embrace a new identity. One of their mottoes, "Hands to work and hearts to God," also embodied enough Calvinist philosophy to bridge the gap between Believers and members of other denominations.

Shaker missionaries used Worley's house at Turtle Creek as their operational base and made journeys into the countryside in search of potential converts. In 1806, Worley's farm and land owned by McNemar became a "place of retreat," which they called Turtle Creek. On June 30, 1806, these Shakers in Warren County drafted a statement of religious principles that differed radically from those established by the founders of the society. It was a thirteen-page document designed to answer questions posed by outsiders and to allay scurrilous rumors. Prior to this time, the Shakers had condemned formal creeds and doctrinal statements, contending that "living witnesses" rather than written documents were needed. Now, their "Candid Statement" held that the Believers alone possessed religious truth, arguing that the "Gospel of the kingdom of Christ" enabled renewal and redemption, while the other denominations, who based their belief on the "law of commandments," could not achieve salvation.

The Candid Statement also held that Christ was revealed in those who possessed his spirit. They called this principle the "Christ within," while the "professors of Christianity" lived not in the spirit of Christ but in the "flesh." Essentially, the Ohio Shakers believed that the other Christians, who continued their carnal knowledge, lived with the spirit of the devil and were in fact anti-Christian. For the Ohio Shakers, the second coming of Christ would not be a physical appearance, but rather the manifestation of his spirit in the Believers who tried to live a righteous life. Distinguishing between Jesus the man and Jesus the Christ by recognizing one as a man and the other as a principle, and by rejecting the sacrament of communion because it occurred under the influence of the devil when the saints were no longer united in Christ, the Shakers considerably upset the members of other denominations on the frontier.

The concept of the "Christ within" developed by the Ohio Shakers made Turtle Creek the theological center for the Shakers on the western frontier. Although the Shakers professed that men and women could be saved only by their own free will, the identification of other Christians with the Antichrist tested the mettle of their neighbors for tolerance. Quickly they found that their austere manner and strange worship services offended the sense of propriety and accepted religious practices of their neighbors. On the frontier, people could believe or not as they pleased, so long as they did not violate accustomed practices. If transgressions occurred, resentment and retribution came quickly. Essentially, people of the frontier were free to believe in the manner of everyone else. Deviant beliefs were radical and dangerous to social order.

Soon many converts known as "Young Believers" joined the Turtle Creek communal society, and their success at recruitment created a great deal of fear, particularly among the Presbyterians. One nearby resident proclaimed that if any Shakers came to his house to delude and draw away any of his family, he would "shoot them with his riffle [sic]." Others charged that the celibate Believers actually practiced "lasciviousness," drank heavily, and physically abused their children. As the Shakers increased in number and prospered, grandparents and relatives often charged that they kidnapped and lured women and held them against their will. Tongues wagged that the Shakers castrated their males, danced naked about their villages, and held sex orgies at night. Rumors spread that the Shakers willfully divided families, destroyed marriages, and controlled all aspects of their members' lives. Once someone was a member of a Shaker community, there allegedly was no escape.

Nonbelievers also charged the Shakers with stealing property in the name of piety and with inciting the Indians against the government, the latter rumor based on the Shaker mission to the Shawnees at Greenville in 1807. In January 1811, the state legislature attempted to provide economic relief to women whose husbands had abandoned them for the Shakers, by authorizing the recovery of real and personal property to the extent a court decreed "just and equitable." The law also prohibited property from passing to the commune as the Shakers required when new members joined their villages.

New Light ministers also resented men such as Bates, Youngs, and McNemar because they aggressively sought converts among their "innocent lambs." In Montgomery County, New Light preacher

John Thompson at Beaver Creek or Beulah, located six miles east of Dayton, considered the Shaker missionaries "ravening wolves . . . that were going about the country in sheep's clothing." Night riders sometimes terrorized the homes of the Shakers and threw stones through their windows, tore down fences, and felled apple trees. Others cropped the ears off Shaker horses and destroyed their sites for worship services in the woods by burning the seats and preaching stand.

The most serious challenge to the order, however, came on August 27, 1810, when New Lights and drunken, armed ruffians marched as a mob on Turtle Creek, bent on driving the Shakers away. Benjamin Seth Youngs, one of the founders, reported that a mob of five hundred men, including many of the "baser sort" from Lebanon, Hamilton, Big Hill, and Springfield, arrived on the grounds before the meeting house, and a committee composed of twelve leaders demanded that they "renounce our faith and practice, our public preaching and mode of worship, or quit the country." The Shakers had been warned several days before that trouble was imminent, and that a band of men would soon march on the village to tar and feather them and "drive the old Shakers out of the country, and restore the rest back to their former faith and manner of living."

About 8:00 A.M. spectators began to arrive at Union Village well ahead of the mob in order to see what would happen. They waited until 1:00, when a group of men marched down the Dayton Road from the north in military order and halted several rods from the meeting house. The men were armed with clubs equipped with bayonets, staves, hatches, and knives. Some of the leaders wore military uniforms, and all "exhibited a very mean and mob-like appearance" to the Believers. Counting the onlookers, more than a thousand people had entered the village. Benjamin Youngs, who went out to meet them, called it a "scene of horror."

The committee demanded in the name of the "people" that Youngs, Peter Pease, and Matthew Houston meet with them in a nearby woods. Presbyterian minister Matthew G. Wallace, speaking for the committee, stated their grievances and charged that Shaker "principles and practice had caused great disturbances in the minds of the people, and led to the extinction of civil and religious society."

The committee also charged that the Shakers "led mankind into bondage and oppression" and that the assembled citizens had come to "prevent evil being done, and perhaps prevent much blood being shed . . . provided we [the Shakers] would comply with the terms they had to propose, as the voice of the people."

The committee then demanded that the Shakers return several children to their grandparents. They also charged that Elder David, "like the Pope, exercises unlimited authority over all under his control," to enjoy a leisurely life supported by the hard work and property of the community's members. The committee reiterated its demand that the Shakers cease their religious practices, including the "dance," which it contended was a practice "reverse from the gospel." If the Shakers did not meet these demands, they would be forced to leave the area by the first Monday in December, pending physical harm. The Shakers responded by asking for these demands to be submitted in writing, but the committee told them that their proposals were "short" and could be easily remembered. Youngs replied that since the demands were short, they could be easily written, but the committee "pointedly refused." By this time an hour had passed, and the Shakers were given until three o'clock to return with their answer. When the appointed time arrived, the Shakers responded that they held no one against their will and that the children should remain in the care of their parents, although grandparents could freely visit them. They said, however, that their faith was "dearer than our lives," and professed, "We will not renounce our faith, nor give up our land." They also demanded that their neighbors respect their right to liberty of conscience "which the laws of our country granted us." If the mob did not, however, the Shakers firmly pronounced, "neither will we take up arms to defend ourselves."

While the two committees met, Youngs reported that a "promiscuous concourse of armed men and spectators" began to mill about the meeting and schoolhouses, "some disputing, some inquiring, others railing out against, and endeavoring to scatter falsehood, and urging the propriety of banishing us out of the country by violence." Youngs observed that "women of the baser sort, who were in fellowship with the riot . . . and others of the same cast were taking an active part in urging on parties of the mob to take away, by force, children of their connections . . . and such like acts of violence." Some of those present, however, began to speak for the Shakers, arguing that they had constitutional rights that had not been "forfeited by any misconduct."

At this moment, Judge F. Dunlavy of the First Circuit of Ohio, who had attended this assembly, perhaps with the intent of ensuring civil order, rode into the crowd and ordered the people to respect the laws of Ohio, and he urged all civil officers present to report anyone who violated them. When a Shaker youth appeared who the mob believed had been murdered by his captors, others also counseled peace and patience while the courts decided custody matters, and some in the crowd began to drift away. But not, Youngs reported, before "some of the party treated the judge with great contempt, and uttered the most bitter invectives against him for his interference."

The mob did not immediately disband after Judge Dunlavy ordered them to do so. Instead, they moved on to the house where the Elders lived and surrounded it, while a Major William Robinson demanded that the Shakers leave the country by December or "suffer the consequences." Then the mob, with uplifted hands and a "general loud and hideous yell," affirmed that order. Robinson and a half-dozen men then demanded to search the house to determine whether any children were being held against their wishes and if they were being subjected to cruelty. The Shakers agreed to the search provided Robinson and his men behaved "civilly." The three young women present were asked whether they wanted to leave, and all said that they wanted to remain with the Shakers. The Shakers offered their interrogators cold coffee, which they accepted before leaving the house of the Elders. Then the house of the Young Believers, that is, the recent converts, was investigated and the children were interrogated.

By this time, the committee, not having discovered any evidence of cruelty toward children or bondage, began to lose its zeal. But it moved on to investigate the schoolhouse, where the leaders asked other children if they had enough to eat and if they had been beaten. Here, too, the committee found everything in order, and evidence that the children were doing good work and making satisfactory progress in their learning. By then the committee members were "wearied and perplexed" and showed signs of "mortifying disappointment." Confronted with a religious enemy who would not fight, and who even went about their daily chores as best they could while the mob milled among them, these frontiersmen were baffled about what course of action to take, and they eventually drifted away. Although bloodshed was averted, this was not the last threat to the Shakers in Ohio. Mob violence occurred again in 1813, 1817, 1819, and 1824, but the incident in 1810 was the most serious.

Despite threats and physical intimidation, the Shakers reported 160 "grown" members or about 370 Believers in the Turtle Creek vicinity by the end of their first year in Ohio, with newly made settlements at Eagle Creek in Adams County and Beaver Creek or Beulah in Montgomery County adding a few souls. Some of these members had converted in Ohio, while others had arrived from other Shaker communities in the East. By 1808, the Turtle Creek community owned 4,500 acres acquired by purchase and donation, and about 1812 the Shakers renamed it Union Village. The Shakers also established the villages of North Union in 1822 (now known as Shaker Heights near Cleveland) and Whitewater in 1823. Moreover, they won converts at the settlements of Straight Creek, Shawnee Run, Cabin Creek, and Darby Plains. All of the successful Shaker communities in Ohio were based on gifts of good land and strong leadership.

Despite harassment, these communal villages achieved economic self-sufficiency and stability and prospered, in part, with financial and organizational support from New Lebanon and other Shaker communities back east. Eastern Shakers, for example, became the elders and eldresses who governed these settlements. Still, distance from the locus of Shaker belief and an absence of tradition kept the settlements of the New Believers weaker and more tenuous than the stable villages of the Shakers far removed from the frontier. By the end of the frontier period, however, Union Village had six hundred members, and it became the communication center and financial conduit that linked the Shakers in the West with those in the East. Oppression on the Ohio frontier served only to isolate and strengthen the Shaker communities rather than destroy them. By 1823, some seventeen hundred Shakers had gathered in

Ohio. Moreover, the expansion of the Shakers into Ohio became the most important achievement of the society during the nineteenth century.

* * *

The Quakers came to Ohio quietly in 1795. By 1800, the Friends had established six settlements—three in Ross, two in Warren, and one in Lawrence County. By 1806, an estimated eight hundred families had immigrated to Ohio. The Quakers neither participated in Pentecostal camp meetings like the Methodists nor suffered threats of physical intimidation like the Shakers. With the exception of a scuffle with several injuries among people to whom non-violence was an article of faith, the members of the Society of Friends lived peacefully and industriously on the Ohio frontier. In 1828 the Society of Friends divided into Hicksite and Orthodox factions over doctrinal matters. In an atmosphere of increasing acrimony, the Orthodox Friends tried to bar the Hicksites from the meeting house, and the fight began. In time the two groups restored harmony, but unity was not so easily achieved, and reconciliation would not occur until after the close of the frontier.

In 1795, George Harlan became the first Quaker to settle in Ohio, taking up land near Deerfield on the Little Miami River near present-day Morrow. Others soon followed from North Carolina, Virginia, and Pennsylvania, making their exodus from the slave South. By the turn of the nineteenth century, they had settled at Quaker Bottom in Lawrence County, at Salt Creek and Grassy Prairies in Ross County, and at Waynesville in Warren County. In January 1800, North Carolina Quakers Joseph Dew and Horton Howard from the Coresound Monthly Meeting in Carteret County and Aaron Brown from the Trent Monthly Meeting in Jones County traveled to Ohio in search of land. They chose the area along Short Creek in Jefferson and Belmont counties and persuaded the entire membership of the Trent and several families of the Coresound monthly meetings to move to Ohio.

Although they left North Carolina in January, they did not arrive in Ohio until September, probably traveling over the future site of the Cumberland or National Road, settling near Colerain. By December 1800, approximately eight hundred Quaker families had immigrated to Ohio. In 1802, others settled near Leesburg in Highland and Jefferson counties, and they had moved the Westland Monthly Meeting from western Pennsylvania to the settlement of High Bank on the Scioto River four miles south of Chillicothe. By 1807, North Carolina Quakers had vitalized the community known as Jesse-Bob Town (after Jesse Thomas and Robert Carothers, who surveyed this Jefferson County town site in 1803). By 1807, the Quakers had stamped their character on it and called it Mount Pleasant.

The Quakers usually came in families and groups, rather than as individuals, and they often wrote encouraging letters home urging kith and kin to join them in Ohio, much like other settlers on the frontier. Because of their numbers and the close proximity of settlement, they worshiped together from the beginning. In April 1801, for example, a dozen families met at Waynesville for services, and they organized the Miami Monthly Meeting in October 1803. The Friends also began meeting regularly at Fairfield in May 1804, while Wilmington in Clinton County became a Quaker center in that year and a place for regular meetings in 1807. Quaker settlement increased rapidly, especially in the Miami Valley, where the membership of the Miami Monthly Meeting reached 1,697 by the summer of 1807. Twenty years later, near the close of the frontier, more than 8,000 Quakers lived in eastern Ohio, particularly Belmont, Columbiana, Harrison, and Jefferson counties.

In 1806, the Ohio Friends petitioned the Baltimore Yearly Meeting for permission to organize a quarterly meeting, and they received authorization to do so at Short Creek, joining the members of the Concord, Short Creek, and Miami monthly meetings. Several years later, in 1810, three quarterly meetings were held in Ohio at Short Creek, Miami, and Salem, and these vigorous and thrifty Quaker communities sought to organize a yearly meeting of elders. A year later, the Ohio Friends petitioned the Baltimore Yearly Meeting for authorization to hold a similar meeting of their own. The elders in Baltimore granted that request in 1812, and authorized the Ohio Yearly Meeting to be held at Short Creek in August 1813. When the Quakers met for their first yearly meeting, between two and three thousand Friends attended. There they made decisions to adopt the Baltimore Yearly Meeting's Book of Discipline until they could write one of their own, and to build a meeting house in Mount

The Quakers came to Ohio in 1795. They established well-ordered farms and worshiped in their quiet way. In 1815, they built this yearly meeting house at Mount Pleasant. It seated two thousand, with the men and women divided by a partition. By the early 1830s, it served fifty-three congregations. COURTESY OHIO HISTORICAL SOCIETY, C. 1984. WILLIAM G. KEENER AND CHRISTOPHER S. DUCKWORTH, PHOTOGRAPHERS.

Pleasant. Construction of the Mount Pleasant Yearly Meeting House began in 1814. When completed a year later, it seated two thousand, with the men and women separated by an intricate hinged wooden panel that rolled into the attic when not in use.

By 1814, the Ohio Yearly Meeting governed 1,693 families. Near the close of the frontier in 1826, fifty-three congregations of Quakers contributed a combined membership of 8,873. By that time, the yearly meeting in Mount Pleasant had become an important social as well as religious occasion similar to the evangelical camp meetings. Parents and elders, however, complained that young Quakers often showed more interest in each other than in the worship services and often had to be reprimanded for "the rolling in of the carriages at midnight, so little becoming the occasion, or the children of Friends."

Most settlers in Ohio considered the Quakers a "peculiar people." Their gentle demeanor, their distinctive dress with the men in black and the women in gray, their manner of speaking, distinguished by the use of "thee" and "thou," their stark meeting houses, their rejection of the arts, either for enjoyment or in practice, and their refusal to celebrate Christmas set them apart as pious and stiff. The Quakers were also peculiar on the Ohio frontier in their desire to establish coeducational schools for their children. They particularly wanted their children to learn math and science for practical applications. In 1824, sheep man Thomas Rotch bequeathed five thousand dollars to the Mount Pleasant boarding school. His contribution, however, was both large and unusual. Most Quaker education was conducted at day schools, where parents paid a subscription to cover the salary of the teacher and expenditures of the governing board. Because these subscription schools accepted only Quaker children, however, their educational practices further defined them as a "peculiar people." The frontier people also recognized that the Quakers were different because of their concept of the "Inner Light," by which they believed that communion with the Holy Spirit could be experienced equally by men and women. By so contending, the Friends composed one of the most democratic religious groups on the frontier. Among the Quakers, both women and men participated in the decision-making process, where all issues were resolved by consensus, with no vote ever taken or any veto ever made.

Despite their peculiar way of dressing and talking and despite the willingness of the Quakers to aid the Indians and runaway slaves, the Society of Friends in Ohio did not suffer persecution during the frontier period. In contrast to the Shakers, the Quakers did not actively attempt to win white converts and thereby threaten the loss of membership and community in the other Protestant sects. The Quakers on the Ohio frontier threatened only the slaveholders south of the river, and those slaveowners could not easily retaliate or make trouble in Ohio. On the religious frontier, the Ohio Quakers kept to themselves, created efficient farms and bustling towns, and worshiped in their own quiet way.

* * *

The Society of Separatists came to Ohio in 1817 from Germany, fleeing William, who ascended the throne to replace his tyrannical and deceased father, Frederick II, king of Württemberg. These Separatists had rejected the practices of the state-supported Lutheran church because it had become too secular. They also disapproved of a new hymnal adopted in 1791 and a liturgy developed in 1808. In protest, they withdrew their children from church-supported schools, refused military service, and rejected all church ceremonies, such as baptism, confirmation, and marriage, substituting a mere agreement before witnesses for the latter formality, and they refused to take oaths. For their deviancy, both state and church persecuted the Separatists with imprisonment, hard labor, and corporal punishment. Some, such as Joseph Baumeler, went underground and moved about to escape the authorities.

Early in 1816, the Separatists sought permission to emigrate from Württemberg to the United States, and William granted their request. With the financial support of the London Society of Friends, some three hundred Separatists sailed from Antwerp in April 1817. They arrived in Philadelphia about four months later, on August 14, where the Quakers provided temporary shelter. Joseph Baumeler, the leader of the Separatists, soon arranged for the purchase of fifty-five hundred acres in eastern Ohio on the Tuscarawas River from a Godfrey Haga. With the purchase price of $15,000, Baumeler considered it "medium good" land and secured it with a mortgage for the Separatists in his name. The Quakers at Philadelphia lent the Separatists $1,500 for the down payment. The first Separatists made their way to their tract in November 1817 and laid out a town which they called Zoar—the refuge of Lot, who fled with his family from the wickedness of Sodom.

The Zoarites supported the beliefs of both the Pietists and Chiliasts. Pietism as a movement emphasized a wholesome lifestyle while the individual sought a spiritual rebirth through the grace of God. As Chiliasts, the Separatists at Zoar also believed the New Testament prophecy of the Second Coming of Christ, which they expected to occur in 1836. Time, then, was of the greatest essence to put their spiritual house in order, and the seclusion of Ohio seemed to be the perfect place, far removed from the secular world.

At Zoar the Separatists maintained their distinctiveness by continuing to speak the Swabian dialect, dressing in Old World style, and greeting friends and strangers with "thee" and "thou," or the familiar "du" in German. In the Tuscarawas Valley, however, these peculiar trappings were nothing compared to their practice of communalism, which made them radically different but no less welcome by their neighbors. Their "Separatist Principles" also provided clear guidelines of acceptable behavior. Although the Separatists resembled the Anabaptists in their belief that men and women could be reunited with God only through Christ, their principles unambiguously distinguished them from other Christians. The Zoarites were especially different from most practicing Christians on the Ohio frontier in their rejection of a formal church in favor of the church within each individual. Baumeler said the clergy merely learned their trade in schools rather than received their knowledge directly from God. Baumeler also spoke for all Zoarites when he held that "the religious needs of mankind are not the same at all times and that, therefore, divine revelation progresses and assumes a character adapted to existing conditions." Put differently, the Separatists at Zoar believed that Baumeler was the "mouthpiece of the Holy Ghost."

Because the Zoarites did not believe in a physical church, they circumvented this organizational problem by holding religious services in a "meeting house." Although Baumeler essentially served as a pastor, he did not hold any official title as the spiritual leader of the Separatists. In addition to not recognizing a formal church or minister, the Zoarites prayed only silently to avoid the appearance of seeking attention. Each Sunday, however, the Separatists held three meetings, with the first beginning at 9:00 A.M. when Baumeler, who believed that God directly inspired him, delivered a two-hour extemporaneous sermon based on an event of the past week. A second service devoted to the children began in the early afternoon, with worship concluding at an evening gathering. The pews in the meeting house, however, faced the doors so that latecomers would suffer embarrassment and, with a scolding from the members, improve their ways. During the evening services, anyone who had transgressed the laws of the society during the week was required to sit in the first pew. The sermon, which they called the "discourse," emphasized the nature of the transgressions of these "sinners of the week," and the service ended with the names of the offenders and the nature of their sins read aloud.

The Zoarites were as earnest in their daily, temporal lives as they were serious about their spiritual well-being. Although the original plan called for the Separatists to pay for their shares of the land from the sale of surplus crops, farming on the frontier took time to achieve commercial success. The threat of mortgage foreclosure worried them, and on April 15, 1819, 53 men and 104 women approved the "Articles of Association," in which they agreed to a community of goods and stipulated that all investments in their society were irreversible; that is, property and capital could not be withdrawn if a member decided to leave the commune. Because the Zoarites did not keep records of any member's contribution of property or capital to the society, disenchanted members had little hope of identifying which property or how much capital should be returned to them if they decided to leave the village. Baumeler kept the property of the Zoarites in his own name. They would later tell visitors, "In heaven there is only Communism, and why should it not be our aim to prepare ourselves in this world for the society we are sure to enter there?" In reality, however, economic necessity forced the Separatists to pool their resources, hold their land in common, divide the workload in the fields and homes, and produce for the economic benefit of the commune.

Similarly, the Zoarites practiced celibacy. About 1822, the Separatists banned marriages. Baumeler professed that marriage was "the result of an impure desire uttered by the first man" and that it had "no other purpose but the preservation of the race whose existence after all cannot be called anything but burdensome and unhappy." Baumeler recognized that marriage had been "instituted by God," but he contended that "such happiness was only temporary and ended with death." In reality, however, the Separatists temporarily rejected marriage for economic rather than religious reasons. Women with small children could not be productive members of the commune during the critical time of establishing its economic viability. Moreover, they doubted that the community could support a great increase in population, where women outnumbered men two to one and their labor was needed in the fields. As a result, the Zoarites abolished the institution of marriage, and they divided the living quarters, some with only men or women and some with both sexes. They identified these households by number. In some households a man presided, and in others a woman. The members of each household had the responsibility of distributing supplies, preparing food, and tending a garden.

About 1830, the Zoarites resumed the practice of marriage. By that time, however, their land had been paid for, and emigrants from Germany increased the labor supply and helped end the need for celibacy. Baumeler also recanted on the importance of marriage, fell in love with a member of the society, and married about the time he lifted the decree prohibiting such unions. Thereafter, a community nursery called the Children's Institution took all children from their parents at the age of three to free their mothers for work in the fields and shops, but that policy occurred after the close of the frontier.

Only members of the Society of Separatists could live in Zoar, and only residents could join the society. Anyone who wanted to join the commune had to serve a probationary year as a member of the first class. During that time, they could participate in all community functions except elections. At the end of the probationary period, an individual could apply for second-class membership in the society. Upon approval, the applicant ceded all property to the commune. If members of the first class chose to leave the society, they could take their property with them, but once second-class membership had been attained, property remained with the society in perpetuity, although each member held an equal share. The requirement for all second-class members to cede their property reinforced religious conviction with economic commitment. Second-class status made leaving difficult, because it meant that all investments of time, money, and work would be lost as well as one's home and sense of place. In order to reach second-class status, members had to convince the community that they believed in the Separatist principles and accepted the communal system as practiced at Zoar.

In contrast to the Harmony Society in Pennsylvania and Indiana, the Zoarites could leave the community, although only Baumeler had the authority to deal with the outside world. He had provided the leadership for migration, and he held the deed to the lands purchased in Ohio, because the seller had required that control. Baumeler alone had the power to buy and sell, sign contracts, and direct and superintend all of the commercial interests of the society. This centralization of authority did not pose a problem for the Separatists, but the unrestricted movement of visitors in Zoar interfered with their privacy and preferred way of life. With the exception of prohibiting their children from talking with guests at the hotel, however, they made no effort to withdraw completely from the world.

Still, Baumeler complained in 1820 that the Zoarite community had "suffer[ed] much persecution since its establishment both from acquaintances and strangers." But the form or extent of that persecution remains unknown. Whatever the persecution that Baumeler had in mind, it apparently did not last long, because the Zoarites lived in peace and harmony with their neighbors. They may have been peculiar in their religious beliefs, but they did not attempt to lure members from other Protestant congregations, and they contributed to the economic prosperity of the area rather than competed with it.

In retrospect, the Zoarites formed one of the most successful communes during the early nineteenth century. They did so because they remained a homogeneous society based on a common nationality, religious belief, culture, and socioeconomic class of poor, uneducated farmers and tradesmen. The Zoarites ensured adequate food, clothing, and shelter for all members of their society, but they did not develop coercive power to force or ensure a specific amount of work from each individual. If a Zoarite disobeyed the regulations of the society, he or she was simply not allowed to attend the meetings, or a trustee might verbally or in writing ask him or her to conform to the standards of the society. Usually those activities seemed to be punishment enough, although expulsion from Zoar served as the ultimate penalty for transgressing the bounds of accepted behavior. The Separatists at Zoar not only knew their place in the universe but also understood the tasks that needed to be completed and dutifully carried out their assignments. The Zoarites led routine and orderly lives in contrast to the regimentation of the Shakers, but in doing so they differed little from the other farmers and tradesmen and -women on the Ohio frontier. During the frontier period, the Zoarites abolished almost all distinctions of rank, Baumeler and a five-member standing committee and a three-member board of trustees being the only exceptions, and they lived as "brethren and sisters of one common family."

Despite their industry and economic success, the Society of Separatists of Zoar (formally incorporated in 1833) remained foremost a religious sect, even though most Ohioans identified them with their commercial activities and peculiar seclusion from the world rather than with any doctrine that upset conventional life or religious practices. Even so, the Separatists at Zoar neither established a communistic society for its own sake nor consciously experimented with socialism. For the Society of Separatists of Zoar, their sense of religious purpose gave their lives meaning. They sought religious freedom and made Zoar a peculiar island on the Ohio frontier.

* * *

Religion brought peace of mind, hope, and a sense of personal commitment. It also meant political power on the Ohio frontier, at least for the Presbyterians. The early settlers at Dayton provide an excellent example of the Christians who brought purpose and order to the frontier and who used their church to foster their own status and influence in the community. The first Presbyterians at Dayton arrived in 1796, and organized a congregation two years later. They hired a regular minister in 1804 and served as the only congregation in the community until the Methodists built a church in 1814. Most important, in little more than a decade after establishment, the young merchants and professionals gained control of the congregation at the expense of the less ambitious rural men who had founded the church. Indeed, between 1813 and 1817, the town-dwelling Presbyterians, who were also evangelical in their beliefs and practices, wrested control from the founders. As a result, the Presbyterians who controlled their church also controlled the town.

Most of the Presbyterians who settled in Dayton and its vicinity migrated from New Jersey and Kentucky. Those who came from the Middle Atlantic region had been strongly influenced by the evangelical theology that swept the eastern seaboard and New England during the late eighteenth century, and which permitted individual initiative for salvation. The Kentuckians had descended from the Scots-Irish in Pennsylvania. They were contentious and sharply divided over strict and more permissive interpretations of Calvinism, especially in relation to the doctrine of God's election or grace for salvation and the necessity and excess of evangelical worship. For these orthodox Presbyterians, physical contortions and shouting at camp meetings indicated poor judgment and worse taste for the public worship of God. The evangelical Presbyterians, however, believed that physical expressions of devotion reflected a necessary and uncontrollable form of communion with the Holy Spirit. Moreover, the evangelical Presbyterian ministers defiantly challenged traditional Calvinist doctrine of predestination and limited grace by preaching a combination of Arminianism and antinomianism.

In Dayton, the evangelical Presbyterian settlers from New Jersey viewed their Kentucky brethren with disdain, because they scorned the concept of free will as the determinant for salvation. Still, both evangelicals and the orthodox members attended the same congregation, and the Presbyterians became associated with leadership and wealth in Dayton. In 1815, approximately 46 percent of the male taxpayers were members of the church. Two years later, a new meeting house contained only expensive private pews, although the poor members could sit in the gallery on a first come, first served basis for services. In 1826, near the close of the frontier period, Presbyterians composed half of the wealthiest 10 percent of the population.

The orthodox members who primarily lived outside of town did not participate in the government of Dayton, and few served in positions of leadership in nonreligious social organizations. In contrast, the young evangelical merchants and professionals, usually in their twenties, contributed most financial support to the church, boosted town economic development, held positions on the boards of the library, bank, and academy, and generally served on the town council. The evangelicals began asserting power within the church and community as early as 1812, when the state legislature approved incorporation of the Presbyterian church. This charter required new and annual elections of church officers, which in 1814 enabled the young, business-oriented members to gain control of the board of trustees, but with considerable ill will evident on the part of the orthodox trustees when they transferred power. The charter also authorized the church to own property and raise subscriptions, which broadened the responsibilities and concerns of the church.

In 1815, the evangelical trustees required residence in Dayton for church membership, thereby consolidating their power base. Between 1818 and 1828, the trustees often suspended church elections, and the members supported their leadership, or perhaps were too apathetic to protest. During that time, the evangelical elders served as moral judges in this frontier community. They heard complaints of drunkenness, swearing, lying, slander, and breach of promise. If personal reform did not result, they held church trials and delivered punishments, such as public rebuke and denial of communion. Although the extent of the elders' power to regulate public morality depended on the individual will of the transgressor, anyone who did not want to lose prestige and influence in Dayton's various institutions and associations had to accept the power of the Presbyterian trustees. Until the mid-1820s, the non-Presbyterian population remained too small for anyone to transgress the church with its comparatively large membership and maintain public respect.

Prior to 1824, only the Methodists competed with the Presbyterians in Dayton for members and moral leadership. The Methodists, however, could not compete in either wealth or numbers, and the evangelical Presbyterians founded and controlled not only the library and academy, but also the Female Bible Society and a "Moral Society," designed to suppress vice. The leadership of each often interlocked with the others. These institutions usually met only the needs of the comparatively elitist Presbyterians. The academy, for example, charged tuition, and the library extended privileges only to those who paid an annual tax. As a result, the poorer and more democratic Methodists began to provide alternatives for education and worked to solve social problems through self-improvement societies during the early 1820s. The Methodists also advocated more equitable tax assessment, particularly after the Panic of 1819 caused economic hardship for Dayton's poorer residents. The Presbyterians, however, dominated the leadership of civic and charitable organizations, such as the Mission Society established to aid the Indians, the Greek Cause Committee organized to champion Greek independence, and the Colonization Society to support the emigration of blacks to Africa as well as temperance and poor relief associations. The church, city government, academy, and voluntary organizations, all dominated by the Presbyterians, collectively provided the social organization of the community.

The Presbyterian entrepreneurs earned their capital for financial development and leadership during the War of 1812 by providing the army with supplies and transportation as well as by furnishing refugees from northern Ohio with food and shelter. When the war ended, Dayton had a population of five hundred, and by 1817 more than a dozen manufacturing enterprises produced nails, saddles, hats, and farm tools as well as flour, beer, and tobacco products. The Presbyterians dominated Dayton's population, economy, political life, and voluntary organizations until the mid-1820s, when new immigrants arrived with wealth to invest. Lured by prospects of canal building, sympathetic to the Jacksonian wing of the Democratic party, and often unchurched, they wielded economic and political power while forsaking the voluntary moral organizations of the Presbyterians. By the end of the frontier period, then, diversity rather than religious homogeneity characterized Dayton's population of eleven hundred. Increasingly, the new immigrants sought political solutions to problems that the evangelical Presbyterians had attempted to resolve through moral suasion, education, and voluntary benevolent organizations.

Prior to 1830, the Presbyterian men in Dayton made a strong showing in the state legislature. They controlled, for example, one-third of the seats in Montgomery County and supported charters for the bank, academy, and churches. They held a majority of the seats for all county offices, thereby wielding power for the construction of roads, bridges, and public buildings. They also supervised tax collections and the issuance of tavern licenses. Dayton's Presbyterians controlled the county judiciary and the justices of the peace for Dayton Township, where they dominated the offices of trustee, overseer of the poor, road supervisors, appraisers, and fence viewers. They also lent money to the county government to support the construction of a courthouse.

In Dayton, the evangelical Presbyterians also monopolized the town council, which exercised considerable legislative, executive, and judicial power. There they occupied more than 50 percent of the council seats between 1805 and 1823, and they held the post of council president for fifteen of those eighteen years. Disagreements among evangelical and orthodox council members, however, plagued their proceedings from incorporation of the town in 1805 until 1815, when the evangelicals gained control of the council. The evangelical Presbyterians who sat on the Dayton city council were reelected more frequently than non-Presbyterians. These evangelical Presbyterians were prominent and wealthy men, and they maintained close ties through their church and businesses, and many served as church trustees. After the evangelicals gained control of the council, they used it to support church-related voluntary beneficent and economic organizations designed to ensure individual betterment and town prosperity. They continued their domination of the church, philanthropic organizations, and town government without party affiliation until Jacksonian outsiders moved into town during the mid-1820s and asserted their own authority through the ballot box, all to the dismay of the Presbyterians, who endorsed Henry Clay in 1824.

The Presbyterians who directed Dayton's politics believed that they had the responsibility to lead because of their social and economic positions. They also supported hierarchy in social and political relationships, and they had great faith in progress. They merged the evangelical Christian's belief in purpose and personal renewal with moral responsibility and public service that transcended the spiritual world into the secular realm of politics. The religious beliefs of the evangelical Presbyterians in this context, then, supported the republican values of government, particularly independence and public service.

* * *

In retrospect, the Calvinist influence in Ohio can be seen in the early "Blue Laws" of the Northwest Territory, when Governor St. Clair and the judges prohibited "idle, vain, and obscene conversation, profane cursing and swearing" as well as drunkenness, fighting, and "servile labor." By all accounts, however, the boatmen along the levee in Cincinnati would have been subjected to immediate and perpetual poverty had the laws against profanity been enforced. In 1805, the state legislature also provided fines for swearing and working unnecessarily on Sunday. Evidently, the Ohio frontier offered considerable work for the religious. Even so, as late as 1818, one traveler who passed through Zanesville reported that churches were "extremely scarce and wretchedly supported," and where churches ministered to the frontier people, the clergy preached conversion, not the social gospel.

Despite the social democracy of the Methodists, the moral elitism of the Presbyterians, as well as the group appeal of the Quakers and Shakers or the utopian zeal of the Society of Separatists of Zoar, however, most men and women on the Ohio frontier remained unchurched. Although the majority of these settlers came from Protestant backgrounds and considered any Catholic to be a "dangerous character," they were not practicing members of any denomination, group, or sect. But they were not irreligious. Given the vastness of the Ohio frontier, individualism, and the diversity of immigrant origins, the religious beliefs of the settlers ranged from atheism to mysticism. On the frontier, nominal Protestantism reigned supreme; that is, settlers professed a belief in Christianity, but they did not do much about it. Located far from a regular minister, many settlers had little contact with organized religion, and many were too poor to support a settled minister. For others, given the choice of accepting or rejecting religion, many chose the second alternative. For the unchurched on the Ohio frontier, freedom of religion meant the liberty to be left alone.

At the same time, religion as practiced by the Methodists, Presbyterians, Congregationalists, and Baptists helped foster the extension of republicanism to the frontier—that is, the concepts of representative government, congregational sovereignty, the abolition of hierarchy, personal discipline, and the will to protect civil and religious liberties. Certainly the churched settlers believed that their stewardship would help ensure freedom on the frontier. At the same time, however, the denominational competition for souls contributed to acrimony, jealousy, and distrust. If anything, religion on the Ohio frontier was a complex institution.

Still, religion had a greater and more universal effect on the frontier people in Ohio than education. It was a unifying element that helped create a sense of community and shared experience that brought settlers together. Religion served as a social and emotional experience that helped break down isolation and ease the burdens of hard work, and it helped enforce moral and social standards that benefited frontier communities. Religion also provided a common basis for the formation of groups beyond the local community and helped bind the people of the new state together in a strong union. Moreover, for many settlers on the Ohio frontier, religion served as the chief form of intellectual stimulation and activity—reading scriptures and controversial tracts, writing sermons, and entering into theological discussions.

While the settlers worked out their religious differences on the Ohio frontier, however, a new Indian war loomed in the West. Soon, many men, women, and children, both Indian and white, would pray to their God for safety and victory.

II.

CONFEDERACY AND WAR

The Treaty of Greenville brought an uneasy peace for the white settlers on the Ohio frontier. It also brought hunger and want for the Shawnees, Delawares, and Wyandots, who were now confined to the northern portion of the state. There they suffered from a depletion in game as well as the further loss of their lands as the frontier people crossed over the treaty boundary. Liquor provided by frontier tradesmen made their lives worse. Many became drunkards prone to violence in their villages and homes. A sense of hopelessness and desperation prevailed in Ohio's Indian communities. Although some Indians, such as the Shawnees under Black Hoof, whose village lay at Wapakoneta on the headwaters of the Auglaize, turned their backs on the past and sought federal assistance to learn agricultural practices in order to "walk the white man's road," others sought a return to their old ways.

By June 1799, rumors circulated that the western Indians were once again preparing for war in desperate hope of defending and keeping the lands they now claimed, if not to recover lost territory. Many whites, however, refused to believe that the Indians planned a new war because they had too much to lose in the form of annual annuities and presents. Even so, these rumors gained substance in early August, when reports arrived in Cincinnati that one hundred Indians, "well armed, painted, and mounted on good horses," had appeared at Fort Loramie, where they talked to a Captain Hamilton. They carried English rifles and full pouches of powder and

lead. After milling about, they took some flour from an army contractor and informed Hamilton that they intended to call a council
of all the tribes to determine whether they would permit the running
of the Greenville Treaty line that would establish the boundary
between Indians and whites. The frontier people were naturally
alarmed, but the Shawnees allayed their fears in mid-August by
sending word that they respected the Treaty of Greenville and meant
no one harm. Not everyone on the Ohio frontier rested assured, but
the peace held.

At least for a time. When Thomas Jefferson became president in
1801, his administration initiated an aggressive land-acquisition
policy. Jefferson operated on the premise that the Indians of the
Northwest would willingly sell additional lands to the federal government whenever white settlers needed more room for expansion.
He also assumed that the Indians would adopt white agricultural
practices and thereby free additional lands for settlers. Jefferson
contended that if the Indians could be taught practical farming
techniques, they would readily adopt an agricultural life because it
would provide both food and security. If they did not do so, Jefferson believed that government traders could so burden the tribes
with debt that they would have no recourse but to trade away their
lands to settle their obligations.

While Jefferson supported both agricultural education and cun-
ning to gain additional Indians lands, he also authorized William
Henry Harrison, governor of the Indiana Territory, to enter into
treaties with the western Indians for additional land cessions. Harrison proved a willing public servant, and between 1802 and 1809, he
pressed the Indians into selling much of the present states of Indiana
and Illinois. Often he dictated rather than negotiated, and the northwestern tribes became increasingly resentful of governmental policy.
The lands promised to them in the Treaty of Greenville were disappearing from their control.

Indian grievances over their continued loss of land festered and
would not heal, and the federal government did nothing to soothe
their wounded pride and sense of right. On July 4, 1805, the Indians
in the Western Reserve surrendered their lands west of the Cuyahoga River and south to the Greenville Treaty line. The Indians in
northwestern Ohio lost additional lands by treaty in 1807 and 1808.

While the government continued to press for more land cessions, the Indians looked to the British in Canada for aid. The British offered encouragement and bided their time.

While the British waited for opportunity, Jefferson continued to press for the acquisition of additional Indian lands and convinced himself that his policy of providing educational instruction on the reservations had achieved remarkable success. In his annual message to Congress in December 1805, Jefferson reported: "Our Indian neighbors are advancing, many of them with spirit, and others beginning to engage in the pursuits of agriculture and household manufacture. They are becoming sensible that the earth yields subsistence with less labor and more certainty than the forest, and find it in their interest from time to time to dispose of parts of their surplus and waste lands for the means of improving those they occupy and of subsisting their families while they are preparing their farms." While Jefferson believed what he wanted, in 1805 a Shawnee by the name of Lalawethika, "the Noisemaker," a younger brother of Tecumseh and later known as Tenskwatawa or the Prophet, offered the Indians in the Northwest an opportunity to redeem their lands and traditional lifestyle, if only they followed his teachings.

Prior to 1805 Lalawethika had been a drunk without respect among the Shawnee people. In April of that year, however, he suffered a seizure that left him unconscious for a considerable period of time. Although his relatives thought that he had died, Lalawethika regained consciousness, at which time he told them that he had died and gone to the spirit world and talked with the Master of Life, who showed him an afterworld divided much like the Christian concept of heaven and hell. In the afterlife those Indians who had wasted their lives with liquor and who had forsaken traditional cultural practices were treated to horrible tortures. The Master of Life then told Lalawethika to lead the Shawnees to cultural redemption. Thereafter, Lalawethika told his people, he would be know as Tenskwatawa or "the Prophet."

The Prophet told the Shawnees that the Americans had been made not by the Master of Life but rather by the Great Serpent, who ruled the powers of evil in the universe. The Master of Life had told him that "they grew from the scum of the great water when it was troubled by the Evil Spirit. And the froth was driven into the woods

Tenskwatawa, better known as the Shawnee Prophet, was the younger brother of Tecumseh. The Prophet sought to rekindle native spiritual beliefs and rituals to help resist white culture that destroyed Indian families. INDIANA HISTORICAL SOCIETY LIBRARY, c546.

by a strong east wind. . . . They are unjust. They have taken away your lands which were not made for them." The Prophet warned that anyone who made peace with the Americans, such as Black Hoof, adhered to the Great Serpent, and he admonished them to avoid them in all ways. The Prophet urged the Shawnees to return to their traditional ways of living. He preached that the Great Spirit had told him that his people suffered because they had forsaken their old ways of hunting and tending their fields. He also told them not to sell their lands, and he admonished them to give up whiskey and to stop fighting among themselves. If the Shawnees obeyed, the Great Spirit would hear and protect them and their lands from the frontier people. The young Shawnees, who had not experienced war, listened to the Prophet, and his word spread among them like wildfire as they envisioned a religious union that would protect them and help them win back Indian lands. By 1806, many Delawares and Wyandots had learned of the Prophet's teachings and joined his newly established village at Greenville.

The Prophet alarmed the settlers on Ohio's frontier. In response to these fears and because the Prophet's village was outside the

Greenville Treaty line, Governor Edward Tiffin asked the federal government to remove them. The crisis seemed to worsen in February 1806, when Tiffin received word from an army patrol in the Mad River region that the Shawnees were preparing for war. At Greenville the young men who followed the Prophet carried "painted and feathered" tomahawks, the symbol of war, while they passed out war belts among the Indian villages in the vicinity. As a result, one small white settlement of eight families on Stoney Creek had fled to the security of more populated areas along the Mad River. Although some residents in Chillicothe believed the Shawnees were a "weak and restless tribe," if events proved that they were "urged by any foreign enemies," proper measures would have to be taken.

Almost as quickly as the Shawnee scare spread across the Ohio frontier, it dissipated. A shortage of food at Greenville and growing hostility by the frontier people encouraged the Prophet and Tecumseh to move their followers to Indiana, where they established the village of Prophetstown at the fork of the Wabash and Tippecanoe rivers. The Shawnees who chose to remain in Ohio professed their intent to remain at peace. In March chiefs Big Snake, Captain Snake, and Captain Lewis declared "in the presence of the Great Spirit above, that we wish no war, but peace and friendship with all the people of the United States, and . . . our hearts are bleeding with sorrow to find our brothers so ready to take our lives innocently." They sent Governor Tiffin a belt of white wampum, a symbol of peace, and professed their desire to begin farming along Stoney Creek. And they offered to shake with their left hands, which signified peace and friendship, rather than their right hands, which symbolized hostility. With that expression of good faith and the absence of war, the settlers who had fled their homes returned to their Stoney Creek settlements.

But their ease did not last long. In mid-April 1806, settlers along the Mad River again reported that the Shawnees appeared to be preparing for war, and they fled their homes and sought protection from the government. Governor Tiffin, however, remained skeptical, saying: "I cannot believe that our red friends will be so far lost to a sense of their duty and best interests, as to entertain a thought of disturbing that peace and friendship which so happily subsists between them and us." Tiffin then sent a white belt to the Shawnees to "brighten up the chain of peace and friendship." He also asked the Shawnees to report "any cause of complaint against our people" so that he could prevent "any serious consequences happening either to your people or ours." He hoped the Great Spirit would touch the hearts of both whites and Indians in Ohio and "keep the chain of peace shinning bright." Once again calm prevailed.

On July 17, 1807, soon after learning about the attack of the British ship *Leopard* on the U.S. Navy frigate *Chesapeake*, a "numerous and respectable collection" of Chillicothe's citizens assembled at Forrest Meeker's Tavern, where, under the leadership of Governor Tiffin, they organized themselves into a committee and proceeded to attack British treachery. Their contempt for the British had no limits, and they even blamed the Burr conspiracy on British influence. Before the assembly adjourned, it resolved to support the government's efforts to seek redress and urged every militia officer to have his men "properly disciplined" and to "excite in them a zeal for the defence of their rights and liberties." The Chillicotheans also resolved to form a committee of correspondence to communicate with other towns and states about all matters pertaining to government actions in the days ahead.

Ohioans did not wait long to learn about the ramifications of the *Chesapeake* affair. On April 18, 1806, Congress had called for the states to provide 100,000 men in case the maritime troubles with Great Britain developed into an armed conflict. The Jefferson administration now asked Ohio to "hold in readiness, to march at a moment's warning" the 291 militia that had been requested from the state. In early September, the citizens of Urbana also began building a blockhouse for their defense upon learning that some five hundred Indians were at Greenville. William Wells, commander and agent at Fort Wayne, reported that the Shawnees and other tribes who were congregating at Greenville were not hostile yet, but he said: "I believe the British is at the bottom of this." Others agreed. The *Western Spy* in Cincinnati reported that the Indians gathering at Greenville had "much alarmed the frontier settlers," and the governor had decided to call out a large portion of the militia in order to march at the first indication of trouble. Reports indicated that many of the Indians had assembled at Greenville to hear the Prophet speak. The frontier people believed that the congregation had been "prompted by a more powerful motive than curiosity—British Gold."

In order to determine the intent of the Shawnees, acting governor Thomas Kirker sent Thomas Worthington and Duncan McArthur to Greenville. There an estimated 505 Indians, 265 women and children and 240 men, resided. Worthington and McArthur arrived at the camp, located about two miles from the fort, on September 13. They reported that the Shawnees were "much agitated and anxious about their safety." The Ohio emissaries then proceeded to remind the Shawnees that they had once fought with the British against the Americans without "cause or provocation." Worthington told them, "You interfered in a family quarrel, in which you had no concern." The English lost that war, and "so far from making any provision for you, who had helped them through the war, they ceded the very lands you live on to your white brethren. This was the conduct of your English friends." Worthington told them that the British had forced the tomahawk into their hands only to "shut their gates against you and drive you away like dogs, although they had before promised you assistance and protection." After General Wayne had defeated them, the Americans treated the Shawnees with "kindness and friendship," and they would have peace if they deserved it.

Worthington told the Shawnees that they had to consider carefully their own interests, because the British had been "lately guilty of taking away the lives of some of your white brethren without cause;—they seek a quarrel without provocation. Your white brethren can bear with them no longer. . . . A war therefore is likely to take place again between your white brethren and the English." Then Worthington told the Shawnees that the Americans did not solicit their aid. Rather, if war came, the United States would send an army that would "march by you to the north; and if they find you sitting still and minding your own affairs, taking care of your wives and children, they will take you by the hand and do you no harm, but help you. But if they find you have let the British put the tomahawk into your hands to be used against them they will destroy you for your folly."

Worthington, then, admonished the Shawnees for moving from their lands north of the Greenville Treaty line "for what purpose we know not." Perhaps, he suggested, the Indians, once again under the influence of the British, intended to make war on the Americans. If they meant to make war, Worthington told them, they would succeed only in destroying a few white families who lived nearby, but they would "suffer severely" for it. Even as he spoke, he reported, their father, the governor of Ohio, was calling five thousand "warriors" to defend against possible attacks. The Prophet, Blue Jacket, and the other Indian leaders listened and promised to give an answer at ten o'clock the next morning.

When they assembled the next day, Blue Jacket delivered the response of the Shawnees, Wyandots, Potawatomis, Tawas, Ojibwas, and others who were present. He said that if the whites went to war, they would "mind their own concerns." Blue Jacket then said, "The disturber of our peace appears to be seated at Fort Wayne [Mr. Wells] who I think is a bad man." Blue Jacket complained that Wells treated his Shawnees "like dogs." He charged that Wells attempted to divide the Indians and keep them from hearing the Prophet. Blue Jacket believed that Wells was "possessed of a Devil," and rather than deal with the agent, he would "as soon go to see a dog with the mange." Despite his hatred of Wells, Blue Jacket told Worthington and McArthur that "we have laid down the tomahawk never to take it up again, if it is offered to us by the French, English, Spaniards or by you, our white brethren, we will not take it," all of which heartened Worthington and McArthur.

The Prophet then spoke and told Worthington and McArthur why he had moved his people to Greenville. He said that about three years before, he had become convinced of the error of his ways and that if he did not change he would be "destroyed from the face of the earth." Accordingly, he learned from the Master of Life that his destiny was to "constantly preach to his red brethren the insufferable situation they were in by nature, and endeavored to convince them that they must change their lives—live honestly, and be just in all their dealings, kind towards one another, and their white brethren; affectionate towards their families; put away lying and slandering and serve the Great Spirit in the way he pointed out; never think of war again." Despite his good intentions, the Prophet said, some Shawnees would not listen but persecuted him. This attack produced a division in the nation. Those who adhered to him moved to Greenville, where he gave spiritual guidance to all the Indians who came to see him. The Prophet told Worthington and McArthur that he did not move his people to Greenville because it was a pretty or valuable place, because it was neither. Rather, he established a village at Greenville because the Master of Life revealed to him that it was the proper place to teach, and he intended to do so as long as he lived.

Worthington and McArthur were impressed by the "sincerity" of the Prophet, and they reported that "there was no hostile appearance—their women and children of which there were about 250 were . . . engaged generally in their ordinary labor." They had been treated with "great hospitality and kindness in their way." Several days later, on September 22, Stephen Ruddel sent a communication to Governor Kirker stating that he had lived with the Indians for seventeen years, that he understood their languages and customs, and that he did not believe the Indians near Greenville had "hostile intentions towards the United States at present." With these reports the frontier people breathed a little easier, but doubts remained and old fears lingered.

* * *

While diplomatic relations deteriorated rapidly with the British over matters of impressment and freedom of the seas, relations with the Indians on the Ohio frontier remained tenuous at best. During the winter of 1807–1808, Sir James Craig, captain general and governor-in-chief of British North America, developed a policy that would keep the Indians loyal to Great Britain. He believed that if war came with the United States, the Americans would use the Indians against the British. To counter that possibility, Craig ordered his subordinates to supply the Indians with provisions and encourage them against the Americans. They were, however, to be held in check until ordered to attack.

At the same time, Tecumseh, brother of the Prophet, began efforts to unite the western tribes in an Indian confederacy that would stretch from Alabama to Minnesota and from Kansas to New England. It would be a confederacy that would have sufficient strength to guarantee the integrity of Indian lands. In 1810, Tecumseh traveled throughout the Northwest Territory urging the formation of an Indian confederacy to prevent the loss of any more land through the cession treaty process. A year later Tecumseh traveled to Alabama, where he attempted to enlist the Creeks in his confederacy. He told them to join together in a confederacy and to break all agreements that they had made with the whites. When the right time occurred, the confederacy would drive the whites back across the Appalachians or kill them to the last man, woman, and child. Increasingly, the tribes of Ohio and the Northwest Territory looked to Tecumseh for leadership. After the Prophet precipitated the Battle of Tippecanoe in Indiana on November 7, 1811, he lost influence among the northwestern tribes, and Tecumseh emerged as the primary leader who would unite the Indians politically rather than religiously.

Specifically, Tecumseh argued that Indians lands could not be sold unless all tribes agreed, and by so doing championed a possessory or exclusive right to the soil and a concept of political and military unity that the Americans could easily understand, if not accept. Tecumseh refused to accept the Greenville Treaty, which required the Indians to give up 25,000 square miles of territory. He considered the agreement nothing less than the theft of Indian lands in Ohio. He turned to the British for support, particularly guns and ammunition, to win those lands back. The British, once again, proved to be a willing ally, and the Indian problem that Ohioans thought had been resolved at Fallen Timbers and with the Treaty of Greenville returned to the frontier.

While affairs with the British deteriorated, James Madison assumed the presidency. Madison continued to follow Jefferson's example by attempting to gain land cessions from the Indians whenever possible. When he sent his annual message to Congress in December 1810, he told the members that peace and friendship between the Indian tribes and the federal government continued to gain strength. Only a few weeks before, however, Tecumseh had met with the British at Amherstburg in Canada and told them that he was prepared for war.

Isolated Indian attacks on frontier settlers increased. In July 1811, Indians killed a white man near Sandusky. His skull was split by a tomahawk, and he was stripped and scalped. Renewed attacks on whites in Ohio, Indiana, and Illinois convinced the frontier people that the Shawnees planned a general Indian war. In response they wanted the federal government to drive the tribes from their "immediate frontiers."

John Johnston, Indian agent at Piqua, attempted to calm the fears of Ohioans by inviting the Shawnees and Wyandots to a council on August 23, 1811, and fifty Indian delegates attended. When the conference broke up the next day, Johnston reported that the results were as satisfactory as could be wished. All had professed their intention to remain at peace and proclaimed their friendship for the United States. "I feel no hesitation," he wrote, "in assuring the public that at present there is not the smallest danger to be apprehended from the Shawanoes, Wyandotts, Delawares, or Miamies, and it is believed that many of the Puttawatomies may be considered as the true friends of the United States." But Johnston's reassurance did little to calm the fears of the frontier people, because in November they learned that the Prophet continued to be "refractory and obstinate" and inclined toward war. "What may be the result," an observer from Vincennes wrote, "God only knows."

While the Madison administration attempted to force British recognition of American rights on the seas by trade sanctions, it also began to prepare for war. Apparently, none too soon. On May 7 a report reached Dayton that the "savages appear engaged on every quarter of our frontier in committing depredations upon the lives and property of the settlers." Everyone assumed that the three men recently found mutilated at the junction of the Auglaize and the Miami of the Lakes rivers had been murdered by Indians. In response, a volunteer militia company from Miami County headed north to investigate. The men sent toward the Auglaize reportedly showed "a determination to kill every Indian they meet with, until they have further orders." They were partly successful—killing two, wounding a third, and taking two women and a boy prisoner. From all appearances, then, by the spring of 1812, both Indians and whites on the Ohio frontier would settle for nothing less than a war, in which they intended to solve their mutual problems of encroachment on their lands.

William Hull, governor of the Michigan Territory, certainly believed that a war with Great Britain would benefit the frontier people and the nation. As the newly appointed commander of the

Northwest Army, he contended that if war came, the British would attack Detroit "with the view to obtain the assistance of the Indians and in the present state of defences in the Northwest country it would be within their power to do it." Hull, however, contended that "a force adequate to the defence of that vulnerable point [Detroit], would prevent a war with the savages and probably induce the enemy to abandon Upper Canada without opposition."

The frontier people agreed that a war with Britain would enable the United States to eliminate the Indian problem once and for all and to seize Canada for redress of British seizures of American ships and goods and the impressment of its merchant seamen during Britain's war with France. Henry Clay, Speaker of the House and war hawk from Kentucky, spoke for most westerners when he said that Canada was "the instrument by which that redress was to be obtained." Jefferson also believed that the seizure of Canada would be "a mere matter of marching." War, then, meant opportunity under the guise of necessity.

* * *

On June 17, 1812, the Twelfth Congress of the United States declared war against Great Britain. Ohio's three-man delegation split over the decision. Senator Thomas Worthington opposed, arguing, "It will be folly & madness to get into a war for abstract principles when we have not the power to enforce them." Yet Worthington did not advocate submission. Rather, while war was "unavoidable," he contended, "we have it completely in our power to choose our own time to make it[.] I cannot take the responsibility on me of entering into it unprepared." Senator Alexander Campbell was absent, but Congressman Jeremiah Morrow voted for war. Governor Return Jonathan Meigs, Jr., called the declaration "a practical renewal of the Declaration of Independence." Most Ohioans believed that war with Great Britain was necessary to solve the Indian problem and bring peace to the frontier. They also believed it was required to defend national honor regarding British impressments and denial of the American principle of freedom of the seas. Once the decision for war had been made, however, events moved quickly in Ohio. Most Ohioans understood that an attack on Canada was essential to achieving the goals of peace and honor.

In March, three months before the declaration of war, Governor Meigs had issued a call for twelve hundred volunteers to rendezvous at Dayton and march north to help defend Detroit, and it was quickly met by mechanics, lawyers, farmers, and merchants. By early May three companies, ranging from fifty to eighty men by state law, had been recruited at St. Clairsville, while two companies had organized in Scioto County. Zanesville and New Lancaster each contributed a company as well. The *Fredonian* at Circleville reported that "political distinctions were unknown," and Colonels Duncan McArthur, James Findlay, and Lewis Cass soon organized three volunteer regiments. Although these volunteers reported with their essential equipment, they lacked blankets, and the stores in Ohio could not provide them. As a result, Governor Meigs made a "pathetic appeal to the patriotism of the ladies of Cincinnati," asking for donations of one or two blankets per family. The next day, five hundred blankets arrived at the nearby volunteers' camp.

Meigs arrived in Dayton on May 7 and quickly sent scouts as well as a volunteer rifle company, under Colonel Jerome Holt, to Greenville and militia reinforcements to Piqua. By the end of the month more than four thousand troops, both militia and regulars, had rendezvoused at Dayton. On May 25, Meigs transferred command of those troops to Michigan governor and brigadier general William Hull, who established his headquarters at McCullum's Tavern. On that day Hull and Meigs received the troops, and the governor gave an inspirational speech in which he said: "Our frontier must be protected from a savage barbarity, our rights maintained and our wrongs avenged." Major James Denny, First Regiment of Ohio Volunteers, wrote to his wife, "The emotions of sympathy which were excited by it cannot well be described. Many shed tears. They were not tears of regret or sorrow for past events, but a burst of manly feelings for the wrongs of their beloved country, and their zeal to revenge them." The reason for war was clear to Governor Meigs and other Ohioans, and he affirmed it in his December 9 address to the legislature, when he said that in the West "hordes of barbarians, stimulated by British influence, tear alike the scalp from the mother, and the infant in her arms, and with relentless fury stain the land of Freedom with the blood of her sons." On the Ohio frontier, Meigs reported, "the war is characterized by the disgraceful alliance of pretended civilization, and inexorable barbarity."

Hull agreed and believed his large army would intimidate the British and force them to evacuate the region. As governor of the Michigan Territory, he had actively solicited an army appointment. Later, when shamed by defeat, Hull claimed that he had accepted command of the Northwest Army only "with great reluctance." One observer who attended the ceremony reported that Hull was a "short, corpulent, good natured old gentleman, who bore the marks of good eating and drinking." Hull also knew how to give a good speech, and he "animated every breast, and great expectations were formed of his prowess and abilities. . . . The frost of time had given him a venerable aspect, and the idea of his revolutionary services inspired the troops with confidence." On June 1, with the formalities out of the way, Hull led the Ohio volunteers north to help protect Detroit. On that same day, President Madison asked Congress for a declaration of war against Great Britain. During the year that followed, regular army units and Ohio and Kentucky militia continually passed through Dayton, traveling north and south to and from the chain of forts that led north to the Auglaize River country, Fort Wayne, Indiana, and Canada.

Hull first led his army to Urbana, where it joined the Fourth U.S. Infantry, commanded by Lieutenant Colonel James Miller, whose men had distinguished themselves in 1811 at the Battle of Tippecanoe. The four regiments then marched to the Maumee and into the Black Swamp, which offered a difficult but direct route to Detroit. Guides blazed trees with their tomahawks to mark the best route, while the soldiers, following with axes and shovels, cleared a trail. On June 16, they built a blockhouse which they named Fort McArthur at the present-day site of Kenton. Colonel Findlay's men then cut the road to Fort Findlay, stopping only because of heavy rain and mud to construct a stockade called Fort Necessity. From Fort Findlay, Colonel Cass's men continued along the road to the Maumee Rapids, which they reached on June 30.

At the Rapids, Hull employed the schooner *Cuyahoga* to transport his baggage and thereby lighten the load on his pack train and speed the reinforcement of Detroit. Hull, however, carelessly sent his personal papers, which documented the American strength and intent to fortify Detroit. On July 2, Hull and his Ohio volunteers reached Frenchtown on the River Raisin, and he received word that the United States and Great Britain were at war. On that same day, the British learned of Hull's intentions when they captured the *Cuyahoga.*

Hull reached Detroit on July 5 and soon sent the regiments under James Miller and Lewis Cass across the Detroit River into British Territory to Sandwich Island in order to prepare an attack on Fort Malden at Amherstburg, while McArthur's regiment attempted to divert the British with a march to Spring Wells. A week later, Hull also issued a proclamation urging the Canadians to join the American cause and promising them protection. But any Canadians who fought with Indians against the United States would be executed. Hull's goal, however, proved greater than his ability. Instead of attacking Fort Malden while it remained relatively weak, he delayed and worried about maintaining his 200-mile-long supply line after learning that the Wyandots had joined the British. While the army waited to attack, Hull sent a message to Governor Meigs that he needed additional supplies immediately or the army would "perish."

Meigs responded quickly by sending 200 militia north from Chillicothe, under Captain Henry Bush, with provisions. Upon reaching the River Raisin about thirty-five miles south of Detroit, Bush feared an attack by Indians and sent word to Hull that he needed reinforcements to proceed safely. Bush's information proved correct. When a detachment of 150 Ohio riflemen under Major Thomas Van Horne from Findlay's regiment attempted to reach the militia, they were driven back by Indians under Tecumseh near Brownstown. Van Horne's men had been caught in an ambush and had taken "heavy fire," with the loss of seven "uncommonly great" officers along with ten privates. Hull learned of the attack on his supply line about the same time that word arrived that British troops would soon reinforce Fort Malden.

Although the Ohio volunteers increasingly grumbled about waiting to attack, Hull retreated with most of his army to Detroit. On August 8, he also sent another escort column to the River Raisin to meet the supply train and break through to Ohio. When the 600-man force, including 200 riflemen and 40 volunteer dragoons from Ohio, under Lieutenant Colonel James Miller, reached Monguagon on August 9, about fourteen miles south of Detroit, it was attacked by approximately 400 British regulars and volunteers and a large number of Indians. During this sharp firefight, Hull reported that the Indians "under the command of Tecumseh fought with great obstinacy," but when his force made a bayonet charge, the British and Indians fled the field. Hull's cavalry, however, failed to pursue them. The Indians left forty dead and the Forty-first Regiment suffered fifteen killed. The losses to the Ohio volunteers went unreported. When the British withdrew, Miller retreated to Detroit because of a "very severe rain storm."

About this same time, Hull learned that the British had captured the American outpost of Mackinac Island between Lakes Huron and Michigan, and he believed this loss "opened the northern hive of Indians and they were swarming down in every direction." As a result, he ordered a withdrawal of the remainder of his army across the Detroit River and abandoned plans to attack Fort Malden. "This fatal and unaccountable step," reported one officer, "dispirited the troops." Hull also suggested that the army retreat back into Ohio, but his officers convinced him that the militia would dissolve if he took that action. With their supply line to Ohio now effectively cut and Hull losing his nerve, however, the militia officers sent a message to Governor Meigs in which they requested "the arrest and displacement of the General." They considered Hull nothing less than a coward, and some even talked about removing him from command, but the plot disintegrated when Colonel Miller, the ranking regular army officer, refused to participate.

While the confidence of the Ohioans in General Hull plummeted, on August 13 British general Isaac Brock arrived at Fort Malden on Lake Erie with a strong force of Canadian militia and British regulars. There he met with Tecumseh, who had about a thousand Indians, including some "extraordinary characters," under his command. Tecumseh impressed Brock, who called him "sagacious" and a "gallant warrior." The Shawnee leader was, Brock reported, "the admiration of everyone who conversed with him." Brock and Tecumseh soon agreed about a plan of attack against the Americans. Two days later, Brock sent a message to Hull demanding the immediate surrender of Detroit. Brock included an ominous warning: "It is far from my intention to join in a war of extermination, but you must be aware, that the numerous body of Indians who have attached themselves to my troops, will be beyond control the moment the contest commences." Hull refused Brock's ultimatum for surrender, and the bombardment of Detroit began.

Confronted with an enemy force that he believed to be stronger than his own and convinced that he was short of supplies, Hull sent Colonels McArthur and Cass to take 400 men and break through the enemy lines on a relief expedition. McArthur and Cass, however, could not locate Brush's company and eventually returned to Detroit. Hull then lost his will to fight and asked Brock to stop the bombardment and to "prepare terms for capitulation," in part to gain a British pledge to protect his women and children from the Indians. Events then moved quickly. At noon on August 16, Hull surrendered his 2,500-man force. "Not an officer was consulted," Colonel Lewis Cass reported. "Even the women were indignant at so shameful a degradation of the American character." One Ohio soldier reported that "Old Gen. Hull became panic struck and despite the entreaties of his officers and private soldiers . . . we were made to submit to the most shameful surrender that ever took place in the world." Other Ohio volunteers considered his actions nothing less than "treachery."

Although Brock held the American regulars as prisoners, he allowed the Ohio volunteers to return home on parole pending good behavior. Although the Ohioans complained bitterly about Hull's incompetency, their own inadequacies helped mar Hull's mission. Even before they left Urbana, some of the militia refused to obey Hull's orders, and they marched north only because the regulars forced them. Along the way, Hull reported, they "kept constantly firing off their pieces," and nearly two hundred even refused to cross the boundary into Canada. Little wonder, then, that when combined with Hull's incompetence, the first engagement of Ohio's military men in the War of 1812 had ended with a humiliating defeat. As a result, by the early autumn of 1812, the Ohio frontier lay open to enemy attack, and the frontier people began fleeing their homes.

* * *

By September 1812, the war went badly for the Americans. The British had foiled an invasion of Canada, the army suffered a lack of training, discipline, and leadership, and national elections loomed on the November horizon. While Madison struggled to bring order out of chaos, on September 17 he bowed to political necessity and appointed William Henry Harrison the new commander of the Northwestern Army, or what there was of it. Harrison had great popularity in the West, and the frontier people believed that the hero of Tippecanoe could best raise a new force of regulars, volunteers, and militia to lead it against the Indians on the frontier and the British at Detroit.

Earlier, on September 5, Harrison, while leading a force of Kentucky volunteers north to Fort Wayne, had issued a call for additional men from his headquarters at Piqua. "The British and Indians have invaded our country," he reported, "and are now besieging (perhaps have taken) Fort Wayne." He asked "every friend of this country, who is able to do so" to "join me as soon as possible, well mounted with a good rifle, & 20 or 30 days provisions." Ammunition would be furnished at Cincinnati and Dayton. Harrison was pleased with the Ohio and Kentucky militia who answered his call. But the Ohioans tended to taunt those from Kentucky, whose "imprudent conduct" caused a "spirit of jealousy" that resulted in several Ohio militia officers' challenging their Kentucky counterparts to duels. Harrison's officers fortunately kept the Ohioans and Kentuckians from fighting. While the Ohioans and Kentuckians squabbled, Harrison longed for an opportunity to march north, not only to attack the British and Indians but also to improve morale among his men. In mid-January one Ohio volunteer reported about the militia: "The enemy will soon be within our reach, [then] they will have an opportunity of gratifying their insatiable appetite for fighting."

Harrison had originally planned to take Detroit and Fort Malden before Christmas after the arrival of consistently cold weather when the Black Swamp froze, thereby making transportation easier. While Harrison waited, he used the autumn to gather his force, and he sent the Ohio militia to harass the Indians to the West. On November 25, Lieutenant John B. Campbell led six hundred men from Franklinton through Dayton and Greenville to attack the Miamis and Delawares along the Mississineway River, which ran into the Wabash. Before winter arrived, Harrison also planned to assemble a strong force at the Maumee Rapids, and he ordered General James

Winchester and his Kentucky militia from Fort Defiance to the Rapids. Harrison also ordered Brigadier General Edward Tupper to use his twelve hundred men to supply Fort McArthur and provision Winchester at the Rapids.

On January 10, Winchester reached the Rapids during bitterly cold and snowy weather, and he began to build a fortified camp along the north bank of the Maumee River. Survival and fort building in the hard northern Ohio winter would have been challenge enough, but Winchester departed from his orders upon learning that Americans not far to the north at Frenchtown (present-day Monroe, Michigan) could be rescued and the village taken, because few British regulars, Canadian militia, and Indians protected the village. Accordingly, on January 18, 1813, Winchester sent 660 Kentucky militia against Frenchtown and captured it. The British, however, quickly regrouped, and Colonel Henry Proctor sent approximately 1,400 men, half of whom were Indians, to surround the overextended Americans at the River Raisin on the night of the 21st.

Winchester had not ordered night patrols or pickets because he assumed that the junior officers automatically took care of those precautions. When Proctor attacked before daylight, his command overwhelmed Winchester's sleeping men. Within minutes more than a hundred Kentuckians lay dead, their scalped skulls steaming in the cold January air. The fighting continued into the early dawn until some three hundred Americans lay dead. Faced with overwhelming odds, Winchester, himself a prisoner, surrendered his force when Proctor promised to protect his men from the Indians. Proctor, however, marched the Americans away, leaving approximately one hundred wounded who were savagely butchered by his allies. When word of the massacre reached Ohio, the rallying cry of the Northwestern Army became "Remember the Raisin."

On January 22, 1813, Harrison learned about Winchester's disaster, the second defeat of the Northwestern Army in seven months, at his Upper Sandusky headquarters, but Winchester's defeat was not his only problem. Secretary of the Treasury Albert Gallatin favored reducing military expenditures in the West to an amount necessary only for "defensive operations." At the same time, Secretary of War John Armstrong preferred to concentrate army activities in the East and mustered little confidence in Harrison. As a result, Armstrong limited Harrison's authority to rely on the militia, stockpile provisions, and attack the enemy. Placed on the defensive by a change of governmental policy, Harrison decided to build a strong fortified position at the Maumee Rapids to prevent a British attack from the Detroit area and to provide a stage for his own attack in the spring, if the situation permitted.

Located on the south bank of the Maumee below the rapids, Fort Meigs became the bastion of the Ohio frontier. Captain Eleazer D. Wood, a West Point–trained engineer, planned and directed the construction. Wood used eight blockhouses with double timbers and four elevated batteries to create interlocking zones of fire for both cannoneers and riflemen along the 2,500-yard circumference of the irregular ellipse-shaped fort. He circled the encampment with fifteen-foot picket logs, reinforced by a thick dirt wall. The men reportedly worked "day and night," hurriedly throwing up breastworks about the pickets and mounting their cannon. Captain Wood wrote that "the weather was extremely severe, and the ground so hard frozen that it was almost impossible to open it with a spade and pick-axe." By spring both Harrison and the British knew that Fort Meigs had become the most important fortress in the western country.

When spring came, reports indicated that the Indians were active in the area of the Maumee Rapids and along the Whitewater. On April 4, the *Zanesville Express* reported that the Indians were "very troublesome" and that a "bloody summer" could be expected. It also noted that small detachments of troops constantly passed through Dayton headed for the Maumee Rapids, in part to replace Kentucky, Pennsylvania, and Virginia volunteers whose enlistments had expired. A week later, the Springfield company of mounted riflemen waited to ride to the Rapids at a moment's notice by order of the governor. On April 26, a rifle company from North Lancaster marched to Fort Meigs. Harrison welcomed these reinforcements because he had learned that six thousand British troops had arrived at Fort Malden to prepare for an attack against his post. "Should that fortress be lost," the *Zanesville Express* reported, "bloody work may be expected on our frontiers." In Marietta, Captain Alexander Hill of the Twenty-seventh Regiment of the U.S. Infantry recruited volunteers from Washington, Athens, and Gallia counties for twelve months of service in Harrison's army.

By mid-April, the construction of Fort Meigs had nearly been completed, and Harrison expected a British attack at any time. On the 18th, he learned from spies that it would come in ten or twelve days. The British had been observed moving out of Detroit, and Tecumseh had rallied the Indians, in part with threats of death and the destruction of their property, if they did not join the attack. Harrison waited with 1,100 men behind the walls of his well-provisioned fort, where he had ordered the sentries to call out "all's well" or otherwise, starting at the main gate every fifteen minutes. On April 27, Proctor's army, consisting of 522 regulars and 462 Canadian militia, arrived at the Rapids by boat on the Maumee from Lake Erie. There they were joined by approximately 1,000 Indians under Tecumseh and a mounted British advance party. Proctor then systematically prepared for a siege. He placed two batteries on the north side of the Maumee and one on the south side to bombard the fort with hot shot in hope of destroying the powder magazine. During that time, Tecumseh's men harassed the fort with musket fire.

On May 1, the British began a four-day cannonade of Fort Meigs. During the shelling, the men huddled in caves that they had dug into the walls of a trench that ran across the interior grounds. One British officer whom the Americans captured and released told General Proctor: "It was powder and shot thrown away to fire at that fort. I can compare the Americans to nothing but an army of ground-hogs." Actually, the men inside Fort Meigs took a pounding in their mud holes. Captain Wood reported that the wounded lay in the trenches "on rails barely sufficient to keep them out of the water, which in many places, from the bleeding of the wounded, had the appearances of puddles of blood."

During the second day of the siege, the British shot and shell fell "as thick as hail." During the lulls the American soldiers "heckled" the British. Before the day ended, Proctor sent an officer under a flag to demand the American surrender, but Harrison refused, saying that the British would gain more honor taking Fort Meigs than by its surrender. Harrison also threatened that if he captured Proctor, "I will dress him in a petticoat, and deliver him over to the squaws, as being an unworthy to associate with men." Later, when the ladies of Chillicothe learned what Harrison had said, they charged that he had slandered them.

Harrison, who directed the defense of Fort Meigs, learned about midnight on May 4 that General Green Clay and his 1,200-man force of Kentuckians were about two hours from the fort. Accordingly, Harrison sent a rider through the lines to Clay with a plan to raise the siege. He ordered Clay and 800 Kentuckians to cross the Maumee and destroy the batteries on the north bank, while he attacked the cannon on the south side of the river. When the batteries on the north side had been taken, the Kentuckians were to recross the river in their boats and fight their way through the Indian forces to the safety of the fort.

At first the attack went according to plan. The Kentuckians under Lieutenant Colonel William Dudley successfully captured and spiked the cannon on the left bank, which had been defended by two hundred British regulars, two companies of Canadian militia, and a "host of Indians." But when the British and their Indian allies fled, the Kentuckians violated orders and pursued them instead of crossing over to the southern bank. In their haste to catch the enemy, the Kentuckians fell into an ambush, in which they lost about six hundred killed or captured. Upon learning about this disaster, Harrison complained that the "excessive ardour" of the Kentucky militia was "scarcely less fatal than cowardice."

The British marched their prisoners to Fort Miamis, but they did not protect them. Instead the Indians formed a gauntlet, "clubbing and tomahawking all they could of their terror-struck prisoners" before the gates. Upon learning that the Indians were murdering and scalping the prisoners, Tecumseh intervened and reportedly chastised Proctor for permitting the slaughter of forty Americans. Proctor wasted little time feeling humiliated by Tecumseh, because his men were engaged in a hard fight across the river, where about four hundred Ohioans and Kentuckians under Colonel John Miller of the Nineteenth Infantry took the lone British battery and fought the Indians to a draw, but lost thirty killed and ninety wounded. When the fighting ended on May 5, however, no clear winner claimed the field.

Proctor repaired his cannon on the north bank and renewed the siege, but his Indian allies soon lost interest and began to drift away with their prisoners and booty taken from the Kentuckians' boats. At the same time, two regiments of Canadian militia informed Proctor that they intended to go home under the pretext that they needed to plant their crops. Before Proctor could resolve these problems, he received word, though false, that a large American force was moving to block his return to Detroit and Fort Malden. Confronted with a threatened American counterattack, low on provisions, with regulars plagued with dysentery and flu and dwindling Canadian and Indian forces, he decided to abandon the siege. It had cost Harrison approximately 273 killed and wounded and the British 14 dead, 47 wounded, and 41 captured. Tecumseh's losses are unknown.

As soon as the British withdrew from the field, Harrison began resupplying Fort Meigs from the South, via Cincinnati and Forts Marys, Amanda, Jennings, Winchester, and Defiance. He also received reinforcements of Ohio militia. Even before the battle ended, Governor Meigs, who learned about the attack, ordered mounted volunteers to assemble immediately at Delaware and Newton for General Duncan McArthur to lead them to Fort Meigs, to secure the military stores at Upper Sandusky, and to calm "the frontier inhabitants from a panic which has besieged them." On May 12, fifty men prepared to march from Zanesville, while one hundred left Newark and three hundred mounted volunteers rode out of Fairfield County, headed for Fort Meigs. Although these reinforcements arrived after the battle, Harrison sent several militia companies to Cleveland and Lower Sandusky. His men, now under the command of Brigadier General Green Clay, also repaired and provisioned Fort Meigs in case the British returned for another strike. Harrison's apprehension about the British proved correct. In late June, he received word that British and Indian forces under Tecumseh were again massing at Detroit for another attack against Fort Meigs. With that news, the repairs quickened. One soldier wrote: "Every man appears to be working for his own safety."

In early July, small parties of Indians began harassing the fort and supply trains. The nearly fourteen hundred tribesmen who had assembled at Detroit, however, had not yet moved south, and they presented a serious supply problem for the British. At the same time, the Indians pressured Proctor to launch a second attack. Thus, faced with logistical and political problems, Proctor decided to move against Fort Meigs even though he wanted additional British troops. As a result, when Proctor returned for another attack on July 20, he came understrength with only about four hundred regulars and several thousand Indians, and six-pound cannon. Harrison waited with two thousand troops, while six hundred Kentucky militia held in reserve at Franklinton and five hundred regulars and one hundred militia held at Lower Sandusky.

The men inside had supreme confidence in their safety. One soldier reported that the men had now grown "indifferent to the sound of bullets." If they had heard the sound of a gun at home, they would have been concerned. "Here," however, "if a man has his glass of grog shattered as he passes it to his lips, it is treated with derision." Even so, General Clay saw fit to remind his men that "should . . . there be anyone so lost to every sense of honor as to shamefully abandon his post, or order a retreat without authority, he shall suffer death."

After a sham battle organized by Tecumseh within earshot but out of sight of the fort failed to lure the troops outside, Proctor shelled the fort for eight days, but he could not take or damage it, and he withdrew down the Maumee into Lake Erie. The second siege of Fort Meigs ended with about a half-dozen Americans killed or captured. Casualties also were light for the British, but their loss of prestige among the Indians proved great, because they had now failed twice to take Fort Meigs. Consequently, Proctor decided to attack Fort Stephenson via the Sandusky River to restore his prestige among the Indians. There, Major George Croghan commanded 160 men of the Seventeenth Infantry. In July Harrison had ordered Croghan to abandon Fort Stephenson to prevent his men from being destroyed by Proctor's army. Croghan, however, believed he could hold the fort and that retreat was more dangerous than to remain. He refused to leave and convinced Harrison to let him stay.

When the British attacked Fort Stephenson on August 1, Proctor sent a Major Chambers under a white flag to demand the surrender of the fort. Croghan sent an Ensign Shipp out to meet him. Chambers told Shipp to observe the number of cannon on the gunboats and the large body of regular troops and Indians. In regard to the latter, Chambers attempted to play on American fears by telling Shipp that Proctor could not control the Indians, and that if the fort had to be taken, the entire garrison would be massacred. Shipp, however, informed Chambers that Croghan intended to defend the fort or be buried in it, and that the British could try their best to take it. When a scuffle developed between Shipp and an Indian who attempted to seize his sword, Croghan, who had been watching from the ramparts, yelled: "Shipp, come in and we will blow them all to hell." With that exchange the negotiations broke off and the bombardment began.

Although Proctor shelled the fort with his gunboats and a five-and-a-half-inch howitzer on the river bank, he could not destroy the walls. When the British tried to concentrate their cannon fire on the northwest corner of the fort to make a breach, Croghan reinforced it with bags of flour from the commissary, and the walls held. Proctor knew, however, that the Indian allies wanted more than a token commitment from the British in this new war against the frontier people. And to satisfy political necessity he sent the regulars in an assault, launching two feints, with the major attack against the northwestern corner, which smoke from the cannon and rifle fire had completely enveloped.

Croghan caught them with his cannon, loaded with musket balls, at the eight-foot-wide and deep ditch that ran before the wall, at a range of thirty feet, while his Kentucky sharpshooters struck their marks with precision, and the attack collapsed. Later, Proctor made a detached analysis of the battle, saying: "The fort, from which the severest fire I ever saw was maintained . . . was well defended. The troops displayed the greatest bravery . . . and made every effort to enter; but the Indians who had proposed the assault . . . scarcely came into fire before they ran. . . . A more than adequate sacrifice having been made to Indian opinion, I drew off the brave assailants."

Proctor had lost approximately two hundred killed and wounded, including twenty-seven dead in the ditch, to one man killed and seven wounded in Fort Stephenson. Indian losses are unknown because most of the dead and wounded were taken from the field under the cover of darkness. Harrison reported: "It will not be amongst the least of General Proctor's mortifications to find that he has been baffled by a youth who has just past his twenty-first year." Suffering a considerable loss, Proctor retreated downriver.

The attack by the British on Fort Stephenson was their last attempt to invade Ohio and the Northwest Territory. A month later, Oliver H. Perry's fleet gained control of Lake Erie. Thereafter, the British could not supply their army by water, and Proctor abandoned Detroit and withdrew across the Thames River away from the American border and Harrison's army. Tecumseh felt betrayed by the British retreat and likened Proctor to "a fat animal, that carries its tail upon its back, but when affrighted . . . drops it between his legs and runs off." Yet, despite Tecumseh's desire to press a new attack on the Americans in Ohio, Proctor based his decision on matters of practical supply rather than an ardor for war. He knew that Harrison would strengthen his army at Fort Meigs and strike north now that the Americans controlled the Great Lakes.

Proctor correctly gauged the American intent, but Harrison faced an immediate problem with his Ohio volunteers, who had mobilized to relieve Fort Meigs because their time would run out before he could complete another campaign. Consequently, he had to call upon Ohio and Kentucky to send him additional militiamen. When Kentucky's Governor Isaac Shelby responded quickly with a promise to lead his militia in the field, more than three thousand men headed north to Fort Meigs. Unfortunately, the patriotic zeal of Ohio's young men set several thousand on the roads to Dayton for a rendezvous. Harrison could not feed and shelter such a large combined force of Ohioans and Kentuckians. The Kentuckians, however, arrived before the Ohio militia responded to Harrison's call, and with about fifty-five hundred regulars and militia at the fort, Harrison had to send home all but twelve hundred of Ohio's volunteers because he did not have sufficient supplies. The Ohioans returned home disappointed and bitter that they would not have the opportunity to deal the Indians and British a death blow in Canada.

Harrison rendezvoused his army at the Portage River in late September 1813. The troops were then transported to Middle Sister Island in Lake Erie by Perry's fleet. On the 26th, the fleet carried them up the Detroit River to within three miles of Amherstsburg. Then they marched north and quickly occupied Detroit and Fort

Tecumseh attempted to establish a military alliance among the tribes in the Northwest Territory to regain lands lost to white settlers and to prevent further American encroachment on Indian lands. Tecumseh was skilled in both diplomacy and war. When he lost his life during the Battle of the Thames in 1813, however, the dream of an Indian homeland north of the Ohio River also died. INDIANA HISTORICAL SOCIETY LIBRARY, SUB. COLL.

William Henry Harrison led the army against the Indians on the Ohio frontier for the last time in 1813. Although no major battle occurred in Ohio during the War of 1812, the military posts and the militia in Ohio helped Harrison drive the hostile tribes from the state. INDIANA HISTORICAL SOCIETY LIBRARY, c5829.

Malden, which the British had abandoned. Harrison then pressed forward with the intent of catching Proctor's retreating army. He caught it near Moraviantown, approximately fifty miles east of Detroit. Proctor's eight hundred regulars and five hundred Indians proved no match for Harrison's superior force of three thousand men. A cavalry charge quickly broke the British resistance, and when word spread through the Indian ranks that Tecumseh had been killed, the opposition disintegrated. The Battle of the Thames ended with victory for Harrison's army. Most important, it had broken British power in the Northwest and destroyed Tecumseh's Indian confederacy.

Although the hostilities in the West had essentially ended except for periodic isolated Indian attacks on civilian teamsters and farmers, the Ohio militia did not go home immediately. By December, two thousand militiamen remained on duty and served as escorts for provisions, munitions, and artillery between Forts St. Marys, Amanda, Jennings, Winchester, McArthur, Findlay, and Meigs as well as Upper Sandusky and Detroit. Indian agent John Johnston also continued to bring the Indians of the Northwest into the American camp. In late February 1814, with Indian and British resistance broken, Johnston held a council at Dayton with several chiefs of the Shawnees, Wyandots, Senecas, Miamis, Potawatomis, Ottawas, and Kickapoos for the purpose of gaining their commitment to take up arms against the British. Johnston chided them for making war on the United States when they had been warned to remain out of the fight. Consequently, he told them: "As war is our trade and you cannot live quiet and take no part in it, your Father is compelled by *necessity and not choice*, to put the tomahawk in your hands. And . . . you must receive the tomahawk from my hands and when you are told you must strike. Our enemies must be your enemies. . . . If you do not, you will be considered enemies and treated as such; but if you are faithful you shall be well paid."

Johnston reported to the Ohio public that the "Government has been reluctantly compelled to yield to this species of force in order to meet them on their own ground; it is a course which has been imposed on us by necessity alone." Accordingly, in July he met at Greenville with delegates from the major tribes, including the

Miamis and a few Potawatomis, whom he called "very sulky." When the chiefs pledged their neutrality in the continuing war with Great Britain, Johnston refused. They could either be the friend or the enemy of the United States, but they could not be neutral. The Miamis and Potawatomis thought it over and decided to join the American cause. On July 22, 1814, with the preliminaries over, Harrison and General Lewis Cass signed the "Treaty of the Wyandots," including the Shawnees, Delawares, Senecas, and Miamis, which obligated them to join the Americans against the British and to end hostilities with the United States. With Harrison's victory and the treaty, peace came at last to the Ohio frontier, but only after a considerable loss of life, a failure of British resolve, and Perry's control of the Great Lakes.

Ohioans now wanted the war to end unless the British were intent on recolonizing the United States. No one talked anymore about seizing Canada. The frontier had been made safe from the Indians, and that was reason enough for peace. By July 1814, many soldiers at Ohio posts also grew restless, and desertions became increasingly frequent. When five solders were shot at Camp Scioto near Cincinnati, the editor of the *Western Spy* hoped the executions would have a "salutary effect on those who witnessed the melancholy fate of the unfortunate culprits."

Those deserters should have waited, because the American peace commissioners were at work at Ghent in Belgium and, on December 24, 1814, signed a peace treaty with the British that essentially restored the *status quo antebellum*. Although no territorial gains had resulted from the war, and while the British still did not recognize the American right to freedom of the seas or give up their right of impressment, the War of 1812 ended the Indian threat on the Ohio frontier. When news of the peace reached Chillicothe on February 22, 1815, most Ohioans considered it an honorable conclusion of the war. Most important, however, on August 31, 1815, peace commissioners met at Detroit with the Wyandots, Shawnees (including the Prophet), Delawares, Miamis, Senecas, Ojibwas, Ottawas, and Potawatomis as well as the Sacs and Winnebagos. There, the chiefs signed a treaty on September 8, 1815, "with considerable ceremony, and apparent sincerity," in which they agreed to bury the hatchet with the United States.

* * *

While the war destroyed Tecumseh's plan for a pan-Indian union, it also boosted Ohio's economy. Indeed, Ohioans learned that war paid, if the enemy did not overrun their farms and towns. The Northwestern Army needed large quantities of pork, beef, flour, and whiskey, and supply and prices increased accordingly. In Dayton and Cincinnati, merchants sold flour at the high price of eight dollars per barrel. In St. Marys it cost two dollars more. Wheat prices doubled, and the cost of whiskey tripled to seventy-five cents per gallon. Farmers near Dayton also sold a large number of horses to the army, and commission men shipped agricultural products down the Ohio and Mississippi rivers to New Orleans to take advantage of high wartime prices. Military roads, such as Hull's Road, which led from Dayton through Piqua to Fort Findlay, and Harrison's Road, which led from Piqua to St. Marys and Defiance, soon provided new avenues for farmers to reach markets.

When the war officially ended in 1815, Ohio's economy boomed. Federal lands could be purchased with credit on easy terms. With the exception of the northwest corner, dominated by the Black Swamp, settlers quickly spread into the vacant lands of the Firelands, the Western Reserve, and the western portion of the state. Although the majority of Ohio's population still lived in the southern river valleys, particularly the Miami, settlement also increased rapidly in towns, such as Columbus, Dayton, Springfield, Zanesville, and Lancaster. When the war ended, residents owned approximately 75 percent of Ohio's lands, while the Western Reserve had the largest acreage held by nonresidents. At that same time, most Ohioans lived on farms or in towns with fewer than 100 people. Only Cincinnati, with a population of 9,642 in 1820, could be called a city. Ohio remained rural, but twilight had come to the frontier.

12.

FARMERS: FIRST AND LAST

Ohio's farm families remained committed to land ownership and a market economy following the War of 1812. The fighting on Ohio's soil during the war had little effect on land sales, particularly after 1813, with the exception of northwestern Ohio and the Western Reserve. During the year following July 1814, the Canton and Cincinnati land offices each sold more than 250,000 acres, while Steubenville and Zanesville together transferred more than 200,000 acres. By 1818, Canton had sold 272,340 acres, and a year later Congress established new land offices at Delaware, Bucyrus, Piqua, Wapakoneta, Lima, Tiffin, Upper Sandusky, and Defiance, primarily to sell the newly opened Congress lands. The Panic of 1819, however, caused by federal banking policy that contracted the currency supply and falling agricultural prices at home and abroad, slowed land sales. Congress responded, in part, with the Land Act of 1820, which ended the purchase of federal lands on credit. Specifically, the legislation provided for the sale of 80-acre tracts for a minimum price of $1.25 per acre. As a result, settlers could purchase a small tract for less money than under the Land Act of 1804, which required the purchase of 160 acres at $2 per acre. Still, while the economic depression lasted, many potential settlers could not afford to pay $100 for federal lands. Most important, however, this legislation suspended forfeitures until March 1821.

Congress provided more immediate relief for debtors with the Relief Act of 1821, which permitted a settler to return part of his land to the federal government if he could not meet his payment, and it extended credit to a debtor for as long as eight years. If the relinquished lands failed to meet the debt on the lands that the settler retained, the government levied a deficiency judgment for the amount due, less a 37.5 percent reduction. This relinquishment policy helped Ohio's debtors retain a portion of their lands until the economy improved to enable them to repurchase their forfeited lands or otherwise meet their financial obligations. In Cincinnati, the *Liberty Hall* reported that the "people of the western country" hailed it with "much satisfaction," while the *Western Herald* in Steubenville contended that "whatever may be said as to the conduct of Congress in other respects, the people of the West cannot but feel grateful for the attention that has been paid to their interests."

Beginning in 1819 through 1821, the federal government also opened the lands acquired by the Treaty with the Wyandot in 1817 and the St. Marys Treaty of 1818 to settlement under the Land Act of 1804. By October 1821, all of the 18,200,000 acres under the jurisdictions of the Marietta, Zanesville, Steubenville, Chillicothe, Cincinnati, Wooster, and Piqua land offices had been surveyed. Only the Delaware office jurisdiction, with 2,321,280 acres, contained unsurveyed lands, which totaled 1,971,840 acres. By that time, the federal government had sold a total of 7,300,000 acres, or 66 percent of the available federal lands; 3,700,000 acres had been sold between 1812 and 1821, an amount not exceeded anywhere on the frontier. In August 1823, James Martin, an English merchant who settled near Bucyrus in Crawford County, reflected on the rapid acquisition of land: "The county is settling fast round me and I will soon have plenty of neighbors," whom he later called "the most trafficking, trading, and quirking people in the world, true children of the great whore." Despite the economic aggressiveness of the Americans, Martin considered the New Englanders "by far the best society and consequently the best neighbors." By January 1, 1826, the federal government had net sales of 8,700,000 acres, after deducting relinquished lands, while sales totaled 892,900 acres for the Ohio Company and 272,540 acres for Symmes. In December 1831, only 317,000 acres remained vacant in the Virginia Military District, and there were 32,724 acres unclaimed in the U.S. Military District by January 1832. By that time, only the least desirable lands remained unpurchased. Federal lands, for example, in Guernsey, Coshocton, and Tuscarawas counties had an average value of only fifty cents per acre.

With the rapid acquisition of land after the War of 1812, Ohio farmers drove a "considerable amount" of cattle, horses, and hogs across the mountains to eastern markets, while flatboats carried casks of flour on the seven-day trip to New Orleans for transshipment to East Coast and international markets. In 1816, prices remained steady on the Cincinnati market—flour and pork brought $5 per barrel, wheat 75 cents and barley 50 cents per bushel, and hemp $100 per ton. In Steubenville, farmers received $1.25 per bushel for their wheat. Peace, however, dramatically decreased military expenditures for agricultural products. In November 1816, the editor in St. Clairsville complained that peace had stopped the "great supply of cash" and that "the supply of cash from emigrations to this part of the country is gradually failing." The "times are hard, business dull and money scarce," he observed. Sometimes country merchants refused to take produce in payment for goods, insisting on cash when little circulated, but most had to accept produce or promissory notes to move their merchandise.

The *Western Herald* in Steubenville urged farmers to fight hard times with productivity. "Every article calculated for export which our soil will produce, should be raised, and the surplus for exportation should be as great as possible," the editor urged. Agricultural exports would pay for imports. Otherwise, needed or desired goods could be purchased only with bank bills that were discounted by 10 percent on the international market. A "vast surplus" for export, he believed, would bring bank paper up to par value and save farmers money.

In 1817, the monetary supply became worse when the federal government attempted to restrain speculation in western lands and regulate state banking practices by requiring obligations, such as payments for public lands, to be paid in specie, U.S. Treasury notes, or notes from specie-paying banks. With insufficient hard money in circulation anyway and more now being withdrawn to the east, Ohio's agricultural economy suffered. By spring 1818, corn and oats dropped to prices ranging from twenty-five to thirty-three cents per bushel at Chillicothe. Wheat soon fell to seventy-five cents per bushel at Steubenville, and dropped to twenty-five cents per bushel in Cincinnati by 1824. The Steam-Mill Company at Marietta, without funds to pay, exchanged flour for wheat at the rate of sixty cents per bushel. In the autumn of 1818, many Ohio banks failed, and an economic depression, called the Panic of 1819, soon gripped the land. By mid-June 1820, Lyman Farwell reported from the Firelands and Western Reserve that times were "cruel hard and business is dull; produce fetches in a manner of nothing."

Low prices, however, did not mean that Ohio's farmers forsook the market economy. Although the Panic of 1819 decreased agricultural prices, farmers tried to produce more to make up for their losses, and businessmen encouraged greater productivity. By January 1820, the Granger Mills in Zanesville offered cash for three thousand bushels of wheat, while another mill with four pairs of stones neared completion, and commission men urged farmers to bring their produce to market on sleds. By the spring of 1823 the economy had improved, and the editor in Zanesville reported that "immense quantities of produce of different kinds have descended our river [Muskingum] this spring for the lower markets." At Coshocton he noted that twenty large steamboats "laden with pork, bacon, whiskey (a good omen) flour, venison, hams, and beans etc. have passed that place from the waters of the Tuscarawas, Whitewoman and Killbuck." He believed that "these vast quantities of produce have a good prospect of meeting a good market." Rather than retreat to subsistence agriculture or attempt self-sufficiency on the farm by expanding home manufacturers, Ohio's farmers sought economic gain in an expanding market economy. "With a few years of such industry," the Zanesville editor reported, "our citizens will not only be relieved from debt, but assume a rank of independence and respectable wealth." Ohio farmers, of course, continued to practice safety-first agriculture; that is, they provided for the essential food needs of their families, but they took advantage of market opportunities whenever possible. Independence for them meant profit, not self-sufficiency.

The late frontier period also provided the opportunity for farmers and laborers to work as part-time teamsters when agricultural work did not demand their time. Just as many farmhands earned money

by cutting trees to buy land, they also often served the transportation needs of local farmers and merchants if they owned a wagon
and team. With a horse costing about fifty and a wagon about
thirty-five dollars near the end of the frontier period, settlers without capital often had to work for wages for two or three years before
they could afford a wagon and team. But once they made the acquisition, they could hire out for a dollar per day and enjoy the elevated
status of an independent businessman.

Teamsters also helped farmers leave subsistence agriculture by
taking their produce to markets both nearby and far away. Often a
farmer with a wagon and a team asked neighbors if they had anything to send to market. He then collected such items as barrels of
pork, casks of butter, jugs of whiskey, and sacks of grain and took
them either to the nearest town or to another location where they
deemed the price would be higher. Then he filled orders for such
staples as salt, sugar, and coffee to haul back home. For these services farmers received some remuneration from their neighbors.
By 1815, Cincinnati had become an important agricultural market
for farmers, who hired itinerant teamsters to make hauls of wheat
and vegetables to the "Queen City" from as far away as fifty miles.
Export markets, such as Cincinnati on the Ohio River or Cleveland
on Lake Erie, also paid higher prices. Farmers who could afford to
hire a teamster to take their wheat to market, for example, often
doubled their price and earned a larger profit, despite transportation charges, than they would have received if they had sold their
crop at the nearest town.

Country merchants, who served as commission men, also used
itinerant teamsters to haul grain, pork, and whiskey to export
towns along the rivers or Lake Erie and to bring back a variety of
mercantile goods from wholesale dealers. During the early 1820s, a
merchant in Zanesville hired teamsters to transport his order of
mercantile goods that arrived by ship at Sandusky. At that same
time, John H. Young, a merchant in Fairfield County's Clearcreek
Township, hired nearby farmers for his freighting needs and credited their account for their services. Depending on the season, teamsters used either wagons or sleds. Most teamsters preferred sleds
during the winter because they glided over snow-covered roads,

while wagons usually bounced over the frozen ruts. Indeed, the first good snowfall usually brought farmers to town with sleds laden with family for visiting and produce for marketing.

Workers could also earn money doing other agricultural tasks. In 1817, for example, a Jacob Stewart paid sixty-eight and a half cents per day for mowing and nine dollars per month for general farm work. Two years later in Hamilton County, Elnathan Kemper paid seventy-five cents per day for plowing. In addition to plowing and mowing, frontier farmers particularly needed extra labor at harvest time, if they had cleared sufficient acreage to merit the surplus production of grain, such as wheat, for market. Because grain can shatter from the heads when ripe, farmers preferred to harvest it before the kernels dried. Once safely bound into sheaves and placed in shocks, it could fully ripen for threshing. Moreover, bad summer weather could easily destroy a crop in minutes. When harvest time came, then, haste became the axiom of the day. But in the absence of horse-drawn machinery and mechanical harvesters, haste meant the employment of workers.

During the early 1820s, itinerant workers earned fifty to seventy-five cents per day harvesting wheat. Although some farmers paid their harvest hands in wheat or corn, agricultural workers usually expected to be paid in cash at the end of each day. Despite an inadequate circulating currency on the frontier, one observer noted that Ohio's farmers "usually contrived some means of getting money to pay the harvest hands," so crucial was their labor to the commercial success of the farm. Most itinerant harvest hands refused payment in grain because they seldom had any means to store or haul it to market. Farmers, who employed hired hands for six months or a year, commonly paid higher wages during harvest time, because the workload increased as well as to provide an incentive for careful work and to encourage them to remain in the farmer's employment during this critical time.

Most small-scale farmers hired workers by the day, while large-scale operators preferred paying hands by the acre. In June 1814, Elnathan Kemper paid James Stewart $1 for a day's work reaping oats and $1.50 to William Scott for cultivating corn, although he hired other workers to cut his wheat and oats with a cradle scythe for thirty-seven and a half cents per acre, or about seventy-five cents per day for reaping two acres. Some merchants who also farmed hired harvest hands and paid them with credit at their stores. Between 1813 and 1821, for example, Elijah Wadsworth, a storekeeper and farmer near Youngstown, extended credit to employees who harvested oats and cut hay on his farm. Occasionally, white labor remained in such short supply that farmers hired black workers. During the War of 1812, Wadsworth, for example, employed two African American men named Peter and Frank to plant and harvest corn, cut hay, and thresh oats. So many men had also enlisted in the army or militia that farmers such as Henry Miskel in Ross County hired black labor to harvest the grain crop.

Although the corn harvest did not involve the critical timing of wheat, oats, and hay, it had become such a large crop by 1815 that farmers often needed help to harvest it. Given the rule of thumb that one person could plow, plant, cultivate, and harvest twenty to twenty-five acres of corn annually that produced from thirty-five to seventy-five bushels per acre, by the late frontier period most farmers raised from twenty to one hundred acres of corn. Because corn did not easily spoil in the husk, it could be harvested in the late autumn or early winter after the fall plowing and other farm chores had been completed. When the corn harvest began, however, it provided considerable work for itinerant agricultural workers and neighboring farmers.

Farmers often paid their workers about fifty cents per day or about five cents per shock to cut corn, bind the stalks, and shock the sheaves. Payment remained similar for husking the ears at a later date. Sometimes local workers took their pay for husking in kind at the rate of about ten cents per bushel of shelled corn or fifty cents per day. A good worker could harvest the equivalent of ten bushels of shelled corn per day. Farmers who harvested their corn in the southern tradition or who picked the ears by the northern method expected their hired workers to harvest at least one acre per day.

Besides an adequate wage, hired workers expected the farmer to furnish good and plentiful meals, which increased the burden on his wife and daughters. They also expected an ample supply of whiskey. Although harvest hands carried water jugs to the fields to refresh themselves, they also believed that liquors of various kinds helped protect their health. They were correct, of course, in this assumption, because water in an age before purification treatment often carried disease, such as typhoid, or caused dysentery. In 1811, John Melish, who traveled through the Old Northwest, observed that "there is unquestionably too much spiritous liquors drank in the newly settled parts of America, but a very good reason can be assigned for it. The labour of clearing the land is rugged and severe, and the summer heats are sometimes so great that it would be dangerous to drink cold water." Farmers who did not provide their workers with spirits had an unhappy crew or found that they had difficulty employing the needed hands.

Women also hired their labor to help country wives with their work. In January 1815, Elnathan Kemper hired Mary Copeland to spin the wool from his sheep into yarn at the rate of twelve and a half cents per day and paid her $3.75 upon completion of the work. Cultural standards usually prevented "hired girls" from working in the fields. Instead, they were employed to help with the housework, process pork at hog-killing time, tend the chickens, cook meals at harvest and threshing time, and perhaps milk cows and make butter and cheese.

Some of Ohio's farmers also sought to improve their agricultural practices and social activities by forming agricultural societies. In April 1817, for example, the Agricultural and Manufacturing Society of Jefferson County formed to encourage farming and manufacturing and the dissemination of useful information. James Wilson, the editor of the *Western Herald and Steubenville Gazette*, urged the society to encourage home manufacturing. He did not mean home manufacturing to enable self-sufficiency, but to provide goods that could be sold for "gold and silver and 'good character notes' that go over the mountains for the purchase of these goods— leaving nothing but paper of doubtful character in their stead." In December 1818, the Agricultural Society of the County of Trumbull also organized at Youngstown, and a group of citizens from Washington County met at McFarland's Tavern in Marietta on February 22, 1819, to form a society "for the promotion and encouragement of improvements in agriculture and domestic manufacturers." The members agreed to meet annually on the second Wednesday of November, a schedule that suggests that they organized primarily for a yearly social gathering rather than for educational reasons, although the "board of managers" had the power to "grant premiums as rewards of merit [for] execution, discovering, or improvement of various branches of agriculture, economy in husbandry and useful domestic manufacturers." Similarly, in July 1819 the Cincinnati Society for the Encouragement of Agriculture and Domestic Economy formed to serve farm families in Hamilton County. Two years later, the Scioto Agricultural Society offered $100 to any person who could discover the cause and provide a cure or preventative for the "Bloody Murain" in cattle. These ambitious goals, however, reflected needs that could not be met in the absence of systematic scientific inquiry and adequate capital or organization, especially on the frontier.

* * *

By 1815, pork packing had become an important industry in Ohio; however, it did not boom until the early 1820s, at the end of the frontier period. Nevertheless, this aspect of the provisions trade was large enough during the frontier years to require strict regulation in Cincinnati as early as 1809. There meat packing could be conducted only with the inspection and approval of the city. By the end of the War of 1812, pork, bacon, and lard ranked second only to flour as an export from Cincinnati, and packing also became important farther to the north at Smithfield and Mount Pleasant in Jefferson County. In 1819, Marietta's merchants packed 30,000 pounds of pork and 33,000 pounds of lard and cured 45,000 pounds of bacon from locally raised hogs for the river trade. Cincinnati became the hub of the industry. A traveler there reported that pork packing had become a bustling enterprise, with dealers busy cutting and salting pork and dray wagons clogging the streets hauling barrels of pork to the docks and the waiting steamboats.

Even though the pork-packing business developed quickly, a chronic lack of salt hindered more rapid expansion of the industry. Prior to 1821, Ohio packers had difficulty obtaining an adequate supply of high-quality salt. Sea salt shipped upriver by steamboat from New Orleans remained prohibitively expensive, and domestic salt from the relatively close Kanawha Valley of western Virginia proved less than satisfactory because high concentrations of lime and magnesium gave it a "dirty red" tinge and spoiled the meat.

Some ship owners refused to carry pork cured with Kanawha salt to New Orleans because it spoiled so quickly. Often Ohio pork had to be repacked in the Crescent City, and it brought a lower price than New England pork on the Atlantic market. Consequently, the severe lack of salt encouraged hog droving to eastern markets. By 1821, however, upstream freight rates declined because steamboats made transportation cheaper, thereby making the use of sea salt economical. At the same time, salt processors began improving the quality of the domestic product. With a plentiful supply of high-quality salt available at an affordable price, the pork-packing industry began to boom, and Cincinnati, the Queen City of the West, became the center of that trade.

Indeed, Cincinnati, located at the southern end of the Scioto and Miami river valleys (the primary corn- and hog-producing regions of the state), was well positioned to become the leading pork-packing center of the West. There, superior waterfront, credit, banking, and supply advantages provided the necessary ingredients for a flourishing meat-packing industry. Furthermore, Cincinnati quickly developed the facilities for an important by-products industry, such as the manufacturing of lard, soap, glue, candles, buttons, shoe polish, brushes, fertilizer, sofas, and mattresses, which further increased the demand and prices for hogs. Indeed, meat packing stimulated the growth of other trades, such as barrelmaking. In addition, because the Ohio River furnished cheap transportation through New Orleans to eastern and international markets, Cincinnati packers could afford to pay higher prices for hogs, and packers could obtain sufficient seasonal workers without difficulty, particularly stonemasons, cellar diggers, plasterers, and others who were idle during the winter months. By the mid-1820s, the concentration of labor, capital, and raw materials at an important intersection of land and water, together with great technological change for processing and transportation, made the pork-packing business a thriving wintertime industry. The Queen City had earned a reputation as the nation's premier hog slaughterer and supplier of cured hams, especially for chic hotels and the tables of affluent eastern families. Cincinnati, with a population of approximately fifteen thousand, also had earned the nickname "Porkopolis."

Indeed, the expansion of the pork-packing industry in Cincinnati was phenomenal, even though prices remained about the same at $2 per hundredweight through the mid-1820s. During the packing season of 1822–23, eleven major firms and several smaller ones processed more than 15,000 hogs, from which 2.7 million pounds of meat were prepared for export. At the market rate of two cents per pound, the total pack was valued at $54,560. By 1826, Cincinnati packers processed 17,000 barrels of pork and 1,280 pounds of lard—roughly double the output for the years 1818–19. At that same time, bacon production increased an estimated 400 percent, to 1.4 million pounds. A year later, during the packing season from mid-November 1826 to mid-February 1827, 40,000 hogs were processed in Cincinnati. Thirty thousand of those animals were slaughtered there; the remainder were killed on surrounding farms and the carcasses hauled by wagon to the packing plants. The total value of the pack now exceeded $250,000. Much of this pork was sold on the Atlantic seaboard, while the lard was primarily exported to Cuba and South America for use as cooking oil and as a butter substitute. Large amounts of the pack were also consumed in the Lower South, and a portion was consumed by the army. The Cincinnati pork-packing industry had by then exceeded that in the city of Baltimore in importance, and it was the unrivaled meat-packing city in the nation.

Pork packing as practiced during the early days of the industry in Cincinnati was far from the specialized process that it would become in Chicago during the late nineteenth century, where packers reportedly utilized every part of the hog except its squeal. Indeed, at this early stage of the industry's development, there was a tremendous amount of waste. Low corn prices encouraged farmers to raise as many hogs as possible. This practice, however, frequently created a surplus of pork, and the packer made little attempt to sell meat cuts that could not be easily salted, pickled, or smoked. During the 1820s, for example, cartload upon cartload of spareribs was drawn to the banks of the Ohio River and dumped into the water, because the packers had no use for them. Not until 1830, when German immigrants began settling in the city, was there a ready market for that cut of pork.

Throughout the frontier period as domestic and international demands for Ohio pork continued to expand, farmers increased their hog production. During the packing season, they usually sold their hogs to drovers, who herded the hogs from the farms to the slaughterhouses with the use of dogs. Both packers and speculators bought up the hog crop, with contracts signed well in advance of the packing season. Cincinnati packers began the contracting practice as early as 1825, because it ensured them at least some pork for high November prices down the Mississippi River. Early contracting was also a common practice in years when the hog crop was small and demand exceeded supply.

In 1828, Frances Milton Trollope, a British visitor to Cincinnati, complained that during the packing season the chances were five hundred to one against being able to cross Main Street without "brushing by a snout." Although Cincinnati's citizens, like those in the other packing towns, grew tired of the mess, smell, and nuisance of hogs in the streets, Ohio's farmers relied on hog raising for commercial purposes. Live hogs and pickled or smoked pork brought needed merchandise and money into the farm home. Hogs helped pay the mortgage on the frontier farmer's land as well as put food on the table. By the late 1820s, when the frontier essentially had disappeared in Ohio, hogs remained essential to the farmer's economic well-being.

Cattle raising also continued to be important to Ohio's agricultural economy during the late frontier period. By 1819, cattle crowded the prairies and pastures from Coshocton to the Miami Valley, in herds ranging from one hundred to three hundred. At that time, a typical "stock farm" in the uplands contained eighteen hundred acres, with one thousand acres fenced. Although cattlemen had used much of the uninhabited land in the Virginia Military District as open range, by 1820 those lands were giving way to fenced pastures. These cattlemen not only put money in the farmers' pocket when they purchased feeder cattle, but they also bought great quantities of corn from nearby farmers for their feed lots. Soon after the War of 1812, then, cattle raising became a moneymaking proposition; it no longer served as a subsistence frontier agricultural activity. Even in the Miami Valley, where cattle raising remained a small-scale endeavor, because of inadequate credit and banking facilities, farmers sold much of their beef in Cincinnati whenever possible.

Ohio's cattlemen at first used a modified open range system characteristic of ranching in the Great Plains late in the nineteenth century. The Virginia Military District provided much of the grazing land because speculators who had purchased land bounty warrants held large blocks of land suitable for extensive cattle grazing until it could be subdivided and sold to small-scale farmers. Moreover, the early settlers avoided the grasslands on the assumption that unforested soil indicated low fertility and did not merit cultivation. At the same time, many of the early settlers had migrated from Virginia, where they had gained experience raising cattle, and they had the financial resources to invest in land and livestock. During the 1820s, cattlemen and farmers began to fence their open grasslands and increasingly to fatten their cattle on corn. Often they raised or bought "stock cattle" or "feeders" about three years of age from local farmers or livestock raisers in Kentucky for the purpose of fattening and driving to eastern markets. These were "native" cattle, not purebreds.

Although Felix Renick attempted to improve his cattle in 1807 when he acquired a herd of "Pattons," which were a mixture of British Longhorns and Shorthorns, general breed improvement did not come until well after the frontier period. In time, breeding improvements came with the use of blooded or grade bulls after farmers learned the benefits of improved breeding and feeding and acquired the capital to afford purebred or improved stock. It also came after they became convinced that purebreds were not weaklings that required special care.

During the early 1820s, Scioto cattlemen bought hardy "Hocking cattle" from that river area and other stockers known as "Bush Creek cattle" from farmers in Highland, Adams, and Brown counties. They also purchased "Barren cattle" in the uplands between the middle Scioto and upper Miami valleys for fattening with corn. By the 1820s, some cattlemen also purchased feeders in Illinois, and they would soon make buying trips to Missouri. Sometimes they drove these cattle eastward and sold them to Pennsylvania, New

York, Virginia, and Maryland livestock men who fattened them to market weight. Or they fattened these stockers themselves and sold the steers as four-year-olds in the eastern stockyards.

By the late frontier period, Cincinnati provided a limited market for cattle, because it had less population than Philadelphia and New York City. During the early 1820s, many pork packers also processed a few cattle. Cincinnati packers, however, emphasized pork rather than beef packing because the southerners preferred pork because of taste and cost. Moreover, farmers in the Miami Valley could earn about as much by raising swine as cattle with less effort and a shorter marketing time. They sold their corn-fattened hogs at about eighteen months of age, but they sold their cattle at four to five years of age. Hogs maintained a quick and consistent cash flow for these farmers, and they preferred to raise swine rather than beef. Even so, they still raised enough cattle to support a profitable leather-manufacturing industry in the Queen City during the early 1820s. Drovers commonly took fat cattle from the upper Miami Valley over the "Montgomery Pike" to the packers in Cincinnati. Still, most cattlemen operated in the Scioto Valley, where by the late 1820s an estimated four thousand to seven thousand cattle fattened annually.

The lush grasslands of central Ohio, the plentiful corn fields in the Scioto Valley, and the close proximity of eastern markets created an ideal region for fattening cattle. Investors, with capital earned from land speculation and commerce, also contributed to the development of the early cattle industry in Ohio. Later, bankers provided financing, with four-month notes with the cattle as security and with the monies deposited in their institutions by the Federal Land Office from the sale of the Congress lands. With profits of 10 percent or more, bankers in Chillicothe, Columbus, and other towns eagerly backed the Ohio cattlemen. Cattle raising in the Scioto Valley particularly offered both livestock men and investors the opportunity to make their fortunes. Beef cattle, which cost less than twenty dollars per head to purchase, when fattened on corn and driven to market sold for as much as thirty dollars per head by the late 1820s. With prices such as these, the cattlemen in the Scioto Valley became the wealthiest agriculturists in the state.

By 1815, the Ohio sheep and woolens industry also continued to expand. Daniel Gregg near Steubenville offered 175 Merino grades for sale in October, while C. Henry Orth in that town advertised to buy wool from full-blooded Merinos for a dollar per pound. Cincinnati had a steam-powered woolen mill, and the Steubenville factory had become one of the most prominent mills in the Old Northwest. In that year, however, with the Peace of Ghent, the boom in the sheep industry collapsed. Sheep men did not have tariff protection, and British woolens flooded the American market. Ohio flockmasters also suffered from a national economic panic, which in 1819 further decreased the price of wool. With prices falling, Ohio sheep men suffered severe monetary losses; like many farmers, Nathan Head in the Scioto Valley sold four hundred head, three-fourths of which were Merinos. Others began to slaughter their fine-wooled Merinos because they could not afford to keep them.

While the market for wool collapsed, the economic depression did not end sheep raising in Ohio, because many farmers were "bent" on raising wool to provide clothing for their families. Most Ohio sheep men, however, continued to grow wool for the local and eastern markets. The fleece sold on the seaboard was generally driven to market prior to the completion of the state's canal and railroad systems. From 1815 through the mid-1820s, drovers took approximately twenty-five thousand head of sheep east to market annually. Those animals followed three routes to market. One route hugged the Lake Erie shore, then passed into the Mohawk Lowland and the Hudson Valley before continuing into Boston or New York City. Drovers also trailed sheep from central Ohio to Pittsburgh and Philadelphia. A third route followed the Ohio River to Wheeling, where it joined the Cumberland Road before ending at Philadelphia or Baltimore.

A few sheep men continued to maintain flocks of purebred Merinos or upbreed their common sheep, and mills such as the Farmers Woolen Factory in Fairfield County provided local markets by taking fleece and weaving cloth "fit for the tailor, [in] any color required." The tariffs of 1824 and 1828 stimulated at least a moderate demand for domestic wool, and Licking County sheep men were extensively engaged in its production. Some of that wool was sold on the eastern market, but most of it was probably sold within the state, where in 1820 woolen mills were operating in thirty counties.

Those mills were small, but they provided the sheep men with custom services for carding, fulling, and dressing their wool. Some of the wool was taken home and mixed with flax for "linsey-woolsey" women's wear, or it was mixed with cotton for men's jeans.

Although the Tariff of 1828 reestablished the eastern woolens industry, even with higher prices, transporting the wool to market was difficult. Given the absence of all-weather roads, much of Ohio's wool could not reach the eastern markets. The opening of the Erie Canal in 1825 did not aid flockmasters substantially because the route to market remained long and costly. Wool had to be hauled from the farm or buyer's office to Lake Erie, loaded onto boats, shipped to Buffalo, reloaded onto canal boats, and eventually floated to New York or other cities. At the same time, the single most important problem for Ohio flockmasters during the frontier period was roaming dogs. Dogs, either singly or in packs, slaughtered hundreds if not thousands of sheep. Wool growers could not afford dog-tight fences around their pastures, and the legislature neglected to provide even modest protection. Roaming dogs had always been a problem for sheep men in the East, and Ohio farmers were no doubt plagued with them from the time the first small flocks were brought into the Northwest Territory. Certainly the problem had been with Ohio sheep men since the spring of 1815, when Thomas Rotch, a Stark County farmer and one of the earliest importers of Merino sheep into the state, had three valuable rams killed by dogs.

As Ohio farmers increased their flocks, the dog problem became worse. In 1814, the legislature debated a bill that would have required the owners of sheep-killing dogs to pay damages and taxes on them, but it failed to pass. Five years later, Rotch recognized the cause of the dog problem when he wrote: "We have met with several severe losses by dogs and there seems no hope of remedying this difficulty until the wild game are destroyed and hunters dogs rendered useless. For while dogs are valued for game no laws for their destruction are expected." The problem of roaming sheep-killing dogs remained unsolved through the frontier years.

* * *

The men and women who farmed the Ohio frontier, then, were a profit-minded people who were interested in agricultural improvement, but most were not wealthy. The ownership of land, however, gave many a sense of security, because it provided subsistence, security, and capital gains. Those who rented land could also feed their families and produce a surplus that could be traded or sold for gain. John Bradbury, a naturalist and writer who traveled through Ohio in 1816, observed that a frontier farmer would need to provide for the subsistence requirements of his family for only two or three years. He noted that to bring "wild land" under cultivation, the frontier people would undergo hardship and suffer privations, but the "state of ease, security, and independence which will assuredly follow, makes ample amends." Not everyone, of course, agreed. In June 1816, Nathaniel Dike, an emigrant from Haverhill, Massachusetts, on his way to Steubenville, met several families in Pittsburgh who were returning to New York and Pennsylvania. They were "fatigued, impoverished, and sick almost to death" of Ohio. They eagerly tried to "dispell the illusions" of anyone who would listen about the "earthly paradise" to the west and professed "they would rather live on one meal a day in their native state than on three in Ohio." These discouraging reports did not cause Dike to lose heart. After his arrival in Steubenville, he soon wrote that the land was cheap and the soil superior to that of Massachusetts and that it produced wheat at the rate of forty bushels per acre in the Scioto River valley. Prospective immigrants preferred optimistic reports such as Dike's to complaints about hardship and failure.

Timothy Flint, a Presbyterian minister and writer who toured the western country in 1818, had a more negative opinion of Ohio than Bradbury and Dike. Flint observed that the settlers along the Ohio River farmed in a "slovenly manner" and were content to raise nothing but corn. "The comforts of these people," he wrote, "must consist chiefly in having enough to eat and drink, and in having no fear of the exactions of the landholder, the tytheholder, or the collector of taxes." Flint, of course, did not see the hogs roaming in the underbrush, and he did not know how corn could both feed a family and bring money into the household when converted to pork and whiskey. He did not understand the extent of the cattle industry or the efforts of farmers to raise a surplus to take advantage of market opportunities. He was correct, however, that the frontier people did not fear landholders, because most were owners themselves. And with ax and plow, they worked the land for subsistence as well as profit.

By 1830, farmers who owned 160 acres of land, that is, a quarter section, had roughly 50 to 80 acres "pretty well cleaned up." According to William Cooper Howells, the frontier people who had a house and a barn, fields of corn and wheat, and a herd of hogs were "well off." These settlers were almost always the sons and daughters of farmers from older settlements. Howells recalled that on the Ohio frontier, "there were no rich, and none very poor." He, of course, was not all-inclusive, but land and agriculture together with increasing access to local and distant markets via the roads and major rivers created economic opportunity, and many men and women took advantage of it, except the Native Americans confined to reservations in northwestern Ohio.

* * *

In December 1816, President James Madison told Congress in his annual message, "The Indian tribes within our limits appear . . . to remain at peace." He also reported that "the facility is increasing for extending that dividend and individual ownership which exists now in moveable property only, to the soil itself; and of thus establishing, in the culture and improvement of it, the true foundation for a transition from the habits of the savage, to the acts and comforts of social life." In Ohio the Indians had no choice other than peace. They also had no choice but to accept the imposition on them of a new lifestyle by the federal government.

In 1817, the federal government began in earnest to remake the Ohio Indians in the white man's image. It did so by confining them to reservations, where they were given agricultural instruction so they could learn to live like small-scale white farmers and eventually achieve assimilation and acculturation in white society. The government began to implement that policy in Ohio when, on September 29, 1817, commissioners Lewis Cass, governor of the Michigan Territory, and Duncan McArthur signed a treaty at the Maumee Rapids, in which the Wyandots, Shawnees, Delawares, Senecas, and Ottawas ceded almost all of their lands north of the Greenville Treaty line. In that "Treaty with the Wyandot," also known as the Fort Meigs Treaty or the Maumee Rapids Treaty, the government agreed to give the Wyandots an annuity of $4,000, payable "forever" in specie annually at Upper Sandusky, provide the Shawnees with $2,000 in perpetuity payable at Wapakoneta, and pay the Senecas $500 annually at Lower Sandusky. The government, however, granted the Delawares only $500 for 1818, but no annuity, while the Ottawas received $1,000 for fifteen years, payable at Detroit.

In addition, the treaty granted the Wyandots a reservation of twelve miles square at Upper Sandusky as well as a number of fee simple patents, that is, titles to small portions of land to the signatory chiefs of the Senecas that totaled about thirty thousand acres along the Sandusky River. The Delawares received a reserve of nine miles square that abutted the Wyandot reserve and which included Captain Pipe's village. The Shawnees received a reservation ten miles square with the center at the council house at Wapakoneta and an adjoining tract twenty-five miles square for the people in their villages along Hog Creek. Shawnee leaders, including Black Hoof, also received fee simple patents to lands within that tract. The Shawnees and Senecas at Lewistown received a tract of forty-eight square miles, while the Ottawas were allotted a tract five miles square on Blanchard's Fork of the Auglaize River and another reserve three miles square on the Little Auglaize River.

The tribal members were to share the reservation lands equally. Each person who received an allotment, upon the approval of the chief, could farm the land or sell it, with the permission of the president of the United States. The Treaty with the Wyandot placed the federal government on course for the development of a general allotment policy. It also provided the government with a means to acquire additional Indian lands, even as it advocated the development of Indian agriculture. Both the fee simple or allotted lands and the communal reserves of the tribes were exempted from taxation. Only the Indians could use the reservation lands, which the federal government held in trust for them in perpetuity, but it reserved the right to build roads across the reserves.

The government also provided that an agent would live among the Indians at their tribal reserves to help them with their new relationship with the federal government and provide agricultural instruction. The commissioners also promised the erection of grist-

and sawmills on the Wyandot reserve as well as for blacksmiths at Wapakoneta, Hog Creek, Lewistown, and the Wyandot reserve. As long as the federal government owned the ceded land, the Indians could hunt on it and use the maple trees for making sugar. For the Indians of these tribes who had remained loyal during the War of 1812, and who had lost property in the fighting, the federal government provided modest monetary compensation.

The Treaty with the Wyandot altered the land base of the Ohio Indians for all time. In October 1817, the *Liberty Hall* in Cincinnati reported: "The cession[s] made by the Indians on this occasion, nearly extinguish their title to this state. The small reservations are of but little consequence to us. The two great objects gained; the security of the North Western Frontier and an opportunity for an immediate settlement of the country, which . . . will compel the few remaining Indians to adopt the habits of civilization, or to migrate to situations more congenial to savage life." Indian agent John Johnston essentially agreed and contended that "the interests of the natives have been properly attended to, and guarded in a manner not heretofore recognized in any Indian Treaty." Perhaps so, considering the government expanded the reserves a bit and modestly increased the annuities soon thereafter, but the reality of the Treaty with the Wyandot meant that the tribes ceded approximately 4.2 million acres of land. It would not be the last.

Until the removal period of the 1830s, however, the federal government and various friends of the Indians attempted to help the Indians on the reserves to practice agriculture in the white tradition as well as to educate and Christianize them. The Quakers showed the most interest in these efforts to assimilate and acculturate the Ohio Indians, and soon after the war they established a mission among the Shawnees at Wapakoneta. John Johnston, who served as the agent, reported in 1819 that "for several years past, the Society of Friends, at considerable expense, have supported an agricultural establishment among the Shawanese." The Quakers built a grist- and sawmill, demonstrated farming techniques to the men, and planned to open a school. They did not, however, attempt to teach the Shawnees the principles of Christianity, because the tribe was "not yet sufficiently acquainted with the arts of civilized life." When Congress appropriated $10,000 in 1819 to help the "civilizing" work of the Christian organizations among the Indians, Johnston urged Secretary of War John C. Calhoun to give the Quakers in his agency preference in the distribution of those funds.

The Ohio Quakers cultivated good relations with the Indians, particularly the Shawnees, by treating them as equals. In 1821, the Friends also demonstrated their concern for the Indians by establishing a school at Wapakoneta. There the Quakers taught their Shawnee pupils the basics of English, writing, and arithmetic. They also showed the boys how to plow, plant, and harvest, while the girls learned the duties of housekeeping. Only nine to eighteen Shawnee children attended the Quaker school at one time; by 1824 only thirty students had been taught, and the Quakers reported that "the children have made but little improvement in learning." The Ohio Friends, however, were encouraged about their success in agricultural instruction. In 1824, a committee reported that the Shawnees "manifest a more steady disposition to engage in agriculture, in which they have made as much progress as could reasonably be expected."

By 1829, the Quaker farm earned enough income to pay most of its expenses and to rely less on the Baltimore Yearly Meeting for support. In that year the Friends at Wapakoneta also reported that "the Indians are mostly settled on farms, and that many of them raise grain and stock sufficient for their own consumption." The Quakers, however, did not have sufficient time to teach the Shawnees to become farmers in the white tradition. Continued white pressure for Indian lands soon forced their removal. In September 1832, the Wapakoneta band left for the Indian Territory, and the Hog Creek band joined them the following summer. When the federal government moved the last of the Shawnees at Hog Creek west of the Mississippi during the summer of 1833, the Quaker school closed.

The Methodists also achieved modest success teaching agriculture to the Wyandots. In 1816, John Stewart, a freeborn mulatto, established a mission at Upper Sandusky. Stewart preached the importance of sobriety, kindness, and honesty, and the Wyandots listened. But when he attacked their traditional feasts, dances, and ceremonies, he created animosity. The Wyandots were particularly perplexed about why a book which the Creator had not given to them, which contained stories of distant lands and people and which they could not read, should rule their lives. Once again they were caught in the netherland of the Middle Ground. Mononcue, a Wyandot chief, felt that ambivalence when he said: "I have some notion of giving up some of my Indian customs; but I cannot agree to quit painting my face. This would be wrong, and it would jeopard[ize] my health."

Stewart was also distressed to see Indian women participating in ceremonial dances. Bloody Eyes, also known as Two Logs, rejected Stewart's preaching against dancing and feasting. "I do not believe the Great Spirit," he said, "will punish his red children for dancing, [and] feasting. . . . Yet I cannot say that he will not punish white people for doing these things; for to me it looks quite possible that the Great Spirit has forbidden these things among the whites, because they are naturally wicked, quarrelsome and contentious; for it is a truth they cannot deny, that they cannot have a dance, a feast, or any public amusement, but some will get drunk, quarrel, fight, or do something wrong." In contrast, he observed, "we have our public amusements in peace, and good will to each other, and part in the same manner. Now, where is the great evil you see." At best, then, the Methodists could expect only selective acculturation.

When Stewart died in 1821, the Methodist Episcopal Church appointed the Reverend James B. Finley to replace him, and he served the Wyandots for a decade and won an increasing number of converts. Finley operated on the premise that all Wyandot cultural practices had to be replaced by white beliefs and that acculturation began with conversion to Christianity. In 1824, the Methodists provided a school and church, demonstrated agricultural practices, and helped the Wyandots organize a system of local government. Although the Methodists did not serve more than 250 Wyandots, their mission became one of the most successful in breaking down traditional Indian cultural practices prior to Removal.

John Johnston, who served as agent at Wapakoneta until 1830, and other government officials were pleased with the adaptation of the Indians to white culture. As early as June 1819, Johnston reported considerable agricultural progress among the estimated 2,407 Indians in Ohio. He reported that the Senecas "labour more steadily, have better houses and farms, and appear more like white

FARMERS:
FIRST
AND
LAST

John Johnston had a long career
as an Indian agent for the federal
government. Stationed at Piqua,
Johnston helped the Ohio tribes
adjust to peace and a life as
farmers after the War of 1812. He
gained great respect among the
Indian peoples for his reliability
and fairness. OHIO HISTORICAL
SOCIETY, SC#2433.

people in their dress and manners, than any other Indians in
Ohio." They raised 250 cattle and 300 hogs at Lewistown, while the
Senecas and Wyandots who lived along the Sandusky River grazed
500 cattle and raised 1,500 hogs. Johnston also noted that "agriculture makes slow but steady progress among [the Shawnees].
Many Indians have taken to the plough." The Shawnees had thirty-
six plows and had begun "turning their attention more and more
to the raising of cattle." In addition to their herd of 125 head, they
also raised 200 hogs. "The stock of the Indians is everywhere
increasing within the limits of this agency," Johnston wrote. "One
individual owns seventy head of cattle." Despite this progress, the
Indians under Johnston's jurisdiction still considered murder a
family matter, and believed the aggrieved should be given a reasonable time to kill the murderer or someone close to him.

At the end of the frontier period, then, acculturation and assimilation remained in the distant future, even with the destruction of
Native American culture well underway, particularly in relation to
agriculture. Among the Ohio Indians, the women had been the traditional farmers. They had tilled the soil and planted, harvested,

and processed the crops. Indian women, not the men, were the first farmers in the Ohio country. Now the federal government and friends of the Indians forced the men to learn agriculture, a practice that they considered degrading as women's work. The government did not provide, and the missionaries could not muster, sufficient financial aid to support significant agricultural training. Inadequate instruction, together with continued pressure by whites for Indian lands, soon brought an end to Indian farming and civilization in Ohio.

13.

SETTLED COMMUNITY

Almost all of Ohio's people emigrated from other states prior to the mid-nineteenth century. Most of them came for economic reasons. The Ohio frontier offered them an opportunity to make their way in the world and improve their lives. In December 1818, John Stillman Wright, who had caught "Ohio mania," stopped in Cincinnati while on a trip from New York to buy land in Ohio. He was both impressed and shocked. Wright thought that "Main street would suffer but little, by comparison with the best of many of the eastern cities." Several churches, a gristmill, and an assortment of steam-powered cotton and woolen manufactories, an ox- and horse-powered sawmill, and steamboat-building and glass-making enterprises, together with a host of other businesses, kept the town bustling.

But not without cost. For Wright, Cincinnati had become the "residence of the great capitalists," where speculators assembled and "the men of *cent per cent* calculation" carried on "monopolizing enterprises." Wright was particularly upset by the "land jobbers, the speculators, the rich capitalists," who were wealthy when they arrived and got richer the longer they stayed. He wrote, "They build elegant mansions, live in style, and diffuse an air of business, life and activity all around them," which created the appearance of wealth and opportunity that deceived thousands. Wright believed this great show of business prosperity to be nothing less than a fraud. Although he correctly gauged the often reckless business practices of the land speculators in Cincinnati, he misjudged the soundness of the economy based on the agricultural hinterland, manufacturing, and the river trade which transformed Cincinnati from a frontier settlement into a town that soon earned the sobriquets of "Porkopolis" and "Queen City of the West."

By 1819, Cincinnati was no longer a frontier town. Instead, it had transformed into a manufacturing city where 1,238 of its 9,642 people produced goods valued at more than $1 million annually. Cincinnati's breweries bought forty to fifty thousand bushels of barley per year. Steam-powered flour and woolen mills provided both services and markets, while steamboats took agricultural produce and locally manufactured products to New Orleans and other river town markets. By 1830, a mechanics' organization represented every important trade, although most workers had not committed to the organization of labor, and tensions increased between freed African Americans and whites over jobs. The value of Cincinnati's manufactured products reached $2.8 million, and manufacturers employed more people than commerce and service occupations by 1830. Although agricultural products, such as flour, pork, lard, whiskey, and tobacco, headed the list of the city's exports, hats, furniture, clothing, and cast iron machinery also made an important contribution to the economy. Cincinnati's imports of salt, sugar, tea, dry goods, and pig, bar, and sheet iron, lumber, and cotton reached $3.8 million in value by 1830, an increase of more than $2.2 million since 1818.

The War of 1812 also stimulated manufacturing and settlement in other frontier towns, such as Dayton and Steubenville. In Dayton, for example, between 1814 and 1821, fifteen new manufacturing enterprises began operation. Craftsmen there made cloth, nails, saddles, flour, beer, mill screws, milling machinery, stills, and kettles. Obadiah B. Conover employed three men to make sickles and other iron products at his blacksmith shop. John Grove made hats, while Christian Oblinger worked as a tinsmith. In 1816, Simon Stansifer established a tobacco factory where he employed seven people to make cigars and plugs soon valued at more than $9,000 per month. Robert Patterson's woolen mill contributed to the frontier economy by producing more than $10,000 in cloth annually. Dayton's economy boomed.

In 1817 the Montgomery County commissioners built a bridge across the Miami River near Dayton, and private investors constructed another bridge two years later to facilitate trade. Dayton's residents also subscribed for the construction of a turnpike to Cincinnati, and in 1820 a weekly stage provided service to the Queen City. By the spring of 1824, so many mill dams created obstructions on the Miami River for the flatboat and keelboat operators who conducted business between Dayton and Cincinnati that some residents talked about vigilante action to remove them. Calmer residents proposed a system of improved channels and locks that would accommodate steamboat service, but fruition of this idea was not achieved until the 1830s.

By 1819, Dayton's state bank, known as the Dayton Manufacturing Company, issued loans totaling more than $100,000 to finance local manufacturing, commercial, and transportation enterprises. Before the collapse of the economy, only the Bank of Chillicothe had more specie in its vaults than the Dayton Manufacturing Company, and the Dayton institution ranked seventh in total assets among Ohio's twenty-eight state banks, with liabilities exceeding its resources by less than 1 percent. Although the Dayton Manufacturing Company suspended specie payments in November 1819, it continued to operate and circulate notes of good reputation until it closed in 1822. By 1825, however, the economy recovered and immigration increased, in large part because of the canal movement in the area. Specialists also began to provide the services of agricultural wholesalers, flour millers, shipping agents, and importers of retail goods. Many of these enterprises were established by newcomers with eastern capital. In Dayton as in other Ohio towns, the market economy governed the lives of both country and town people.

Steubenville businessmen also focused on the national market structure rather than on the frontier, and they talked about building their own steamboat to enhance trade on the Ohio River. Although the estimated cost of $10,000 seemed daunting in 1815, they believed the amount would be justified for the export trade alone. With the woolen factory reaching the production of twelve hundred yards of cloth per month, and with a steam-powered flour mill and a brewery nearing completion, they needed transport for these and other products both up- and downriver. Moreover, a steamboat could easily bring British articles such as coffee, indigo, tea, and sugar to the town as well as Spanish hides for the tanneries. Economic prosperity in Steubenville depended, the local editor believed, on a steamboat. Steubenville and other river towns, such as Marietta and Cincinnati, which also longed for steamboat traffic, had become less transitional frontier villages and more settled communities.

Only New York and Pennsylvania surpassed Ohio in the value of manufactured goods by 1820, and the state ranked fifth nationally in the capital invested in its manufacturing enterprises, most of which drew upon the land for materials, such as wood for furniture, wagons, and barrels; hides for leather, shoes, and saddles; corn for distillers; wheat for millers; and pork for meat packers. Most of these manufacturers employed fewer than 10 employees, although the iron works at Zanesville ranked among the largest in the nation with 158 employees.

By 1819, Ohio's twenty-eight state-chartered banks, an increase of twenty in four years, flexed their lending power based on military and land office deposits. Unchartered or "wildcat" banks also issued paper money, usually based on insufficient specie or gold reserves to support it at an equal exchange rate. These institutions issued paper money without regulation, and speculation became the basis of daily operation. In addition, the federal government continued to extend easy credit for the purchase of the public domain, and manufacturing and commerce expanded and thrived, particularly in the river towns.

Easy credit from bankers and the federal government promoted social leveling and created a democracy of debt. While still linked to the frontier, Ohio's economy also become intertwined with national and international affairs. The economic well-being of residents in Cincinnati, Chillicothe, and Marietta as well as settlers in the U.S. and Virginia military districts and the newly opened Congress lands depended on decisions made in New York, Philadelphia, Washington, D.C., and London. Although many areas of Ohio still remained relatively isolated, the entire population, no matter where they resided, had become interdependent on both national and international events. When a British financial crisis in 1818 caused bankers to demand payment of loans issued to American banks in specie, it

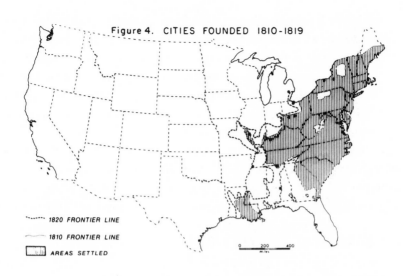

Figure 4. CITIES FOUNDED 1810-1819

------- 1820 FRONTIER LINE

········· 1810 FRONTIER LINE

▭ AREAS SETTLED

0   200   400
      Miles

By 1820, the Ohio frontier had essentially ended. Only the
northeast corner of the state remained empty because the
great Black Swamp blocked settlement. From Howard J.
Nelson, "Town Founding and the American Frontier,"
Association of the Pacific Coast Geographers Yearbook 36
(1974): 7–23.

had a ripple effect throughout the banking community. Most state
and wildcat banks had overextended their loans and could not pay
hard money to their creditors on demand, and the economic boom
collapsed.

The Panic of 1819 brought Ohio's economy to a near halt, and
proved its interdependency with national and international events
and with that dependency the end of the frontier. Indeed, by the
early 1820s, the frontier as borderland was quickly disappearing
as settlers gave increasing emphasis to commercial agriculture. Certainly they still produced to meet family needs, but they took advantage of market opportunities whenever possible. Merchants in
the towns vied for the farm trade and, despite temporary setbacks
such as the Panic of 1819, expanded their activities and services in
the towns.

By 1830, most Ohioans, particularly in the major river valleys,
no longer lived on the frontier. Lands had been purchased, cleared,
and planted, and a diversified agriculture provided a sound eco-

nomic base. Although the remaining public lands could still be purchased for $1.25 per acre, improved lands near Cincinnati brought as much as $100 per acre, while good lands under private ownership that had not been cleared brought from $2 to $5 per acre in the interior. Steamboats reduced freight rates and provided farmers, commission men, merchants, and manufacturers with relatively swift and reliable access to markets on the major rivers. Farmers and merchants had established a market economy based on the mutual dependence of agriculture and trade and, in some towns, such as Cincinnati, Steubenville, and Dayton, manufacturing.

Poor roads, however, often hindered economic development, and Ohioans supported road improvements. The state legislature proved supportive except for funds, and left the financing and construction to the counties. The legislature, however, granted liberal charters to turnpike companies, required adult males to work on the roads annually, and levied a special state tax that the counties could use for road construction. Work on the National Road began again in 1825; a year later it extended thirty miles west of Wheeling, and an additional twenty-eight miles had been contracted. By 1830, freight wagons traveled Ohio's roads on regular schedules. Postal roads increased in number, particularly radiating from the capital at Chillicothe until 1809, then from Zanesville, where the legislature met, until 1812 before returning to Chillicothe. When the state capital moved to Columbus in 1816, roads soon led to the center of the state like spokes on a wheel.

As Ohio's economy became more integrated with the national economy, the interests of its people also became less local and more national. By 1816, for example, the Quakers in Ohio had become embroiled in the slavery controversy. They held as an act of faith that no one could be a slave. Because of this belief and the proximity of slave territory south of the Ohio River, they quickly became involved in helping bondsmen escape from Virginia and Kentucky. Mount Pleasant became a center for abolitionist activity and well-known as a place where runaway slaves could receive aid on their way north via the Underground Railroad. In Mount Pleasant during 1817, Charles Osborn began publishing *The Philanthropist*—the first newspaper in the United States to champion the abolition of slavery. There, four years later, Benjamin Lundy first printed the *Genius of*

Universal Emancipation, thereby gaining fame as the "Father of Abolitionism." By the end of the frontier period, the Quakers in the Mount Pleasant vicinity had gained a national reputation for creating the hub of the antislavery movement in the United States.

The passing of the frontier can also be seen in the census records. In 1800, Ohio had a population of approximately 42,000, or a little more than 1 person per square mile. By 1810, the state's population had increased to 230,760, or about 6 people per square mile. During the next decade, immigrants continued to make their way to Ohio in large numbers. By 1820, the population had increased by 353,586 for a total of 581,434, or 14.5 people per square mile in fifty-nine organized counties. In 1825, Ohio had a population of approximately 800,000, making it the fourth most populous state in the Union. Five years later Ohio's population tallied 937,903. Migration accounted for this rapid increase in population, and it would continue to do so until the decade beginning in 1840, when the state lost 76,762 people or 5.05 percent of the population to emigration. Although the Western Reserve and the northwestern corner remained sparsely populated, Ohio's population was sufficiently large and widespread to end the frontier as borderland between an uninhabited area and settled communities.

The immigrants who came to Ohio after 1815 usually located near areas that had been developed. Towns and neighbors provided markets, services, and social interaction, and the new settlers preferred to take advantage of those opportunities whenever possible. Most of the state's residents lived in the southern river valleys, particularly the Miami, Scioto, Muskingum, and Hocking, where Cincinnati, Dayton, Springfield, Columbus, Zanesville, and Lancaster were thriving communities. At the same time, most Ohioans continued to live in towns with fewer than 100 people or on farms. By 1820, only 48 towns with 35,000 total residents each exceeded a population of 100. Only Cincinnati, with 9,642 residents, could be called a city. By 1830, Ohio still remained rural and agricultural.

* * *

Although rapid settlement and the acquisition of land followed the War of 1812, that conflict destroyed the Federalists for all time. The Federalists as a political party became dormant after statehood in 1803, but deteriorating relations with Great Britain over impressment and freedom of the seas and Jefferson's embargo in 1807 temporarily revitalized them, and they became spokesmen for peace. Although the Federalists occupied an increasingly shrinking political base because immigration from New England did not match the number of newcomers from Pennsylvania and Virginia, who cast their lot with the Jeffersonians, they could influence Ohio's politics because the Republican party in the state was divided by political philosophy and geography. During the early nineteenth century, the Federalists wielded significant minority strength in Marietta, in the towns of the Miami Valley, in the Quaker settlements of eastern Ohio, and among the New Englanders in the Western Reserve.

In the contest for political influence, the conservative branch of the Republican party favored the state courts and postured as the protectors of order, while the more liberal wing of the party championed the authority of the assembly. Republicans beyond Chillicothe also resented the power of the southerners who dominated politics in the Scioto Valley. Many merchants and bankers, who financed the export of agricultural produce and the import of needed goods, also resented Republican foreign policy that damaged their trading relations with Great Britain. Shipbuilders at Marietta, such as Benjamin Gilman, adamantly supported the Federalist party.

In 1808, George Denny and George Nashee established a Federalist newspaper called the *Supporter* in Chillicothe, the heart of the Republican camp in Ohio. Soon they sold subscriptions across the state, and more than a few readers agreed with their attacks on the Republicans and their charges that "we have long groped in the dark paths of raging democracy," while Jefferson dallied with his mistress, "black Sal." In order to put things aright, the Federalists successfully supported Samuel Huntington, a conservative to moderate Republican, whom the *Supporter* called a "federal republican," during the gubernatorial election in 1808. Huntington won and carried Marietta and the counties that had been settled primarily by New Englanders. Running candidates alone, however, the Federalists could marshal only between 25 and 33 percent of the votes for any particular office. Still, if they joined with Republicans on specific issues, they could influence state politics. In 1810, for example, the Federalists endorsed Return J. Meigs, Jr., for governor. Meigs, a conservative Republican, had once been a Federalist, and he carried the state with little difficulty. Meigs ran particularly well in Marietta and Dayton, where Federalist newspapers championed his candidacy. This election proved that the Federalist-Republican coalition had power, and one observer even attributed Meigs's victory to the "*Yanky* Swarms" that had settled in Ohio.

The Federalists, however, needed the Republicans more than the Jeffersonians needed them. As relations with Great Britain deteriorated, the Republicans either solved their differences or put them aside to form a united front. By 1812, Ohio's Republicans believed that Great Britain had to be checked and that the return of the Federalist party to power would have a devastating effect on American trade abroad and the security of the frontier at home. Without offices and with little hope of achieving them, the Federalists could challenge Republican policies only through their newspapers, such as the *Western Spectator* in Marietta, the Zanesville *Express*, the Dayton *Ohio Centinel*, and the St. Clairsville *Ohio Federalist*, or in tolerant Republican newspapers such as the Chillicothe *Fredonian*, where the editors wanted to maintain relatively large Federalist subscriptions, or in the neutral *Western Spy* in Cincinnati.

After Congress declared war, however, the Chillicothe *Supporter*, which had become the chief Federalist newspaper in the state, urged all Ohioans to support the war, contending that "it now becomes the duty of every citizen to cling to his country and rise or fall with it." And in July 1814, the Zanesville *Express* contended that peace would come soon "unless England is determined to *recolonize* us; and such a mad scheme cannot enter into her policy." Charles Hammond, editor of the *Ohio Federalist*, was not as magnanimous or supportive. He vociferously and often vitriolically opposed the war, claiming that British impressments essentially reclaimed deserters, that an invasion of Canada would be immoral and impractical, that the Republicans were essentially French bootlickers, and that war would cause New England to secede. When the British attacked Washington, D.C., forcing Madison to flee, Hammond claimed that this was the first evidence of presidential activity. His commentaries won him a seat in the state senate, where he continued to annoy his Republican colleagues.

Throughout the war, however, Ohio's Federalists played little role other than to harass the Republican party. When the war ended, their newspapers folded, and they ceased to exist as an organized party. Had Jefferson and Madison not led the nation into war, the Federalists might have been able to assert political influence on the state level by joining Republican factions to achieve specific agendas. But the Indian threat together with British violations of American rights and honor easily placed most Ohioans in the Republican camp.

After the War of 1812, politics in Ohio began to change dramatically. The Panic of 1819 caused many to question the value of an unregulated economy, and an increasingly diverse population made public consensus difficult. As a result, Ohioans revived the old political differences between those who favored governmental authority, control, and direction and those who opposed a powerful government on any level and who favored independent action in the frontier tradition. Economic hard times and immigration brought a host of new and dissatisfied voters to the polls. After the Panic of 1819, the state's politics centered on issues of credit, monetary policy, taxation, and internal improvements, particularly canals. During the 1820s, gubernatorial and congressional elections usually hinged on personalities rather than policies, although the public remained indifferent to presidential politics until after 1824. Thereafter, issues that affected Ohio ended bipartisan politics and crystallized positions that led to the creation of a new two-party system in the state. Those issues particularly involved the rechartering of the Bank of the United States and the extension of slavery. But those matters were not frontier concerns, but rather issues of consequence to a settled state with a commercially based economy.

Although the economy had begun to improve by 1824, Ohioans had learned that they needed better transportation systems to enhance the marketing of their agricultural surpluses and manufactured products. As a result, they became receptive to Kentuckian Henry Clay's program for the federal government to support internal improvements, such as roads and canals, and to aid manu-

facturers with a protective tariff. But Andrew Jackson, who harangued against corruption and the Bank of the United States, caught the fancy of many independent and often undisciplined frontier people. Although the Jacksonians espoused the slogan of "No intrigue, No corruption, Andrew Jackson" during the presidential election of 1824 they did not have the support of Ohio's newspapers and public officials beyond Cincinnati and the southwest. As a result, the Jacksonians could not organize effectively; only eight of sixty-four counties sent delegates to a state convention. Even so, the presidential election of 1824 caused the reemergence of the two-party system in the nation and Ohio, with the followers of Henry Clay becoming National Republicans and the Jacksonians emerging as Democratic Republicans.

In the presidential election of 1824, Clay received votes across Ohio. He polled more than two-thirds of the vote in the areas of the northwest that had been opened to settlement in 1818. Most of the hill counties of southeastern Ohio enthusiastically supported him as well as the residents along the proposed route of the National Road that construction crews began building west from Wheeling in 1825. John Quincy Adams received most of his support among New Englanders in the Western Reserve and settlements such as Worthington, and among settlers who opposed a state canal system because its location would not serve them. Jackson carried Cincinnati and the southwestern counties, where he polled 60 percent of the vote, and where the deflationary policies of the Bank of the United States most affected merchants and the agricultural trade.

Jackson's support in southwestern Ohio stemmed from the Panic of 1819. In October 1820, the Cincinnati branch of the Bank of the United States closed and demanded repayment of all outstanding loans. According to the cashier, "The sudden withdrawal of the Branch, and the unexampled oppression practiced upon its debtors, closed the doors of at least two-thirds of the business houses of the city. . . . Many of the commercial houses thus unnecessarily and wantonly prostrated, never recovered the blow. The city at large groaned under the infliction for many years." Henry Clay, who supervised the bank's legal business in Ohio, prosecuted defaulting debtors and caught the blame for the bank's policies, even though many of those voters favored federal support for internal improvements, particularly canals. For them, Jackson seemed the only alternative to the abusive and corrupt power exemplified by the Bank of the United States and its agents. In the eastern counties of Jefferson, Harrison, and Columbiana, Jackson also polled more than 54 percent of the vote among the Scots-Irish and Germans from Pennsylvania who identified with his victory over the British at New Orleans. In all, Jackson carried seventeen to Clay's forty-three counties.

When the election officials counted the ballots, however, Clay received 19,255 votes to Jackson's 18,489, while John Quincy Adams polled 12,280 votes. With a total vote of only 50,024, probably half of Ohio's voters remained at home. Because no candidate received a majority of the electoral votes, the election had to be settled in the U.S. House of Representatives, where each state cast one vote, based on the decision of that delegation's majority. Because Clay finished fourth behind William H. Crawford, he was excluded from consideration as provided by the Twelfth Amendment to the Constitution.

In late December 1824, Acting Governor Allen Trimble wrote Congressman Duncan McArthur in relation to the upcoming resolution of the election in the Congress. Trimble believed the "'reflecting' part of the people of Ohio would prefer Adams to Jackson, but I have no doubt but Jackson would in an election, have a majority of votes." Certainly, personality played a role. McArthur wrote: "God keep us from such an administration as we might expect from such a man as Genl. Jackson," primarily because he acted impetuously and did not support "western interests" as defined by Ohioans. In the end, Ohio's fourteen-man congressional delegation gave ten votes to Adams and two each to Jackson and Crawford, which gave their one congressional vote to Adams. The Ohio delegation evidently believed that Clay's supporters favored that action, because Adams as a northerner also advocated the American System, particularly internal improvements, and he had both ability and experience.

In general, the public supported the decision of the Ohio delegation. By 1827, however, Jackson appealed to many Ohioans who believed that Adams favored government by the wealthy elite, and the country people preferred Jackson for the presidency to "revolutionize the country." The organizational efforts of the Jacksonians paid off during the presidential election of 1828, although his victory in Ohio was due more to his personality than to the advocacy of policies. Jackson polled 67,597 votes to Adams's tally of 63,396, for a margin of 4,201 votes.

The supporters of Adams were astounded. The editor of the *Ohio State Journal* wrote: "For an event as mortifying as it was unexpected, it would, perhaps, be impossible to account satisfactorily, otherwise than by attributing it to the momentary influence of one of those fits of political delirium, of which the history of the human race affords too many examples. . . . Where the Jackson votes came from is, in sober truth, a perfect mystery." Yet Jackson's victory should not have been a surprise, especially for seasoned political observers. Essentially, Jackson won because he was a westerner, and Ohioans, who had fought Indians and the British and cleared land, and who disliked the elitism and alleged corruption of the Adams administration, identified with him. Jackson, not Adams, personified and symbolized the frontier.

By 1828, voters' dissatisfaction stemmed largely from their belief that a corrupt aristocracy wielded political power that violated their own economic and political liberties. The national debate over slavery helped polarize political positions and contributed to the identity of political parties in Ohio and across the nation. In addition, Jackson's advocacy of strong government, as personified by the president, to protect state powers and guarantee individual liberties, appealed to Ohioans. As a result of dissatisfaction with federal banking policy and the Adams administration, together with Jackson's personal appeal and continued immigration, the number of voters who cast ballots more than doubled from the election of 1824 to 130,953 votes four years later, which represented 90 percent of the electorate.

* * *

Throughout the 1820s, Ohio's politicians increasingly understood that the state's economy and society had become complex and interdependent with others, all of which required greater governmental action, regulation, and organization. The Ohio of the 1820s was not the state that it had been at its creation in 1803. New leaders, such as Governor Ethan Allen Brown, Micajah T. Williams, Alfred Kelley, and Ephraim Cutler, believed that government, especially state government, should be used to support the public interest. In 1825, men of this ilk were responsible for creating the state's public school system with tax money and directing the organization of school districts and the employment of qualified teachers, all of which decreased the local autonomy of the past regarding education.

Although the Northwest Ordinance had proclaimed that education would be "encouraged," it did not provide a school system for the Northwest Territory; nor did the state of Ohio until near the end of the frontier period. Settlers from New England generally had some exposure to the schools in that region, while immigrants from the Pennsylvania, Virginia, and Kentucky frontiers usually were less educated and more concerned about making their way on the new land, and they had little formal education, time for it, or willingness to pay for schooling. Consequently, private education in the form of academies provided the only structured education in Ohio until the 1820s.

The quality of education at these academies depended, as in the past, on the breadth of knowledge and ability of the teacher. The better academies granted diplomas after four years of study and a public examination. One woman observed at a graduation ceremony of the Cincinnati Female Academy that the young ladies "blushed so sweetly, and looked so beautifully puzzled and confounded, that it might have been difficult for an abler judge than I was to decide how far they merited the diploma received." She wondered whether this training would help them "stand the wear and tear of half a score of children and one help." The practical expectations of education reigned supreme.

In Ohio the academies remained the predominant educational institutions until after 1830 and the end of the frontier period, and they were most prevalent in the Western Reserve. Even so, Ohio became the first and most successful state in the Old Northwest to establish a system of public schools. Newspaper editors were among the champions of public education to increase the number of potential subscribers, while many parents wanted to enhance the opportunities for their children. Others believed that public education would improve morality and help prevent crime. In January

1825, a legislative committee reported: "A wise legislature will endeavor to prevent the commission of crimes—not only by the number and rigor of her penal statutes—but by affording the whole rising generation, the means of moral and virtuous education; by extending its benign influence to all the paths of private life and social intercourse, and by strengthening the ties of moral duty." Two years later, a "Citizen" writing in the *Ohio State Journal*, published in Columbus, observed: "Witness, fellow citizens, the throng of ragged, profane, vicious, whiskey drinking, noisy, mischief doing boys from five to twenty years old, who are rambling and prowling about on streets, two or three, or more nights every week, damaging property, disturbing repose of the quiet, and worst of all ruining themselves, both for this world and for that which is to come." School and homework would prevent this degradation, he evidently believed. For an increasing number of Ohioans, then, the creation of public schools could solve a host of social problems.

Several years earlier, in 1821, the legislature had attempted to provide such a system when it passed the first general educational act for the state. It authorized towns to form districts that included between twelve and forty homes, establish schools, and levy taxes. Most of the funding, however, would still come from the rental of school lands, donations, and assessments of parents. Moreover, the act did not require taxation to support public education. By so doing, it did little more than call attention to the necessity of state funding.

By 1824 the major political issues in Ohio involved state funding for canals and schools and taxation. Those who supported taxation to pay for schools joined with the legislators who advocated financing a canal system with levies to support legislation of mutual interest. As a result, on February 5, 1825, the state legislature approved a statute that mandated the establishment of school districts in incorporated townships and required taxation of property to support the schools. It did not, however, provide for the enforcement of the act's provisions. Governor Jeremiah Morrow noted in his message to the legislature in December 1826 that more needed to be done to support public education, and he criticized the statute. "It contains," he observed, "not sufficiently the principle of either compulsion or inducement to insure its general operation, and experience has shown that without one or the other of these the chances for its being carried into effect is in the reverse ratio to the necessity of its use."

Morrow was correct in his assessment. The 1825 act provided tax support for the creation of a public school system in Ohio of only one-half mill on a dollar, that is, one-twentieth of 1 percent, based on property valuations in the counties. The school law provided, however, that if a township did not organize school districts within five years, it would not receive either tax money or other state funds for educational purposes. The state legislature also authorized county officials to collect and distribute the school tax, while a board of examiners, appointed by the court of common pleas, would license teachers. But unless the counties levied the property tax and enforced its collection, public schools could not be supported.

Indeed, taxation was essential to finance the creation of a public school system because the revenues generated from the rental of section 16 in each township to support education as provided by the Land Act of 1785 had proved insufficient. Between 1803 and 1827, Ohio leased the designated school lands in those township sections, although some adjustments had to be made for the Virginia Military District, the Western Reserve, and the U.S. Military District, where more than 10.5 million acres were originally beyond congressional authority in the Land Act. In time, Congress provided for the rental of lands in the Virginia Military and U.S. Military districts and the Western Reserve, which gave Ohio a total of 711,871 acres to support education. All too often, however, township trustees leased those lands to friends and politicians at low rates, a practice that could not generate sufficient revenue to support public education.

In general, few settlers preferred to lease lands in section 16 of their townships, because they could buy their own acreage with little difficulty. "Only the lowest class of the community" tended to rent these lands, and they did little to make improvements. Because lands reserved to support public education returned so little revenue, the state asked Congress for permission to sell them. Beginning in 1827, the state legislature authorized the townships or school districts to sell the lands in section 16, and a host of laws followed that provided for sales, revaluations, and payments over time. Once again, however, these land sales generated little revenue, in part because speculators, such as those in the Virginia Military District, bid only ten cents per acre. The funds generated, however, were deposited in the state treasury and credited to the townships or regions, such as the Western Reserve. By 1836, nearly $1 million had been earned from the sale of these lands. A year later the state legislature provided for the distribution of funds raised from selling school lands among the counties, most of which local officials used to support canal building rather than public education. In 1827, the legislature also provided that all fines levied by justices of the peace for immoral practices would be contributed to the school fund. Four years later, in 1831, the legislature required teachers to be certified annually for moral character and educational qualifications.

Still, while most townships organized school districts after 1825, these institutions remained poor in quality and uneven in distribution. Usually they could not afford to operate during more than three months of the year. Low population density often prevented the organization or adequate support of public schools in some areas. Moreover, the operators of the private academies opposed tax-supported public education, as did members of the lower class who did not have the ability or the willingness to pay the required levies. Others, who merely opposed taxation or who did not have children who would benefit, also obstructed the establishment and development of public education, as did chronic underfunding well past the close of the frontier period.

By 1838, however, the editor of the *Cincinnati Daily Gazette* was encouraged by the progress of public education in the state. "The common schools of Ohio," he wrote, "are rapidly gaining popularity. We scarcely open an exchange paper, from towns around us, that we do not see some article in praise of them." Still, much needed to be done. In Cincinnati alone during 1836, only an estimated two thousand of the fifty-five hundred children aged six to sixteen attended the public schools, which had been in operation since 1829. And in May 1839, when an examiner asked a prospective teacher whether the world was round or flat, the candidate answered: "I can teach her either way." Clearly, by the time Ohio adopted the German grammar school system in 1840, and with teachers required to be familiar only with reading, writing, and arithmetic, considerable improvements needed to be made before the state's public education reached the level of adequate. Still, by the early 1830s, Ohio's children would be educated by state mandate in order to live in an interdependent political and commercial world in which the frontier would be only a memory.

College education fared somewhat better on the Ohio frontier. Two townships in the Ohio Company Purchase and one township in the Symmes Purchase had been reserved to support colleges. In 1804, the legislature chartered Ohio University to be located in Athens, although an academic department was not created until 1808, and the first two graduates did not receive their diplomas until 1815. Until about 1820 the university primarily offered secondary-level education. Throughout the frontier period, however, despite reports of its "flourishing condition," it struggled with inadequate funding. As late as 1828, Ohio University graduated only ten students, including one African American male. To the west, Miami University in Oxford received a charter in 1809, but it also served as little more than a grammar school until 1821, when it temporarily closed. In 1824 it reopened, adding faculty and students, and by the end of the frontier period it had earned a reputation second only to Kentucky's Transylvania College in the trans-Appalachian West. During the frontier period, the rental of the reserved lands in the Ohio Company and Symmes purchase areas primarily financed both "Athens College" and Miami University, although each also received modest state funding from the beginning.

Religious denominations, however, established most of Ohio's colleges during the frontier period, such as Kenyon by the Episcopalians (1824), Western Reserve by the Presbyterians (1826), Athenaeum and Xavier by the Catholics (1829 and 1831), and Oberlin and Marietta by the Congregationalists (1833 and 1835). The University of Cincinnati began as a nonsectarian medical school in 1819. Oberlin encouraged the enrollment of African Americans in 1835, and it admitted women two years later.

* * *

African Americans and mulattoes were denied admittance to Ohio's public schools. Although the Northwest Ordinance and the state constitution prohibited slavery in the Old Northwest, neither document could prevent prejudice. Most Ohioans held much the same racial views as other northern whites, and many settlers had migrated from the Upper South and harbored racial beliefs similar to those of the slaveholders in the region. While most Ohioans abhorred slavery, they did not oppose servitude or believe in social equality or civil liberties for blacks. Early in the frontier period, for example, southern immigrants brought African Americans, particularly women, into Ohio as indentured servants. Black children were also indentured until the age of twenty-one. Southerners such as Thomas Worthington, who moved to Chillicothe in 1798, freed their slaves before arrival but brought their servants with them. Soon Chillicothe's population included a small but noticeable number of manumitted slaves.

Although Ohio provided a major route north for the Underground Railroad, few blacks stayed in Ohio. Slave owners in Kentucky commonly advertised in the newspapers of the Ohio River towns for the return of runaway slaves and paid handsome rewards. At the turn of the nineteenth century, only 337 African Americans lived north of the Ohio River. That population increased to 1,890 by 1810, to 4,723 in 1820, and to 9,586 a decade later, as a result of both fugitives and the natural increase. Most African Americans lived in the towns along the Ohio River and in the Scioto River valley. Throughout the frontier period, African Americans could not vote, serve on juries, or testify against whites. In 1804, the state required any African American who entered Ohio to post a $500 bond to guarantee their good behavior, to ensure that they would not become wards of the state, and to discourage their immigration. They also had to show evidence that they were free men or women.

In 1816, as the black population increased, whites began to support a "back to Africa" movement in the form of the American Colonization Society, but little came of these efforts because of inadequate funding and increased births and flight from the South. Cultural beliefs that African Americans were inferior as well as their increasing competition for jobs led to a race riot in Cincinnati in 1829 and to the citizens of Portsmouth forcing the removal of eighty blacks from the town a year later. White settlers in the Scioto Valley also drove black farmers from their lands. Throughout the frontier period, then, with the exception of the Quakers and other abolitionists, such as Presbyterian minister John Rankin at Ripley, Ohioans did not welcome African Americans, and the frontier did not serve as a land of equal opportunity when matters of race determined relationships.

* * *

On July 4, 1827, the *State of Ohio* bore down on Cleveland at the rate of three miles an hour. The excitement on board muffled the clop of hooves along the towpath and the gentle wash behind the keel as the governor and other public dignitaries celebrated the opening of the Ohio and Erie Canal. Thousands of onlookers lined the canal banks between Akron, where the boat was launched, and Cleveland to wave and marvel at the beginning of a new era in Ohio. On this Independence Day, more than state pride contributed to the spirit of celebration. Those who watched the canal boat glide quietly along and who participated in the ceremonies knew that the Northwest now lay open to the commercial riches of the East, and that the day would not be long coming when the waters of Lake Erie would mingle with those of the Ohio River. The canal would provide trade, communication, and ease of travel that had been only a dream. It would also help build a strong Union, and on this Independence Day, Ohioans were nationalists to the core. The canal, however, also clearly indicated that the Ohio frontier had come to an end.

And so the *State of Ohio* came slowly on. Twelve hours and thirty-eight miles later, during which time it dropped four hundred feet and passed through forty-one locks and crossed three aqueducts, the fifty-ton boat deposited its cargo of dignitaries on a wharf in Cleveland. While the governor and his party hurried off to make proclamations and to toast the dawn of a new age, another canal boat bound for Cleveland left Portage Summit. It was loaded with flour and whiskey—products which, more than speeches, helped build the state. Although the name of that vessel is lost in the distant past, it in reality began the canal era and marked the end of the frontier in Ohio.

The excitement of the people who lined the banks to watch the first boat through this portion of the canal was as great as their need. The only alternative to crossing the difficult and distant mountains over uncertain roads to reach eastern markets was to descend the Ohio and Mississippi rivers to New Orleans. Then goods and passengers had to be reloaded upon sailing vessels for transport to the ports beyond. The time and expense required to cross the mountains or to reach the East Coast by first traveling west and south frequently proved prohibitive. Ohio's farmers needed quick and cheap access to market, and the state's rich natural resources, such as coal and timber, would remain underdeveloped until these transportation problems were solved. Moreover, those who lived in Ohio could enjoy only a rough standard of living as long as the consumer goods of the East remained unavailable to them. In 1825, however, the opening of the Erie Canal changed all of that. Now eastern markets became available to the farmers and merchants along the Lake Erie shore. The people in the interior, however, were unwilling to have only a few individuals profit from the benefits of the Erie Canal. They, too, wanted ready access to market, and they sent out a call for canals that would link the state's interior with the lake and the Ohio River.

Those demands did not fall on deaf ears. As early as December 1816, Governor Thomas Worthington asked the state legislature to join the state of New York in the construction of the Erie Canal. Although the house approved his idea, the senate rejected it. Two years later Worthington also unsuccessfully appealed to William H. Crawford, secretary of the Treasury, for federal support for an Ohio as well as an Erie Canal. Ethan Allen Brown, who succeeded Worthington, continued to press the issue as well. In his inaugural address on December 14, 1818, Brown urged the state legislature to support the construction of a canal in order to promote industry, commerce, and trade, and to enhance the development of the state's natural resources. Brown told the legislature in his message on January 8, 1819, "Roads and canals are the veins and arteries to the body politic."

Brown, however, had a difficult time convincing the legislature to accept the responsibility for building inland waterways. Some legislators wanted to leave the matter to private enterprise. Others believed the state should first spend its money to improve the road system. Still others argued that canal work was the responsibility of the federal rather than the state government. During the next several years, Brown lobbied long and hard for the state support of a canal. He maintained not only that Ohio's merchants would profit from higher prices for goods gained through timely shipments, but that the volume of traffic would generate sufficient revenue to pay for construction costs and operating expenses.

With these thoughts in mind, in addition to the hope that the federal government would provide support, the legislature made a preliminary commitment. In January 1822, it authorized the governor to employ an engineer and a seven-man Board of Canal Commissioners to oversee the survey of potential routes and to determine expenses. The canal commissioners, including Thomas Worthington and Ethan Allen Brown, quickly turned to the task at hand, only to discover that no qualified civil engineers resided in Ohio. Confronted with the lack of local expertise, they employed James Geddes, one of the most prominent engineers working on the Erie Canal. Eight months and nine hundred surveyed miles later, the commissioners selected five potential canal routes. Planning continued until early 1825, when the commissioners reported to the legislature that the time had come to start digging. A "canal spirit" had spread throughout Ohio.

After a lengthy debate, the legislature responded to the enthusiastic report of the canal commissioners on February 4, 1825, by authorizing the construction of two canals. The legislature also provided for the continuance of the Board of Canal Commissioners on a permanent basis. Although the board was to have the power of eminent domain, disputes between landowners and the state were to be settled by an impartial board of arbitration. The legislature also created a three-man Board of Commissioners of the Canal Fund, whose responsibilities were to borrow money and issue bonds backed by the full faith and credit of the state. The Canal Fund commissioners were to pay out money, upon authorization of the Board of Canal Commissioners, to retire the long-term debt, and to keep the financial records during the construction process. Only representatives from areas far removed from the proposed canal lines opposed this legislation, but the legislature's approval of extensive improvements for roads solved this problem.

The two canals that were to be built met both economic and political needs. The first and largest, the Ohio and Erie Canal, was to link

the Ohio River with Lake Erie by following a route through the
Scioto-Muskingum river valleys between Portsmouth and Cleveland, a distance of slightly more than three hundred miles. The
second canal, known as the Miami and Erie Canal, was to follow the
Great Miami River and link Dayton with Cincinnati. The commissioners supported the construction of these canals to include as
many people as possible and thereby win legislative support, particularly since the estimated construction costs reached $3 million,
or about 10 percent of the property valuation in the state. Although
northeastern and southwestern Ohio had the greatest concentration
of population, a diagonal route across the state was not feasible. Not
only was the divide between the Scioto and Miami river valleys
higher than the source of water for a canal, but the water supply was
also insufficient to fill it.

Because of the magnitude of the undertaking, the Ohio and Erie
Canal could not be built at one time. Consequently, the commissioners first decided to construct a portion of the canal that would open
the state's interior to Lake Erie as well as to begin the "deep cut" on
the Licking Summit which separated the Muskingum and Scioto
watersheds. They also agreed to start digging the Miami Canal between Middletown and Cincinnati. With these priorities established,
the state engineers laid out the precise canal lines, and the Board
of Canal Commissioners appointed Micajah Williams and Alfred
Kelley to the positions of "acting" canal commissioners to oversee
construction and daily affairs. In order to support that construction,
the Canal Fund commissioners also sold bonds worth $400,000 at
5 percent interest to investors in New York.

On July 4, 1825, with the management and funding in place, the
formal spade work began at the Licking Summit, located three miles
west of Newark. Governor DeWitt Clinton of New York, together
with Ohio's Governor Jeremiah Morrow and former governors Ethan
Allen Brown and Thomas Worthington, addressed the audience with
optimistic speeches, after which they raised symbolic spades of
dirt—accompanied by the applause of the audience, the spit-and-
polish drill of a militia troop, and the blare of several neighborhood
bands. The lesser dignitaries scuffled for the honor of lifting additional spades of dirt. Then the governor's party adjourned in order
to repeat the ceremony on July 21 at Middletown to hail the be-

ginning of the forty-two-mile Miami Canal. While the onlookers dreamed of future wealth, the real work now began.

By the end of November 1825, approximately two thousand men labored with picks, axes, shovels, and blasting powder on the segment of the Ohio and Erie Canal between Portage Summit and Cleveland. They had cleared timber and grubbed roots and stumps for thirty miles along the canal line. Even so, the work was piecemeal. Because no construction company in Ohio had the ability to tackle this project alone, the canal was completed in sections, and each section or "job" was let as a single contract. The commissioners estimated the costs of each portion, then, through newspaper announcements, opened the work to bids. At first, the competition for canal contracts was heavy. In 1826, nearly six thousand contractors submitted bids for the 110 sections of the Ohio and Erie Canal south of Portage Summit, for an average of fifty-four bids per section. Many of those bids, however, were made by inexperienced contractors or by those who saw an opportunity to make a quick profit at state expense, all of which forced the state to relet contracts whenever a particular contractor failed to meet his obligations.

At first the contractors hired local workers, and farmers and tradesmen earned needed cash by digging on the canals. Later, as the canals expanded, newly arrived Irish and German immigrants made their way to Ohio to work on them. The utopians at Zoar also reportedly earned $21,000 of needed income for their community by contracting to dig a portion of the Ohio and Erie Canal that ran through their neighborhood. Although the work progressed at a feverish pace, the Ohioans who lived along the projected routes waited impatiently for the completion of the canals. In 1827, a resident in Portsmouth wrote: "Business of every kind is very dull here; but we all hope to live on milk and honey and without labor when we get the canal."

No matter who labored on the canals, however, the work was hard and not without danger. First, the entire length of the canal had to be cleared of trees, stumps, and roots for a distance of at least twenty feet on each side of the projected channel. Next, the ditches had to be excavated and embankments built to provide a towpath and to contain the water. Wood and stone had to be cut and crafted into locks, aqueducts, and culverts. Where the canal cut through rock, the work became more difficult, even with the aid of blasting powder. When a channel passed through swampy country, canal workers completed the "mucking and ditching" while standing in water. During the summer months the mosquitoes preyed on bare backs, necks, and arms; malaria took its toll, sometimes halting the digging for weeks at a time while the workers shivered, trembled, and fought to regain their health. Because of malaria, although no one as yet had made the connection, construction usually stopped about mid-July and resumed only after the first frost killed the mosquitoes. Then it continued until winter weather forced the workers indoors. When the ground thawed in the spring, the digging began again.

For their sacrifice, workers at first received only thirty cents per day, or about eight to ten dollars per month, including board, for twenty-six working days, each of which began at sunrise and ended at sunset. This was the first real money that many of the farm boys had earned. At first, a "jigger" of whiskey, equal to a quarter-pint, was issued at least once each day, and in some localities at sunrise, ten o'clock, noon, and suppertime. After the first four months, however, canal commissioners Williams and Kelley ended the daily allotment of whiskey because they believed it took too much time to dispense and because it reduced the efficiency of the men. If the workers were disappointed with this ruling, their wages soon began to rise to twelve to fifteen dollars per month as a result of competition for their labor from Pennsylvania and Indiana, which also began canal projects.

The scale of work completed is both fascinating and overwhelming. The Ohio and Miami canals were to be a minimum of 40 feet wide at the water line, tapering to 26 feet at the bottom with a depth of 4 feet. These "prism" dimensions, however, were minimum standards, and a substantial part of both canals was much larger—in some places stretching to 150 feet at the water line with a depth of 12 feet. This variance was by design. The canal commissioners expanded the size of the canals whenever possible, provided the extra dimensions did not increase the construction costs. In some cases, only the towpath embankment was built, thus allowing hills on the opposite side to contain the water. This procedure, however, caused the water to spread across low-lying land, and farmers were quick to file damage suits against the state.

The canals, of course, were worthless without water, and the chief limiting factor which determined prism size was the amount of water available. The larger the prism, the more water was needed to fill the canal. The locks on the Ohio and Erie Canal, for example, averaged a nine-foot lift, while those on the Miami Canal averaged eight feet. Consequently, the more times the locks were used during the course of a day, the more water was needed to fill them from above. The canal season, however, extended from April to November, which included the driest portion of the year. To ensure a ready water supply in the absence of adequate stream flow, the canal commissioners turned to the construction of reservoirs. Both the Ohio and Erie and the Miami canals crossed lands that could not provide enough water to keep the boats out of the mud. At the same time, the water supply had to be above the highest portion of the canals so that it could flow into the channels without pumping. Because of this need, reservoirs were built on the summits of each canal. On the Ohio and Erie Canal, two summits existed—one in Portage County and the other in Licking County—where reservoirs of the same names were constructed to feed the waterway. Later, on the Miami and Erie Canal, the St. Marys, Loramie, and Lewistown reservoirs provided the water supply.

Prism size also determined the maximum dimensions of the canal boats, which in turn had economic ramifications for shippers. With a water surface of only 40 feet, the canal boats had to be less than half that width in order to pass each other up and down the line. In addition, the locks usually were only 100 feet long and 25 feet wide. Consequently, canal boats in Ohio customarily were 14 feet wide and 60 to 70 feet long, with a capacity of about 60 tons. At the ports, such as Cleveland and Dayton, basins had to be constructed to enable the boats to turn around. At Cleveland, for example, the basin was 120 feet wide and nearly a mile long.

Upon completion of the Miami Canal from Dayton to Cincinnati in December 1828 and the Ohio and Erie Canal from Cleveland to Portsmouth in October 1833, the public pressed the legislature to expand the canal system to other portions of the state. Even though the Ohio and Erie Canal cost $4.3 million, more than a third above the original estimate of slightly more than $3 million in 1825, primarily because of escalating labor expenses, and although the Miami Canal cost $900,000 (a little more than $200,000 above the original estimate), every section of the state appealed to the legislature and to the canal commissioners to favor it with a canal. To be without access to a canal seemed to promise no less than economic strangulation and a continuation of frontier conditions.

Fortunately for Ohio, previous federal action helped alleviate the financial problem. On May 24, 1828, Congress transferred 500,000 acres of federal lands to the state, which it in turn sold over time to help meet construction costs. Congress also granted more than 438,000 acres in a five-mile-wide stretch from Dayton to the mouth of the Auglaize River. Within that corridor, Congress gave the state every other section in a checkerboard fashion. Not only did the sales of these lands help meet the state's investment in canals, but once the Miami and Erie Canal was completed to Lake Erie, the value of those lands increased substantially, thereby boosting the tax revenue of the state. Consequently, Ohio benefited from these grants in two ways. Later, Ohio received an additional 294,000 acres of federal land to facilitate the construction of the Wabash and Erie Canal from Lake Erie to the Indiana Line. Canal officials and state legislators were confident that this form of financial support would solve the problem of continually having to seek loans from beyond the confines of the state to support canal construction. The only provision that Congress attached to these grants was that the canals, constructed with funds generated from the sale of federal lands, were to remain public highways and that federal freight and agents were to travel over them without cost. Although those lands did not generate as much revenue to help with construction as the optimists had hoped, those federal grants played an instrumental role in the completion of the canal system.

Essentially, at the end of the frontier period, then, Ohio's farmers and merchants near the canal system now had improved access to market for wheat, flour, oats, lard, whiskey, pork, lumber, iron ore, coal, and various manufactured products. With access to markets via the canals, the price of wheat jumped from twenty-five cents per bushel in 1825 to seventy-five cents per bushel in the interior counties and to even higher prices at the warehouses in Toledo and Cleveland, where buyers represented millers from distant markets. Moreover, while the price of exported commodities increased, the cost of imported items declined. Surprisingly, however, those markets remained primarily local, with the exception of substantial agricultural exports. Little through traffic, however, crossed the Ohio canals. Neither the Ohio and Erie nor the Miami and Erie systems saw much transshipment of goods through the state from northern or southern points of origin.

Even so, the cumulative benefits of the canal system proved significant. Akron, for example, not only owed its existence to the Ohio and Erie Canal, but it also drew on the canal for water power, as did other cities and towns. Moveover, with the creation of business and jobs, more opportunities existed in the canal towns than in those that were passed by. The population of Cincinnati, Dayton, Toledo, Circleville, Newark, and Zanesville, among others, also increased, in part because of the canals. In addition, new markets and trade made the hinterland along the canals more valuable than ever before, and real estate values increased rapidly.

Several problems, however, prevented the development of lucrative through traffic that would have generated significant revenues in tolls for state coffers. First, the canals were plagued with inadequate water supplies, particularly during periods of drought. Transportation over the Ohio and Erie Canal was too undependable. Second, the canals were slow. Both major routes had an exorbitant number of locks that had to be negotiated, and that took time. In addition, at the very moment that the canal system was on the verge of completion, a new, quicker, more reliable system of transportation entered the state in 1836—the Erie and Kalamazoo Railroad.

Beginning in 1816, then, the canal movement helped improve travel and transportation and break down local isolation, petty jealousies, and parochial prejudices—all of which provided a unifying effect on the people of the state. As a result, the standard of living and the quality of life improved, and the people of Ohio became more linked than ever before with the world beyond its borders. Moreover, in little more than twenty years after the conclusion of the War of 1812, the Ohio and Erie and Miami and Erie canals cut through Indian lands where not long before the Delawares, Wyandots, and Shawnees had lived and hunted. Indeed, by 1840, then, with Ohio on the verge of losing population to other states for the first time, and with two major canals completed, a two-horse hitch on the towpath and canal boats symbolized as well as anything the end of the Ohio frontier.

Bibliographical Essay

The most comprehensive collection of primary and secondary materials relating to Ohio's frontier history is located at the Ohio Historical Society in Columbus, Ohio. Anyone conducting research on the Ohio frontier must read the early newspapers. The most important guides to the newspaper collection are the "Ohio Newspaper Catalog: 1991 Microfiche Edition," and Stephen Gutgesell, *Guide to Ohio Newspapers, 1793–1973* (Columbus: Ohio Historical Society, 1974). Among the most useful newspapers for the frontier period are the *Centinel of the North-Western Territory* (Cincinnati), *Liberty Hall and Cincinnati Mercury, Western Star* (Lebanon), Zanesville *Express, Muskingum Messenger* (Zanesville), *Ohio Centinel* (Dayton), *Fredonian* (Chillicothe), *Scioto Gazette* (Chillicothe), *Independent Republican* (Chillicothe), *Monitor* (Columbus), *Western Herald* (Steubenville), *American Friend* (Marietta), *Ohio Federalist and Belmont Repository*, and the Toledo weekly *Blade*.

For an introduction to the manuscript collection, see Andrea D. Lentz, ed., *A Guide to Manuscripts at the Ohio Historical Society* (Columbus: Ohio Historical Society, 1972), and Linda Elise Kalette, *The Papers of Thirteen Early Ohio Political Leaders . . . An Inventory to the 1976–77 Microfilm Editions* (Columbus: Ohio Historical Society, 1977). The latter collection includes the "Northwest Territory Transcripts," as well as the papers of Arthur St. Clair, Winthrop Sargent, Edward Tiffin, Thomas Kirker, Samuel Huntington, Return J. Meigs, Jr., Othniel Looker, Thomas Worthington, Ethan A. Brown, Allen Trimble, Jeremiah Morrow, Charles Hammond, Micajah T. Williams, and "Letters from the Executive of Ohio and Ohio Governors' Letters." In addition, see the Description and Travel Collection for early reports about life in Ohio. Also on microfilm are the records of the U.S. General Land Office, Moravian Mission, Society of Friends, and Society of Separatists of Zoar. The Lyman C. Draper Collection also contains useful sources. Before beginning with the Draper Collection, see Josephine L. Harper, *Guide to the Draper Manuscripts* (Madison: State Historical Society of Wisconsin, 1983). For a guide to the most recent research and writing about Ohio, see *America: History and Life*. This index is published quarterly by ABC-Clio, Inc., and it can also be accessed via CD-ROM or with an on-line computer search. See also the *Timeline: Index*. This source is periodically updated by the magazine's editorial office, and it provides an excellent subject, author, and title index.

Anyone beginning the study of Ohio's history must consult the best one-volume history of the state: George W. Knepper, *Ohio and Its People* (Kent, Ohio: Kent State University Press, 1989). This study not only provides a solid, brief overview of the frontier, but it also includes several maps that show the location of Indian towns, forts, military expeditions, land surveys and subdivisions, and canal routes that cannot be found in other sources. More detailed but older general histories include the first three volumes in the series known as The History of the State of Ohio, edited by Carl Wittke and published by the Ohio State Archaeological and Historical Society. Those volumes are Beverley W. Bond, Jr., *The Foundations of Ohio* (1941), William T. Utter, *The Frontier State, 1803–1825* (1942), and Francis P. Weisenberger, *The Passing of the Frontier, 1825–1850* (1941). R. Carlyle Buley, *The Old Northwest Pioneer Period, 1815–1840*, 2 vols. (Indianapolis: Indiana Historical Society, 1950), includes a great deal of information about social life in the region, with examples from Ohio. See also Beverley W. Bond, Jr., *The Civilization of the Old Northwest: A Study of Political, Social, and Economic Development, 1788–1812* (New York: Macmillan, 1934). An engaging narrative written for the general reader is Walter Havighurst, *Wilderness for Sale: The Story of the First Western Land Rush* (New York: Hastings House, 1956). See also Thomas H. Smith, *The Mapping of Ohio* (Kent, Ohio: Kent State University Press, 1977).

The historical literature on the Native Americans in the Old Northwest is extensive and almost unmanageable. For an introduction to the major tribes in Ohio, see Bruce G. Trigger, ed., *Northeast*, vol. 15 of *Handbook of North American Indians*, ed. William C. Sturtevant (Washington, D.C.: Smithsonian Institution Press, 1978). Important ethno-cultural studies of major tribes in Ohio include James H. Howard, *Shawnee: The Ceremonialism of a Native Indian Tribe and Its Cultural Background* (Athens: Ohio University Press, 1981), and Vernon Kinietz and Ermine Wheeler Voegelin, "Shawnese Traditions: C. C. Trowbridge's Account," *Occasional Contributions from the Museum of Anthropology of the University of Michigan*, no. 9 (1939). For a cultural survey of the Hurons (Wyandots), Miamis, Ottawas, Potawatomies, and Chippewas (Ojibwas), see W. Vernon Kinietz, "The Indians of the Western Great Lakes, 1615–1760," *Occasional Contributions from the Museum of Anthropology of the University of Michigan*, no. 10 (1940). A brief history of the Shawnees for the general audience is Jerry E. Clark, *The Shawnee* (Lexington: University of Kentucky Press, 1977). Useful studies designed for the scholar are Ermine W. Voegelin, "Some Possible Sixteenth and Seventeenth Century Locations of the Shawnee," *Proceedings of the Indiana Academy of Science* 48 (1939): 13–19; John Witthoft and William A. Hunter, "The Seventeenth-Century Origins of the Shawnee," *Ethnohistory* 2, no. 1 (1955): 42–57; and Ermine Wheeler Voegelin, "The Place of Agriculture in the Subsistence Economy of the Shawnee," *Papers of the Michigan Academy of Science, Arts, and Letters* 26 (1940): 513–20.

An important introduction to the Delawares can be found in two books by C. A. Weslager, *The Delaware Indians: A History* (New Brunswick, N.J.: Rutgers University Press, 1972) and *The Delaware Indian Westward Migration* (Wallingford, Pa.: Middle Atlantic Press, 1978). For a cultural study of Delaware women, see Anthony F. C. Wallace, "Women, Land, and Society: Three Aspects of Aboriginal Delaware Life," *Pennsylvania Archaeologist* 17, nos. 1–4 (1947): 1–35. Two other important studies of the Delawares are Francis Jennings, "The Delaware Indians in the Covenant Chain," in *A Delaware Indian Symposium*, ed. Herbert C. Kraft (Harrisburg, Pa.: Pennsylvania Historical and Museum Commission, 1974), 88–101, and in the same publication Melburn D. Thurman, "Delaware Social Organization," 111–34.

Excellent studies of intercultural relations between the Native Americans and whites that apply to the Old Northwest are Richard White, *The Middle Ground: Indians, Empires, and Republics in the Great Lakes Region, 1650–1815* (New York: Cambridge University Press, 1991); Daniel K. Richter, *The Ordeal of the Long-house: The Peoples of the Iroquois League in the Era of European Colonization* (Chapel Hill: Published for the Institute of Early American History and Culture, Williamsburg, Virginia, by the University of North Carolina Press, 1992); and Michael N. McConnell, *A Country Between: The Upper Ohio Valley and Its Peoples, 1724–1774* (Lincoln: University of Nebraska Press, 1992).

For early Indian and white contacts, see George A. Wood, "Céloron de Blainville and French Expansion in the Ohio Valley," *Mississippi Valley Historical Review* 9 (March 1923): 303–19. Important firsthand accounts are William M. Darlington, *Christopher Gist's Journal* (1893; reprint, Ann Arbor, Mich.: University Microfilms, 1966), and Reuben Gold Thwaites, *Early Western Journals, 1748–1765* (Cleveland: Arthur H. Clark Co., 1904), which contains the journals of Conrad Weiser (1748), George Croghan (1750–1765), and Frederick Post (1758). See also James P. McClure, "The Ohio Valley's Deerskin Trade: Topics for Consideration," *Old Northwest* 15 (Fall 1990): 115–33, and W. Neil Franklin, "Pennsylvania-Virginia Rivalry for the Indian Trade of the Ohio Valley," *Mississippi Valley Historical Review* 20 (March 1934): 463–80. For late eighteenth- and early nineteenth-century relations, see two biographies by R. David Edmunds, *The Shawnee Prophet* (Lincoln: University of Nebraska Press, 1983) and *Tecumseh and the Quest for Indian Leadership* (Boston: Little, Brown and Co., 1984). Harvey Lewis Carter, *The Life and Times of Little Turtle: First Sagamore of the Wabash* (Urbana: University of Illinois Press, 1987), traces the life of the most skilled war leader of the Miamis.

A good introduction to the diplomatic problems of the Ohio country is Michael N. McConnell, "Peoples 'In Between': The Iroquois and the Ohio Indians, 1720–1768," in *Beyond the Covenant Chain*, ed. Daniel K. Richter and James H. Merrill (Syracuse: Syracuse University Press, 1987), 93–112. Paul A. W. Wallace, *Conrad Weiser: Friend of Colonist and Mohawk* (New York: Russell and Russell, 1945), is the standard biography of Pennsylvania's diplomat to the Ohio Indians. See also Nicholas B. Wainwright, *George Croghan: Wilderness Diplomat* (Chapel Hill: Published for the Institute of Early American History and Culture, Williamsburg, Virginia, by the University of North Carolina Press, 1959). A succinct study of Old Briton's attempt to assert independence from both the French and British, while relying on British trade and protection, is R. David Edmunds, "Old Briton," in *American Indian Leaders: Studies in Diversity*, ed. R. David Edmunds (Lincoln: University of Nebraska Press, 1980), 1–21. See also Reginald Horsman, *Expansion and American Indian Policy, 1783–1812* (East Lansing, Mich.: Michigan State University Press, 1967), and Francis Paul Prucha, *American Indian Policy in the Formative Years: The Indian Trade and Intercourse Acts, 1790–1834* (Cambridge: Harvard University Press, 1962).

An important study of the attempt to create a confederacy based on a re-newal of nativism is Gregory Evans Dowd, *A Spirited Resistance: The North American Indian Struggle for Unity, 1745–1815* (Baltimore: Johns Hopkins University Press, 1992). For Pontiac's role in the resistance of the western Indians, see Wilbur R. Jacobs, *Dispossessing the American Indians: Indians and Whites on the Colonial Frontier* (New York: Charles Scribner's Sons, 1972). See also Charles E. Hunter, "The Delaware Nativist Revival of the Mid-Eighteenth Century," *Ethnohistory* 18 (Winter 1971): 39–49; R. David Edmunds, "The Thin Red Line: Tecumseh, the Prophet, and Shawnee Resistance," *Timeline* 4 (December 1987– January 1988): 2–19; and Terry Rugley, "Savage and States-man: Changing Historical Interpretations of Tecumseh," *Indiana Magazine of History* 85 (December 1989): 289–311.

The military history of the Ohio frontier is extensive. For perspective on the colonial wars, see Howard H. Peckham, *The Colonial Wars, 1689–1762* (Chicago: University of Chicago Press, 1964). An excellent detailed history that is essential for a thorough overview of European-Indian relations is Fran-cis Jennings, *Empire of Fortune: Crowns, Colonies, and Tribes in the Seven Years War in America* (New York: W. W. Norton and Co., 1988). Firsthand ac-counts in the American Culture Series, 1493–1875: A Cumulative Guide to the Microfilm Collection, edited by Ophelia Y. Lo (Ann Arbor, Mich.: University Microfilms, 1979), are *Journal of Captain William Trent from Logstown to Pickawillany, A.D. 1752* (Cincinnati, 1871) and *An Historical Account of the Expedition against the Ohio Indians in the Year MDCCLXIV under the Com-mand of Henry Bouquet* (Philadelphia, 1766). See also "An Account of the Captivity of Hugh Gibson among the Delaware Indians of the Big Beaver and the Muskingum, from the Latter Part of July, 1756, to the Beginning of April, 1759," *Massachusetts Historical Society Collections* 6, 3d series (1837): 140–53, and Beverley W. Bond, Jr., ed., "The Captivity of Charles Stuart, 1755-57," *Mississippi Valley Historical Review* 13 (June 1926–March 1927): 58–81. Two important secondary sources are Paul K. Adams, "Colonel Henry Bouquet's Ohio Expedition in 1764," *Pennsylvania History* 40 (April 1973): 139–47, and Paul E. Kopperman, "The Captives Return: Bouquet's Victory," *Timeline* 7 (April–May 1990): 2–14. Other secondary sources concerning the French and Indian wars include William J. Eccles, "Iroquois, French, British: Imperial Ri-valry in the Ohio Valley," in *Pathways to the Old Northwest: An Observance of the Bicentennial of the Northwest Ordinance* (Indianapolis: Indiana Histori-cal Society, 1988), 19–32; R. David Edmunds, "Pickawillany: French-Military Power versus British Economics," *Western Pennsylvania Historical Magazine* 58 (April 1975): 169–84; and Leroy V. Eid, "'A Kind of Running Fight': Indian Battlefield Tactics in the Late Eighteenth Century," *Western Pennsylvania Historical Magazine* 71 (April 1988): 147–71.

For the period of the Confederation and American Revolution, see Archer Butler Hulbert, ed., *Ohio in the Time of the Confederation* (Cleveland: Arthur H. Clark Co., 1918). The military activities in Ohio during the American Revolution have been traced from the Draper Manuscripts; see Reuben Gold Thwaites and Louise Phelps Kellogg, *The Revolution on the Upper Ohio, 1775–1777* (Madison: State Historical Society of Wisconsin, 1908); *Frontier De-fense on the Upper Ohio, 1777–1778* (Madison: Wisconsin Historical Society,

1912); and Louise Phelps Kellogg, *Frontier Advance on the Upper Ohio, 1778–1789* (Madison: State Historical Society of Wisconsin, 1916). Other documentary evidence can be found in Reuben Gold Thwaites and Louise Phelps Kellogg, *Documentary History of Dunmore's War, 1774* (Madison: State Historical Society of Wisconsin, 1905). An important collection of essays that involve the American Revolution in the Ohio country is David Curtis Skaggs, ed., *The Old Northwest in the American Revolution* (Madison: State Historical Society of Wisconsin, 1977). See also Reginald Horsman, "The Collapse of the Ohio River Barrier: Conflict and Negotiation in the Old Northwest, 1763–1787," in *Pathways to the Old Northwest: An Observance of the Bicentennial of the Northwest Ordinance* (Indianapolis: Indiana Historical Society, 1988), 33–46. A good study that shows how the British attempted to isolate the Shawnees is John M. Sosin, "The British Indian Department and Dunmore's War," *Virginia Magazine of History and Biography* 74 (January 1986): 383–428. For the Native American perspective, see Francis Jennings, "The Indians' Revolution," in *The American Revolution: Explorations in the History of American Radicalism*, ed. Alfred F. Young (De Kalb: Northern Illinois University Press, 1976), 321–48, and Colin G. Calloway, "'We Have Always Been the Frontier': The American Revolution in Shawnee Country," *American Indian Quarterly* 16 (Winter 1992): 39–52. A good study written for the general reader is Thomas I. Pieper and James B. Gidney, *Fort Laurens, 1778–1779: The Revolutionary War in Ohio* (Kent, Ohio: Kent State University Press, 1976).

Anyone coming to the subject of the military history of the Northwest Territory and Ohio for the first time should consult Francis Paul Prucha, *The Sword of the Republic: The United States Army on the Frontier, 1783–1846* (New York: Macmillan, 1969). An older but still good overview of the army in the Ohio country is James Ripley Jacobs, *The Beginning of the U.S. Army, 1783–1812* (Princeton: Princeton University Press, 1947). An important study of army organization is Richard H. Kohn, *Eagle and Sword: The Federalists and the Creation of the Military Establishment in America, 1783–1802* (New York: Free Press, 1975). See also Randolph C. Downes, *Council Fires on the Upper Ohio: A Narrative of Indian Affairs in the Upper Ohio Valley until 1795* (Pittsburgh: University of Pittsburgh Press, 1968). Although the sources are sometimes dated and the quoted material should be used with care, see Wiley Sword, *President Washington's Indian War: The Struggle for the Old Northwest, 1790–1795* (Norman: University of Oklahoma Press, 1985).

Portions of General Harmar's journal and the diary of Lieutenant Denny as well as several other primary documents can be found in Basil Meek, "General Harmar's Expedition," *Ohio State Archaeological and Historical Quarterly* 20 (January 1911): 74–108. See also the journal of Colonel John May, May 1788 to September 1788, in the collections of the Ohio Historical Society, and Howard H. Peckam, "Josiah Harmar and His Indian Expedition," *Ohio State Archaeological and Historical Quarterly* 55 (July/September 1946): 227–41.

For the military and political affairs of Arthur St. Clair, see William Henry Smith's annotated *The St. Clair Papers: The Life and Public Services of Arthur St. Clair*, 2 vols. (1882; reprint, New York: Da Capo Press, 1971). Other important primary sources include Milo M. Quaife, ed., "A Picture of the First United States Army: The Journal of Captain Samuel Newman," *Wisconsin*

Magazine of History 2 (September 1918): 40–73; Frazer E. Wilson, ed., *Journal of Capt. Daniel Bradley* (Greenville, Ohio: Frank H. Jobes and Son, 1935); and "Winthrop Sargent's Diary While with General Arthur St. Clair's Expedition against the Indians," *Ohio Archaeological and Historical Society Publications* 33 (July 1924): 237–73. See also J. Martin West, "Arthur St. Clair," *Timeline* 5 (April–May 1988): 51–56.

A number of journals written by members of Anthony Wayne's campaign have been published. Several of the most easily accessible are R. C. McGrane, ed., "William Clark's Journal of General Wayne's Campaign," *Mississippi Valley Historical Review* 1 (December 1914): 418–44, and M. M. Quaife, ed., "General James Wilkinson's Narrative of the Fallen Timbers Campaign," *Mississippi Valley Historical Review* 16 (June 1921): 81–90. In relation to Wilkinson, see also two articles by David A. Simmons, "The Military and Administrative Abilities of James Wilkinson in the Old Northwest, 1792–1793," *Old Northwest* 3 (September 1977): 237–50, and "An Orderly Book from Fort Washington and Fort Hamilton, 1792–1793," *Cincinnati Historical Society Bulletin* 36 (Summer 1978): 125–44. A list of the published journals along with another journal by an unknown officer can be found in Richard C. Knopf, "A Precise Journal of General Wayne's Last Campaign," *Proceedings of the American Antiquarian Society* 64 (October 1954): 273–302. Knopf has also published "Two Journals of Kentucky Volunteers, 1793–1794," *Filson Club History Quarterly* 27 (July 1953): 247–81, the second journal of which is by an unknown author who participated in Wayne's campaign. For an account by an unknown soldier that was critical of Wayne's daily operations, tactics, and maneuvers, see Dwight L. Smith, ed., "From Green Ville to Fallen Timbers: A Journal of the Wayne Campaign, July 28–September 14, 1794," *Indiana Historical Society Publications* 16 (1952): 239–326. At the Ohio Historical Society see the John Carmichael diary, June 16, 1795–December 3, 1795, and the journal of Dr. Joseph G. Andrews. The Isaac Craig Papers at the Ohio Historical Society also contain materials concerning military affairs in Ohio during the 1790s, especially in relation to logistics and outfitting.

The secondary literature on Wayne's campaign is voluminous. For the British concerns, see Reginald Horsman, "The British Indian Department and the Resistance to General Anthony Wayne, 1793–1795," *Mississippi Valley Historical Review* 49 (September 1962): 269–90. Studies that focus on Fort Miamis include Richard C. Knopf, "Fort Miamis: The International Background," *Ohio State Archaeological and Historical Quarterly* 61 (April 1952): 146–66. Dwight L. Smith has provided brief overviews of Wayne and the Greenville Treaty in "Wayne's Peace with the Indians of the Old Northwest, 1795," *Ohio State Archaeological and Historical Quarterly* 59 (July 1950): 239–55, and "Wayne and the Treaty of Greene Ville," *Ohio State Archaeological and Historical Quarterly* 63 (January 1954): 1–7. For a discussion of the Indian villages along the Auglaize River at the time of Wayne's campaign, see Helen Hornbeck Tanner, "The Glaize in 1792: A Composite Indian Community," *Ethnohistory* 25 (Winter 1978): 15–39. Paul David Nelson has written the best biography of Anthony Wayne, entitled *Anthony Wayne: Soldier of the Early Republic* (Bloomington: Indiana University Press, 1985). Wayne's correspondence from 1792 to 1796 has been published in Richard C. Knopf, ed., *Anthony Wayne: A Name in Arms* (Pittsburgh: University of Pittsburgh Press, 1960).

Related studies include Colin G. Calloway, "Simon Girty: Interpreter and Intermediary," in *Being and Becoming Indian: Biographical Studies of North American Frontiers*, ed. James A. Clifton (Chicago: Dorsey Press, 1989), 38–58, and James K. Richards, "A Clash of Cultures: Simon Girty and the Struggle for the Frontier," *Timeline* 2 (June/July 1985): 2–17. For a recollection about the killing of Colonel Crawford, see "Narrative of the Capture of Abel Janney by the Indians in 1782: From the Diary of Abel Janney," *Ohio Archaeological and Historical Society Publications* 8 (1900): 465–73. See also David A. Simmons, "Simon Kenton," *Timeline* 5 (April–May 1988): 56–58.

The historical literature on the War of 1812 is also extensive. The researcher will do well to begin with Dwight L. Smith, *The War of 1812: An Annotated Bibliography* (New York: Garland Publishing, 1985). The best synthesis of the war can be found in Donald R. Hickey, *The War of 1812: A Forgotten Conflict* (Urbana: University of Illinois Press, 1989), but it does not contain much about Ohio. An excellent study of the causes of the war that stresses the importance of European affairs can be found in Reginald Horsman, *The Causes of the War of 1812* (New York: A. S. Barnes and Co., 1962). The best brief military history of the war that includes analysis of the conflict in the West remains Harry L. Coles, *The War of 1812* (Chicago: University of Chicago Press, 1965). For a more detailed narrative history of the engagement, see John K. Mahon, *The War of 1812* (Gainesville: University of Florida Press, 1972). A contemporary study still worth consulting is Robert Breckenridge McAfee, *History of the Late War in the Western Country* (1816; reprint, Ann Arbor, Mich.: University Microfilms, 1966). A descriptive, uncritical source, but of some value for the study of the most significant aspect of the war in Ohio, is Larry L. Nelson, *Men of Patriotism, Courage, and Enterprise: Fort Meigs in the War of 1812* (Canton, Ohio: Daring Books, 1985). The most detailed study of Fort Meigs is Rex L. Spence, "The Gibraltar of the Maumee: Fort Meigs in the War of 1812" (Ph.D. diss., Ball State University, 1988). Firsthand accounts of the War of 1812 include Sally Young, Robert Reid, and Ronald Reid, eds., *To the Rapids: A Journal of a Tour of Duty in the Northwestern Army under the Command of Major-General William H. Harrison* (Columbus, 1990), and "The Siege of Fort Meigs Year 1813: An Eye-Witness Account by Colonel Alexander Bourse," *Northwest Ohio Quarterly* 17, no. 4 (1945): 139–54. This account is continued in volume 18, no. 1 (1946): 39–48. See also "The Pittsburgh Blues by Captain John H. Niebaum," *Western Pennsylvania Historical Magazine* [Part I] 4 (April 1921): 110–22; [Part II] 4 (July 1921): 175–258; [Part III] 4 (October 1921): 259–70; and Lee A. Wallace, Jr., "The Petersburg Volunteers, 1812–1813," *Virginia Magazine of History and Biography* 82 (October 1974): 458–85. For extracts of newspaper articles published in the *Trump of Fame* (Warren) in Trumbull County, see "Ohio in the War of 1812," *Ohio Archaeological and Historical Society Publications* 28 (1919): 286–368. David Arthur Simmons provides a good look at post life and construction in "Fort Hamilton, 1791–1797: Its Life and Architecture" (Master's thesis, Miami University, 1975).

For removal and Indian/white affairs following the War of 1812, see John Johnston, "Account of the Present State of the Indian Tribes Inhabiting Ohio," *Transactions and Collections of the American Antiquarian Society* 1 (1920): 269–99, and Leonard U. Hill, *John Johnston and the Indians in the Land of the Three Miamis* (Columbus, Ohio: Stoneman Press, 1957), especially for

Johnston's recollections. Grant Forman, *The Last Trek of the Indians* (Chicago: University of Chicago Press, 1946), provides a detailed survey. See also Joseph E. Walker, "Plowshares and Pruning Hooks for the Miami and Potawatomi: The Journal of Gerald T. Hopkins, 1804," *Ohio History* 88 (Autumn 1979): 361–407, and Harlow Lindley, "Friends and the Shawnee Indians at Wapakoneta," *Ohio State Archaeological and Historical Quarterly* 54 (January–March 1945): 33–39; Dwight L. Smith, ed., "An Unsuccessful Negotiation for Removal of the Wyandot Indians from Ohio, 1834," *Ohio State Archaeological and Historical Quarterly* 58 (July 1949): 305–31; Max L. Carter, "John Johnston and the Friends: A Midwestern Indian Agent's Relationship with Quakers in the Early 1800s," *Quaker Quarterly* 78 (Spring 1989): 37–47; and Martin W. Walsh, "The 'Heathen Party': Methodist Observation of the Ohio Wyandot," *American Indian Quarterly* 16 (Spring 1992): 189–211.

Early travel accounts provide an excellent view of the Ohio country and its people. Manasseh Cutler, *The First Map and Description of Ohio, 1787* (Washington, D.C.: W. H. Lowdermilk and Co., 1918), is a promotional piece for the settlement and acquisition of land in the Ohio Valley. Three books that include observations about frontier Ohio are by Timothy Flint: *Recollections of the Last Ten Years Passed in Occasional Residences and Journeyings in the Valley of the Mississippi* (1826; reprint, New York: Da Capo Press, 1968); *Letters from America*, in *Early Western Travels, 1748–1846*, ed. Reuben Gold Thwaites, vol. 9 (Cleveland: Arthur H. Clark Co., 1904); and *The History and Geography of the Mississippi Valley* (Cincinnati, 1832). See also F. A. Michaux, *Travels to the West of the Allegheny Mountains in the States of Ohio, Kentucky, and Tennessee, and Back to Charleston, by the Upper Carolinas* (1805; reprint, Ann Arbor, Mich.: University Microfilms, 1966), John Bradbury, *Travels in the Interior of America in the Years 1809, 1810, and 1811* (1817; reprint, Ann Arbor, Mich.: University Microfilms, 1966). John Stillman Wright, *Letters from the West; or a Caution to Emigrants* (1819; reprint, Ann Arbor, Mich.: University Microfilms, 1966), provides often negative impressions of the Ohio Valley in 1819. See also Joseph E. Walker, ed., "The Travel Notes of Joseph Gibbons, 1804," *Ohio History* 92 (1983): 96–146, which provides a good look at everyday life; Dwight L. Smith, ed., "Nine Letters of Nathaniel Dike on the Western Country, 1816–1818," *Ohio Historical Quarterly* 67 (July 1958): 189–220; and Brian P. Birch, "A British View of the Ohio Backwoods: The Letters of James Martin, 1821–1836," *Ohio History* 94 (Summer–Autumn 1985): 139–57.

Land policy in relation to the Ohio frontier is best studied in *The American State Papers* and the *Territorial Papers of the United States*. Good sources on land speculators include the Zalman Wildman Papers for the Firelands and the Joseph Kerr Papers for the Virginia Military District, which are located in the Ohio Historical Society. See also Ellen Susan Wilson, "Speculators and Land Development in the Virginia Military Tract: The Territorial Period" (Ph.D. diss., Miami University, 1982); Beverley W. Bond, Jr., *The Correspondence of John Cleves Symmes* (New York: Macmillan, 1926); and R. Pierce Beaver, "The Miami Purchase of John Cleves Symmes," *Ohio State Archaeological and Historical Quarterly* 40 (January 1931): 284–342. A good, brief introduction to Symmes is Dwight L. Smith, "John Cleves Symmes," *Timeline*

5 (April–May 1988): 20–23. *The Memoirs of Rufus Putnam and Certain Official Papers and Correspondence* (Boston: Houghton, Mifflin and Co., 1903) is good for Putnam's perception of land, settlement, and Indian affairs. Anyone studying land policy in Ohio would do well to consult Malcolm J. Rohrbough, *The Land Office Business: The Settlement and Administration of American Public Lands, 1789–1837* (New York: Oxford University Press, 1968; reprint, Belmont, Calif.: Wadsworth Pub. Co., 1990). A general reference for land policy is Paul Wallace Gates, *History of Public Land Law Development* (1968; reprint, New York: Arno Press, 1979). John Opie provides a brief interpretive discussion of American land policy that includes the Ohio country in *The Law of the Land: Two Hundred Years of American Farmland Policy* (Lincoln: University of Nebraska Press, 1987).

A technical assessment of the equipment and procedures for surveying can be found in William D. Pattison, *Beginnings of the American Rectangular Land Survey System, 1784–1800* (Columbus: Ohio Historical Society, 1970). The complexity of surveying the Seven Ranges can be studied in C. Albert White, *A History of the Rectangular Survey System* (Washington, D.C.: Government Printing Office, 1983). This study includes excellent maps. In addition, see B. H. Pershing, "A Surveyor on the Seven Ranges," *Ohio State Archaeological and Historical Quarterly* 46 (July 1937): 257–70, and William D. Pattison, "The Survey of the Seven Ranges," *Ohio Historical Quarterly* 68 (April 1959): 115–40.

The histories of land speculation and settlement are inextricably linked. Good places to begin are Brian Harte, "Land in the Old Northwest: A Study of Speculation, Sales, and Settlement on the Connecticut Western Reserve," *Ohio History* 101 (Summer/Autumn 1992): 114–39, and Andrew R. L. Cayton, "'A Quiet Independence': The Western Vision of the Ohio Company," *Ohio History* 90 (Winter 1981): 5–32. Timothy J. Shannon emphasizes economic motives in "The Ohio Company and the Meaning of Opportunity in the American West, 1786–1795," *New England Quarterly* 64 (September 1991): 393–413. For an analysis of land ownership, see Lee Soltow, "Inequality amidst Abundance: Land Ownership in Early Nineteenth Century Ohio," *Ohio History* 88 (April 1979): 133–51. See also David T. Stephens and Alexander T. Bobersky, "The Origins of Land Buyers, Steubenville Land Office, 1800–1820," *Material Culture* 22 (Summer 1990): 37–45.

The maneuvering of the Ohio and Scioto companies is complex, but the consensus view of the details can be found in E. C. Dawes, "The Beginnings of the Ohio Company and the Scioto Purchase," *Ohio Archaeological and Historical Society Publications* 4 (1895): 1–29, and "The Scioto Company and Its Purchase," *Ohio Archaeological and Historical Society Publications* 3 (1890/91): 109–40. Archer B. Hulbert published two useful articles, "Andrew Craige and the Scioto Associates," *American Antiquarian Society* 23 (October 1913): 222–36, and "The Methods and Operations of the Scioto Group of Speculators," *Mississippi Valley Historical Review* 1 (1914): 502–15.

The best study of the French settlement remains Theodore Thomas Belote, *The Scioto Speculation and the French Settlement at Gallipolis* (New York: Burt Franklin, 1907). Anyone investigating this aspect of settlement on the Ohio frontier must also consult Lee and Margaret Soltow, "A Settlement That

Failed: The French in Early Gallipolis, an Enlightened Letter, and an Explanation," *Ohio History* 94 (Winter/Spring 1985): 46–67. In addition see John L. Vance, "The French Settlement and Settlers of Gallipolis," *Ohio Archaeological and Historical Society Publications* 3 (1890/91): 45–81; Lawrence J. Kenny, trans., "Memoir of Antoine LaForge: A Gallipolis Manuscript (1790)," *Ohio Archaeological and Historical Society Publications* 26 (1917): 43–51; and John Francis McDermott, "Gallipolis as Travelers Saw It, 1792–1811," *Ohio State Archaeological and Historical Quarterly* 48 (1939): 283–303.

Useful studies of town and commercial development on the frontier include George Jordan Blazier, ed., *Joseph Barker: Recollections of the First Settlement of Ohio* (Marietta, Ohio: Marietta, 1958). A good secondary source for an introduction to the settlement of Marietta is Andrew R. L. Cayton, "Marietta and the Ohio Company," in *Appalachian Frontiers: Settlement, Society, and Development in the Preindustrial Era*, ed. Robert D. Mitchell (Lexington: University of Kentucky Press, 1991), 187–200. Other useful studies include Daniel F. Preston, "Market and Mill Town: Hamilton, Ohio, 1795–1860" (Ph.D. diss., University of Maryland, 1987), and George C. Crout, "The Economic Development of Middletown Ohio, 1796–1865" (Master's thesis, Miami University, 1941). See also William Ganson, *Cleveland: The Making of a City* (Kent, Ohio: Kent State University Press, 1990), and Andrew Denny Rodgers, "Lucas Sullivant and the Founding of Columbus," *Ohio Archaeological and Historical Society Publications* 37 (1928): 162–76. For works on the Western Reserve, see Robert A. Wheeler, "Land and Community in Rural Nineteenth-Century America: Claridon Township, 1810–1870," *Ohio History* 97 (Summer/Autumn 1983): 101–21, which focuses on Geauga County. Studies designed for the general reader include Harlan Hatcher, *The Western Reserve: The Story of New Connecticut in Ohio* (Kent, Ohio: Kent State University Press, 1991); Harry F. Lupold and Gladys Haddad, *Ohio's Western Reserve: A Regional Reader* (Kent, Ohio: Kent State University Press, 1988), and Robert D. Wheeler, "The Town in the Western Reserve, 1800–1860," *Western Reserve Magazine* 6 (May–June 1979). More general though scholarly studies that will prove useful are Michael McManis, "Range Ten, Town Four: A Social History of Hudson, Ohio, 1799–1840" (Ph.D. diss., Case Western Reserve University, 1976); "The New England Presence on the Midwestern Landscape," *Old Northwest* 9 (September 1983): 125–33; and Kenneth V. Lottick, "Culture Transplantation in the Connecticut Reserve," *Bulletin of the Historical and Philosophical Society of Ohio* [Cincinnati] 8 (July 1959): 155–66.

Historians have given considerable attention to Cincinnati. The best accounts are Daniel Aaron, *Cincinnati: Queen City of the West, 1818–1838* (Columbus: Ohio State University Press, 1992); Richard T. Ferrel, "Cincinnati, 1800–1830: Economic Development through Trade and Industry," *Ohio History* 77 (Autumn 1968): 111–29, and "Internal-Improvement Projects in Southwestern Ohio, 1815–1834," *Ohio History* 80 (Winter 1971): 4–23; and Harry R. Stevens, "Samuel Davies and the Industrial Revolution in Cincinnati," *Ohio Historical Quarterly* 70 (April 1961): 95–127. See also Richard C. Wade, *The Urban Frontier: The Rise of Western Cities, 1790–1830* (Cambridge: Harvard University Press, 1959), but be aware that his interpretation has provoked considerable debate. In this regard see Howard J. Nelson, "Town

Founding and the American Frontier," *Association of the Pacific Coast Geographers Yearbook* 36 (1976): 7–23.

Anyone interested in the early settlement of Ohio should consult Robert P. Swierenga, "The Settlement of the Old Northwest: Ethnic Pluralism in a Featureless Plain," *Journal of the Early Republic* 9 (Spring 1989): 73–105. See also Joan Howison Fabe, "The Trial and Error Period of Euro-American Settlement in Hamilton County, Ohio, 1773–1795" (Ph.D. diss., University of Cincinnati, 1988). For a survey of ethnicity and immigration, see Robert E. Chaddock, "Ohio before 1850," Columbia University, *Studies in History, Economics and Public Law* 31 (1908): 1–155; and John D. Barnhart, "Sources of Southern Migration into the Old Northwest," *Mississippi Valley Historical Review* 22 (June 1935): 49–62. For the Pennsylvania influence, see William L. Fisk, Jr., "The Scotch-Irish in Central Ohio," *Ohio State Archaeological and Historical Quarterly* 57 (April 1948): 111–25.

Studies of everyday life include works on architecture, country stores, road building, and education. The place to begin is Malcolm J. Rohrbough, *The Trans-Appalachian Frontier: People, Societies, and Institutions, 1775–1850* (New York: Oxford University Press, 1978; reprint, Belmont, Calif.: Wadsworth Pub. Co., 1990). The house-building concerns of the frontier people are admirably discussed in Donald A. Hutslar, *The Architecture of Migration: Log Construction in the Ohio Country, 1750–1850* (Athens: Ohio University Press, 1986). Hutslar has also studied gunsmithing on the frontier; see "Lock, Stock, and Barrel: Ohio Muzzle-Loading Rifles," *Timeline* 9 (June–July 1992): 2–17. For an early reflection on daily life, see William Cooper Howells, *Recollections of Life in Ohio from 1813 to 1840* (Cincinnati, 1895). Two older studies include Beverley W. Bond, Jr., "American Civilization Comes to the Old Northwest," *Mississippi Valley Historical Review* 19 (June 1932–March 1933): 3–29, and John D. Barnhart, "Southern Contributions to the Social Order of the Old Northwest," *North Carolina Historical Review* 17 (1940): 237–48. See also Edward A. Miller, "History of the Educational Legislation in Ohio from 1803 to 1850," *Ohio Archaeological and Historical Society Publications* 27 (1919): 1–261. The standard history of the country merchant remains Lewis E. Atherton, *The Frontier Merchant in Mid-America* (Columbia: University of Missouri Press, 1971). The most detailed study of Zane's Trace is John Bernard Ray, "Zane's Trace, 1796–1812: A Study in Historical Geography" (Ph.D. diss., Indiana University, 1968).

The role of women on the Ohio frontier has not been extensively, rigorously, or critically studied, but the researcher can begin with Mildred Covey Fry, "Women on the Ohio Frontier: The Marietta Area," *Ohio History* 90 (Winter 1981): 55–73, and Hermina Sugar, "The Role of Women in the Settlement of the Western Reserve, 1796–1815," *Ohio State Archaeological and Historical Quarterly* 46 (January 1937): 51–67.

Essential studies of politics and government in frontier Ohio include Andrew R. L. Cayton, *The Frontier Republic: Ideology and Politics in the Ohio Country, 1780–1825* (Kent, Ohio: Kent State University Press, 1986), and Jeffrey Paul Brown, "Frontier Politics: The Evolution of a Political Society in Ohio, 1788–1814" (Ph.D. diss., University of Illinois at Urbana-Champaign, 1979). See also Cayton's "Land, Power and Reputation: The Cultural Dimension of Politics in the Ohio Country," *William and Mary Quarterly* 47 (April 1990): 266–86, as well as Brown's "The Ohio Federalists, 1803–1815," *Journal of the Early Republic* 2 (Fall 1982): 261–82; "Chillicothe's Elite: Leadership in a Frontier Community," *Ohio History* 96 (Summer–Autumn 1987): 140–56; and "Samuel Huntington: A Connecticut Aristocrat on the Ohio Frontier," *Ohio History* 89 (Autumn 1980): 420–38. Another useful study is James Herbert Stuckey, "The Formation of Leadership Groups in a Frontier Town: Canton, Ohio, 1805–1855" (Ph.D. diss., Case Western Reserve University, 1976). Older but useful studies are John Theodore Grupenyoff, "Politics and the Rise of Political Parties in the Northwest Territory and Early Ohio to 1812 with Emphasis on Cincinnati and Hamilton County" (Ph.D. diss., University of Texas, 1962); and John D. Barnhart, "The Southern Influence in the Formation of Ohio," *Journal of Southern History* 3 (February 1937): 28–42, and "The Southern Element in the Leadership of the Old Northwest," *Journal of Southern History* 1 (May 1935): 186–97. For a reproduction of the laws passed by the territorial legislature, see "Legislature of the Northwestern Territory, 1795," *Ohio Archaeological and Historical Society Publications* 30 (1921): 13–53. Regarding the statehood debate, see the works of Cayton, Brown, and Randolph C. Downes, "The Statehood Contest in Ohio," *Mississippi Valley Historical Review* 18 (September 1931): 155–71. See also E. O. Randall, "Location of Site of Ohio Capital," *Ohio Archaeological and Historical Society Publications* 25 (1916): 210–34; and William R. Barlow, "Ohio's Congressmen and the War of 1812," *Ohio History* 72 (July 1963): 176–94. The best overview of the importance of the Northwest Ordinance is Andrew R. L. Cayton and Peter Onuf, *The Midwest and the Nation: Rethinking the History of an American Region* (Bloomington: Indiana University Press, 1990). An introduction to later political affairs can be found in Harold E. Davis, "Economic Basis of Ohio Politics, 1820–1840," *Ohio State Archaeological and Historical Quarterly* 47 (October 1938): 288–318; and Donald J. Ratcliffe, "The Role of Voters and Issues in Party Formation: Ohio, 1824," *Journal of American History* 59 (March 1973): 847–70.

The early agricultural history of Ohio can be researched in the account books of farmers, such as those of Elnathan Kemper and Elijah Wadsworth in the Ohio Historical Society. A detailed topical study, primarily composed of his published articles, can be had with Robert Leslie Jones, *History of Agriculture in Ohio to 1880* (Kent, Ohio: Kent State University Press, 1983). A broader and more analytical study for the late frontier period is Clarence H. Danhof, *Change in Agriculture: The Northern United States, 1820–1870* (Cambridge: Harvard University Press, 1969). The best study of agricultural labor in the Old Northwest is David E. Schob, *Hired Hands and Plowboys: Farm Labor in the Midwest, 1815–1860* (Urbana: University of Illinois Press, 1975).

Important sources for the livestock industry include William Renick, *Memoirs, Correspondence, and Reminiscences of William Renick* (Circleville, Ohio: Union-Herald Book and Job Printing House, 1975). See also Charles Sumner Plumb, "Felix Renick, Pioneer," *Ohio Archaeological and Historical Society Publications* 33 (1924): 3–66. An important study that has implications for the development of the cattle industry in Ohio is Richard McMaster, "The Cattle Trade in Western Virginia, 1760–1830," in *Appalachian Frontiers: Settlement, Society, and Development in the Preindustrial Era*, ed. Robert D. Mitchell

(Lexington: University of Kentucky Press, 1991), 127–49. The most thorough study of the early cattle industry in Ohio is Paul C. Henlein, *Cattle Kingdom in the Ohio Valley, 1783–1860* (Lexington: University of Kentucky Press, 1959). See also David L. Wheeler, "The Beef Cattle Industry in the Old Northwest, 1803–1860," *Panhandle-Plains Historical Review* 47 (1974): 28–45.

For the swine industry see Stephen C. Gordon, "The City as 'Porkopolis': Some Factors in the Rise of the Meat Packing Industry in Cincinnati, 1825–1861" (Master's thesis, Miami University, 1981), and William H. Hildreth, "Mrs. Trollope in Porkopolis," *Ohio State Archaeological and Historical Quarterly* 58 (January 1949): 35–51. Anyone interested in the sheep industry should see the Rotch Family Papers in the Ohio Historical Society as well as Charles Sumner Plumb, "Seth Adams," *Ohio State Archaeological and Historical Quarterly* 43 (January 1934): 1–34.

The most recent religious study relating to the Ohio frontier is Earl P. Olmstead, *Blackcoats among the Delaware: David Zeisberger on the Ohio Frontier* (Kent, Ohio: Kent State University Press, 1991). See also Edmund de Schweinitz, *The Life and Times of David Zeisberger* (1871; reprint, New York: Johnson Reprint Corp., 1971). William Warren Sweet was one of the most prolific historians of American religion. Among his most important works that include material about Ohio are *Religion in the Development of American Culture, 1765–1840* (New York: Charles Scribner's Sons, 1952); *Religion on the American Frontier: The Baptists, 1783–1830* (New York: Henry Holt and Co., 1931); *Religion on the American Frontier, 1783–1832: The Presbyterians* (Chicago: University of Chicago Press, 1936); *Religion on the American Frontier, 1783–1840: The Methodists* (Chicago: University of Chicago Press, 1946); and *Religion on the American Frontier, 1783–1850: The Congregationalists* (Chicago: University of Chicago Press, 1939). For another study of the Presbyterians and Congregationalists, see Colin B. Goodykoontz, *Home Missions on the American Frontier: With Particular Reference to the American Home Missionary Society* (1939; reprint, New York: Octagon Books, 1971). A detailed study of the importance of the Presbyterians in the social, economic, and political life of a frontier community is Emile Pocock, "Evangelical Frontier: Dayton, Ohio, 1796–1830" (Ph.D. diss., Indiana University, 1984). Other useful studies include Margaret Burr Des Champs, "Early Presbyterianism along the North Bank of the Ohio River," *Journal of Presbyterian History* 38 (December 1950): 207–20; and James Haldane Brown, "Presbyterian Social Influences in Early Ohio," *Journal of Presbyterian History* 30 (December 1952): 209–35.

The literature on Methodism in Ohio is also large. For an introduction, see William Warren Sweet, ed., *The Rise of Methodism in the West, Being the Journal of the Western Conference, 1800–1811* (Nashville: Smith and Lamar, 1920), and I. F. King, "Introduction of Methodism in Ohio," *Ohio Archaeological and Historical Society Publications* 10 (1901): 165–219. Paul H. Boase has written extensively about Methodism in Ohio. The researcher would do well to begin with his "The Fortunes of a Circuit Rider," *Ohio History* 72 (April 1963): 91–115. See also Charles A. Johnson, "The Frontier Camp Meeting: Contemporary and Historical Appraisals," *Mississippi Valley Historical Review* 37 (June 1950): 91–110, and "Early Ohio Camp Meetings, 1801–1816," *Ohio State Archaeological and Historical Quarterly* 61 (January 1952): 32–50.

A good, detailed study of the Shakers can be found in J. P. Maclean, *Fugitive Papers concerning the Shakers of Ohio, with Unpublished Manuscripts* (Philadelphia: Porcupine Press, 1975). An excellent doctrinal study is Stephen J. Stein, "'A Candid Statement of Our Principles': Early Shaker Theology in the West," *Proceedings of the American Philosophical Society* 133 (March 1989): 503–19. An uncritical study of the Shakers, particularly regarding dates, but still worth seeing is Caroline B. Piercy, *The Valley of God's Pleasure: A Saga of the North Union Shaker Community* (New York: Stratford House, 1951). More useful studies of the Shakers include Edward D. Andrews, *The People Called Shakers: A Search for the Perfect Society* (New York: Oxford University Press, 1953), and Marguerite Fellows Melcher, *The Shaker Adventure* (Princeton: Princeton University Press, 1941). Two studies on the Shakers that will help provide context, although neither specifically concerns the Ohio experience, are Priscilla J. Brewer, *Shaker Communities, Shaker Lives* (Hanover, N.H.: University Press of New England, 1986), and Marjorie Procter-Smith, *Women in Shaker Community and Worship: A Feminist Analysis of the Uses of Religious Symbolism* (Lewiston, N.Y.: Edwin Mellen Press, 1985). See also "The Shakers of Ohio: An Early Nineteenth-Century Account," *Cincinnati Historical Society Bulletin* 29 (1971): 126–37; Benjamin Seth Youngs, "An Expedition against the Shakers," *Ohio Archaeological and Historical Society Publications* 21 (1912): 403–15; and Lenna Mae Gara, "An Expedition against the Shakers," *Timeline* 10 (May–June 1993): 46–53.

The best study of the Quakers in Ohio is James L. Burke and Donald E. Bensch, "Mount Pleasant and the Early Quakers of Ohio," *Ohio History* 83 (Summer 1974): 220–55. A brief older study is Harlow Lindley, "The Quakers in the Old Northwest," *Mississippi Valley Historical Association Proceedings* 5 (1912): 60–72.

The most detailed studies of Zoar remain George B. Landis, "The Society of Separatists of Zoar, Ohio," *Annual Report of the American Historical Association* (1898): 165–220, and Edgar Burkhardt Nixon, "The Society of Separatists of Zoar" (Ph.D. diss., Ohio State University, 1933). A more recent study that emphasizes the theoretical aspects of the economy of Zoar is David William Meyers, "The Machine in the Garden: The Design and Operation of the Separatist Society of Zoar" (Master's thesis, Ohio State University, 1980). See also E. O. Randall, "The Separatist Society of Zoar," *Ohio Archaeological and Historical Society Publications* 8 (1900): 1–105; Edgar B. Nixon, "The Zoar Society: Applicants for Membership," *Ohio Archaeological and Historical Quarterly* 45 (October 1936): 341–50; Harvey Leroy Holshoy, "The Educational Opportunities of the German Separatists in Their Communistic Settlement at Zoar, Ohio" (Master's thesis, Kent State University, 1942); and Wilfred Freed McArtor, "Arts and Industries of the Zoarites, 1817–1898" (Master's thesis, Ohio State University, 1939).

The most detailed economic study of the Ohio canals is Harry N. Scheiber, *Ohio Canal Era: A Case Study of Government and the Economy, 1820–1861* (Athens: Ohio University Press, 1968). For a well-illustrated study designed for the general reader, see Jack Gieck, *A Photo Album of Ohio's Canal Era, 1825–1913* (Kent, Ohio: Kent State University Press, 1988).

Index

R. DOUGLAS HURT

is the editor of *Agricultural History* and Professor and Director of the
Graduate Program in Agricultural History and Rural Studies at Iowa State
University. He has written and edited more than a dozen books.